Branches & Byways
Sussex and Hampshire

Branches & Byways
Sussex and Hampshire

John Vaughan

An imprint of
Ian Allan Publishing

Dedication
This book is dedicated to John Marshall Frith,
a special, much valued and lifelong friend

Front cover:
With large numbers of railway enthusiasts paying their last respects to the Hayling Island branch, A1X class No 32650 is seen at Langston during the last days of service, on 2 November 1963. *R. C. Riley*

Back cover (top):
A green 350hp diesel shunter with yellow coupling rods arrives at the Kemp Town terminus in Brighton with the daily freight, in June 1971. *JV*

Back cover (top):
One of the few electrified branch lines in Sussex and Hampshire is the Lymington branch. Passing the closed Ampress Works halt is 3-car EMU No 1199, a 4-CEP derivative, in March 2003. *JV*

Half title:
Of the 25 primary branch lines and byways described within this volume, 21 have completely closed to passengers and just two remain open for freight traffic only, such has been the demise of minor railways over the years. Fortunately for posterity six preservation societies operate over short sections of former Sussex and Hampshire branches. Well over 30 years ago, on 4 January 1970, the loading gauge frames ex-LBSCR Class A1X 'Terrier' No 72 *Fenchurch* as it departs from Horsted Keynes for Sheffield Park on the now well-established 'Bluebell Railway'. *A. Eaton*

Title page:
Of all the motive power used on Sussex and Hampshire branches over the past century, only the English Electric 'Hampshire' diesel-electric multiple-units and their variants could rival the LSWR 'M7', SECR 'H', LBSCR 'A1X' and 'E4' (and cousins) classes of tank in terms of longevity. The 'Thumpers', as they were affectionately known, operated until the year 2004 when they were finally removed from the Uckfield branch and the Ashford to Hastings line. No 1112 is seen south of Hailsham with a train for Polegate and Eastbourne on 22 August 1967. *JV/TTT*

First published 2004

ISBN 0 86093 585 X

Published by Oxford Publishing Co

an imprint of Ian Allan Publishing Ltd, Hersham, Surrey KT12 4RG.

Printed by Ian Allan Printing Ltd, Hersham, Surrey KT12 4RG.

Code: 0408

Contents

Introduction

TO attempt to produce a book that includes every significant branch line and byway in the large counties of Sussex and Hampshire is a formidable task. In the space available it has been necessary to carefully balance the coverage and content to produce 25 chapters describing the more obvious candidates for inclusion. In order to achieve this objective, this weighty tome includes over 450 photographs, over 130,000 words and hundreds of relevant facts. It has, however, been necessary to refer briefly to other lines in a Miscellany.

As was the case with my *Branches & Byways: Cornwall*, some thought had to be given to the definition of the words incorporated in the title. Inevitably there has been some author's licence, but where a branch leaves a main line and ends in a terminus it has been included. Many cross-country lines were operated on branch-line principles and they have also been included. A handful of secondary lines could reasonably be called branches even though they enjoyed through trains from Sussex and Hampshire to London. Where branches run into other counties a judgement has had to be made regarding whether they should be included here. Main lines have been excluded, as have street tramways, most narrow gauge lines, industrial complexes, some military lines, works and quarry sidings, dock lines, airport 'people-movers' and 'pleasure-park' lines. However, a selection of the above are mentioned in the Miscellany in addition to a selection of 'Byways'.

A realisation that emerged while writing *Branches & Byways: Sussex and Hampshire* was how the minor line networks in both counties have been truly decimated over the years. Of the lines featured in the first 25 chapters only two remain open to passengers, Seaford and Lymington; two are partly open, Uckfield and

Chandlers Ford; and two are open for freight-only working, Ardingly and Fawley. Some lines closed during the purge of the 1930s, after the great depression, while BR closed others in the 1950s. However, the 1960s 'Beeching era' produced the greatest carnage of any decade, when the majority of loss-making minor lines succumbed to the criteria imposed by the BR Modernisation Plan. Many closures were fully justified as the public preferred their automobiles, or in some areas far more convenient buses, while the trains ran empty. There is no doubt that during the 1950s/60s a way of life changed for ever and many of the photographs within now simply ooze nostalgia. It was not only the lines that were lost but also the wonderful infrastructure surrounding the country station and all that that entailed.

I was well aware of the existence of branch lines in my local area in the 1950s but it would be the mid-1960s before a reasonable camera could be afforded, not to mention having sufficient disposable income to purchase a small motorcycle to travel the area. By 1965/66 steam had all but disappeared and the surviving branches with a passenger service were nearly all worked by English Electric diesel-electric multiple-units. At the time of writing, these venerable 46-year-old units are just about to be withdrawn. From my trainspotting days I remember most of the small tank classes of steam locomotive featured in this book, and happily many types have been preserved for posterity. It is difficult to believe that many of my own photographs were taken 40 years ago; time has passed so quickly. One thing is certain — I will not be writing another book 40 years from now!

The large area of Sussex (East and West) and Hampshire is far more rural than most people imagine, and long sections of land on former branch lines are still sparsely populated. In addition to agriculture, the other overwhelming influence in both counties is the English Channel and the plethora of important ports and associated docks. These ports were the *raison d'être* for many of the lines featured in this book, and with a combination of naval interests, cross-Channel traffic and commercial shipping there was a real need for connection to a national rail network. The railways had a significant influence on population growth in the 20th century and in later years many towns and villages in both counties joined the 'commuter belt'. However, with the closure of so many branch and secondary lines, distant 'park and ride' sites now have to be used.

I hope that all readers enjoy this weighty tome as much as I have enjoyed compiling it. The process has brought back many happy memories for me, and scenes that will never be witnessed again have generated many moments of great nostalgia. My wish is that *Branches & Byways: Sussex and Hampshire* will become a valuable 'all in one' reference book for current and future generations. Finally, this book could not have been completed without the co-operation of many close friends and fellow photographers, and I thank them on the Acknowledgements page.

John A. M. Vaughan
Goring by Sea, West Sussex

Below:
This volume features mainly LBSCR and LSWR branches and byways with just a hint of the SECR. A happy mix of an LSWR Drummond 'M7' class locomotive working an LBSCR line shows how post-Grouping operations fogged the boundaries of the pre-Grouping companies. With Bramber station just visible in the background, No 30048 works a Horsham to Brighton train in the early 1950s. *E. R. Wethersett*

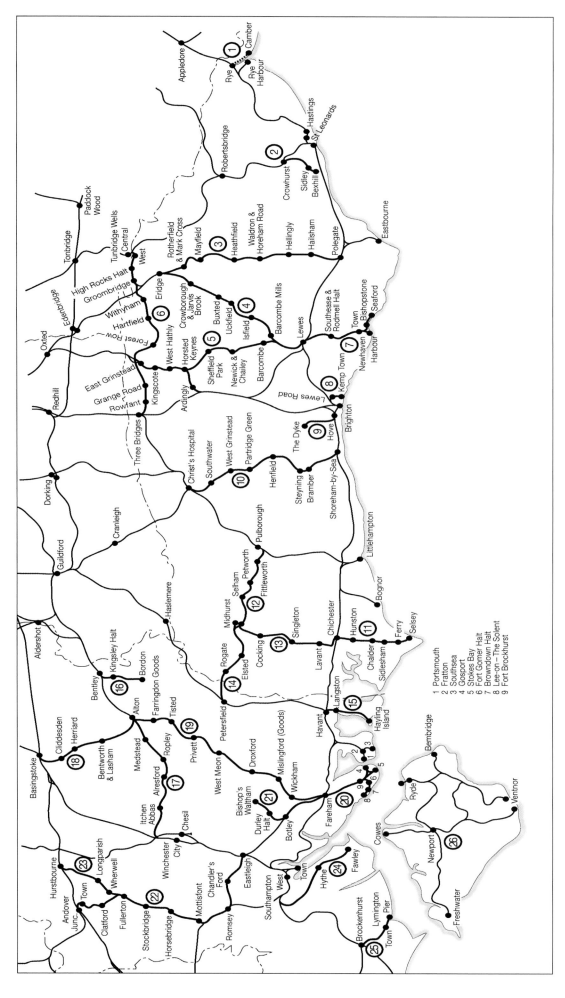

Map of the railways of Sussex and Hampshire at the time of the Grouping in 1923.
The branch lines are numbered according to the chapter numbers in this book.

1 Portsmouth
2 Fratton
3 Southsea
4 Gosport
5 Stokes Bay
6 Fort Gomer Halt
7 Lee-on – The Solent
8 Browndown Halt
9 Fort Brockhurst

1. Rye & Camber Tramway

ALTHOUGH various branches, byways, sidings and industrial installations are referred to in this book, the only narrow gauge line covered in any detail is the Rye & Camber Tramway. Rye is an ancient town just inside the (East) Sussex border where the River Rother spills into the sea. It also stood on the Royal Military Canal that ran across the marshes towards Hythe in Kent. The main town is slightly inland, about 2 miles from Rye Harbour and, beyond it, the sea. Rye was the most important town between Hastings and, in the 1850s, the rapidly growing town of Ashford (then New Town, previously Alfred Town) in Kent. It was connected to the outside world by rail when the line from Ashford to Hastings opened in February 1851. As the population began to travel more, the fine sands in the area of Camber on the coast, just a couple of miles from Rye, were recognised for their recreational potential. Approaching the end of Queen Victoria's reign, the population of Rye exceeded 4,000 inhabitants and, with the facilities required to support a population of this size, such as the availability of food and accommodation, the area became a target for holidaymakers. However, it was the growth in

the popularity of the game of golf that we will be primarily concerned with here!

Rye Harbour, to the south of Rye and on the west side of the small river estuary, had become sufficiently important for the South Eastern Railway to build a siding down from the 'main' line in 1854, although it must be emphasised that the line was only for goods traffic. The siding was built from the 1851 main line, mentioned above, along the south side of the river. Over 40 years later, in 1894 — but before the advent of the motor car — a new golf course had been built just across the river from Rye Harbour and some local wealthy businessmen thought it would be useful for members to have a rail connection from Rye to the new club, some 1½ miles away. Capital of £2,300 was made available and a strip of land purchased, sufficient to support a narrow gauge railway, or tramway, together with some essential infrastructure items, such as stations, and a locomotive and carriage shed. The land for the Rye terminus was leased from the local authority. Being businessmen they recognised that as there was no passenger service on the SER siding across the river, it made sense to run any tramway to a point

Below:
The Rye & Camber Tramway was effectively a 3ft-gauge railway running 1½ miles from the ancient East Sussex town of Rye to a golf course located across the river from Rye Harbour. From 1908 it was extended by a further ½ mile to a remote terminus set amongst the sand dunes. Although near to the beach, Camber Sands Station was about ½ mile from the small town of Camber. The first locomotive purchased was a small 6-ton Bagnall 2-4-0T locomotive, named *Camber*. Here the locomotive pauses at Rye terminus with station roof advertising for the short-sighted being only too obvious. *SLS*

opposite Rye Harbour, so that both golfers and any residents or visitors to the harbour could use the line, the latter finishing their journey by ferry.

The Rye & Camber Tramways Company was registered in the first half of 1895. The company quickly appointed Holman F. Stephens as line engineer and charged him with designing and equipping the proposed tramway. There are whole books dedicated to the life and works of Holman F. Stephens, later to become the famous Colonel Stephens. Born in 1868, he became synonymous with minor, light and narrow gauge railways from Cornwall to Kent and from Sussex to Shropshire, and a whole lot in between (see Chapter 11 on the Selsey Tramway)! He was involved in one capacity or another with over a dozen minor railways until he died in 1931. His offices were in Tonbridge, Kent. His 'economic' station building design was one of his trademarks, as was his interchange of locomotives between lines. Stephens studied civil engineering in this country and also spent some time in Germany. He cut his railway engineering teeth with the Metropolitan Railway, then with a railway company and a public utility in Kent. However, his early claim to fame was building the first railway under the Light Railway Act of 1896, the Rother Valley Railway, the line that later became the Kent & East Sussex Railway. The Act opened the floodgates for applications for the construction of minor railway lines that were subject to strict speed limits. The Act was not relevant to the Rye & Camber.

His task in completing the Rye & Camber Tramway was executed with almost lightning speed. The construction company involved, Mancktelow Bros of Horsmonden, worked quickly and to a very tight budget to lay the 3ft-gauge track, build two stations and a two-road locomotive/carriage shed with such effect that the line was ready for opening by July 1895. A further two-road shed was added to the trackwork at the down end of the station at a later date. The track was 26lb Vignoles-type rail spiked to wooden sleepers. The track layout was very simple: a single track with run-round loops at both stations and sidings to corrugated iron carriage and locomotive sheds. There were no signals because there was never more than one train, or one engine in steam, on the line. Stephens had initially favoured a locomotive using an internal combustion engine, but at that time there was little that could be purchased 'off the peg' and the company bought a small 6-ton 2-4-0 steam locomotive from W. G. Bagnall Ltd. The normal service speed was 10mph. A single bogie coach was ordered from the same engineering company, a 3-tonner that could accommodate 32 passengers in two classes of travel, First and Second. The coach had entrance platforms at both ends. A couple of small three-plank four-wheeled wagons were also acquired. A year after opening, a second, locally built, bogie carriage was purchased for Third Class passengers. This vehicle could accommodate 25 seated passengers, but there was an entrance platform at one end only. One year later still, in 1897, a second Bagnall 2-4-0 locomotive was purchased and this turned the scales some 12cwt heavier than its sister engine. The two were named *Camber* and *Victoria* respectively, and, as delivered, were in lined light green and blue livery respectively. In 1900 two sturdier wagons were purchased, and although these were used to convey sand they were later adapted for use by passengers as an overflow during busy periods. The only other vehicle on the line at this time was a permanent way trolley.

The terminus station at Rye became well known for its giant-size advertising lettering on the roof, which read 'TRAM STATION', allegedly so that it could be seen from the town of Rye. The building had a booking office and waiting room. A low brick and concrete platform was provided on the down side of both stations. From Rye the line was absolutely straight for about ½ mile, when it crossed Broadwater Stream; bridge abutments were necessary to support the small railway bridge. The line then ran across some shingle at Northpoint Beach and passed a sprinkling of dwellings,

after which passengers gained a fine view of the river estuary and Rye Harbour. Just 1½ miles from Rye the line terminated at Golf Links station, at that time known as 'Camber'. The station was similar to Rye but without engine or carriage sheds. There was a run-round loop and the station was well positioned for the golf club.

The line being ready for service, there was a grand opening on Saturday 13 July 1895. The Mayor and Mayoress of Rye were top of the guest list, followed by other Mayors, the Chairman of the Rye & Camber company, members of the clergy, the contractor and many in the upper echelons of Rye's social circle. Detonators sounded and the crowds cheered as the first train pulled out. Upon arrival at Camber the VIPs trudged across the golf course for a slap-up lunch at the Royal William Hotel. The general public were then allowed to use the trains, with the fare set at 4d single and 6d (2½p) return First Class and 2d single and 4d return Second Class. Special regular-traveller deals were available for golfers and fishermen. For a fee of 4d parcels could be delivered to Rye Harbour Village, which included the cost of the ferry. In the first six months of operation no fewer than 18,000 tickets were sold and, as mentioned above, an additional coach and a second engine had to be procured to cope with the summer traffic.

Although the line was a success, finances were at best marginal and by the beginning of the Edwardian era the railway was looking to the golf club for a subsidy, which it duly paid. By 1903 the Directors of the Rye & Camber Tramway announced that the tramway would be closed in the winter months unless they received a subsidy of £50. The golf club paid £25, with other clubs and the Mayor stumping up a similar amount, and thus the trains continued to run. The line hovered on a more or less break-even basis but with the combination of better receipts in 1906 and the increasing number of day trippers intent on spending a day on the sands, the company decided to extend the line by half a mile to Camber Sands. They had to find £650 to pay for the extension, but as with most investments it was the future income potential that was in focus. Camber Sands was located amongst the sand dunes, about half a mile from the hamlet of Camber. The extension was opened on 13 July 1908, from which date the original terminus was renamed Golf Links. Camber Sands had just a low wooden platform made from old standard gauge railway sleepers. Initially there was no building or shelter, but later a wooden hut was provided. There was a good crowd to see the opening of the extension, and although there were some dignitaries present it was, perhaps understandably, not on a scale of the original opening.

The new extension was popular in the summer months, and 10 round trips per day were made, with a couple of extras on Saturdays. However, the line was hardly used when the season turned, and consequently all winter services terminated at Golf Links. An occasional wagon of sand for local builders was hauled from the beach at Camber, but otherwise it was merely the golf club subsidy that kept the line going in winter. In the 1920s, as with most branch lines of the era, bus competition began to make inroads into traffic and some of the golfers were amongst the early car owners. Gradually the golf club got fed up with making handouts to the railway, and the last £25 subsidy was paid in 1925. In order to make economies, the company purchased an unusual-looking petrol locomotive from the Kent Construction Company of Ashford, Kent. *Victoria* was withdrawn soon after the 0-4-0 petrol locomotive's arrival and sold for scrap in 1926, after just 29 years of service, and from that date *Camber* was rarely used, it too being sold in 1937. Another economy, although it cannot have saved much money, was the abolition of First and Second Class seating, making the railway 'all Third'. The passing loop at Golf Links was abandoned. Tickets had, except for the very early days, always been issued on the train, so there was no room for manpower economies. Off peak, the tramway employed only two staff, with casual help being taken on

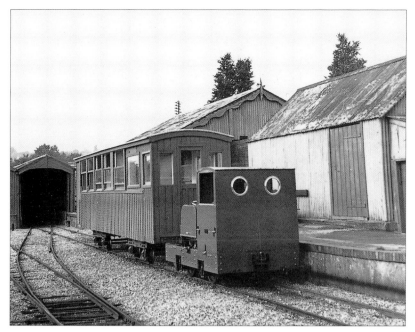

Upper left:
From 1925 the staple motive power for the Rye & Camber Tramway was a small petrol locomotive purchased second-hand from the Kent Construction Company of Ashford. Upon the arrival of the diminutive locomotive the second steam locomotive, called *Victoria*, was sold for scrap and *Camber* was rarely used. The railway owned only two coaches and a few wagons, and in October 1937 the petrol locomotive and the original 1895 coach were sufficient to accommodate the number of passengers travelling. *SLS/J. F. Roberts*

Lower left:
The little line closed with the onset of World War 2. It was taken over by the Admiralty, but by the time hostilities finished in 1945 the infrastructure had become so run down that the chances of the tramway reopening, which even in the good times had operated at the margins, were nil. Accordingly the company was formally wound up and all assets were disposed of. In this remarkable view taken on 19 April 1946 the original passenger coach stands abandoned and derelict while in the background the original locomotive and carriage sheds look to be in a sorry state of repair. *S. C. Nash*

Below:
During the war the Admiralty converted the railway alignment into a road/railway by almost encasing the track in concrete. This section of track to the west of the golf club has survived the ravages of time and was still clearly recognisable when photographed in 2003. In the background can be seen the buildings of Rye Harbour located on the other side of the River Rother. *JV*

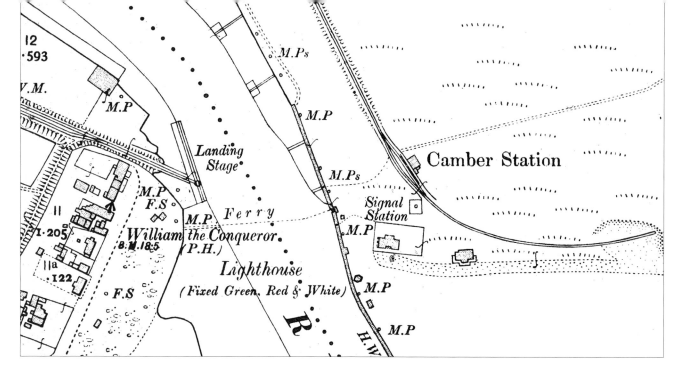

Above:
This pre-1908 Edwardian map shows the location of the original Camber Station, later Golf Links Station, just across the River Rother from Rye Harbour. As can be seen, the Rye Harbour branch, from the Ashford to Hastings 'main' line at Rye, terminated just across the river, and a ferry service was in operation. The Rye & Camber Tramway was extended to Camber Sands Station in 1908. *Crown Copyright*

during the summer. Sadly, receipts continued to fall, and although the railway tried to maintain an hourly service in the middle of the day — between approximately 10am and 6pm — it continued to struggle financially. It should be mentioned that at Northpoint Beach a local company set up a business digging out shingle, and its short 2ft-gauge railway passed underneath the Rye & Camber.

The onset of World War 2 put the little tramway out of its misery because in 1939 it was obliged to close and, as it transpired, it never reopened. During the war the Admiralty took over the Rye to Golf Links section of track to convey materials for the building of a 1,000ft jetty on the Camber side of the River Rother. It also built a short spur from Golf Links to a jetty on the River Rother and reinstated the run-round loop at Golf Links, to facilitate access to the spur and for other movements. At some locations the Admiralty laid strips of concrete either side of the narrow gauge track to form a road. After the war the stock and the railway were in very poor shape and, with no prospect of reopening, the Rye & Camber Tramway Company was wound up, Rye station demolished and the track taken up. Today the only relics of note are the station at Golf Links, which not only survives but which has some track set in concrete in front of the building, and ½ mile of trackbed used as a road. It is only the vigilant and tenacious enthusiast who can trace other features of note, although part of the original Bagnall coach survives; after being used as a summerhouse and a chicken shed, it

is presently at the Amberley Chalk Pits Museum in West Sussex.

The little line served a purpose for over four decades, but although it made a profit in a handful of years, its finances were always tight. Crossing that fairly bleak open country on a wet February day must have been depressing, while a trundle down to the sands in an open wagon on a hot summer's day must have been a sheer delight. There would have been no place for the line today in a workaday sense, although as a summer novelty act it could have attracted a percentage of the visitors and enthusiasts who still visit the relatively nearby Romney, Hythe & Dymchurch Railway and, for that matter, the Kent & East Sussex Railway, Northiam station being only about 8 miles distant.

As already mentioned, a 1¾-mile goods branch from Rye to Rye Harbour was opened in March 1854, and it survived for no fewer than 108 years, closing in 1962. The line never had a passenger service and for many years the main source of traffic was an oil depot and a chemical works. There was a daily train until the final years. Now only the remains of a river crossing and a shallow embankment, together with an old coach body opposite the William the Conqueror public house, survive. As an aside, the non-electrified and therefore diesel-worked Hastings to Ashford via Rye line remains open. Although closure was approved in 1969, the line was reprieved, although part was singled and infrastructure rationalised in 1979.

Left:
There is little to see by way of remains of the freight-only branch from Rye in the Rye Harbour area. The line opened in 1854 and was in regular use until closed and lifted in 1962. Now the only relic giving anything of a railway flavour is this old coach body on the banks of the river opposite the William the Conqueror public house and just in sight of the former Golf Links Station across the river. *JV*

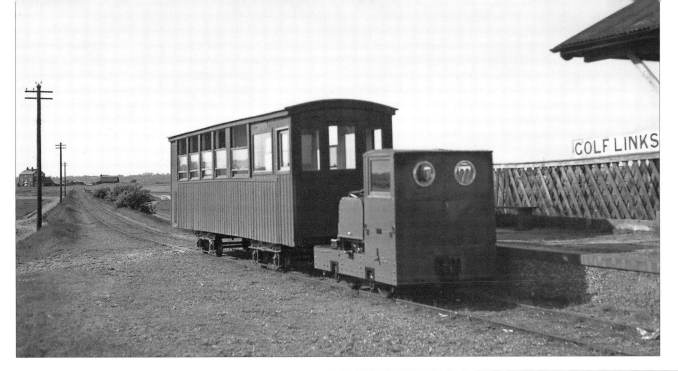

Above:
This is quite possibly the very last photograph of a public service train ever to be taken on the Rye & Camber Tramway. Photographed in June 1939, just weeks before passenger services were withdrawn and the line was taken over by the Admiralty, the petrol locomotive and a single coach arrive at Golf Links from Rye. During the summer, peak-period trains often comprised both coaches plus two open wagons with bench seats to accommodate the number of passengers. *SLS/R. F. Roberts*

Upper right:
This very rare view of Golf Links station, recorded on 19 April 1946, shows the spur line and the lead to the 1,000ft-long pier on the River Rother constructed by the Admiralty. Used during World War 2 to transport men and materials, the track was still *in situ* but clearly disused at this time.
S. C. Nash

Lower right:
Golf Links station was a typical Colonel Stephens-type structure with corrugated iron sheeting over a wooden frame. Nevertheless, several examples have withstood the elements for more than 100 years. After closure of the tramway the building was modified and the former awning area was filled in to provided more internal accommodation. In this 30 October 1964 view the building was being used by M. J. Haynes, Boat Repairer. *SLS/R. F. Roberts*

Above:
One of the great joys of exploring long-closed railway lines is the discovery of original infrastructure that has survived the passage of time. Such an example is Golf Links station, originally Camber station. Other than for service personnel, the last passenger used the platform in 1939. In 2003 the 3ft-gauge track was still visible, albeit embedded in concrete, and traces remain of the main line, the passing loop and (branching to the left) the spur down to the Admiralty Pier. *JV*

Below:
At the end of the 2-mile line was Camber Sands station. Unlike the other sites, only a primitive wooden hut
was provided as a passenger shelter, and the station, which was remotely located amongst the sand dunes, was some ½ mile from
Camber village. Once popular motoring and omnibuses became established there was no chance of the tramway surviving.
In October 1937 the glowing petrol locomotive waits to depart for Rye with a single coach — note the run-round loop.
Nothing now remains of the tramway at this location. *SLS/R. F. Roberts*

2. Bexhill West Branch

IT would be reasonable to say that except for a long-term devotee of branch lines or those living in the Bexhill to Hastings area, the Bexhill West branch was one of the lesser-known branches, especially when compared with, say, the nearby Kent & East Sussex Railway. In fact, the double-line 'branch' was not built as a branch but as a main-line terminus, in a rapidly growing town and resort, for trains to and from London via South Eastern Railway lines.

The railway had reached Bexhill as long ago as 27 June 1846 by a line from Brighton promoted and built by the Brighton, Lewes & Hastings Railway. The 1844 Act stipulated that the undertaking would then be sold to the London & Brighton Railway, which by amalgamating with the London & Croydon Railway became the London, Brighton & South Coast Railway on the same date that the line from Lewes to Bulverhythe, near St Leonards, was opened throughout. Direct access from London to Bexhill was available from October 1847 when the line from Keymer Junction, on the London to Brighton main line, was opened to Lewes, where it

joined the 1846 Brighton to Lewes and St Leonards line. As mentioned in the Cuckoo Line chapter, branches to Eastbourne and Hailsham were opened in 1849, and in 1852 the SER completed its line from Tonbridge via Tunbridge Wells Central to St Leonards and Hastings. The line from Lewes later joined up with the SER line at a new junction, called Bopeep Junction, at St Leonards.

The family name of a local dignitary and landowner still perpetuated in the Bexhill area, where the main pavilion is named after him, is De La Warr. Earl De La Warr was very keen to ensure that Bexhill became one of the leading resorts on the South Coast. From 1880 he had been aware that the key to achieving his objectives was having a first-class railway service between Bexhill and the capital. At the time it was considered that the 'Brighton' route via Lewes to London was something of a 'great way round' for Bexhill inhabitants and visitors. The SER route via Tonbridge was likewise inconvenient, for the same group of people had to travel towards Hastings and change trains for a journey back along the coast. There were a number of proposals for new routes into

Below:
The Bexhill West branch was built to rival the LBSCR line that ran along the coast between Lewes and Hastings. The SECR was keen to serve a growing town and wanted to exploit its shorter route to London. The junction station from the London/Tonbridge/Hastings main line was at Crowhurst. In May 1958, when steam was being replaced by diesel, a classic main-line-to-branch interchange scene is depicted. Arriving from Charing Cross and bound for Hastings is all-green DEMU No 1015, one of the Class 201 units that had narrow bodies so that trains could pass within the tolerances of the restricted tunnel clearances on the Hastings line. In the bay platform a SECR 'H' class on a push-pull working will shortly be leaving for Bexhill West. *Michael E. Ware*

Bexhill during the 1884 to 1889 period, including a Bexhill Direct Railway from a point south of Battle into the town.

As the population of Bexhill grew to some 12,000 inhabitants, so did the frustration of local landowners and businessmen, and, after a number of meetings were held by a high-powered local committee, the Crowhurst, Sidley & Bexhill Railway (CSBR) was formed in 1896. Its objective was to build a double-track standard gauge line from the SER's Tonbridge to Hastings route at a point near the small village of Crowhurst, which in 1901 had a population of 574 (including the surrounding area). The company had the full support of the SER, which not only promised a significant financial contribution towards the construction of the proposed line but also agreed to work it using SER motive power and rolling stock. The capital authorised was a staggering £135,000, with a further £45,000 in borrowing powers, a significant sum for a mere 4½ miles of railway line. The main reason for the cost was the need to build deep cuttings south of Crowhurst and at Sidley, but mainly to construct a truly spectacular viaduct, in terms of length, across some marshland between Crowhurst and Sidley.

There seems little doubt that just as the LBSCR had made considerable efforts to keep potentially rival railways out of its area, the SER saw the proposed line as a way of attracting much of the Bexhill traffic to the financial detriment of the LBSCR. To rub salt into the wound, it must also be remembered that the LBSCR was paying a proportion of its receipts to the SER in respect of Eastbourne traffic, carried via the Cuckoo Line (see Chapter 3). Also, the Board of the CSBR included a number of prominent members of the SER Board! Royal Assent for construction of the line was given on 15 July 1897, and no doubt the SER cheque-book was wielded to such an extent that construction commenced in January 1898. The major problem encountered in construction was the viaduct, where the foundations for some of the supports of the 17 arches were difficult to locate on terra firma, in this case hard blue clay far below the marshy surface of peat, soft clay and shingle. Piles for foundations gave way and were substituted by enormous blocks of concrete, each of which was bigger than the

average two-storey house. These blocks extended 40ft below the ground, the viaduct was 67ft above the ground, and the total length was 417yd. It took a total of two years to build, and it was alleged that some 9 million bricks were included in the structure. Construction of the viaduct commenced in December 1898 and it was completed on 21 September 1900. As an aside, the SER became part of the South Eastern & Chatham Railway from January 1899.

Some 700 navvies were employed on the construction of the railway, and the contractors used a variety of small locomotives to assist with spoil removal and for incoming materials. A number of these locomotives carried the names of local towns, presumably temporary names applied for 'PR' purposes. It is interesting to note that a temporary spur from the coastal LBSCR line was laid towards the site of the new Bexhill West terminus so that spoil and chalk could be transported by rail. In addition to a new junction station, Crowhurst, and of course the Bexhill terminus, there was to be one intermediate station at Sidley, which would also be provided with a goods yard, goods shed, signalbox and pedestrian overbridge. The stations were all impressive and, although brick-built, they were all embellished in slightly different ways. Crowhurst station, on the down side, was built using both red and yellow brick, Sidley had Bath stone dressing, and Bexhill was very decorative (see photograph) with a fine central clock tower. There was nothing conservative about the track layout at Crowhurst, which had two centre through lines, two platforms serving through loops, and south-end bays on both sides of the station for local Bexhill branch trains. Signalboxes were sited at both ends of Crowhurst station, which had a new access road and a new hotel nearby. The actual junction for Bexhill was at the south-west end of the station. Up branch trains would use the up bay platform, then be shunted across the main line to the down bay, to await a down main line connection.

From the junction the double-track line passed through a notable cutting past several farms before approaching the slight dip into and out of the valley. Descending towards the viaduct the severest gradient on the line, a relatively short stretch at 1 in 90, was encountered. Sidley was originally known as Sidley Green, but

Below:
A dramatic contrast at Crowhurst some 45 years after the date of the last photograph, with through roads removed, station buildings demolished, manual signalling replaced and both the up and down Bexhill West branch bay platforms lost beneath weeds and undergrowth. In June 2003 Class 375 No 375305 arrives at the station with a London-bound train, and two elderly passengers are being watched by CCTV as they make their way to the train and try to find out how to open the sliding doors! *JV*

Above:
**Framed by Crowhurst's delightful home signal gantry is 'Schools' class No 30923 *Bradfield* at the head of the 1.30pm
Charing Cross to Bexhill West express, which comprises some old compartment stock and four Maunsell coaches, on 22 April 1950.
As the years went by, the number of through trains and through coaches greatly diminished, but at this time trains were using
the Bexhill West branch as Bopeep Tunnel at St Leonards had been closed for repairs.** *S. C. Nash*

Below:
**The little LBSCR 'A1X' class 'Terriers' were aptly named, and could turn their hand to most things.
In this case the great Kentish tradition of hop-picking, where working-class people from the poorer parts of London
spent working holidays in the fields picking hops for use primarily in the brewing industry, was the reason for this working.
Hop-pickers normally travelled down to the country (and back) by special train. On 29 September 1956 Nos 32636 and 32678
head for Robertsbridge with a returning empty stock working from Bexhill West to Bodiam on the Kent & East Sussex line.
In the right background is the impressive Sidley Viaduct.** *S. C. Nash*

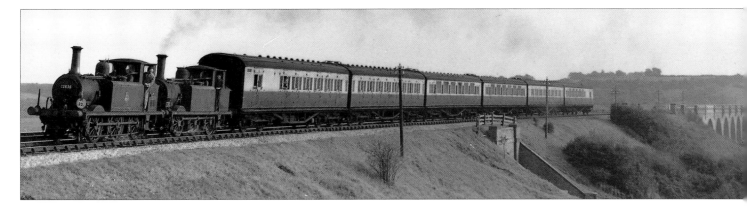

over the years it had been absorbed by the ever-growing Bexhill to become a suburb of that town. The station was located in a shallow cutting and its platforms were 490ft long. The 20-lever signalbox was at the end of the down platform. Sidley also boasted a goods yard at the up end of the down platform and a large brick-built goods shed, which was, surprisingly, sold out of use by the Southern Railway as early as 1929. The line then broadly descended to the Bexhill (West) terminus, to the west of the town, where the extensive goods yard and sidings were built mostly on reclaimed land, or at least land that had been heightened by the deposit of huge quantities of spoil from the aforementioned cuttings on the line. The specification of the new terminus reflected the almost wild optimism of the proposers. The goods shed was some 133ft long and contained two cranes. There were also loading docks, cattle pens, a weighbridge, a heavy crane and a yard signalbox with

no fewer than 123 levers, 80 of which were connected. There was a commodious locomotive shed capable of housing four locomotives, with a 54ft 9in turntable. This was a sub-shed of Hastings and later St Leonards, but was closed and sold to a building company in 1938. On the west side of the station were four carriage sidings. A second signalbox was unusually located at the buffer-stop end of the station, and this had a more modest 12 levers in a 22-lever frame. The station buildings contained every facility including a handsome refreshment room. The two platforms were an impressive 700ft long and 30ft wide with deep canopies that covered the first 400ft from the main building. Adjacent tracks were used as a locomotive release road.

The completed line was ready for an inspection by the Board of Trade on 25 April 1902. After travelling from London in the First Class coach of a special train, Major Pringle measured, observed,

Right:
The only intermediate station on the 4½-mile branch line was Sidley. The station building was attractive with red brick embellished by Bath stone dressing. In 1938 the Southern Railway let the building, and for many years it was used as a garage. The building was at street level and passengers descended to the platforms, located in a shallow cutting below. Sadly the building was demolished in 1970. *IAL*

Left:
The Bexhill West branch opened in May 1902 and closed 62 years later in June 1964. Trains had been steam-hauled for most of that time, but in 1958/59 English Electric DEMUs took over most branch services, by which time they had become Bexhill West to Crowhurst shuttles. On 14 June 1964, the last day of service, a 2H/4S six-car formation comprising Nos 1120 and 1007 arrives at Sidley with the 11.5am from Crowhurst. *S. C. Nash*

Right:
Sidley station once boasted up and down platform buildings, a signalbox and goods yard. Some 40 years after closure, the only remnant of the railway is the old goods shed, located at the down end of the up platform. The shed was sold out of railway use in 1920 and the faded lettering of a builder's merchant can just be seen. Note the awning over the road vehicle loading platform and the double doors across the old railway access. *JV*

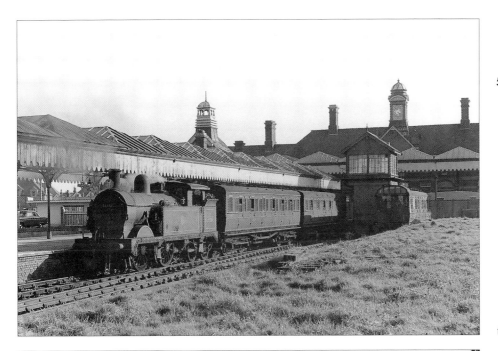

poked and prodded all aspects of the railway's infrastructure, fixtures and fittings before retiring to the Hotel Metropole in Bexhill for lunch. He then continued his inspection and, having spent some 7 hours on the line, returned to the capital. In a report published a few days later he gave his blessing to the opening of the line subject to some very minor alterations. Accordingly the opening ceremony was set for 31 May 1902, with public services starting the day after, Sunday 1 June.

The weather was kind on the opening day and the stations were gaily decorated with banners and bunting. The inaugural train left Bexhill at noon and the train locomotive was also highly decorated. The train was to travel to Crowhurst where it would connect with a special train from London, containing a really impressive list of VIPs who were amongst the most influential politicians and railway officials of the day, ranging from the Home Secretary to the Directors of the SECR. Both the train from Bexhill and the one arriving from London were packed, and crowds congregated at every vantage point. The down train had left Charing Cross at 11.10am, London Bridge at 11.15am and, after what must have been a stirring run, pulled into Crowhurst at 12.30pm. The combined trains then travelled slowly to Bexhill so that the visitors could have a good view of the new line. At Bexhill there were large crowds and, in the style of a modern railway enthusiast special, the local paper reported that 'snap-shooters were dodging about all over the place'! Although speeches were made on the platform, mostly praising the new railway and Bexhill, the principals and their entourage made off for a beano, again at the Hotel Metropole, while tables were set out at the station for the station staff and other railway employees to have their free lunch. A special train returned to London at 4.30pm.

The new Bexhill station was at the end of a route that, at 62 miles, was 9 miles shorter than the LBSCR route to London, and, as if to emphasise the point, the initial service included a through train to London that completed the journey in about 1 hour and 40 minutes, compared with the best LBSCR time of around 2 hours. In addition, there were four up and three down trains that comprised through carriages for either Victoria or Charing Cross. A local service was also provided, with passengers travelling beyond Crowhurst changing trains at the junction station. In total there were 13 trains per day in each direction. There was subsequently a juggling of names because the new CSBR/SER station had been opened as Bexhill-on-Sea, while the LBSCR station was known simply as Bexhill. After the Grouping in 1923 the LBSCR station was renamed Bexhill Central and the SECR station just plain 'Bexhill', although in 1929 this was changed again to Bexhill West.

It seems strange to relate that although the Bexhill West branch trains offered many advantages in elapsed journey time to London, it was difficult to shake the population of Bexhill out of its time-honoured traditions, which after all had been in existence for 56 years, and large numbers continued to use the LBSCR route. Although the SER offered some through carriages, there was of course no change of train needed along the coastal route. Also, the 'Brighton' station was nearer to the centre of Bexhill and nearer to the sea. By 1913 the through train from Bexhill West to London had been withdrawn. Another body blow to the SECR line was the onset of World War 1 and its impact on the economy, when, in January 1917, the line was temporarily closed. Goods services were reinstated later in the year, but passenger trains did not start to operate again until March 1919, and Sidley was not reopened until the middle of 1920. As with, *inter alia*, the Devil's Dyke and Kemp Town branches, the wartime closures had a serious impact on subsequent passenger receipts at a time when road transport was beginning to be competitive, especially on local journeys. After the war the through train to London was reinstated and through carriages continued, but the Bexhill West line continued to be secondary.

In 1927 there were about 15 workings over the branch in each direction, including both London trains/carriages and locals. Curiously the January 1927 Bradshaw shows a train that ran only on Wednesday nights, leaving Charing Cross at 5 minutes past midnight, with through carriages, arriving at Bexhill (West) at 2am! One goods train per day worked over the branch. The traffic graph of Bexhill West took a further dive when in 1935 the by then Southern Railway coastal route from Lewes, Haywards Heath and Brighton was electrified through to Ore, east of Hastings. Bexhill West was then reliant on a handful of commuters who travelled to London and those who made middle-distance journeys to Tunbridge Wells and Tonbridge. For many years there was also a school train. However, the off-peak local traffic was low in volume and, almost by default, the Bexhill West line had become a branch line! In fact, from the 1940s all through carriage workings were abandoned, and push-pull trains started shuttling between the terminus and Crowhurst. There was a period during 1949/50 when former glories were recalled. Bopeep Tunnel at St Leonards had to be closed for urgent engineering work, and main-line trains from Charing Cross to Hastings worked to and from Bexhill West, as seen in Sid Nash's excellent accompanying photographs. From time to time the carriage sidings at the terminus were the home of empty stock workings, especially hop-pickers' specials. The line was dieselised in 1958 and English Electric multiple-units replaced the old 'H' class steam locomotives, although there was a brief resurgence in 1959. Some aspects of the infrastructure had by then been run down, such as the loss of one of the platform awnings at Bexhill West, and the volume of goods traffic had diminished. At the beginning of the 1960s all British Railways lines were under critical review, and it was hardly surprising that the Bexhill West line failed to make the grade and was included in a long list of future closures. The freight service was withdrawn just six months after the publication of the Beeching report, and on 15 June 1964 the line closed completely. Those six months were used by local pressure groups, including some 250 regular commuters, to try and save the line, but despite petitions and protests it seemed that closure was a *fait accompli*, presumably because of the losses and the viable alternative route to London from Bexhill Central.

The last train from Bexhill West to Crowhurst, a seven-coach diesel train, left at 10.20pm on 14 June 1964, packed with locals and enthusiasts. Although there were attempts to reopen the line, the demolition gang arrived in 1965 and the entire track was lifted, various bridges were removed, and infrastructure razed. However, the most spectacular part of the decline of the Bexhill West branch was when the massive 17-arch viaduct across the Crowhurst marshes was blown up in May 1969. It was a story beloved of all news editors, who always want to end their broadcasts with a 'bang', and film crews were everywhere to record the occasion. Crowhurst station, albeit without its grand station building and with hugely rationalised track layout, is still open. Sidley station was demolished in 1970, but the brick goods shed remains. The ornate Bexhill West terminus is still in everyday use and is occupied by a firm of auctioneers. The old engine shed is still being used commercially within the industrial estate that now covers the old goods yard.

The Bexhill West branch had less variety of motive power compared with many other branch lines featured within this volume. In the early days most of the main-line through trains from Bexhill West were powered by various SECR 4-4-0s, and even in the 1950s 'D', 'E' and 'L' class locomotives appeared. 'Schools' class engines were regular visitors to the line, especially in the 1949/50 period, and they also dominated services on the main Hastings line. In push-pull days, the LBSCR 'D3' class worked the line until replaced by the SECR 'H' class. 'A1X' tanks were seen from time to time, and 'Cs' or 'Q1s' normally hauled

Above:
There is little left of the old Bexhill West branch, but happily the jewel in the crown is the magnificent terminus building, presently used by an established firm of auctioneers. With decorative brick and stone work, the facilities once included booking hall, ticket and parcels offices, station master's and inspector's offices, general and ladies' waiting rooms, refreshment rooms, ladies' and gentlemen's toilets and porters' and lamp rooms! *JV*

Below:
Bradshaw's timetable of 1910.

HASTINGS, ST. LEONARDS, BEXHILL, TUNBRIDGE WELLS, TONBRIDGE JUNCTION, and LONDON.—South Eastern & Chatham.

[Bradshaw's railway timetable, Up direction, Week Days and Sundays, with stations including Hastings, St. Leonards, West St. Leonards, Bexhill, Sidley, Crowhurst, Battle, Robertsbridge, Etchingham, Ticehurst Road, Wadhurst, Frant, Tunbridge Wells, Southborough, Tonbridge Junc., Victoria, London Bridge, Cannon Street, Waterloo Junction, and Charing Cross.]

NOTES.

a Stops by signal at 9 mrn. to take up 1st class London Passengers on notice being given to the Station Master.

b Stops to take up only.

c Stops by signal at 9 17 mrn. for Passengers from or to the Kent and East Sussex Line.

d Stops at 8 56 aft. to take up on 10 minutes' notice being given to the Stationmaster.

goods trains. From 1958 English Electric diesel-electric multiple-unit formations handled passenger services, and a diesel shunter appeared on freight trains.

The branch had a life of only 62 years and, despite the double track, the permanence of the structures and the grand opening, it never quite fulfilled its theoretical promise. The Grouping, then nationalisation, damaged the line and it seems that after 1923 little was done to actively promote it. The sad thing is that even in 2004 train times from Bexhill to London still cannot match those 1902

1hr 40min timings of the early days, and now passengers from Bexhill to London have the great frustration of travelling all the way from Willingdon Junction at Hampden Park to Eastbourne and back before they even get as far as Polegate. Presently the best time for the journey is about 1hr 49min! Anybody taking the trouble to drive to Crowhurst and ride the train can reach London in 1hr 27min on the now electrified line, so even though Crowhurst is of course not Bexhill, it would seem that the old 'Chatham' route still has something to offer.

3. Cuckoo Line

ALTHOUGH the Cuckoo line, the Uckfield line and the 'Bluebell' line were in some ways secondary through routes, in all other ways they were classic branch lines meandering through pleasant rural and pastoral countryside serving a number of small communities ranging in population from a few hundred to about 6,000 inhabitants. The opening dates of all of these lines pre-dated the motor car and motor lorry and it is easy to envisage the hopes and aspirations of the original railway promoters. The commercial opportunities afforded by the railway in opening up huge areas of Sussex by facilitating the movement of people and goods in terms of both cost and time were, in the eyes of the promoters, infinite. Certainly the farming community could take advantage of sidings at stations in exporting its produce, including milk, to other parts of the country while importing seeds and fertilisers to help boost production. The cost of domestic fuel would be slashed as coal moved in bulk by rail could more easily be distributed from local goods yards.

Although it seems somehow normal to think of lines radiating from London being built from north to south, it was often the case that the southern sections of such lines were built first. The first part of what was to become the Cuckoo line (named after the Cuckoo Fair held at Hailsham in April) is very old indeed. Early plans to connect the important town of Hailsham to the railway network were promoted in the 1840s. The London, Brighton & South Coast Railway opened its line from Brighton to St Leonards in June 1846, and in the same month an Act of Parliament authorised the construction of a branch line from Polegate to Hailsham (and incidentally a line from Polegate to a rapidly growing Eastbourne). As we will see, the railway had a profound effect on Hailsham, and between 1846 and 1901 it grew in population from 1,500 to over 4,000. Hailsham was the administrative centre for the area and was the location of police headquarters and local government offices. It was also an important market town in the heart of an agricultural area.

Construction commenced and the rate of progress was such that both the Hailsham and Eastbourne branches were opened on 14 May 1849. We are concerned here only with the Hailsham line, and although the Directors of the LBSCR and various officials headed initially for Eastbourne, there was nevertheless great celebration at Hailsham. The first train left Brighton at 8.40am, arriving at Polegate just over an hour later, where passengers from

Above:
The Cuckoo line enjoyed an almost infinite variety of motive power over the years. Some of the least likely examples that worked the line in the 1949/50 period were the huge Billinton 'J' class tanks, which were normally employed on a through Victoria to Eastbourne via Hailsham working. No 32325, formerly named *Abergavenny*, was built in 1910 and withdrawn from service during 1951. Here the 11.8am Victoria to Eastbourne train nears Polegate on 30 June 1950. *E. R. Wethersett*

Right:
Only pedestrians, dog-walkers, cyclists and horse-riders now pass this spot between Hailsham and Polegate, as the old trackbed has been converted into the 'Cuckoo Trail'. Passing a rural crossing, with the crossing keeper's cottage on the up side, two-car unit No 1119 with a '31' headcode stretches its legs between Hailsham and Polegate with a down working in September 1968. *JV/TTT*

Left:
The line between Hailsham and Eridge, including stations at Hellingly, Horam Road, Heathfield, Mayfield and Rotherfield & Mark Cross, closed to passengers from 14 June 1965, but the Eastbourne to Polegate and Hailsham service lasted until 9 September 1968. On the last day of service, 3H unit No 1112, forming the 12.16 departure, is, according to the old-fashioned destination board, bound for 'Hailsham only'. A new slightly relocated but featureless Polegate station has now been built. *JV/TTT*

a train from the Hastings direction joined the first train. In the wonderful terminology of the mid-Victorian era, newspaper reports referred to 'Hailsham being devoted to much pleasure'. Class consciousness came to the fore as it was reported: 'The poor were up and stirring with the lark and watched with no small degree of interest in the proceedings on the local common, where a feast of roast beef with plum pudding to follow as well as oranges and nuts was to be provided later in the day.' Large numbers of children attended, many from the nearby Union Workhouse. The Hastings band played rousing music and it seems a good time was had by all. The dignitaries, having 'done' Eastbourne, arrived at Hailsham by special train during the afternoon. Unfortunately the day was marred by a fatal accident to a train guard who was hit by a gate when standing on the step of one of the carriages. Nevertheless, at a formal dinner at The Crown Inn a toast to the 'prosperity of the town of Hailsham' was proposed.

The initial train service timetable was rather frugal and there were complaints that only a solitary locomotive was available to work both the Eastbourne and Hailsham lines, but by the early 1850s little four-wheeled coaches trundled to and from Hailsham about nine times per day. Although further railway development proposals emerged in the 1860s and 1870s, Hailsham was, surprisingly, to remain a terminus for a total of 31 years. Again, the prime cause for development was the LBSCR's fear, some might say almost paranoia, of the South Eastern Railway invading what is nowadays known as 'South Central' territory. In 1865 the LBSCR made proposals through Bills to cover much of what is now East Sussex with railways. Among these Bills was a plan to extend the railway north of Hailsham, but construction plans were abandoned some three years later after a national recession.

In 1873 the SER promoted a narrow gauge line from Hailsham to Tunbridge Wells. However, the idea of a narrow gauge line was dropped and an Act incorporating the Tunbridge Wells & Eastbourne Railway Company was passed in August 1873. Again, finance and delays resulted in little progress, and the 'Brighton' company was approached to take over the project. Although it initially refused the proposal, a deal was eventually done with the SER whereby the LBSCR was to construct and operate the line but the SER was to have running powers over it. A further Act was passed in 1876 that changed the alignment of the original proposal between Rotherfield and Hellingly. This Act specified that stations be provided at Rotherfield, Mayfield, Cross-in-Hand (for

Heathfield), Horeham (original spelling) and Hellingly. In July 1879 financial arrangements between the companies regarding the allocation of receipts was also agreed, and construction of what was to become the Cuckoo line commenced. The content of legislation required the LBSCR 'to provide a reasonable service between Tunbridge Wells and Eastbourne', presumably so that the SER could link into a London to Eastbourne route via connections between the Tunbridge Wells stations.

The line from Lewes to Tunbridge Wells via Uckfield had opened in 1868. The line from Hailsham to Tunbridge Wells was to join this line at Redgate Mill Junction, 1¼ miles south of Eridge, so it was not necessary to build a new railway for the whole of the distance between the aforementioned towns. However, with the planned through service to Eastbourne in mind, the junction at Polegate was facing Brighton to the west, whereas the Eastbourne line was to the east of Polegate. Therefore the station had to be moved some distance to the east and the track realigned to permit through running. The changes were completed on 3 October 1881. At the other end, at Redgate Mill Junction, the Cuckoo line ran parallel to the Uckfield line into Eridge until 1894, when the Uckfield line was doubled and the lines from Eridge to Redgate Mill became up and down tracks respectively used by train on both lines.

Construction continued apace and although the line was to be single track with passing places at all stations except Hellingly, some provision was made for the possibility of future double track. The first section of line completed was from Hailsham to Heathfield, some 7¾ miles, and this opened on 5 April 1880. The line to Redgate Mill and Eridge, nearly 10 miles further on, opened in September the same year. During 1884 and 1885 the SER flexed its muscles by invoking the through working clause dating back to the original agreement, and for over 18 months two express trains worked through from Charing Cross to Eastbourne and return. However, they were not successful and from that point until the Grouping the SER merely took its share of line revenues from the LBSCR. By 1888 there were seven trains in each direction on weekdays. Throughout the life of the line most trains ran from Eastbourne to Tunbridge Wells, but in the early days there were through coaches for London, attached/detached at Groombridge, and in Southern Railway days there was a sprinkling of through trains to and from the capital. By 1927 there were about 10 trains per day in each direction together with a few 'shorts' between Eastbourne and Hailsham. In 1950 there were eight or nine trains in each direction

Left:
The service between Eastbourne, Polegate and Hailsham (originally and latterly the terminus of the line) was always more intensive than through trains to either London or Tunbridge Wells West. For many years push-pull trains operated the Hailsham shorts. On 13 September 1952 the 5.44pm to Eastbourne leaves Hailsham and passes Hailsham South signalbox, being propelled by 'D3' class No 32384, of 1893 vintage. *S. C. Nash*

Top right:
The next station north of Hailsham was Hellingly. The station had an up-side goods yard, but also down-side sidings for the nearby hospital, originally a lunatic asylum. The hospital had its own railway, which was operated by electric power via an overhead 500V DC wire. On the right of this 1939 photograph are the remains of the dedicated hospital platform built to separate travelling inmates and visitors from the general public, which was removed in 1933. One of the overhead wire supports can just be seen. A down train headed by a 'Brighton' tank is approaching. *IAL*

Centre right:
Motive power for the Hellingly Hospital Railway came in the form of the diminutive 9-ton 0-4-0 that was provided by the original contractor, seen here at Hellingly on 19 September 1953. The 1¼-mile line had a passenger service until 1931, and an electric tramcar that could seat 12 passengers (six on each side) was used. The main incoming traffic was coal, but when the hospital boilers converted to oil-firing in 1959 the little railway was doomed. *S. C. Nash*

Lower right:
Although freight continued to visit Heathfield twice weekly until April 1968, the goods yard at Hellingly station, seen here, closed in 1964. The last passenger train called at Hellingly in June 1965, but the station building has survived and is now a private residence. The old trackbed is now part of the 'Cuckoo Trail' and is used for recreational purposes. This was the scene in 2002. *P. G. Barnes*

Above:
This was the only occasion that the author photographed the Heathfield freight while the train was still steam-hauled.
The weather was appalling on this April day in 1965 as Standard tank No 80089 departed from Horam Road in torrential rain,
with just four wagons and a brake-van. The locomotive had been noted earlier in the day shunting at Polegate. *JV/TTT*

Below:
A revisit to Horam Road (formerly known as Waldron & Horeham Road) was made in September 1971, and although
now historically interesting it made a sad sight. The tracks had been ripped up, the station and signalbox had been boarded up,
and debris was being burned in the goods yard, although the station and awning were perhaps surprisingly intact.
The only sign of life was the local coal merchant, who was still using the erstwhile goods yard. *JV*

TUNBRIDGE WELLS, HEATHFIELD, HAILSHAM, and EASTBOURNE.—L. B. & S. C.

Miles	Down. West End Station.	Week Days mrn	mrn	mrn	mrn	n	aft	aft (Saturdays only; also on 6th and 20th inst.)	n	aft	aft	aft	aft (Wednesdays and Saturdays.)	Sundays mrn	aft	aft
	190 VICTORIA .... dep.	5 25	7 44	....	9 10	1115	12 5	....	3 45	4 50	5 3	....	8 5	8 50	2 30	7 10
	190 LONDON BRIDGE. "	5 20	7 25	....	9 5	1056	1225	....	2b3	4o47	5 22	....	8 12	8 35	....	6 53
—	Tunbridge Wells ... dep.	7 10	9 10	....	1055	1220	1 50	....	4 35	5 55	6 40	....	9 34	1020	4 15	8 27
3	Groombridge	7 19	9 18	....	11 4	1227	1 57	....	4 44	6 2	6 49	....	9 41	1027	4 22	8 35
5	Eridge	7 24	9 23	....	11 9	1232	2 2	....	4 49	6 6	6 54		9 46	1032	4 27	8 41
8¾	Rotherfield & Mark Cross	7 32	9 31	....	1118	1241	2 12	....	4 59	6 15	7 2	....	9 55	1041	4 36	8 50
11	Mayfield	7 41	9 40	....	1127	1250	2 21	....	5 9	6 24	7 11	....	10 4	1050	4 46	8 59
14¾	Heathfield .... [Road	7 53	9 53	....	1139	1 2	2 33	....	5g27	6 36	7 23	8 20	1016	11 3	5 0	9 11
17¼	Waldron and Horeham	8 2	10 2	....	1148	1 15	2 42	....	5 36	....	7 32	8 28	....	1112	5 9	9 20
20¾	Hellingly	8 12	1011	1119	1157	1 24	2 50	4 32	5 45	....	7 41	8 37	....	1121	5 19	9 29
22¼	Hailsham	8c24	1018	1124	12 2	1 29	2 57	4 36	5 50	....	7 49	8 44	....	1129	5 25	9 34
25¼	Polegate 176, 180	8 32	1026	1131	1210	1 38	3 5	4 44	5 58	....	7 57	8 52	....	1140	5 33	9 42
27¾	Hampden Park †	8 38	1033	....	....	....	3 13	5 9	6 6	....	8 4	8 59	....	....	5 44	10 4
29¾	Eastbourne .... arr.	8 44	1038	....	1220	1 47	3 18	5 15	6 12	....	8 10	9 5	....	1150	5 50	1010

Miles	Up.	Week Days mrn	i	i	mrn	aft	aft	aft (Saturdays only; also on 6th and 20th inst.)	aft	aft	aft	aft	aft (Wednesdays and Saturdays.)	aft (Wednesdays only.)	Sundays mrn	mrn	aft
	Eastbourne .... dep.	6 46	8 0	10 0	1040	1240	3 40	4 0	4 45	6 20	....	7 30	....	1020	7 18	1020	6 15
2	Hampden Park †	6 50	....	10 3	....	1244	3 44	4 4	4 49	6 24	....	....	....	1024	7 22	1024	6 19
4½	Polegate	6 56	8 11	10 9	11 2	1250	3 51	4 15	4 55	6 30	....	7 39	....	1031	7 30	1030	6 25
7½	Hailsham	7 3	8 21	1016	11 9	1258	3 59	4 22	5 3	6 37	....	7 46	....	1038	7 38	1037	6 34
9	Hellingly .... [Road	7 8	8 28	1021	1114	1 3	4 4	4 27	5 8	6 42	....	7 51	....	1047	7 44	1042	6 40
12½	Waldron and Horeham	7 17	8 38	1030	....	1 14	4 13	....	5 18	6 52	....	8 0	....		7 54	1051	6 50
15	Heathfield	7 26	8 47	1039	....	1 23	4 22	....	5 27	7 1	7 25	8 8	1025		8 2	11 2	7 0
18¾	Mayfield	7h43	9 0	1051	....	1 35	4 34	....	5 40	....	7 36	8 20	1036		8 14	1114	7 12
21½	Rotherfield & Mark Cross	7 53	9 9	11 0	....	1 44	4 42	....	5 49	....	7 45	8 29	1045		8 23	1123	7 21
24¾	Eridge 196	8 3	9 20	11 9	....	1 53	4 51	....	5 59	....	7 54	8 38	1054		8 32	1132	7 30
26¾	Groombridge 191	8 8	9 25	1114	....	1 58	4 56	....	6 4	....	7 59	8 43	1059		8 37	1137	7 35
29¾	Tunbridge Wells 241 arr.	8 16	9 34	1122	....	2 5	5 5	....	6 13	....	8 7	8 51	11 7		8 45	1145	7 43
67¾	191 LONDON BRIDGE. arr.	9 42	1045	1243	i	3 36	6 30	....	7 46	....	....	1047	....		1018	....	9 10
67¼	191 VICTORIA (W.E.) "	9 40	1038	1225	....	3 30	6 22	....	8 20	....	....	1027	....		1020	1 30	9 0

b Leaves at 2 25 aft. on Saturdays. *c* Arrives at 8 17 mrn. *g* Arrives at 5 22 aft. *h* Arrives at 7 38 mrn.
i Through Carriages, Eastbourne Line Stations to Victoria. *i* 1 & 2 class Passengers arrive at 12 27 aft.
n Through Carriages, Victoria to Eastbourne Line Stations. *o* Leaves at 4 22 aft. on Saturdays.
† Station for Willingdon.

☞ For **LOCAL TRAINS** between Hailsham and Eastbourne, see page 198.

Above:
Bradshaw's timetable for April 1910.

with even more trains shuttling between Eastbourne and Hailsham. Many of the Eastbourne to Hailsham short workings were operated by push-pull sets powered by a variety of tank locomotives.

The line from Polegate ran northwards through pleasant unspoiled countryside and climbed up to Hailsham, some 3 miles distant. Hailsham had all facilities commensurate with its importance on the line, including a substantial goods shed and yard on the up side at the southern end of the complex, a goods yard crane, private and public sidings, a substantial station building and up and down platforms. Until the line was extended northwards in 1880 there was also a small locomotive shed. There was a large signalbox at the south end of the complex on the down side, and a smaller one at the north end of the up platform. The line then entered a deep cutting and the climb continued to Hellingly at 4¾ miles. The simple sidings at Hellingly were best known for the connection to Hellingly Mental Hospital, but there was also a three-road general goods yard and shed on the up side. Hellingly station was on the up side and there was a small signalbox at the up end of the platform, which closed in February 1930. The large hospital, originally the East Sussex County Asylum, was located about a mile from the station. A standard gauge railway was built at the beginning of the 20th century, which was initially used to convey construction materials to the asylum site. In total it was 1¼ miles long. In 1902 the managing committee decided to electrify the line by a trolley system using electricity generated within the asylum's own power plant. A small 0-4-0 electric locomotive was purchased, capable of hauling a couple of loaded coal wagons. There was also a 12-passenger single-deck tramcar. The committee reached agreement with the LBSCR not only to maintain the asylum's dedicated sidings but also to build a wooden platform for use by visitors to the asylum. Another platform was of course built at the asylum end of the line. The asylum opened for patients in 1903. The passenger service to the asylum ceased in 1931 and in later years the tramcar body was in use locally as a sports pavilion. In the late 1950s changes in the hospital's power plant meant that the electricity supply to the railway would cease, and sadly the last wagon traversed the line in March 1959. A full history of the little line has been written and published by Peter A. Harding (see Bibliography).

The Cuckoo line continued to climb from Hellingly to Horam (current spelling), 8¼ miles from Polegate. Sometimes referred to as Horam Road, the station was originally known as Waldron & Horeham Road, then Waldron & Horeham and, in the latter days of the line's life, simply Horam! Horam had the Express Dairy processing plant on its doorstep and there was plenty of milk traffic conveyed in glass-lined 3,000-gallon tankers until the contract was lost in the early 1950s, after which the milk travelled by road. The station and the goods yard were on the up side of the line with a modest shelter and awning being provided on the down side. Originally there was a north and south signalbox, but a lever frame on the platform replaced both. After climbing at 1 in 50, a height of 500ft above sea level was reached just beyond Heathfield, 10¾ miles out. The 266yd Heathfield Tunnel penetrated Battle Ridge to the north of the station. Heathfield, located 46 miles from London, was an important point on the line, especially for freight traffic. In fact, in 1965 all freight facilities on the line were withdrawn except those at Hailsham and Heathfield. Large volumes of outgoing milk and incoming coal were handled in the down-side yard as well as a wide range of other commodities, including agricultural produce. The main brick-built station building was at street level, high above the platforms. For many years the running-in board proclaimed 'Heathfield — Cross In Hand'. There were two signalboxes, but the north box was later reduced to a ground frame. A source of natural gas was discovered at Heathfield, supposedly the first such discovery in the UK, when a borehole was made for a water supply. The gas was harnessed to provide station lighting for many years as well as for powering a water pump.

Beyond Heathfield Tunnel the line descended the southern side of the River Rother valley and ascended the northern side at gradients of 1 in 50 to reach Mayfield, 14½ miles. Mayfield also had a substantial red-brick station building, and although originally there were two signalboxes, a 22-lever example to the north and a 12-lever frame on the up platform, after 1931 there was just a single 22-lever frame on the down platform. Mayfield had a goods yard and shed at the up end of the down platform. In the 1930s some 300,000 gallons of milk were shipped from the yard, but unfortunately the traffic was lost in the 1950s. The main station building was also on the down side, and refreshment rooms were available for the public. A subway connected the two platforms. Between Mayfield and Rotherfield & Mark Cross, 17¼ miles, up and down gradients in the 1 in 50/52 band were encountered, as well as 24-chain-radius curves and Argos Hill Tunnel. Rotherfield village was ¾ mile to the west of the shared-name station, while Mark Cross was 1¼ miles to the east. The station was on the down side of the track and the attractive little signalbox was at the down end of the down platform. There had been a larger north signalbox, but this was closed as an economy measure in 1935. The goods yard was at the up end of the down platform and as usual a goods shed was provided. The line then descended at 1 in 56 to Redgate Mill Junction, where the single-track Cuckoo line joined the double-track Uckfield line.

The variety of motive power that worked the Cuckoo line was, in Brighton terms, hugely varied, and all of the classes mentioned in the Uckfield line text in Chapter 4 are largely relevant here. There was also the usual sprinkling of ex-SECR power in the shape of 4-4-0 tender locomotives and 'H' class tanks. Worthy of special mention was the appearance on the Cuckoo line of Marsh's massive 'J' class tanks during the 1949/50 period; once main-line stalwarts, they ended their days on the Cuckoo 'branch'. After steam the usual three-car English Electric diesel-electric multiple-units took over, and during the period of steam/diesel transition Class 33 'Crompton' diesels worked both passenger and freight workings.

In 1956 British Railways made a big effort to encourage traffic on the branch by introducing an hourly service between Eastbourne and Tunbridge Wells. But by then the line was clearly a loss-maker, and with the increase in motor car ownership, with its great flexibility making inroads into the population's travel patterns, the situation could only decline. In the 1960s the line failed to meet financial viability criteria and, like many of the other lines in East Sussex, the Cuckoo line was listed for closure. Also, by then the timetable was less favourable than hitherto. The ensuing process resulted in the passenger service between Eridge and Hailsham being withdrawn in June 1965. At this time services were shared between three-car DEMUs and Standard 2-6-4Ts, normally hauling three corridor coaches. The last steam train had the inscription 'Farewell Faithful Servant' chalked around the smokebox, and some modest floral decoration was provided. After this partial closure, passenger services continued to run as far as Hailsham and freight trains worked to both Hailsham and Heathfield yards. The author visited the line in 1965 and was steam-hauled from Polegate to Horam. In 1967 he 'rode the freight' to Heathfield behind a Class 33/2 'Slim Jim' diesel, and in 1968, in 'Hailsham only' days, the train comprised a three-car 'Hampshire' unit.

The coal train to Heathfield ran three times a week, as required, but after a road bridge was damaged by a crane travelling on the back of a lorry in April 1968, freight ran only to Hailsham. This too ceased in August 1968, leaving just the DEMU shuttle to Hailsham, which was also doomed as closure notices were posted. The last day of service was Sunday 8 September 1968. The very last train comprised a two-car and a three-car DEMU to accommodate some 150 revellers who were determined to personally administer the last rites. As the train left, detonators exploded and the diesel sounded its horn, briefly drowning out the strains of 'Auld Lang Syne'. It was ironic that the first section of track opened, from Polegate to Hailsham, was to be the last to close, albeit some 119 years later! Eventually, long after closure, Polegate station was 'moved', a new station being built almost on the site of the original pre-1881 one. The old station building is now a public house.

The track was duly ripped up and the trackbed suffered a variety of fates. At Rotherfield the old station is now a well-preserved and highly desirable private residence, while nearby at Mayfield the station is semi-derelict and a road now runs along part of the trackbed. Heathfield station is at street level and survives, but the platform and goods yard area is completely covered by an industrial estate. The old tunnel entrance can still be traced. However, from Hellingly to Polegate the old trackbed, bar a housing estate or two, now forms part of the 'Cuckoo Trail', built for the enjoyment of hikers, cyclists and horse-riders. The trail is a delight to cycle on a fine day, although it is hard to imagine that trains traversed the route. Hailsham station has been razed, but Horam and Hellingly survive, the latter complete with awning!

Below:
After one abortive attempt to travel on the Heathfield freight, which was cancelled due to the absence of a train guard, the journey up from Polegate in the brake-van of the twice-weekly freight was finally achieved on 15 November 1967. The power provided for the train was Class 33/2 'Slim Jim' No D6597 (later No 33212), the very last Class 33 to be delivered in May 1962. By then the only commodity handled was coal. Here the locomotive is shunting the yard by Heathfield signalbox. The last freight ran about five months later. *JV/TTT*

This double-page spread is dedicated to the work of Sid Nash of Eastbourne who sadly passed away during the preparation of this book. In the post-war years and until many of the lines closed, he spent much of his time photographing branches in Sussex and Hampshire (and elsewhere). The photographs also show the immense variety of motive power found on the Cuckoo line.

Top left:
Clanking southward with a typical branch freight from Tunbridge Wells West to Polegate is 'C2X' class No 32541, near Argos Hill on 9 April 1952.
S. C. Nash

Centre left:
There is something graceful about a large-driver 4-4-0. With a 'Birdcage' set in tow, Wainwright SECR 'E' class No 31166 of 1905 vintage gallops towards Otham Court Crossing with the 1.56pm Tunbridge Wells West to Eastbourne on 27 March 1954. The tender was painted just after nationalisation with the clearly visible legend 'British Railways'. In the Summer 1955 Ian Allan *ABC*, No 31166 was the only 'E' class remaining in service.
S. C. Nash

Lower left:
One of the chunky 60-ton Billinton 'E5s', No 32585, has an easy load to handle at Argos Hill near Rotherfield on 9 April 1952. The train is the 1.50pm from Tunbridge Wells West, which would arrive in Eastbourne at 3.16pm. The locomotive was born in 1902 and withdrawn from service in 1954. *S. C. Nash*

Above:
Sid must have been really 'chuffed' on 12 May 1951 when, some three years after nationalisation, Class I1X No 2002, still in its Southern Railway livery and number, emerged from Heathfield Tunnel with the 4.39pm Eastbourne to Tunbridge Wells West train. It was clearly a warm evening, as most of the windows along the three-coach train are open. *S. C. Nash*

Below:
This is a truly remarkable sight, even though at that time a Bulleid Pacific regularly worked a morning Eastbourne to Hailsham service as a filling-in turn. Simply toying with its two-coach branch train, now preserved 'West Country' class No 34027 *Taw Valley* curves away from Polegate with the 8.16am Eastbourne to Hailsham 'short'. *S. C. Nash*

Above:
The railway line at Mayfield has been obliterated and its alignment now rests several feet below the tarmac of a local relief road. However, even though the station was in a sorry state when photographed in 2003, it was at least still standing, despite being devoid of railway passengers for 38 years. This is the view down the station approach road — just look at those chimneys! *JV*

Upper left:
Towards the end of the line's life, steam was rapidly disappearing from the Southern Region and diesel units operated some services. The lines towards the east of the region had an allocation of Class 207 'Oxted' (or 'East Sussex') units, which were 3 inches narrower than the 'Hampshire' Class 205 units. One of the 19 units, No 1310, pauses at Mayfield with the 9.56am Tonbridge to Eastbourne service on 11 June 1965, just a couple of days before complete closure of the line north of Heathfield. *J. Scrace*

Lower left:
The junction of the Cuckoo line with the Lewes to Tunbridge Wells via Uckfield line was at Redgate Mill Junction, 1¼ miles south of Eridge. Originally the two routes ran from here to Eridge as independent single tracks, but when the Uckfield line was doubled in 1894 trains on both routes shared the lines. On 13 January 1962 a Standard 2-6-4T is about to pass the signalbox with the 11.45am Eastbourne to Tunbridge Wells West service.
E. Wilmshurst

Top right:
A Victorian view of Rotherfield station showing three station staff on the up side (with two of them hoping that a train is not due) and two ladies in their 'Sunday best' on the down side. The sign shows the station name as Rotherfield, but for most of its life the station was known as Rotherfield & Mark Cross, the two villages being ¾ mile and 1¼ miles respectively from the Cuckoo line station. *IAL*

Lower right:
In early Southern Railway days, a typical branch train of the era approaches Rotherfield & Mark Cross. The headcode on 'D3' class No 2379 indicates a Tunbridge Wells West to Eastbourne service. Wagons can be seen in the down-side goods yard. Infrastructure items include oil lamps, upper-quadrant signal and water crane. Although there were through trains over the line, few could argue that in many ways the line was operated as a branch. *IAL*

Below:
The conversion of Rotherfield & Mark Cross from station to private residence must be one of the most impressive in the entire UK. This ornamental pond is an attractive feature that has been incorporated in the gap between the old up and down platforms. The main building is clearly discernible and the down-side awning has been incorporated in a large building extension. Compare the nearest station chimney with the Victorian photograph at the top of this page. The author thanks the current owner for the opportunity afforded to photograph his home. *JV*

4. Uckfield Line

THE Lewes & Uckfield Railway is an old line dating back to 1858, and was another brick in the London, Brighton & South Coast Railway's defensive wall to keep rival railway companies out of its area. The LBSCR intended to build two routes to Tunbridge Wells, from Three Bridges via East Grinstead and from Lewes via Uckfield and Eridge. In 1857 the Lewes & Uckfield Railway was authorised by Act of Parliament to build a 7-mile line from Lewes to the town of Uckfield, to the north-east of what is now the East Sussex county town. The line would follow the valleys of the Rivers Ouse and Uck, and the cost of building was a modest £66,500. Construction was rapid and within a year of Royal Assent of the Act the line was complete.

The line opened on 11 October 1858, although the public time-table was introduced one week later. There was much excitement locally and a public holiday was declared in Uckfield. As many free tickets as there were seats available on the first down train from Uckfield were issued on a first-come-first-served basis. However, the most spectacular sight was the first return train from Lewes, which departed at 12.15pm, comprising no fewer than 16 carriages and two wagons that were hauled by two highly decorated loco-motives. At Uckfield the church bells rang, the band played, there was a procession, and there were sports and games aplenty. There was an official dinner for 100 invited guests at the Maiden's Head Hotel. The day ended with a bonfire and fireworks that coincided with the departure of the last train of the evening from Uckfield.

In 1864 the LBSCR purchased the Lewes & Uckfield Railway, and in 1868 a new 3-mile stretch of railway was opened, giving the railway independent access to Lewes, avoiding Lewes Tunnel. The new line deviated from the old near the village of Hamsey to join the Brighton to Hastings line immediately east of Lewes station.

In 1861 powers had been granted to the Brighton, Uckfield & Tunbridge Wells Railway to build a railway north of Uckfield, but by 1864 these powers had been transferred to the LBSCR. Work commenced in 1863, and by 1 October 1866 the section from Tunbridge Wells to Groombridge had been opened. Also in 1866 the line from East Grinstead to Groombridge (and therefore Tunbridge Wells West) had been opened under the auspices of the LBSCR. However, south of Groombridge a 1,020yd tunnel some 158ft below the Wealden Heights ridge needed to be built, and both the 11-arch Sleeches Viaduct and the 10-arch Greenhurst Viaduct between Rotherfield (later Crowborough and Jarvis Brook) and Buxted, each named after local farms, were taking time to com-plete, their brick-arch structure no doubt being an obstacle. The line was inspected in July 1868 and formally opened on 3 August, thereby linking Tunbridge Wells to Brighton by rail. The first-day trains were well patronised, but celebrations were not quite as extravagant as those that had occurred in 1858.

From Lewes on the 1868 route the line crossed some goods lines on a girder bridge followed by another bridge that crossed Cliffe High Street in the heart of Lewes, closely followed by a bridge

Below:
Lewes, the county town of East Sussex, has always been a focal point for railway activity. At one time trains departed from the junction station for London, Brighton, Seaford, Eastbourne, Horsted Keynes (and beyond) and Uckfield (and beyond). Trains to the last two destinations are now history, and certainly this through working from Chatham via Tonbridge to Brighton is but a memory. In the early 1920s SECR 4-4-0 No 1079, with its outside-sprung tender, and a train of compartment coaches, with carriage boards, waits to leave for Brighton. *JV collection*

Above:
The heavy and powerful 85-ton LMS Fairburn 2-6-4Ts worked hard over many East Sussex branches until enough
BR Standard tanks were constructed at Brighton Works. Here No 42090 crosses the River Ouse on Every's Bridge at Lewes,
just beside Harvey's famous brewery, with the Sunday 8.50am Victoria to Brighton through train. *S. C. Nash*

Below:
Running down through Hamsey, between Barcombe Mills and Lewes, with the line elevated on an embankment above the flood
plain of the River Ouse, is 'L' class No 31778 heading the three-coach 3.4pm from Tonbridge. These locomotives were introduced
in 1914 to a Wainwright SECR design, but were later altered by Maunsell, the CME of the Southern Railway from 1923 to 1937.
F. J. Saunders

across the River Ouse, just south of Harvey's famous brewery. The Ouse is an important feature in this area, and between Lewes and Uckfield the river and its tributaries would be crossed no fewer than eight times! After passing near the village of Hamsey, and about 3 miles and 20 chains from Lewes, Culver Junction was reached, although the site only became a junction when the Lewes and East Grinstead line opened in 1882. Originally opened as Barcombe, the first station out of Lewes was Barcombe Mills, about half a mile from Culver Junction. The original 1858 station was extended in 1900. A signalbox was located by a road crossing at the north end of the station. On the down side was a goods yard and there was a lengthy siding down to the local corn mill. Many fishermen alighted at the station to fish the River Ouse. A couple of miles along the way was Isfield station, serving a village with a population in 1901 of 431. There was a road crossing at the south end, a signalbox on the down side, and a goods yard on the up side. The station became a railway preservation site 110 years after opening.

The market town of Uckfield, 8½ miles from Lewes, was by far the largest centre of population on the original line, with a population in 1901 of 2,895 souls. At Uckfield there were two signalboxes, a handsome goods shed on the down side, and various sidings. The railway ran through the town at the lowest point of the valley, and downhill roads approached the level crossing on both sides of the line. This point has always been susceptible to flooding, courtesy of the nearby River Uck. From Uckfield the line continued through wooded country to Buxted, at 10 miles and 60 chains, which had all the facilities associated with a 'Brighton' country station of the era, including a handsome station building. North-west of Buxted the line crossed the 185yd Greenhurst Viaduct, and a mile later the 183yd Sleeches Viaduct. Climbing at 1 in 75, Crowborough (originally Rotherfield) Tunnel was reached, and after emerging therefrom trains reached Crowborough & Jarvis Brook, 15 miles and 20 chains from Lewes. The station was opened as Rotherfield in 1868, but the name was changed to Crowborough in 1880, and to its current name in 1897. A name 'split' was relevant because Crowborough was some 1½ miles from the station! A significant goods yard graced the down-side area beyond the station, and as with many other stations on the line a pedestrian overbridge was provided, linking the platforms. One of the signal-boxes was located about half way along the up platform, and there was another further south.

Beyond Crowborough & Jarvis Brook the line descended at 1 in 75 to Redgate Mill Junction at approximately 17 miles and 60 chains, the junction for the Cuckoo line from 1880 until 1965. It is historically significant that the entire line from Lewes to Redgate Mill Junction via Uckfield was doubled by 1894. The next station, at just over 19 miles from Lewes, was Eridge. The station is situated in something of a cutting with the station building at road level. The platform comprised two island platforms, although in later years the two outer roads were merely stubs, effectively bay platforms. Goods facilities, including a goods shed, were originally provided, with signalbox and sidings necessarily situated in a rather confined space. Until 1985, particularly after the Three Bridges to Tunbridge Wells line closed in 1967 and the Ashurst Junction to Groombridge Junction line closed in 1969, passengers from the north and the south changed at Eridge for Groombridge and Tunbridge Wells West and vice versa. North of Eridge the line veered to the east at a point that became Birchden Junction, 20 miles, towards Groombridge Junction and Groombridge station. In 1888 the line that ran down from Oxted via Hurst Green, Edenbridge Town, Hever, Cowden, Ashurst and Ashurst Junction (not included in this volume) was opened and a spur line from Ashurst Junction (where the Three Bridges line joined the route) to Birchden Junction, on the Uckfield line, was later constructed, producing a very large triangle. The line beyond Groombridge through High Rocks to Tunbridge Wells West is dealt with in Chapter 6.

From October 1858 there were five trains per day to and from the Uckfield railhead. A horse-drawn coach service was provided to make connections between the railway at Uckfield and Tunbridge Wells. By 1888, 20 years after the opening of the entire line, there were nine trains in each direction at Uckfield, although three were short workings to and from Lewes. Through trains between Brighton and Tunbridge Wells had a total journey time of 1hr 20min. By 1927 there were some 20 trains in each direction covering all route permutations, including through trains to and from London (London Bridge and Victoria). Many trains ran beyond Tunbridge Wells West to Tonbridge, thereby invading 'Chatham' territory, and in the 1930s there was a daily through train from Brighton to Chatham via Maidstone. Overall the frequency of trains was good for an area that was not heavily populated.

In recent times, since the truncation of the line at Uckfield (see below), an hourly regular-interval service has been provided. Most trains run to and from Oxted, where trains connect into electric services plying between London and East Grinstead. However, commuters are still catered for by a through train to Victoria and another to London Bridge in the morning and return workings in the evening. There were many unusual workings over the years, ranging from through trains from the Medway towns, such as Gillingham, to Brighton, particularly in pre-war times, to 'Bicycle Belle' specials from London for cyclists wishing to partake of their hobby in the countryside.

In common with so many other branch and secondary lines or byways that opened with such optimism, there followed a period of consolidation where, over several decades, the Lewes and Uckfield line performed a useful function, mainly for local communities but also as part of a through route. However, after World War 2 there was a period of rundown leading eventually, in the 1960s, to financial scrutiny and consequent partial closure. Nearly all of the 'Wealden' lines were uneconomic by the 1950s, and most were identified as candidates for total closure in Dr Beeching's reports and the BR Reshaping plan. Certainly when the author travelled from Brighton to Tonbridge in 1956, changing at Tunbridge Wells West, he recalls lightly loaded trains. So it came to pass that the broadly parallel 'Bluebell' line closed finally in 1958, the Three Bridges to Tunbridge Wells West line closed on New Year's Day 1967, the Ashurst Junction to Groombridge spur closed in 1969, and, alas, after 110 years of operation, the first section of the line to be built, from Lewes to Uckfield, was closed on 24 February 1969. The line between Uckfield and Lewes had been scheduled for closure on 6 January, but due to replacement bus service problems a stay of execution was granted. There were structural problems with a viaduct just outside of Lewes, and a special train shuttle service was provided until the line finally closed.

Things could have been much worse, but in 1969 it was announced that the Minister of Transport had refused to give consent to the closure by the Southern Region of the line between Hurst Green and Uckfield and the line from Eridge (Birchden Junction) to Tunbridge Wells West. The Minister decided that there was a case on social and economic grounds for a grant to be paid under Section 39 of the Transport Act 1968 to maintain 'modified services' on both sections of this route, as part of grant-aid for the London commuter services as a whole. Nevertheless, some 16 years later, in July 1985, the line from Eridge (Birchden Junction) to Tunbridge Wells West (and on to Grove Junction) did finally close, depriving Eridge of its junction status and leaving Tunbridge Wells to be served only by its 'Central' station on the Tonbridge to Hastings line.

There were many other changes executed on the remaining railway, with parts of the line down to Uckfield being singled. At Eridge, a once important junction station, only the former up main platform is used, a dramatic contrast with the four usable platforms of yesteryear. The signalbox has closed and the only encouraging signs are the well-populated commuter's car park on the site of the

Top right:
Rails warped by excessive heat during the summer months is not a new phenomenon: on 5 July 1923 LBSCR 'D1' class No 253 was leaving Culver Junction with the 4.27pm Brighton to Tunbridge Wells West when it spectacularly derailed due to the road spreading. Note the coal in the foreground that has spilled from the bunker, and also the signal wires on the right. Only the driver was slightly injured. *A. B. McLeod*

Centre right:
Perhaps the classic goods engine for Sussex branches was the 'C2X', a Marsh rebuild of the Billinton 'C2' class, introduced in 1908. Photographs of the daily goods actually doing business at Barcombe Mills station are extremely rare, but in this view No 32441 shunts the freight siding while leaving the main part of its train on the down line. The purpose of the loading gauge perfectly positioned above the locomotive's cab is obvious. The train is a through working from Tunbridge Wells West to Lewes. *Norman Simmons*

Lower right:
The line between Uckfield and Lewes opened in 1858 and was closed in May 1969. The first station out of Lewes was Barcombe Mills, and this view looking north shows the station during the winter following closure. The old crossing gates, signalbox and weed-covered track are still in place, but soon the track will be recovered. Happily the station has been saved and is now in use as a residence and restaurant. *JV/TTT*

CHEAP DAY - 2nd
Brighton
to   (No. 1)
**BARCOMBE
MILLS**
via Lewes
(S)
5964

Top left:
Some 5¾ miles from Lewes was Isfield station, although as usual the station was not well placed for the village. The delightful lower-quadrant LBSCR signal is 'off' for this down train during the reign of King Edward VII. Some work is progressing on the up platform because the running-in board is on the ground on the platform slope.
IAL

Lower left:
Nearly 80 years separate this photograph and the above view, but contrary to the usual depressing comparisons little has changed, except that through trains to Lewes no longer run. Photographed in September 1983, the station and signalbox had been fully restored resulting in a 'Best Restored Station' award in 1985. The crossing gates and the fencing look immaculate and, continuing with the good news, the Laughing Fish public house on the left is still open!
P. G. Barnes

Below:
After closure of the line, 14 years elapsed before British Rail sold the station, and it was purchased by the Milham family, who set about restoring the building and the site. Track was relaid and various stock items were imported. This eventually led to the creation of the 'Lavender Line', with steam and diesel trains running on public open days. On 29 March 1997 Class 73 electro-diesel No E6003 runs along the restored track towards the station with a shuttle train. Shunting the depot on the left, on the site of the old goods yard, is the rare Bulleid Class 12 No 15224. *P. G. Barnes*

Above:
The distant farm overbridge links this photograph from the 1950s with the previous plate. The signal is 'off' for 'L' class No 31763 as it eases out of the station with a Tunbridge Wells West train. For many years there has been talk of restoring the line and the train service between Uckfield and Lewes, using an old pre-1868 alignment at Lewes. Sadly this proposal is for the railway romantic who would be unable to persuade a public or private undertaking to invest millions of pounds, with no prospect whatsoever of profit, unless subsidised by car-owning Council Tax-payers. *Hugh Davies*

Upper right:
There is no sadder sight than revisiting a closed station, which just months earlier (and for the past 110 years) had been providing a public service, even if only for a handful of people. This view shows an abandoned Isfield station during the winter of 1969/70 and should be compared with the following photograph. *JV/TTT*

Lower right:
With a rather incongruous 'Elizabethan' headboard, Ivatt 2MT 2-6-0 No 46443 faces the down direction at the up platform while waiting for a tank locomotive and brake-van to clear the line before proceeding to 'Dingley Dell'. The shuttle service was being provided on 28 January 1995 at the Lavender Line's winter gala. *P. G. Barnes*

Left:
Preparing to stop at Isfield for absolutely no reason other than to comply with the timetable, 'Hampshire' three-car DEMU No 1118 rolls in with a Victoria to Brighton train on 28 December 1968. It had been many years since the oil lamp provided any illumination, but the footprints in the light snow show that more than one person other than the photographer had used the up platform earlier in the day. *JV/TTT*

Below:
The largest intermediate station on the line was Uckfield, but for the first 10 years of its existence it was the terminus of a line from Lewes. The original station was replaced by this magnificent double-gabled building in 1901. Posing on the down platform soon after opening are 18 members of staff, with the boy in the foreground looking pleased with himself, probably because he is sitting in front of the bearded stationmaster. The latter would be outraged to know that in 1986 his office was being used by a taxi firm (see below right). Note the substantial goods shed in the background. *IAL*

Above:

This photograph, looking down the main A22/A26 road(s) at Uckfield on 7 January 1989, shows the acute problems caused by the railway crossing. Twice each hour (the up and down hourly trains) the old manual gates needed to be opened and closed and manual upper-quadrant semaphore signals operated. Eventually the lovely old station building featured opposite was closed and demolished and a new single-faced concrete platform was built to the right of this scene, on the other side of the road. No 207011 leaves for Oxted with the 14.39 departure. *JV/TTT*

Below:

This fine picture is worthy of inclusion not only because the awning-less station can be compared with the earlier view but also because anybody prepared to photograph the up locomotive-hauled commuter service to London at 07.00 hours on the wet morning of 23 January 1986 deserves a medal. Having worked down to Uckfield as 2L63, the 05.48 service from East Croydon, Class 33 No 33042 has run round its stock and, after positioning the train at the up platform, will form train 2L80, the 07.11 Uckfield to London Bridge. *B. K. Addis*

Above:
Four old-timers at Uckfield! The pace is leisurely and there is time for a chat as elderly 3H DEMU No 205012 rests at the new but featureless Uckfield station in September 1991. A miserable small open shelter is the only passenger comfort. The track and the gates in the foreground were subsequently removed, but the signalbox found use as an office and survives to this day. *JV/TTT*

old goods yard and the surviving station building at street level. At Uckfield the old original station and adjacent road crossing were abandoned so that terminating trains no longer had to cross the main road through Uckfield, which had caused delays to traffic. In 2000 the grand station building and the substantial goods shed were demolished. Over the years there have been plans to electrify the remaining line from Oxted to Uckfield. Indeed, the line from Oxted to East Grinstead was electrified in 1987, but the money was never found for a third rail to Uckfield. Nowadays the line does allow an increasingly rare opportunity: to travel on a single line in Sussex by scheduled service train under diesel power. There have been moves to reopen the Uckfield to Lewes line, but its use as an alternative through route from London to Brighton was discounted years ago, and in 2004, with no money available for primary railway projects, it seems that such notions are merely for the romantic amongst the railway fraternity. The car is king in this part of Sussex, and the notion that a proposition could ever be self-financing is, sadly, for the nearby 'cuckoo' land.

As with so many other Brighton byways, the usual range of 'Brighton' locomotives worked the line over the years. Other than during the earliest days, such locomotives as Stroudley 'single' 2-2-2s were regular performers, as were Classes 'Gladstone' 0-4-2; B4, D, E, L and 'Schools'; H2, K, N and U1; C2, C2X and Q; D1, D3, I1X and I3; 'West Country'; Standard, Fairburn LMS and Ivatt tanks, and I have no doubt many more! Class 33 diesels also worked the line, and once steam disappeared 3D, 3H and 3R diesel-electric multiple-unit types were regular performers for some 40 years. Indeed, at the end of 2003 the service was still in the hands of these 46-year-old veterans, fondly nicknamed 'Thumpers'. By 2004 services were in the hands of modern two-car sliding-door Class 170 'Turbostar' units. Enthusiasts' specials have of course traversed the line, with perhaps a Class 45 visitor in 1986 being the most interesting interloper.

In addition to the surviving section of line down to Uckfield, the length of line between Lewes and Tunbridge Wells West is perhaps unique in having two railway preservation centres now operating on closed sections of the original route, within 25 miles of each other. The 'Lavender Line' is located at the closed station of Isfield, and the Spa Valley Railway is based at Tunbridge Wells West (see Chapter 6). Isfield station closed in 1969, and in 1983 the Milham family purchased what was by then a rather forlorn building. They established a railway centre and completely refurbished the site, including the station building and signalbox. They extended the buildings, provided 'facilities' for the public, built a bookshop and café, and a large restoration and storage shed on the site of the goods yard. Various items of motive power and rolling stock were acquired, and the 'Lavender Line' was born. The name came from the firm of A. E. Lavender & Sons of Ringmer, which once operated from the goods yard. A length of trackbed north of Isfield, to a site colloquially known as Dingley Dell, was purchased, and on open days trains operate over the extended line for the benefit of the public. Isfield station won the 'Best Restored Station' award in 1985. The Milham family pulled out in 1992 and other enthusiasts became more involved in site restoration projects. Some of the line was washed away in the floods of 2000, and although some stock has recently been transferred away, the attractive site is still an active preservation centre featuring both steam and diesel traction.

There is no doubt that the Uckfield stub is now something of an anachronism. On the one hand there is a growing population in the small towns served by the railway and in their general 'parkway' catchment area. Many commuters have decided that living in the countryside while working in London is, despite the arduous nature of the journey, a preferred lifestyle. On the other hand the line is served by diesel units with, seemingly, little hope of line electrification. Off-peak train loadings are poor and the line is likely to remain as a mainly single-line stub. However, for the present it seems to be secure, but the old expression 'use it or lose it' must always be uppermost in the minds of locals, and there is absolutely no room for complacency.

Above:
A splendid, if conventional, shot of a LBSCR Class I3 in British Railways livery. Sporting the 'lion and wheel' emblem on the side tanks, 1910-built No 32030 nears Eridge on 1 June 1950 with an up Cuckoo line train. Note the surviving LBSCR lower-quadrant signal. *E. R. Wethersett*

Upper right:
The next station north of Uckfield is Buxted. The station is a focal point for a number of surrounding communities, a fact supported by the number of commuters' cars in the station car park. With the high land of Ashdown Forest in the distant background and with the advanced starting signal 'off', 'West Country' class No 34012 *Launceston* heads south with a Victoria to Uckfield ramblers' excursion on 2 July 1963. *S. C. Nash*

Lower right:
Until August 1880 Crowborough & Jarvis Brook station was known as Rotherfield, but this changed with the opening of the Cuckoo line that year. The village of Rotherfield was much nearer to the Cuckoo line, hence the naming of Rotherfield & Mark Cross station on that route (see Chapter 3). The new 1905 station had a sizeable goods yard with a substantial goods shed, and is featured in this Edwardian scene as a Brighton tender locomotive heads a southbound train. *IAL*

The timetable for November 1888.

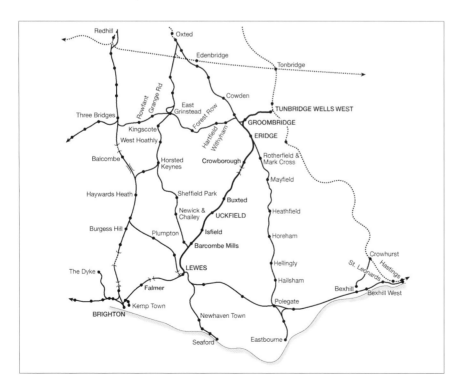

Above:
North of Crowborough & Jarvis Brook, but just over 1 mile south of Eridge, was Redgate Mill Junction, where the Cuckoo line joined the Uckfield line. Eridge was a wonderful country junction station with little by way of population in the immediate vicinity. Once Uckfield became a terminus it became the target for a number of railtours, but a most unusual visitor turned up on 27 December 1986 when a Pathfinder tour brought 135-ton 'Peak' class 45/1 1Co-Co1 No 45104 *The Royal Warwickshire Fusiliers* to the line. In failing light the interloper is passing the diminutive Eridge signalbox on its way south. *JV/TTT*

Upper left:
The timetable for November 1888.

Lower left:
Map of the Uckfield line and connecting lines.

2nd - SINGLE   SINGLE - 2nd
3698   Eridge to
Eridge / Tunbridge Wells / Central
TUNBRIDGE WELLS CENTRAL via Groombridge
(S)   1/8   Fare 1/8   (S)
For conditions see over   For conditions see over

42

Upper right:
During its heyday Eridge station comprised two island platforms providing two up and two down platform faces. Leaving the up central platform, prior to replacement of the lower-quadrant LBSCR signals with BR upper-quadrant examples, 'D' class No 31728 heads the 11.19am Brighton to Tonbridge train. The wooden goods shed was demolished long ago and the land now comprises a surprisingly busy rail travellers' car park, a good example of 'park and ride'. *SLS/R. F. Roberts*

Lower right:
In more recent times economies on the Uckfield line have been introduced, including centralised colour-light signalling and the singling of long sections of track. With the abandoned down road on the right and the closed signalbox being overwhelmed by undergrowth on the left, No 207203 approaches Eridge with a train from Oxted to Uckfield on 16 April 2003. Note the 4-CEP trailer from a withdrawn Kent Coast electric unit. *JV*

Below:
In the days when Eridge was a true junction with cross-platform interchanges, 'Oxted' Class 207 unit No 1317 waits in what was by then the up bay platform with an Eridge to Tonbridge working. This service was withdrawn in July 1985 when both Groombridge and Tunbridge Wells West finally lost their regular train service. The photograph shows the rural setting of Eridge station, although the bathroom facilities could perhaps be a little more private! *JV/TTT*

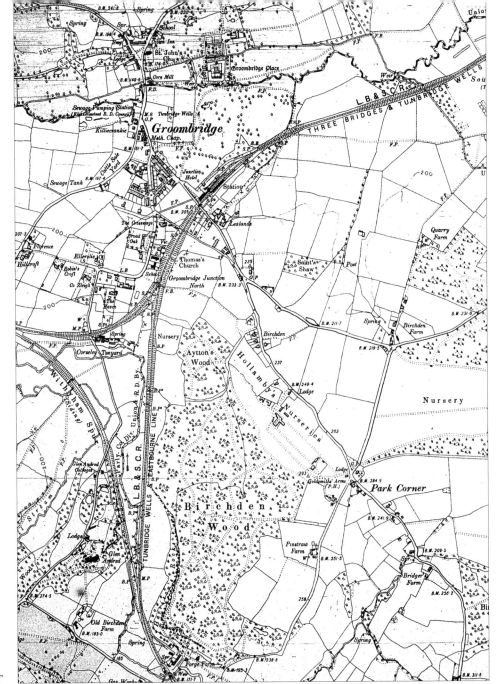

Right:
This early *circa*-1910 map shows the triangle formed between Birchden Junction near Eridge at the bottom, Groombridge Junction at the top and Ashurst Junction to the left. Both Uckfield and Cuckoo line trains to Tunbridge Wells West used the right-hand spur (now part occupied by the Spa Valley Railway) while both East Grinstead and Oxted to Tunbridge Wells West trains used the north chord, at the top. The left-hand spur is now the only survivor in everyday use — by Oxted to Uckfield trains. However, it is interesting to note that at this early date the line is shown only as 'Withyham Spur (Siding)'; it was only used as a through route from 1914.
Crown Copyright

Below:
The remote Birchden Junction signalbox controlled the junction of the Groombridge and Tunbridge Wells West line (right) and the Oxted to Uckfield line (left). Passing the signalbox in October 1983 is a fascinating Class 33 diesel-hauled train: a 'Bicycle Belle' special from London Bridge to Crowborough & Jarvis Brook. The four leading GUV vans contain dozens of bicycles, with the cyclists being accommodated in the six Mark 1 coaches behind. *JV/TTT*

5. Bluebell Railway and Ardingly Branch

Right:
No book on branches and byways in Sussex would be complete without a fairly weighty chapter on the Bluebell Railway. At its southern end the line diverged from the Uckfield route at Culver Junction, north of Lewes. Joining the double-track Uckfield line from the single-track Bluebell line is 2-6-4T No 80011 on 15 March 1958, the penultimate day of service, with the 2.28pm East Grinstead to Lewes train. *Norman Simmons*

THERE is little that has not been written about the now famous Bluebell Railway that BR closed in 1958. Since the formal reopening of the line in 1960, scheduled train services have been running in a preservation environment for some 44 years — well over one-third of the total time that has elapsed since the line was first opened in 1882. The Bluebell Line was one of the pioneers in standard gauge preservation and for that it deserves the degree of fame and the size of patronage that it has attracted. In fact, so much time has elapsed since the Bluebell Railway was reopened that photographs of the 1960 period are now historic!

This chapter deals only with the railway line that was built from East Grinstead (Low Level) to Culver Junction and Lewes via Horsted Keynes and the short Ardingly branch that connected Horsted Keynes with Haywards Heath on the London to Brighton main line. The 1830s was a remarkable decade for railway development throughout the country, and plans of varying viability competed with each other as the wealthy put their brains into overdrive on how they might earn 'a fast buck' by investing in the new form of transport with all its attendant advantages to the community. Bills for presentation to Parliament were thicker than flies and many were in direct competition with each other. Tactics were like a game of chess, where established railway companies proposed not only primary 'bread and butter' routes but lines that would prevent other companies from penetrating their 'patch', thereby maximising income, increasing profits, and hence returns for the investors and landowners.

As far as the London, Brighton & South Coast Railway (formerly the London & Brighton Railway) was concerned, its main opposition for through routes to the South Coast, especially Brighton, came from the constituent companies of the South Eastern & Chatham Railway, or those local companies that would be looking to the SECR to run services over their lines. East of the main London to Brighton line the land was virgin in railway terms, and the plans for new railway routes were thick on the ground in the 1835 to 1880 period, and far too numerous to detail here. In 1855 the LBSCR reached East Grinstead from the Three Bridges direction, but, as mentioned in the Kemp Town Branch chapter, the battle between the competing railways came to a head in 1863 when the South Eastern Railway backed the Beckenham, Lewes & Brighton Railway, which intended to head south through East Grinstead, Newick and Lewes to terminate to the east of Brighton in the Kemp Town area. A further scheme was proposed in 1865.

With the extension of the Three Bridges and East Grinstead line to Tunbridge Wells in 1866, completion of the Uckfield line throughout in 1868, and the 'Cuckoo line' in 1880, the LBSCR very much 'ring-fenced' its domain. Furthermore, in 1864 the LBSCR planned to build the Ouse Valley Railway from the south of the Ouse Valley Viaduct on the London to Brighton main line, eastward through Lindfield, north-east of Sheffield Park, Uckfield and Hailsham towards St Leonards and Hastings. Work actually commenced on the line, but as a result of the great recession in the mid-1860s,

Above:
Barcombe station had only a single platform face but that did not stop the railway building a substantial station building, which survives today as a private residence. Here 'C2X' class No 32440 leaves with the 12.28pm SO service from East Grinstead to Lewes. This working commenced in January 1955 in connection with Brighton & Hove Football Club matches at Hove, with cheap through ticket availability. There are two wagons in the small goods yard. *A. W. Burges*

Left:
After closure, nature soon took hold and in many cases it was some years before BR disposed of redundant property, resulting in a scene of total abandonment and considerable dereliction. This view shows Barcombe in September 1971, with nature gradually reclaiming its ground. The building is now well preserved, although substantial trees now afford casual passers-by only a glimpse of the erstwhile station. *JV*

Below:
Few would now believe that a down evening train to Lewes commenced its journey from Newick & Chailey station. In this truly idyllic rural branch line scene, LBSCR 'E4' class No 32482 and its two elderly coaches catch the last rays of the sun as they approach Barcombe with the 7.28pm from Newick on 5 May 1955. *S. C. Nash*

Above:
In LBSCR days, heading a northbound train comprising a couple of six-wheeled vehicles and some bogie coaches is 1893-built 'D3' class No 373. As can be seen from the road bridge in the background, the line was built for double track but only station passing loops were provided between Culver Junction and Horsted Keynes. After the line closed in 1955 Barcombe was one of the stations that never reopened. *IAL*

Right:
The short 61yd Cinder Hill Tunnel was located about ¼ mile south of Newick & Chailey station, and was one of only three tunnels built by the Lewes & East Grinstead Railway. In this November 1965 view the track had been removed but the foliage had not then obliterated the scene. *IAL*

Below:
This Sid Nash classic has been published many times before, but in view of its rarity, sharpness and lighting it deserved inclusion in this tome. On 25 May 1955 the 5.18pm Brighton to Victoria train was unusually powered by LSWR 'T9' class No 30718, returning to Nine Elms shed. The train comprises a Maunsell three-set with Pullman car *Savona* at the rear, returning from Preston Park Works to Stewarts Lane. The train is climbing away from Barcombe.
S. C. Nash

Left:
The Culver Junction to East Grinstead line was set to close on 13 June 1955, but due to a strike by BR employees the last rites were administered on 28 May. A story told many times relates to the discovery that the wording of the original Act of Parliament approving the construction of the line stated that the line could only be closed by another Act and not by the railway company. Accordingly, British Railways was obliged to run four trains per weekday from 7 August 1956 until 16 March 1958. With much local excitement, the first 'reinstated' train, headed by Billinton 'K' class Mogul No 32342, arrives at Newick & Chailey.
Hugh Davies

Right:
The re-instated service did not provide any useful connections and through ticketing was not available. BR was clearly irritated at being beaten by protesters, and its actions at this time could have been interpreted as being bloody-minded. Less than three weeks after the reopening, 'C2X' class No 32434 pauses at Sheffield Park with the 3.30pm Lewes to East Grinstead service. By then the up platform had been abandoned because there was only one train on the route at any one time.
S. C. Nash

Left:
A couple of months before the first formal closure date, one of the purposeful Brighton-built Standard tanks, No 80016, pauses at Sheffield Park with the headcode discs denoting a Victoria to Brighton train. Photographed on 16 April 1955, the substantial station building still dominated the scene, with tapered oil lamps adding to the platform decoration. Within five years the platforms would be swarming with visitors to the Bluebell Railway headquarters. *S. C. Nash*

Above:

Railway services under the auspices of the Bluebell Railway officially commenced on Sunday 7 August 1960. In the early days mostly small locomotives were used, such as 'P' and 'A1X' classes and a North London 0-6-0T, but in later years a huge variety of locomotives appeared including Pacific 4-6-2s and even a '9F' class 2-10-0! One of the great curios, no longer on the railway, was this Aveling-Porter locomotive that once worked for the Blue Circle Cement Company. The unusual device was photographed hauling the LNWR observation saloon and a van north of Sheffield Park on 17 October 1964. *G. D. King*

Below:

An atmospheric backlit view of the trackwork south of Sheffield Park in 2002 finds two locomotives in steam, 'Q1' class No 33001 on the left and SECR 'C' class No 592 on the right. The Bluebell Railway has now celebrated its 40th anniversary, and throughout that time it has operated a steam-only policy. Only time will tell whether this policy is short-sighted — it will be fully justified if future generations who have only known diesel traction continue to visit the line in large numbers.
To this extent a diet of 'Thomas the Tank Engine' may prove invaluable. *John Hicks*

which affected capital investment in railways throughout the country, work came to an abrupt halt and was never restarted.

In 1876 a group of residents and landowners collaborated in creating the Lewes, East Grinstead & London Railway. The three-part proposal comprised the sections north and south of East Grinstead and a branch from Horsted Keynes to Copyhold Farm, north of Haywards Heath (near the site of the present Copyhold Junction). Even the formidable list of noblemen and gentry associated with the LEGLR could not raise sufficient funds to build the proposed line, and the Chairman of the company, Lord Sheffield, approached the LBSCR. By 1878 that company had two members on the Board of the LEGLR, and it looked as though 'loads of money' would be earmarked for the proposed line, but only between Lewes and East Grinstead. Work commenced and a line to very high standard was built, not only in terms of permanent way but also in terms of stations, which were rather grand for the essentially rural area served. The signalling system was praised, although at a dozen signalboxes in total the specification did seem rather lavish!

Construction was relatively straightforward, notwithstanding tunnels just south of West Hoathly (Sharpthorne Tunnel) and south of Newick & Chailey (Cinder Hill Tunnel), the impressive 10-arch Imberhorne Viaduct, a few chains from East Grinstead (Low Level), together with several deep cuttings. Finances dictated that except for passing loops in stations and goods yards, the line south of Horsted Keynes as far as Culver Junction would be single track. North of Horsted Keynes would justify double track, particularly with the Ardingly route services in mind. Between East Grinstead and Lewes, stations were sited at or near Kingscote, West Hoathly, Horsted Keynes, Sheffield Park, Newick & Chailey and Barcombe. At the southern end of the line, at a location that became known as Culver Junction, the Lewes & East Grinstead joined the 1858 line from Lewes to Uckfield, which had itself been diverted just outside Lewes in 1868. Having passed inspection, the line through from East Grinstead to Lewes opened in August 1882, by then totally in the hands of the LBSCR.

There were fun and games in the village of Barcombe. When the southern section of the Uckfield line opened the station on that line was called Barcombe. When the LBSCR opened the East Grinstead line the station on that line became New Barcombe, which in the Act of Parliament was to be known as Barcombe Cross, after the estate it served. However, this resulted in confusion, and in 1885 Barcombe became Barcombe Mills and New Barcombe became Barcombe!

The branch from Horsted Keynes to Copyhold Junction near Haywards Heath was authorised in 1880. The double-track line (from shortly after the date of opening) had its own pair of running lines right into Haywards Heath station, to avoid operational problems and congestion at the junction with the main London to Brighton line. The main features were a single intermediate station at Ardingly, and Lynwood Tunnel, between Ardingly and Horsted Keynes. The line opened in 1883 and, by routeing trains via East Grinstead, provided the LBSCR with an alternative route from London to Brighton. North of East Grinstead the route was via the Croydon, Oxted & East Grinstead Railway, which had opened as a double-track line in 1884.

Initially, from 1882, six return services over the line from Lewes were scheduled, but from 1884 the number of trains north of Horsted Keynes doubled. By 1888 Bradshaw shows five down and six up trains via Sheffield Park and eight up and nine down trains calling at Ardingly, although two of these in each direction started and finished their journeys at Ardingly. On Sundays there were two trains on the Lewes section and no trains at all on the Ardingly branch. By 1927 there were either eight or nine trains per day in each direction (depending on the day of the week) on the Sheffield Park section, while on the Ardingly branch there were between 10 and 12 trains each way. By 1950 there were some nine workings each way via Sheffield Park and over twice as many on the Ardingly branch, which by then had been electrified. In 1950 the Sheffield Park line was still used as a through route, the 8am ex-Brighton arriving at London Bridge at 10.40am. There was also, for example, a 12.3pm from London Victoria, which, having taken water at Sheffield Park and paused for 8 minutes at Lewes, arrived at Brighton at 2.54pm.

At the southern end the East Grinstead route effectively commenced at Culver Junction, but in respect of stations Lewes was the focal point. The Lewes & East Grinstead Railway branched away from Culver Junction as a single track and travelled initially in a north-westerly direction to Barcombe, about 1 mile from the junction. A goods yard was provided at the north end of the single-platform station. It was never a passing place and, unsurprisingly, the signalbox closed in 1932. All of the station buildings on the line were substantial. The line then travelled north through the 61yd Cinder Hill Tunnel to Newick & Chailey. In common with other country stations with split names, the station was in neither community, with Newick, the nearest village, being a mile away from the station. In the 1901 census Chailey had a population of 1,363 and Newick 953. The station, 4 miles and 50 chains from the junction, was set on a curve and in a deep cutting, and consequently the main building was a three-storey affair. The station incorporated both up and down platforms, and an overbridge was provided. There were two signalboxes, north and south, with a goods yard on the down side at the south end of the station. These closed in 1914 and 1939 respectively, with only a ground frame being left for access to the sidings.

A station at 6 miles and 20 chains from Culver Junction was, in accordance with the Act of Parliament, to be called Sheffield Bridges, but was opened as Fletching & Sheffield Park. However, following objections from the most important dignitary in the area, the Earl of Sheffield, it was changed to the more familiar Sheffield Park. Set in the valley of the River Ouse, the goods yard was at the down end of the down platform, but there were also sidings on the up side including one to an important sawmill. Sheffield Park was a significant point on the line for watering locomotives, and many service trains were scheduled to stop there for several minutes for that purpose. A passing loop between the platforms and a signalbox were part of the railway infrastructure. After crossing the River Ouse the line veered to the north-west, then north again to reach the junction of Horsted Keynes, 10 miles and 60 chains from Culver Junction. It should be noted that in later years, under the auspices of the Bluebell Railway, minor halts were both opened and closed between Sheffield Park and Horsted Keynes.

Being a junction station, the area covered by the entire Horsted Keynes site was considerably larger than other stations on the line, although the station building was no grander. The station was built about a mile from the village it served, which had a population of 888 in 1901. The basic layout was a little unusual because there was a platform face adjoining the station building on the west side together with two large island platforms, but because only a single line passed between the single platform and the nearest island platform face, there were five platform faces but only four tracks through the station. During World War 1 the line serving the outer platform face of the second, east-side, island was lifted, leaving only four usable platform faces. The sole track remaining on the outer island was later electrified and used mainly by electric trains travelling to and from Haywards Heath (and beyond) via Ardingly. Access between the platforms was by subway. There were sidings on both sides of the station, with the goods yard being at the down end of the down platform. In Edwardian times the LBSCR used the west-side sidings as a dumping ground for withdrawn steam locomotives. For some considerable time Horsted Keynes was the northern end of Bluebell Railway operations, but the line has since been extended in stages towards East Grinstead, the railway's operational target.

Above:

The double-track branch from Copyhold Junction, north of Haywards Heath on the London to Brighton main line, to Ardingly and Horsted Keynes, on the Lewes & East Grinstead Railway, was opened on 3 September 1883. It was later electrified, but that fact did not prevent the line closing to passengers on 28 October 1963. All that now remains is a single track 'siding' to a Hanson stone and gravel distribution centre near the site of Ardingly station. On 15 May 1993 the track was included in the itinerary of Hertfordshire Railtours' 'Cattle Grid' special, which was topped by Class 47 No 47820 and tailed by Class 56 No 56059. The 10-coach train is seen at Copyhold Junction. *P. G. Barnes*

Below:

BR Construction sector Class 60 No 60099 and a long rake of empty bogie wagons, which turn the scales at 100 tons when loaded, creep along the old bullhead rail near Copyhold Junction on their way back to Acton Yard and Whatley Quarry in Somerset, during the winter of 1997. The locomotive will run round the wagons at Haywards Heath. In 2004 these workings ran twice weekly, as required. *JV/TTT*

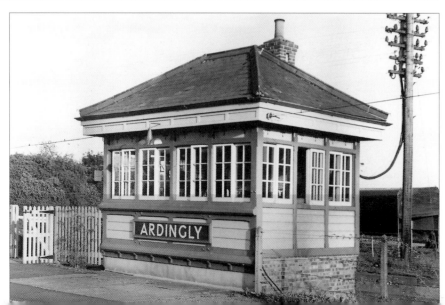

Above:
This April 2003 view shows the scale of operations at the Hanson (formerly ARC) depot at Ardingly. Stone is transferred from the unloading point by conveyor belt to hoppers for mixing, grading and crushing in order to meet precise customer requirements. It is then transferred to bays for storage. Distribution from the works is, of necessity, by road. This is a 'hard hat' site and photography was with the kind permission of the Hanson Works Manager. *JV*

Upper left:
In December 1994 one of the excellent North American-built General Motors Class 59s, No 59005 *Kenneth J. Painter*, waits at the head of its wagons under the unloader at Ardingly. The locomotive had failed and it was many hours before this rare event was remedied, because technicians from Acton had to travel down to Ardingly by road. *JV*

Lower left:
The attractive signalbox at Ardingly was located on the down platform. Although the line from Copyhold Junction to Horsted Keynes was double track throughout, in its last years only the up line was in use, the down line being used for the storage of new electric train stock and later for condemned coaches and wagons. *IAL*

Above:

The line from Horsted Keynes to Haywards Heath closed to passengers in October 1963, and by the time the author visited Ardingly for the first time in 1967 the old station was in an advanced state of decay. The Ardingly stone train worked in the early morning and photography was possible only in the summer months. Here Class 73 electro-diesel No E6029 (later No 73122) has just arrived at Ardingly on the down road and the shunter is uncoupling the locomotive and brake-van from the hopper wagons so that they can run round. *JV/TTT*

Upper right:

Everything in this 1969 view looking towards Horsted Keynes, except the distant road bridge and the buildings at road level, has been swept away, and now just a rough works road runs where the trains once passed. The line was electrified in July 1935, but the conductor rail was of course removed when the line was closed to passengers and truncated to the ARC works. The track here was used only for arrival and run-round, and even this has now been lifted following a reconfiguration at Ardingly. *JV/TTT*

Lower right:

The main structures on the Ardingly branch were the six-arch Sheriffs Mill road bridge and the 215yd Lywood Tunnel. One of the lovely old 2-BIL two-car electric units, No 2149, leaves the latter on the up road with a down Horsted Keynes to Seaford train on 9 May 1959, showing the correct '37' headcode stencil.
S. C. Nash

North of Horsted Keynes the line gradually climbed through the damp 731yd Sharpthorne Tunnel to the station of West Hoathly. The station, at the 13 miles 10 chains mark, was about a mile from the village, which had a population in 1901 of about 1,500. The station had an overbridge connecting the up and down platforms, with the station building on the up side. The goods yard was also on the up side, with goods dock and coal yard. There was also a down-side siding and a signalbox at the up end of the down platform. Just under 2 miles along the track was Kingscote station (15 miles), originally to be named Turners Hill, the only place of significant population in the area. The station boasted a goods yard at the up end of the up platform and a signalbox in a similar position to that of West Hoathly. Again, the station building was on the up side and an overbridge of similar design connected the platforms. The line continued on to East Grinstead across the 10-arch red-brick 262yd-long Imberhorne Viaduct.

Lewes to East Grinstead trains (and those to Oxted) used East Grinstead Low Level, while Three Bridges to Tunbridge Wells West trains used the High Level station. However, the track layout was more than a mere crossroads, because two connecting spurs between the lines were used by a number of trains, including freights, but particularly passenger trains running from the Oxted area to Tunbridge Wells West via East Grinstead. In 1939 there were plans by the Southern Railway to electrify the line from Croydon and Sanderstead to East Grinstead and Horsted Keynes to link with the already electrified branch from Haywards Heath. However, this did not come to fruition; had it done so, the route would probably have been saved from eventual closure. As it was, the line from Oxted to East Grinstead was electrified, but not until 1987.

The double-track route from Horsted Keynes to Haywards Heath was some 4¾ miles in length, less to Copyhold Junction. The only intermediate station, Ardingly, some 2 miles from Horsted Keynes, was no less than 1½ miles from the village it served! The running-in board proclaimed 'Ardingly for Ardingly College', some half a mile distant. Again, a substantial station was provided, with overbridge, signalbox and goods yard on the down side. The main features encountered in construction were the 218yd-long Lywood Tunnel and the Sheriffs Mill road bridge, in fact a six-arch viaduct. Also, in climbing up towards Horsted Keynes a 1 in 75 gradient was necessary. As already mentioned, the line had a dedicated pair of tracks provided into Haywards Heath so as not to conflict with the London to Brighton main line, but in later years this was modified so that main-line trains shared the tracks with the 'branch' trains south of Copyhold Junction.

Train services over the route have already been mentioned, but following the electrification of the Ardingly line in July 1935 many trains ran through from Horsted Keynes to Seaford. Electrification also increased the longevity of the line. In 1959 it had been run as a single line, due to storage on the down line of new Kent Coast electric train units, and later, in 1960, redundant steam stock dis-placed from the newly electrified Kentish lines. The line soldiered on after the main LEGLR closed, but it became a detached stub and was vulnerable to economies in operation resulting in closure to passenger services on 27 October 1963. The six-arch Sheriffs Mill road viaduct was blown up after closure. Part of the line was destined to reach its centenary, but only as a single-track freight siding from Copyhold Junction to Ardingly. For the past 40 years stone trains from Somerset have continued to run to a distribution depot at Ardingly; once owned by ARC and now Hanson, the depot normally receives two trains per week (see photographs).

The LEGLR line became a well-established secondary route running through many small agricultural communities and serving villages rather than towns. Passengers were plied with refresh-ments at both Horsted Keynes and Newick & Chailey, but those buffets succumbed in the mid-1930s. Through trains to and from London continued to run, but overall journey times were very slow.

Some trains worked only to Lewes while others served Brighton. Similarly, some trains terminated at East Grinstead while others ventured further north. Agricultural freight traffic volumes were seasonal, but a wide range of other goods was handled such as coal, feedstuffs and building materials inwards and timber and milk outwards. However, after World War 2 it was clear that the entire operation was becoming uneconomic.

All of the usual financial viability pressures were experienced by the line, such as an unimaginative timetable, increasing motor car ownership and the reduction of freight by rail. By the early 1950s, for every pound of income the line cost £7 to run — an unsustainable loss. The line became a candidate for abandonment, and by 1954 rumours of impending closure were circulating. Early in 1955 the closure posters confirmed that as from Monday 13 June 1955 Lewes to East Grinstead services would be withdrawn. It was ironic that one of the seemingly frequent footplatemen's strikes of the era resulted in the line being closed prematurely, on 28 May 1955. A special train over the route had to be cancelled, but after the strike ended, as a concession, it was allowed to run on 14 August 1955, after which total closure took place.

However, what then happened will be carved in the granite of railway history for all time, when a Miss Bessemer took the trouble to study the original Act of Parliament, which required four trains to be run over the route each day calling at specific stations. The closure had contravened the conditions of the Act, and the British Railways Board was obliged to reintroduce a train service. There was a remarkable reaction in the national press, and it would be fair to say that it resulted in bad publicity for BR. As a result BR grudgingly reintroduced the minimum service required by the original Act, run at inconvenient times with no effort made to connect with other trains, and excluding Barcombe and Kingscote stations, which were not mentioned in the original provisions. For a further 19 months the service was run, but new closure notices were posted after the railway had taken all necessary steps to legally remove its obligations under the Act. Sometimes trains comprised a single coach, but on the last day of service BR did have the decency (or could it have been sense?) to provide a six-coach rake and a whopping nine coaches for the very last train from East Grinstead! Finally, on Sunday 16 March 1958, the last scheduled train traversed the old Lewes & East Grinstead. However, the line remained dormant but usable for some while; at the northern section in particular there were wagon movements, ramblers' excursions and, in 1959, even specials run by the newly formed Bluebell Railway Preservation Society. Some of these stock movements ran into 1960, by which time the Bluebell Railway had run its first service train.

Over the years the line had been a bastion for 'Brighton' locomotives, viz 'Gladstone' 0-4-2s, 'A1X' class 'Terriers' and Classes D1, D3, E4, E5, B4, C2 and C2Xs, I3s and Ks. 'Chatham' locomotives were seen from time to time, including various 4-4-0s and 'C' class 0-6-0s. Later LMS-type Ivatt and Fairburn tanks and Standard 2-6-4Ts were regular visitors, as were SR Moguls and even Bulleid Pacifics. Various electric types worked the Ardingly branch, including 2-NOL, 2-BIL, 2-HAL and, less often, 4-LAV units. In the days of freight-only operation Class 33 diesels and Class 73 electro-diesels were the mainstay of operations in the 1960s to the 1990s, but the Ardingly stone trains were later worked by Classes 56, 59, 60 and 66 diesel-electric types. At the northern end of the line, after closure of the route to the south, diesel-electric multiple-units worked down to East Grinstead, and after electrification in 1987 electric multiple-units took over. A three-car DMU worked the Ardingly centenary shuttle.

Although there had been stock movements and one-off specials, the Bluebell formally opened on 7 August 1960. Once it became established, a huge variety of steam locomotive types appeared on the line, including not only the Bluebell's permanent stock, but also

Above:

This photograph of great historical significance shows the Bluebell Railway's first train, which comprised 'A1X' class No 55 (alias BR No 32655) *Stepney*, of 1875 vintage, and coaches S320S and S6575S, arriving at Horsted Keynes from the Ardingly direction on 17 May 1960. By this time the Culver Junction to East Grinstead line had closed, but the Ardingly branch was still open — note the conductor rail *in situ*. Some wagons populate the goods yard. Once the track was removed, the land to the right became heavily overgrown. *IAL*

Upper right:

More than 43 years later, on a bleak 9 November 2003, and at 128 years of age, *Stepney* was still to be found in action at Horsted Keynes. With a female 'fireperson', No 55 is coupled to a former SECR brake-van during a one-day footplate experience course for eight fortunate participants. *JV*

Lower right:

The driver of green-liveried 2-BIL No 2115 notches his controller over as the 2.20pm service to Seaford departs from Horsted Keynes on 27 October 1962 — the service has just one year to live. The up island platform has a trackless outer face and the Bluebell Railway's delightful 'E4' class No 473 (BR No 32473) can be seen steaming in the background. *S. C. Nash*

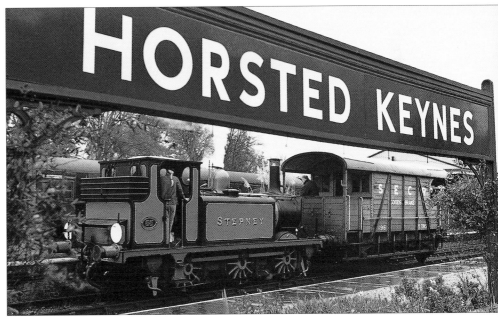

visiting locomotives from all over the country. In the early days preserved LBSCR 'A1X' and 'E4' tanks worked the line with an SECR 'P' 0-6-0T. A North London tank was also on the roster, followed by an Adams Radial 4-4-2T, as well as such curios as the Blue Circle Cement Company's Aveling-Porter machine and the 0-4-0T *Baxter*. In no particular order, 'Dukedogs', Classes H, Q and Q1, Standard 4-6-0s and 2-6-4Ts, 'West Country' Pacifics and '9F' 2-10-0s, 'C', 'U' and 'Schools' classes, and an array of other motive power that would have been unimaginable in 'Brighton' days, have been seen in action. It must be noted that no diesel classes are mentioned because it has been Bluebell policy to remain a preserve of steam and for that situation not to be diluted at any price. Some consider this extremely short-sighted on the grounds that railway history did not stop in 1960. Even Thomas the Tank Engine has diesel stablemates and many young enthusiasts are diesel-orientated and have never seen steam locomotives in everyday service. Also, it must be said that the 'corruption' of a diesel-hauled train is no worse than the contrived gimmick of a 'triple-headed' steam-hauled service or an artificially renumbered locomotive. However, the author has to admit that the sight of an original Brighton tank hauling a couple of pre-war coaches along a rural single track is a wonderful spectacle!

For a period of over 40 years the Bluebell Railway has renovated stations, signals, locomotives and stock, improved facilities and gradually extended the track northwards towards its East Grinstead goal. Battles have been won, sometimes in the courts, but a positive approach to expansion has been maintained throughout the years. From the original five-year lease taken out with BR in 1960 on 5 miles of line, to the ownership of the line and future East Grinstead and Ardingly options, the Bluebell has gone from strength to strength, while in the process carrying millions of visitors of all ages from every part of the UK. The railway's marketing has been excellent and there are numerous special events in its adventurous calendar. At one such event more than a dozen locomotives were in steam! In the year 2000 the Bluebell Preservation Society celebrated its 40th anniversary. As one of the pioneers of standard gauge preservation with a loyal band of supporters, its continued success in the 21st century in keeping its part of the old Lewes & East Grinstead alive is richly deserved.

As regards the closed part of the line, there is little to see now and, four decades on, some of the trackbed has been ploughed up while at some locations trees and grasses now cover where the trains once trundled. However, Barcombe station is still extant as a smart private residence, and the scar of the line on the countryside can be seen in several places. Ardingly station building at street level and one of the platforms can still be seen in Hanson's yard, which is of course private property. With occasional stone trains to Ardingly and with Bluebell operations likely to expand, the old 1883/4 lines are far from dead!

Below:
Timetables for November 1888 (*left*) and January 1927 (*right*).

Above:
Over the past 43 years millions of visitors have experienced the delights of the Bluebell Railway, and with sights and trains such as this it is hardly surprising. In this 'all SR' line-up, 'U' class Mogul No 1618 (BR No 31618) and 'Schools' class No 928 (BR No 30928) *Stowe* have just arrived at Horsted Keynes from Sheffield Park. At this time the extension to Kingscote had not been opened. As an aside, the refreshment rooms on the platform serve real ale, whereas the locomotives will be replenished at Sheffield Park! *JV/TTT*

Below:
The Bluebell Railway has featured in many films and TV series. In this tremendous night shot at Horsted Keynes, the North London tank is featured in the multi-million-pound 1966 production *Khartoum*, starring Charlton Heston, Laurence Olivier, Richard Johnson and Ralph Richardson. On the right General Gordon is following Mr Gladstone into the stationmaster's office! *Courtesy United Artists*

Above:
After closure of the line, sections were used by British Railways to store large numbers of condemned goods wagons. Over a period of time these wagons were gradually removed, and in this April 1960 view 'U1' class No 31890 is seen departing from a derelict West Hoathly station bound for Newhaven, where they were all cut up for scrap. *Derek Cross*

Upper left:
West Hoathly station was 11¾ miles from Lewes, and just north of Sharpthorne Tunnel. Sadly the station did not survive the demolition process, being reduced to rubble in September 1967. In 1974 the Bluebell Railway did manage to secure the West Hoathly station site and the Kingscote station building, which will be important features of any future extension to East Grinstead. This post-war photograph, looking south, shows the white bands painted on the awning supports to increase visibility at night during 'blackouts', when all lights had to be extinguished. *IAL*

Lower left:
By comparison this shot in September 2002 shows a similar view, with Standard 4MT No 75027 exiting Sharpthorne Tunnel with five coaches in tow, passing the crumbling remains of West Hoathly's up platform during the Bluebell Railway's Somerset & Dorset weekend. *P. G. Barnes*

Top right:
Kingscote station suffered from being situated in a remote location and was the least used on the entire line. Although there was a lack of passengers, carriage of agricultural materials, milk, coal, timber and bricks kept goods traffic buoyant. As with Barcombe, the station never reopened after the 1955 closure. Although contractors cleared most of the site, unlike West Hoathly the station was not demolished and luckily an opportunity arose for the Bluebell Railway to purchase the building in later years. This 1991 view shows the station looking north, before track re-laying. At present the station is the northern terminus of the line. *J. Bloom*

Centre right:
During the 1956/58 period, when BR was forced against its will to run a four-trains-per-day 'sulky service' between Lewes and East Grinstead, a minimum-length one-coach train passes East Grinstead South signalbox and arrives at the Low Level station behind a Standard 2-6-4T. The down starting signal was still a lower-quadrant example. *Norman Simmons*

Lower right:
They say that all good things must come to an end, and after the formal closure in 1955 and the drama of the reopening in 1956, the various statutory processes duly took place and final closure was set for 16 March 1958. With all the publicity that had surrounded the events of the previous three years, the public turn-out on the last day was phenomenal. With the platforms at East Grinstead Low Level lined with passengers, the last train to Lewes, appropriately headed by No 80154, the last ever Standard 2-6-4T built at Brighton Works, waits to shunt across to the down platform. The old East Grinstead High and Low Level stations were swept away many years ago, and the only remaining rail link to the town is the line from Oxted, which was electrified in 1987. *Norman Simmons*

6. Three Bridges to Tunbridge Wells West

THE story of the largely east-west branch between Three Bridges, on the London to Brighton main line, and Tunbridge Wells can, historically, be divided into two sections: Three Bridges to East Grinstead, and East Grinstead to Tunbridge Wells West. Although in the mid-1840s there had been a grandiose scheme involving the LSWR, LBSCR and SER to link the naval towns of Portsmouth and Chatham, which would have traversed the approximate route of the line that was eventually built, the plans never came to fruition. However, with a population of about 6,000, the town of East Grinstead was an obvious target for the railway companies in the golden age of railway development. The LBSCR obtained Parliamentary authority to build a line from Three Bridges to East Grinstead in 1846, but in the following years no actual construction took place. In 1852, before powers lapsed, it was a newly formed East Grinstead Railway Company (in close co-operation with the Brighton company) that issued a prospectus in an attempt to raise the £50,000 required for construction. The money was raised and agreement was reached with the LBSCR

whereby it would fully operate the line and retain the income, save for an annual rent of £2,000. The first sod was cut on 22 November 1853, steady progress was made, and, after some hiccups caused by a recalcitrant landowner, all of the land was acquired. The single line opened in July 1855. Initially the only intermediate station was Rowfant, although Grange Road was added to the railway map in 1860. In 1861 the LBSCR took over the EGRC completely.

The second half of the route, from East Grinstead to Tunbridge Wells, was a continuation of the original line, and yet again it was the result of local activity that the project got off the ground. Prominent local businessmen and landowners formed the East Grinstead, Groombridge & Tunbridge Wells Railway Company, which was incorporated in 1862. The Act to build the line received Royal Assent on 7 August 1862, subject to the usual conditions and stipulations. The money was duly raised, but yet again it was close co-operation with the LBSCR, which agreed to operate the line, that ensured early progress. The first sod was cut in July 1863 and construction work was steady rather than spectacular. In 1864 the

Top right:
Rowfant was a very old station, dating back to the opening of the line in 1855. The landowner gave the necessary land to the railway company in exchange for a station being provided, in a sparsely populated area. In the late autumn of 1966 a six-car formation headed by 'Oxted' unit No 1302 enters the station with a Tunbridge Wells West train. The two local passengers will probably leave the train at East Grinstead. Note the compact signalbox on the up platform. *JV/TTT*

Centre right:
By 1969 the scene was one of total dereliction with the track removed, the signalbox demolished and the telegraph posts felled. Instead of a DEMU, the only focal point on the former trackbed is an abandoned car. Either side of Rowfant the branch was single track, but the station provided a useful passing loop. *JV/TTT*

Lower right:
Eventually the entire site was acquired for commercial use, and in April 2003 the Colas company was using the site as a distribution centre. Happily the old down-side station building and the railway house have survived and the original bargeboards have been retained. The old goods yard used to be on the left of this view, and there was once a long siding to the local brickworks. The trackbed here is now part of the Worth Way foot and cycle path. *JV*

Left:
Although the train is described by the photographer as an 'autotrain', the crowd of youngsters at Three Bridges seem to be fascinated by some coupling activities between the locomotive and the leading coach. This delightful study of the East Grinstead and Tunbridge Wells West branch bay platform, with its dedicated overall roof, is seen on 2 March 1963. By that time steam traction on the branch was doomed. *Michael J. Fox*

LBSCR took over the local company completely. The line opened for service in October 1866 with intermediate stations at Forest Row, Hartfield, Withyham and Groombridge.

As can be seen from the railway map it is interesting to note that while the Three Bridges to East Grinstead branch ran on an east-west axis, later in the 19th century a number of north-south lines connected with the route at East Grinstead and in the Ashurst Junction/Groombridge Junction areas. The Lewes & East Grinstead Railway (opened in August 1882) ran south via Horsted Keynes to join the Lewes to Tunbridge Wells via Uckfield line at Culver Junction. From the north, the Croydon, Oxted & East Grinstead arrived in East Grinstead in March 1884. Further east the line from Lewes to Tunbridge Wells joined the Three Bridges line just outside Groombridge in August 1868, and 'Cuckoo line' trains also used this part of the route from September 1880 (see Chapter 3). In October 1888 a direct service commenced from Oxted to Tunbridge Wells via Edenbridge, which joined the Three Bridges line at Ashurst Junction (before heading east to Groombridge). In total this represented 30 years of remarkable railway development in what was essentially a rural and sparsely populated area, supported mainly by agriculture.

Returning to Three Bridges, in February 1848 it became a junction between the London to Brighton main line and the line down through Crawley to Horsham (and later beyond). The station area boasted freight sidings, an engine shed, stock storage sidings and a siding that served an adjacent gasworks. The track configuration in the area changed many times and the station was rebuilt on more than one occasion, but from the opening in 1855 trains for East Grinstead and later Tunbridge Wells always left the station on the down side in a southerly direction from a bay platform that was graced with an overall roof. There were major changes in 1907 when the main line was converted to quadruple track, and a new station was built in 1911. The main line was electrified in 1932 and colour lights replaced semaphores during the same decade. The single track veered away eastward and passed through some attractive woods, over level crossings and beneath bridges in the Pound Hill and Worth areas before reaching the remote station of Rowfant, about 1½ miles from Three Bridges.

Rowfant was flattered by a station only because the original landowner gave the necessary land to the railway on the condition that a station was built, a situation that was not without precedent in the early days of the railway building era. An ornate station building was constructed on the down side and a gated road crossing was located at the west end. At the beginning of the 20th century a passing loop was provided, and this resulted in an up platform and a cast-iron footbridge being added to the local railway infrastructure. There was a signalbox by the road crossing, and a small goods yard with a goods shed and a long siding that ran down to Rowfant Brickworks south-east of the station. Beyond Rowfant the single line continued for 2¾ miles before Grange Road was reached. This station, with a single platform face on the up side of the line, did not open until March 1860. In the early years the station rejoiced in the cumbersome name of 'Grange Road for Crawley Down and Turners Hill', villages to the north and south of the line. Again, a small goods yard with a loading dock and gauge was provided. The station was enlarged in 1877/78 and, in common with Rowfant, an iron pedestrian overbridge was erected simply for people to cross the railway when the crossing gates at the east end of the station were closed! The small signalbox was located north of the line at the east end of the station.

Some 2¾ miles beyond Grange Road was East Grinstead. The original 1855 East Grinstead station was a simple affair and, of course, a terminus. A second station was required when the line to Tunbridge Wells opened in 1866, and this was a more substantial structure. It was located on the London road with the upper floor of the building and the booking hall at street level, with the platforms below. When East Grinstead became an important railway crossroads in 1882/84, a third station was necessary and the 'high level/low level' complex was built. This station was only about 300yd west of the second station and both were conveniently situated for the growing town. The Low Level station had an up and a down platform, but the High Level station had two large island platforms providing four platform faces. The high-level lines were used by Three Bridges to Tunbridge Wells trains and the lower ones by trains from Oxted and/or those travelling over the line to Horsted Keynes, Lewes and Brighton. There was a connecting loop line from the Oxted line to the high-level lines that was used, *inter alia*, by Victoria to Tunbridge Wells West through trains. There was a connecting freight spur from the south (low level) to the east (high level) lines, avoiding the station platforms altogether. There were once four signalboxes at each end of the platforms of both high-level and low-level lines. There was a large goods yard and goods shed at the east end of the high-level lines and additional sidings on the east side of the low-level ones. The 1882 station had all creature comforts for passengers, ranging from commodious waiting rooms to refreshment rooms at both levels.

The decline of railways in the East Grinstead area started with the withdrawal of services towards Horsted Keynes and Lewes in March 1958. Although the Bluebell Railway took over part of the line, and has long-term aspirations to run its tracks back into East Grinstead, it will probably be half a century from the date of closure before this comes to fruition. Once the Three Bridges to Tunbridge Wells line closed in January 1967, there was another significant rebuilding as the whole of the High Level station was demolished. Freight facilities were withdrawn just three months later, but the abandoned goods shed hung on until 1976, when it too was demolished. Much of the old railway alignment, including embankments, was later removed to facilitate the town's new road system, and some of the former railway ground became a car park. About 1970 East Grinstead's third station was completely demolished, and a new modern single-storey building and footbridge constructed. There is nothing architecturally meritorious in the town's fourth station! From 1967 the line down from Oxted comprised East Grinstead's only rail service, and its future seems assured, especially as the line was electrified in September 1987.

Leaving the High Level island platforms, the line soon reverted to single track for the 3¼-mile downhill run into the Medway Valley and on to Forest Row station, which for many years was marketed as 'Forest Row for Ashdown Forest'. In 1897 a passing loop, down platform and pedestrian overbridge were provided to increase the potential line capacity. The station was located on the edge of town, but a growing town, which resulted in Forest Row having the highest takings of all the intermediate stations on the line, excepting East Grinstead. There was a signalbox, goods shed and siding adjacent to the station. A further 3½ miles east of Forest Row was the single-platform Hartfield station. By 1901 Hartfield and the surrounding area had a population of some 1,500 people and it was therefore entirely reasonable to site a station there, albeit a short way north of the village. As with other stations on the line a substantial station house was provided on the up side of the line. There was a small signalbox at the Tunbridge Wells end of the site, a large goods shed and a couple of goods sidings, all on the up, or south, side of the branch.

Withyham, just 1¼ miles from Hartfield, was very similar in terms of infrastructure to its neighbour in that it had a single platform, large station building, platform awning, goods shed, sidings and a signalbox. The only difference was that at Withyham the box was located at the eastern end of the station in order to control a road crossing, whereas at Hartfield a north-south road crossed the line via an overbridge. The line continued via what in later years was Ashurst Junction, where the line down from Oxted and up from Uckfield met the Three Bridges route. The 1914

Left:
Grange Road station opened in March 1860 and for many years rejoiced in the grandiose name of Grange Road for Crawley Down and Turners Hill (the villages to the north and south of the station). Although the station had a goods yard it was provided with only a single platform face. With delightful period infrastructure all around, 'H' class No 31551, heading the 11.8am Three Bridges to Tunbridge Wells West train, pauses for custom on 23 June 1962. *J. H. Aston*

THREE BRIDGES, EAST GRINSTEAD, and TUNBRIDGE WELLS.—London, Brighton, and South Coast.

Down. — Week Days / Sndys

Down.	mrn	mrn	mrn	mrn	aft	aft	aft	aft	aft	aft	Sndys mrn	Sndys aft
VICTORIA 72..dep	....	7 35	10 5	11 40	1 30	1 30	2 5	4 0	5 52	7 8	8 20	6 30
72 LONDON BRIDGE	5 45	7 50	9 45	12 0	....	....	4 55	5	7 20	....	8 30	6 40
Three Bridges..dep	7 15	9 10	11 18	1 5	2 35	3 30	5	5 52	8	....	9 30	8 25
Rowfant	7 20	9 15	11 23	1 10	2 40	3 35	5 13	5 57	8 35	....	9 35	8 30
Grange Road	7 25	9 21	11 28	1 15	2 43	2 45	3 40	5 18	6 2	8 40	9 40	8 35
East Grinstead { ar	7 35	9 29	11 33	1 25	2 51	2 54	3 50	5 27	6 12	8 50	9 50	8 45
(High Level) { dp	8 17	9 36	....	1 28	2 53	....	3 51	5 29	6 53	8 55	9 58	8 47
Forest Row	8 24	9 43	....	1 35	3 0	....	3 58	5 37	6 59	9 1	10 5	8 54
Hartfield	8 32	9 51	....	1 43	3 8	....	5 45	a	9 10	....	10 13	9
Withyham	8 36	9 55	....	1 46	3 12	....	5 49	....	9 14	....	10 17	9 6
Groombridge 70, 77	8 42	10 1	....	1 51	3 16	....	5 54	7 11	9 19	....	10 22	9 11
Tunbridge Wells 90	8 50	10 10	....	2	3 25	....	7 18	9 27	....	10 36	9 19	

Up. — Week Days / Sndys

Up.	mrn	mrn	mrn	mrn	mrn	aft	aft	aft	aft	aft	Sndys mrn	Sndys aft
Tunbridge Wells dp	....	7 25	9 0	10 0	....	11 25	2 20	3 32	6 15	....	7 15	5 55
Groombridge	....	7 31	9 6	10 6	....	11 31	2 26	3 38	6 21	....	7 21	6 1
Withyham	....	7 38	9 12	b	....	11 36	2 31	3 43	6 26	....	7 26	6 6
Hartfield	....	7 43	9 17	....	....	11 40	2 35	3 47	6 30	....	7 30	6 10
Forest Row	....	7 51	9 25	10 17	....	11 48	2 43	3 54	6 38	....	7 38	6 18
East Grinstead { ar	....	8 0	9 34	10 26	....	11 57	2 52	4 2	6 47	....	7 47	6 27
(High Level) { dp	6 45	8 7	9 36	....	11 45	11 59	2 55	4 6	6 53	....	7 49	6 29
Grange Road	6 51	8 16	9 43	....	11 51	12 5	3 1	4 12	6 59	....	7 55	6 35
Rowfant	6 56	8 21	9 48	....	11 56	12 10	3 6	4 17	7 4	....	8 0	6 40
Three Bridges 74	7 3	8 29	9 56	....	12 4	12 17	3 14	4 24	7 12	....	8 6	6 48
74 LONDON BDGE.arr	8 17	9 45	10 45	11 25	....	1 17	4 20	5 43	8 33	....	10 27	8 15
VICTORIA 74	8 27	....	11 0	11 23	....	1 44	4 27	5 43	....	....	10 56	8 16

a Stops to set down from London. **b** Stops by signal to take up 1st class London Passengers.
For **other Trains** between Tunbridge Wells and Groombridge, see pages 70 and 77.

Above:
Bradshaw's timetable for November 1888.

Below:
The train in this striking study, bound for Tunbridge Wells West, has travelled from London Bridge via Oxted and is seen exiting the spur from St Margaret's Junction on the climb up to East Grinstead High Level. 'I3' class No 32091, in BR lined black livery, was built in 1913, and immediately behind the locomotive is a Maunsell coach, a common sight when this train was photographed on 20 October 1951. Note the Westinghouse brake mechanism in front of the side tank. *E. R. Wethersett*

Top left:
The photographer provides a wonderful view that shows the juxtaposition of the High Level and Low Level East Grinstead stations. Looking north, the low-level lines can be seen disappearing towards St Margaret's Junction and Oxted, while at the high level 'H' class No 31518 propels the 1.27pm to Three Bridges out of the station. The spur linking the two levels is out of sight, several hundred yards to the left.
G. D. King

Centre left:
On a bleak winter's day in 1966 the driver of green 'Oxted' unit No 1310 surrenders the single-line token for the section from Grange Road and enters East Grinstead High Level station with a train from Three Bridges, sporting the correct '37' headcode. The spur to St Margaret's Junction and Oxted can be seen on the right.
JV/TTT

Lower left:
A view of East Grinstead High Level station, looking towards Tunbridge Wells West on 28 December 1966. The island platform on the left tended to be used by trains travelling to and from Oxted/London, while the island on the right was for up and down trains on the Three Bridges to Tunbridge Wells West line. The water tower was erected in 1920. *JV/TTT*

Top right:
The station at Forest Row was (with the exception of East Grinstead) the busiest intermediate station on the Three Bridges to Tunbridge Wells route. A passing loop was provided and an overbridge installed in 1897, and there was a busy goods yard and substantial goods shed adjacent to the station. This shows the attractive small signalbox, and behind it are some compartment coaches in a siding. Some peak-period trains were extended from East Grinstead to terminate at Forest Row. *IAL*

Centre right:
By 17 December 1966 the goods yard sidings at Hartfield had been lifted, but the local coal merchant was still using the site — note the fine goods shed. Closure is just two weeks away as Class 207 No 1310 pauses on its way from Tunbridge Wells West to Three Bridges. After closure the station became derelict, but many years later it was restored and is now used as a residence and a playschool. *JV/TTT*

Lower right:
Another rural station on the line was Withyham. The single platform face was more than adequate for the amount of traffic generated, although with a population of over 2,000 in 1901 the village justified a station. A goods yard was provided to the east of the station on the south side and, in common with Hartfield, a goods shed was part of the infrastructure. Both stations had a small signalbox, and the Withyham example has been preserved. *SLS/W. A. Camwell*

signalbox, which remained open until the Three Bridges line closed, contained 35 levers. The line then continued to Groombridge via Groombridge Junction, where the branch met the line from Birchden Junction and Eridge (the Uckfield/Lewes and Heathfield/Polegate 'Cuckoo line' routes). East of Ashurst Junction the branch was double track into Tunbridge Wells West.

The commodious station at Groombridge, 2½ miles from Withyham, was built at the same time as the line opened in 1866 and was considerably enlarged in 1897. The parish straddles the Sussex/Kent border. The station had staggered platforms, one of which was an island platform (see photograph); for many years before the Ashurst Junction to Birchden Junction link was established and in everyday use, those travelling from north to south and vice versa changed at Groombridge and reversed direction. Either side of the turn of the 20th century, carriages for Eastbourne were detached from London to Tunbridge Wells trains, and London to Eastbourne trains reversed direction before continuing their journey south, again passing Groombridge Junction, half a mile to the south-west. A 35-lever signalbox and goods shed and sidings were located at the north end of the station. A modern box replaced the original in the late 1950s. By the 1970s the station canopies had been dismantled, goods traffic having been lost some years previously.

Beyond Groombridge a small halt with staggered wooden platforms on either side of a road bridge opened at High Rocks on 1 June 1907. Its primary use was for visitors and ramblers visiting outcrops of sandstone rock located in nearby Broadwater Forest. The halt gradually became decrepit and, after a three-year period of closure during World War 2, it finally closed in May 1952. The line continued into Tunbridge Wells West, 3 miles from Groombridge, with Three Bridges services often running into a bay platform rather than occupying the through platforms towards Tunbridge Wells Central on South Eastern lines. Tunbridge Wells West was a Mecca for a number of LBSCR services, and the station was very impressive, even by Victorian standards. Originally the two main Tunbridge Wells stations were known as either 'SER' or 'LBSCR', but after the Grouping they were known as Central and West respectively. This place was incredibly busy, and in the 1950s there could be 70 passenger and five freight trains using the station every weekday. Multiple sidings, goods yard and shed, locomotive depot, signalboxes at each end of the complex with an array of semaphore signals, bay platforms at each end of the main platform and, from 1884, two island platforms were all part of this substantial site. Beyond this huge complex a modest single line with narrow clearances disappeared into Grove Tunnel, and at the nearby Grove Junction made a connection with the SER, facilitating through train working from Brighton to Tonbridge. However, in the main, passengers changed at the West station for stations on the Tonbridge line (and beyond). At one time some 40 steam locomotives were shedded at Tunbridge Wells, and even after steam was finally replaced in 1965 Tunbridge Wells West was still an important stabling and signing-on point, with up to 30 diesel units berthed in sidings overnight.

As regards the Three Bridges to Tunbridge Wells services, the early timetable to East Grinstead only provided for six trains in each direction on weekdays, with two on Sundays. This level of service was continued after the second half of the line to Tunbridge Wells opened in 1866. In 1888 there were still six trains each way, with one or two extra on the Three Bridges to East Grinstead section, later increased to nine. A delightful note appears in the 1888 Bradshaw in respect of the 10am Tunbridge Wells West to London Victoria train, which stopped at Withyham 'by signal to take up 1st class London passengers', a wonderful example of class discrimination! One interesting working was a down coach that was 'slipped' from a London train at Three Bridges, with the coach continuing to Forest Row behind a branch locomotive. In 1938

there were 10 weekday trains east of East Grinstead and a dozen to the west, with a reduced Sunday service. In 1950 there were one or two extra workings, but by 1955 there were an unbelievable 17 workings between Three Bridges and East Grinstead. Diesel-electric multiple-units took over services during 1965 and although a good service was provided on the mainly single track, the economies that came with dieselisation were insufficient to save the line.

The motive power working over the line was hugely varied and I will deal here with only the last years of the line's life. After World War 2 various tank locomotives were regular performers; these included the ex-LBSCR 'E4' and 'I3' classes, SECR 'H' class, LSWR 'M7' class, LMS-designed 2-6-2Ts and Fairburn and Standard 2-6-4Ts. Some passenger services were worked in push-pull mode. Early Chatham 4-4-0s appeared at the Tunbridge Wells end of the line, and various Moguls of the 'N', 'N1' and 'U' classes were regulars in the area. Freight traffic was in the hands of 'C', 'C2X', 'Q', 'Q1' and 'K' classes. Class 205 'Hampshire' and Class 207 'Oxted' diesel units worked all passenger trains on the line in the last years its life, with occasional Class 33 diesel locomotive appearances on engineers' workings.

The Three Bridges to Tunbridge Wells West line was an integral part of a large railway network in the Sussex Weald area. The line served the area faithfully for 111 years in respect of the section west of East Grinstead, and just three months over 100 years in respect of the eastern section. I travelled the line in the mid-1960s and the off-peak loadings were very light indeed. There was a modicum of commuter traffic, but most of this was north of East Grinstead, necessitating some locomotive and stock workings rather than DEMUs. There was a little school traffic, but overall there was little chance of making money. Towards the end of the line's life freight had all but disappeared, many of the stations were run down and there was little scope for cost saving without getting into an even more severe downward spiral of fewer trains and even fewer passengers. The last day of service was 1 January 1967; there was to be no Happy New Year between Rowfant and Withyham inclusive.

The trackbed through Rowfant is now a foot and cycle path called the Worth Way. The station building has, remarkably, survived and is now on land owned by Colas, a tarmac distribution company. Grange Road has long disappeared under housing development in an area where the population is now, somewhat ironically, growing rapidly. At East Grinstead there is no trace of the old station, although the original 1855 building does survive. As already mentioned, there is now just a functional building at what was once the low-level site. Beyond East Grinstead part of the old trackbed is now a road that bypasses part of the town. Forest Row station has been flattened and the land is now used as an industrial estate. The Worth Way, using the old trackbed, continues through Hartfield and Withyham to Groombridge. After lying derelict for some considerable time, both Hartfield and Withyham stations have survived and are now in private hands; the former doubles as a playschool. It is hard to define the alignment of the railway either side of the Uckfield line at what was once Ashurst Junction.

After the closure of the Three Bridges to Tunbridge Wells West service the only section of line to remain open was a shuttle service between Eridge, Tunbridge Wells West and Tonbridge. The diesel unit used a down bay platform at Eridge that was once the outer face of the down island platform. This service lasted until July 1985, when both Groombridge and Tunbridge Wells West stations were closed. However, all was not lost in that a preservation movement enjoying the name of the Tunbridge Wells & Eridge Railway Preservation Society, with the perhaps unfortunate acronym of TWERPS, commenced a long journey in reopening services between Tunbridge Wells West and Eridge, thus re-establishing a connection to the 'outside world' via the Uckfield branch. Now generally known as the Spa Valley Railway, the line was inspected by the Department of Transport in 1993 and a Light

TUNBRIDGE WELLS, EAST GRINSTEAD, and LONDON.—London, Brighton, and South Coast.

Up. Week Days—Continued.

	aft	aft	aft	m		aft	aft	aft	aft	aft	aft	aft		aft	aft	aft	aft	aft		aft	aft	aft	aft
Tunbridge Wells ¶ dep.				1 5		2 20				3 35				4 53				6 10					8 20
Groombridge				1 13		2 26				3 41				4 59				6 16					8 26
Withyham				1 20		2 32				3 47				5 5				6 22					8 32
Hartfield				1 24		2 36				3 51	m			5 9				6 26					8 37
Forest Row †				1 31		2 43				3 58	4 45			5 17				6 34					8 45
East Grinstead arr.				1 46		2 51	m			4 5	4 53			5 25				6 43					8 53
East Grinstead dep.				1 48			2 53	3 10		4 6				5 28						6 57			
Grange Road				1 56			2 59	3 17		4 13				5 35						7 4			
Rowfant				2 1			3 4	3 22		4 18				5 40						7 9			
Three Bridges arr.				2 8			3 11	3 29		4 25	m			5 47	m					7 17			
East Grinstead dep.			1 50			2 55				4 8			5 3			6 5				6 57			9 0
Dormans			1 55			3 1				4 13			5 8			6 11				7 2			9 5
Lingfield	m		1 59			3 5				4 17			5 13			6 15				7 8			9 9
Tunbridge Wells ¶ dep.	1 20	2 5							3 28				5 0			6 15				7 40			
Groombridge	1 28	2 12							3 35				5 7			6 25				7 46			
Ashurst	1 34	2 18							3 40							6 31				7 52			
Cowden	1 41	2 24										5 16				6 38				7 59			
Hever	1 46	2 29										5 21				6 43				8 4			
Edenbridge Town ¶	1 50	2 34							3 53			5 27				6 48				8 8			
Oxted 274	2 4	2 46	2 13			3 18			4 5	4 31			5 26	5 39		6 30	6 59			7 21		8 19	9 22

Up. Week Days—Continued. / Sundays.

	aft	aft	aft	aft	aft				mrn	mrn	mrn	mrn	aft	aft	aft	aft	aft
Tunbridge Wells ¶ dep.				9 40					7 15					5 55			
Groombridge				9 46					7 21					6 2			
Withyham				9 52					7 27					6 8			
Hartfield				9 56					7 31					6 12			
Forest Row †				10 4					7 39					6 21			
East Grinstead arr.				1013					7 48					6 30			
East Grinstead dep.		8 54							7 49					6 31			
Grange Road		9 1							7 55					6 38			
Rowfant		9 6							8 0					6 43			
Three Bridges arr.		9 14							8 8					6 51			
East Grinstead dep.					1150 c				10 0						8 5		
Dormans									10 5						8 10		
Lingfield			m						10 9						8 16		
Tunbridge Wells ¶ dep.	8 55		9 40						8 32		1148		4 55		7 35		
Groombridge	9 1		9 46						8 44		1156		5 1		7 44		
Ashurst	9 7		9 52						8 51		12 2		5 7		7 51		
Cowden	9 13		9 59						8 59		12 9		5 15		7 58		
Hever	9 18		10 4						9 4		1214		5 20		8 3		
Edenbridge Town ¶	9 22		10 7		1157 y				9 9		1218	1 10	5 25		8 8		
Oxted 274	9 33				12 8				9 21		1023	1230	1 21	5 37	8 20	8 30	

(Saturdays only / Wednesdays only columns noted in left margin)

Above:
Bradshaw's timetable for April 1910.

Railway Order was granted, although it was not until 1996 that services recommenced on a short part of the line, and then on 23 August 1997 were extended to a new station at Groombridge. Much of the old station area at Groombridge was covered by a housing development, but with the co-operation of the various parties involved, provision was made for the railway.

At Tunbridge Wells the grand building with its clock tower was preserved and converted for commercial use, while a Sainsbury's supermarket with a large car park was built on the station and goods yard area. Sainsbury's was of great help to the preservation movement and subsidised certain activities, such as the restoration of the four-road LBSCR engine shed. Although it was not possible to use either of the original stations, the locomotive depot was a handsome consolation prize. In August 1998, with the support of a local pub-owner, a new platform was completed at the site of High Rocks Halt and opened for Spa Valley Railway traffic, enabling visitors to visit the rocks or the High Rocks Inn! In 2004 the railway ran timetabled services over the 3-mile section to Groombridge, and in future years it plans to signal the line and open the remaining 2½ miles to Eridge. It has a comprehensive collection of diesel and steam locomotives and rolling stock, while normal service trains comprise ex-BR Mark 1 coaches. The railway has a single-platform station and sidings at Tunbridge Wells West, and an ex-Midland Railway signalbox is being readied for service. Beyond the new Groombridge station, towards Groombridge Junction, the line is fenced and used for stock storage. It may be a long haul, but the SVR has great ambitions and, given funds and manpower together with public support, it will no doubt achieve its long-term objectives.

Right:
The chimneys of this fine residence are a sure giveaway that the building is in fact Withyham station, photographed in April 2003, 36 years after the line closed. This view looking towards Ashurst Junction and Tunbridge Wells shows that the trackbed is now the Forest Way footpath. *JV*

Top left:
After the Eridge to Tunbridge Wells West and Tonbridge service ceased in 1985, there were the usual attempts to preserve the line. The difference in this case was that the Eridge Line Action Group was successful in securing part of the line. J. Sainsbury greatly assisted the preservationists at Tunbridge Wells West, where the company had built a supermarket and car park. As explained in the text, a Light Railway Order was granted in 1993, but it was 21 December 1996 before the first fare-paying passengers were conveyed over the 3-mile route. On 6 December 1998 Peckett 0-6-0ST *Fonmon* runs round a 'Santa Special' in the loop at Groombridge. *P. G. Barnes*

Centre left:
Although now generally known as the Spa Valley Railway, for many years the popular name for the society was the Tunbridge Wells & Eridge Railway Preservation Society, producing the acronym of TWERPS! For the number of working members involved, the organisation has made considerable progress, despite the number of years that have elapsed since the line closed. An intermediate halt at High Rocks was opened in August 1998. On 23 June 2002 *Fonmon*, from the Peckett stable, and *Spartan*, a Polish TKH 0-6-0T, are seen near Tunbridge Wells with the 11.03 from Groombridge. *P. G. Barnes*

Lower left:
One of the main assets of the Spa Valley Railway is the old LBSCR locomotive shed, formerly 75F, which was preserved with the assistance of J. Sainsbury. The original Tunbridge Wells West station building has also survived, but is now in use as a family restaurant. The Spa Valley Railway station is beside the engine shed. Here the majority of the hard-working Engineering Department and one Labrador dog pose beside No 3135 *Spartan* on 8 October 2000. *P. G. Barnes*

Above:
With some remnants of snow on the ground in the bad winter of 1962/63, 'H' class No 31551 steams away from Groombridge with a two-coach train for Three Bridges. Note the stagger in the platforms, the large goods shed in the background and two spare coaches in the bay platform. By way of comparison with the photograph below, the alignment of the track through the outer face of the island platform should be noted. *IAL*

Below:
The fine awnings on both the up and down platforms were removed long before closure, and colour lights replaced the semaphore signals. After closure a small housing estate was built on the site, which prevented the preservationists from using the original primary route. However, sufficient land was provided for the preserved railway, approximately following the line of the outer island platform, and a new station to the south was built on the other side of the adjacent road bridge. Here 0-4-0ST No 2315 arrives from Tunbridge Wells with three Mark 1 coaches on 16 April 2003. *JV*

Top right:
High Rocks Halt between Groombridge and Tunbridge Wells West opened on 1 June 1907. A nearby outcrop of rocks became a popular tourist destination in Edwardian times, and motor trains of the era stopped here. The wooden halt was closed for part of World War 2, and completely on 5 May 1952. As can be seen in this view, the wooden platforms were staggered on either side of a road bridge. The Spa Valley Railway has built a permanent single-faced station here and the main attraction these days is the High Rocks Inn!
IAL

Centre right:
Tunbridge Wells is of course in the county of Kent, but it was the destination for many of the trains over three of the Sussex branches and byways featured in this book. Although a single track connected the SECR station on the Hastings line to the splendid LBSCR station, it was only after the formation of the Southern Railway in 1923 that they became Central and West respectively. One of the sturdy Fairburn 2-6-4Ts, No 42088, prepares to leave the impressive station with a London Victoria train on 14 September 1958. A Brighton tank engine is in the background.
A. W. Martin

Lower right:
Oops! Stroudley 2-2-2 No 342 *St Lawrence* was already using the Tunbridge Wells West turntable on 11 March 1905 when a 'C1' class 0-6-0 tried to share the facility and ended up in the pit. The locomotive was recovered only to be involved in a further accident at Eridge nine months later. The locomotive shed now houses much of the stock of the Spa Valley Railway.
IAL

Above:

A local resident once told the author that living in the environs of Tunbridge Wells West station in diesel days was a nightmare because at 5 o'clock in the morning the large number of 'Thumpers' stored there overnight were started up, and at its peak there could be a couple of dozen units in the sidings! In this October 1983 shot there are a dozen units berthed in the sidings as No 1317 has the road to Grove Junction and Tunbridge Wells Central. Note the magnificent building and the goods and engine sheds in the left and right background. *JV/TTT*

Below:

With only a few weeks of service to go, thereby ending 119 years of railway history, 'Oxted' 3D unit No 1304, of 1962 vintage, passes beneath the surviving signal gantry on its way from Tonbridge to Eridge in April 1985. Even at this late stage the area was fully signalled, not only for the hourly train service but also for the large number of stock movements in the yard. The island platform was established in 1884. This entire area is now a supermarket car park. *JV/TTT*

7. Newhaven and Seaford Branch

OF the many small ports strung out along the Sussex coastline, Shoreham, at the mouth of the River Adur, and Newhaven, where the River Ouse joins the sea, were to become the most important, and their traffic potential was given a high priority in the railway companies' plans for expanding and developing their networks. Most of the small ports had histories going back hundreds of years, but by modern standards their operations were small-scale. However, Newhaven was in a different category because even before the railway arrived it was being used not only by local fisherman and some coastal shipping, but by shipping plying across the English Channel to exploit the lucrative European traffic.

In July 1837 an Act of Parliament authorised the construction of a railway between London and Brighton with branch lines to Newhaven and Shoreham, to the east and west of Brighton. The line from Brighton to Shoreham was opened on 12 May 1840, more than 12 months before Brighton was connected with London by rail. Some of the materials for building the London & Brighton Railway's lines were landed at Shoreham. The Brighton main line opened in September 1841, and the line beyond Shoreham towards Worthing opened in November 1845. Work was proceeding on the Newhaven (via Lewes) branch and it was duly opened from Brighton as far as Lewes, county town of East Sussex, in June 1846.

The line running eastward towards Polegate and St Leonards on the Sussex coast was opened later in the month, although it would be 1849 before East Bourne (*sic*), to the south of Polegate, and Hailsham, to the north, would be rail connected. There was frantic railway building activity at this time as Lewes gained direct access to London when the line from Keymer Junction, south of Haywards Heath, opened on 1 October 1847. Just a couple of months later, on 8 December, the line was extended from Lewes to the town of Newhaven, although it seems that goods services may have commenced the previous month. The Newhaven branch left the Polegate line at Southerham Junction, just under a mile from Lewes station. Initially stations were located at Newhaven Town and Newhaven Wharf (later Harbour). There was a signalbox at Southerham Junction, where the Newhaven line turned south and ran down the east side of the River Ouse. Near Southerham in later years there was a private down-side siding serving a cement works. Beyond what was to become Southease & Rodmell Halt (2½ miles), the line ran closer to the river before passing the acres of sidings north of Newhaven Town station (5¼ miles), including an area known as Cedar Sidings.

Originally the River Ouse spilled into the sea at Seaford, but in the 17th century the movement of shingle banks resulted in the river meeting the sea at the village of Meeching, renamed Newhaven in 1620. A Harbour Authority had been set up by 1730, but operations were essentially small-scale. A few years before the railway arrived at Newhaven there had been some developments, with the east pier being extended to 210ft and the west pier to 330ft, but the arrival of the railway was the catalyst for significant change. At this time small packet boats left Newhaven (and Shoreham) for France, calling at Brighton Pier before steaming to Dieppe. By the 1860s the LBSCR had a firm foothold, and the company even built a 370-ton cross-Channel vessel. The packet service was soon transferred away from Shoreham. By the mid-1860s cross-Channel

Below:
**Trying to emulate the exhaust emissions of a steam locomotive, the driver of Class 56 No 56070, having slowed
for the speed restriction through Lewes station, opens the power handle with a Crawley to Newhaven train of empty aggregate
hoppers in 1996. The train is coming off the line from Haywards Heath. This traffic eventually petered out.**
JV/TTT

Above:
To the east of Lewes lies Southerham Junction, where the Newhaven and Seaford branch leaves the Lewes to Eastbourne and Hastings main line, designated the East Coastway line. The double-track Newhaven line can be seen curving to the right in the background as 4-VEP No 3112, forming an Eastbourne to Brighton local, heads for Lewes in September 1988. There were four tracks at this spot until 1976. *JV/TTT*

Upper right:
South of Southerham Junction the only intermediate station (halt) between Lewes and Newhaven Town stations is Southease & Rodmell. Located on the eastern side of the valley of the River Ouse, the small station remains open to serve two hamlets that are some distance away on the west side of the valley. Approaching the station on 22 July 1995 with the 10.35 Newhaven to Crawley New Yard aggregates train is Class 60 No 60001. *P. G. Barnes*

Lower right:
After the demise of the 2-BIL and 2-HAL units, but before more modern stock was introduced, ex-'Pompey line' units, then designated 4-COR, were regular performers on local trains. On 6 September 1972 No 3123 crosses a local gated road crossing and enters Southease & Rodmell with the 15.02 Lewes to Seaford working. The station is a typical Southern Railway concrete structure. The small signalbox at the up end of the up platform has now been abolished, having for the whole of its life carried the name Itford Crossing. *J. Scrace*

traffic was dominated by the LBSCR and the French company Chemin de Fer de l'Ouest, with some 40,000 passengers being carried annually. Until World War 1 the LBSCR route to France was rivalling the South Eastern Railway's London/Folkestone/Boulogne service. In 1889 sufficient work was done at Newhaven to almost eliminate the 'tidal' label (see below), and cross-Channel shipping could sail regardless of the state of the tide. By 1893 services carried over 110,000 passengers, and in early Edwardian times the 200,000 milestone was passed. Unfortunately the harbour was closed to all commercial traffic during World War 1, between August 1914 and March 1919. By 1928 more than 250,000 passengers used the port, and by 1938 usage had grown to 383,000.

Returning to the railways, at the time the line to Newhaven was being constructed, an extension to Seaford was already under consideration. However, in the 1840s Seaford, despite its ancient history, had a very small population and it had yet to become a resort or residential area of any significance. By the 1860s events were changing, and an omnibus connection with the railway at Newhaven was advertised. In 1860/61 further plans were lodged for the building of an extension of the Newhaven branch to Seaford, and a Newhaven & Seaford Railway Company was formed. It would be the LBSCR that would exercise these plans, and after all the usual formalities had been dispensed with, construction of the line commenced. The Seaford line would run from Newhaven Wharf (Harbour) station to within 80yd of Seaford parish church. The line climbed away from Newhaven past the original Bishopstone station and through a 36ft-deep cutting before descending to Seaford. The maximum gradient was 1 in 100 and the extension was just over 2¼ miles in length. It opened on 1 June 1864, with six trains a day working the branch and half that number on Sundays. The fastest journey time from London to Seaford was 2hr 16min, a considerable improvement on previous timings involving other modes of transport.

There had been significant changes at Lewes in 1857, and later in 1889, as the number of lines converging on the town increased and as both passenger and freight volumes grew. The original terminus was used from 1847 to 1857, but to reduce very complex movements a new station (effectively two stations) opened in 1857. The line to Uckfield opened in 1858, but this was re-aligned in 1868. Finally in 1889 a brand new station (the present one) was built, but there is insufficient space here to relate the full and detailed history of railway developments in Lewes.

Back at Newhaven there were developments aplenty, most of them with LBSCR involvement. A large goods yard was constructed north of Newhaven Town station, freight sidings served most of the important wharves, and a tramway was built on the east side of the harbour. An iron swingbridge across the Ouse was opened in 1866, although a railway line across it giving access to the West Quay sidings was not built until 1880. The bridge was opened manually, requiring eight fit men to operate the mechanism. Once the age of the motor car arrived there were sometimes long delays of up to half an hour on the main A259 coast road as ships left or entered the upper harbour. The swingbridge lasted until 1976, when a new flyover was built. In 1878 a Newhaven Harbour Company was formed with the primary task of running the harbour operations. Railway sidings on the quaysides were initially shunted by horses, but from 1881 the company purchased its first steam locomotive and in 1898 LBSCR 'A1X' class No 72 Fenchurch was acquired.

At Newhaven the line passed through Newhaven Town station to Newhaven Wharf, where the pretentiously named London & Paris Hotel was located. The 1848-built hotel was put to military use during World War 2 and damaged during the war years; it was demolished in 1956. In 1884 some of the land to the south of the original Wharf station (later Newhaven Harbour) was reclaimed, which was used to site a new station, in recent times known as Newhaven Marine but in the past regarded as part of a two-section

Harbour station (and, just to complicate things, often referred to as Newhaven Continental). However, the junction with the Seaford section was unchanged so that there were in fact two adjacent stations, Harbour and Marine, joined by a footbridge and a walkway. The track layout in the Newhaven area expanded and there were to be sidings on both sides of the river. A long East Pier was built and a 2,800ft mole along the river to the west of the port was constructed, not only to protect the port from gales but also to avoid shipping movements having to rely on the state of the tide. The work included costly deep dredging. Additional wharves were built upstream and the East Harbour Tramway was extended, partly to reach the source of shingle used in the construction of the mole. By about the year 1900 the Port of Newhaven was, in broad terms, complete, and developments in future years were minor by comparison with the late Victorian era. At the 1901 census the population of Newhaven was 6,373, Seaford 2,675, with Bishopstone turning the scales at 301, Rodmell at 231 and Southease at 66! By comparison, Lewes, at 11,249, was larger than the combined populations of all the towns and villages on the branch.

The size of the growing town of Newhaven and the local track layout became impressive. There was a large brick goods shed north of Town station and another on the railway wharf located further south. There was a four-road engine shed with a turntable and an engineering shop. Sidings served all manner of industries including coal wharves, a tarpaulin factory, chalk from nearby pits, a granary, a sawmill, aggregates and general merchandise. There was of course a Customs Shed and sidings to accommodate merchandise being loaded and unloaded from cross-Channel vessels. At one stage there were four goods trains per day between Lewes and Newhaven, with one continuing to Seaford. Freight traffic was heavy until the early 1960s.

Over the years the vessels using the port changed considerably, and the world of sail gradually gave way to steam power. In Victorian times many of the early passenger-carrying vessels were paddle-steamers of a fairly small tonnage. They in turn gave way to turbines in the Edwardian era, but even they were small compared with today's cross-Channel ferries, which would completely dwarf the ships frequented by the pioneers of the packet services. Another interesting development that occurred once Newhaven became established was the advent of 'Boat Trains', run as expresses specifically for passengers using Newhaven as part of a London to Paris route. Overall timings of about 1hr 50min between London Victoria and Newhaven Wharf in 1867 were gradually whittled down so that the best steam run to Newhaven Marine in 1931 was 1hr 26min. Even after electrification, the boat trains were still steam-hauled because the 'third rail' did not extend into Newhaven Marine until 1949. On occasions during peak periods there were even relief boat trains. Gradually over the years through workings from London to both Newhaven and Seaford diminished, and are now confined to a single commuter train to and from Victoria, which takes 1hr 16min to Newhaven Harbour.

Just to the east of Newhaven was a small coastal village known as Tide Mills, and a siding from the Seaford extension ran down to the mill from Bishopstone station. At one point the track ran down the village street to the actual mill. About 60 locals worked at Tide Mills, but by the 1880s all of the activities were in decline and the population reduced significantly. The site was used as a bonded warehouse for a while, but when that ceased about 1900 the line to Tide Mills was abandoned and the village gradually became a ghost town, there being nothing to keep the population in the immediate area; the owner of the mill and adjacent land sold much of the area to the Newhaven Harbour Company. The extended East Harbour Tramway also reached the site just above the shingle beach. Many of the cottages were used to house railway employees, but by 1940 the last of them had been removed. The Royal Navy used the site during World War 2 and it gradually became derelict. By the

Above:
There is an air of dereliction in this 1988 shot just north of Newhaven Town station. There were once acres of sidings at Newhaven, but over the years they have been gradually eroded, with freight traffic being totally eliminated by the Millennium. Here a Class 33 locomotive and eight 'Seacow' ballast hoppers wait just off the main line while on the right an old box van seems to be marooned in front of the substantial but abandoned goods shed. The A259 road flyover can be seen above the signalbox in the background. *JV/TTT*

Below:
With Newhaven's star in the descent and with the age of the boat train all but finished, it was surprising in May 1986 when a scheduled Newhaven to Manchester service was inaugurated. On 11 January of that year there was a dress rehearsal for what was to come when the Brighton main line was closed for engineering works and the Brighton to Manchester service started from Newhaven Marine. Passing acres of abandoned sidings, the train of empty stock drops down into Town station behind Class 47 No 47408 *Finsbury Park*. *JV/TTT*

end of the war the village had completely disappeared, except for a few boundary walls. In 1922 Bishopstone station (a misnomer because Bishopstone was some distance away) was reduced to unmanned halt status and the station goods sidings were lifted. Once the station master had gone the railway demolished his house. The Southern Railway built a new Bishopstone station between the halt and Seaford, and this opened in September 1938. The old station closed briefly, but reopened in 1939 as Bishopstone Beach Halt, mainly to serve a small community living nearby in old railway carriages. Although even this closed on 1 January 1942, the remains of the platforms can still be detected.

The track beyond Newhaven had been doubled in July 1904 and at Seaford both a long main platform and a bay platform to the north were provided. From the opening, goods facilities were provided at Seaford, but they were of course a fraction of those described at Newhaven. The original goods yard was on the up side of the line opposite the station platform, and a goods shed was provided. From about the time the line was doubled a large coal yard was constructed on the down side of the branch, and a further goods shed was part of the infrastructure. At the very end of the line a 'sector plate' was used during locomotive run-round operations rather than conventional space-consuming points. The railway was having an influence on the growing seaside town, which was taking on more of a residential character. Although it is perhaps too easy to gloss over the decades, the Newhaven and Seaford line settled down, providing a reliable service for local people and an ever-increasing number of European travellers.

On 1 September 1906 Southease & Rodmell Halt between Southerham Junction and Newhaven Town was opened. The hamlets the halt served were some way from the station — in fact, both were on the other side of the valley across the River Ouse. It was the advent of World War 1 that saw Newhaven at its busiest, with troop, supply and ammunition trains at the forefront. Yet more sidings were laid in the only space available, north-east of Newhaven Town station. After the war the railways were in a bad shape, and this eventually resulted in the 'Grouping' of the railway companies into the 'Big Four' in 1923. The resulting Southern Railway extended third-rail electrification to the Newhaven and Seaford branch line in July 1935.

Returning to the early days, the passenger timetable at the time of opening comprised half a dozen round-trip workings per day, a frequency that was retained until after the opening of the Seaford branch in 1864. By 1888 there were eight trains on weekdays and two on Sundays. In Edwardian times railmotors were introduced, and no fewer than 22 trains per day traversed the line between Lewes and Seaford. There was a slight reduction in services during the 1920s, but when the line was electrified in 1935 an almost unbelievable 50 trains per day worked the line. In 2003 about 32 trains arrived at and departed from Seaford, with the minimum off-peak service being half-hourly.

Interestingly, some local trains originated at Horsted Keynes on the Bluebell line, travelling to Seaford via Ardingly and Haywards Heath. As with World War 1, the 1939 to 1945 World War 2 period saw much additional traffic and general activity on the branch right up to D-Day, such was the strategic importance of Newhaven. Several bombs landed in the dock area and much damage was caused from time to time. Over the years there have been many permutations to the timetable. In addition to the now discontinued Newhaven boat trains, which ran for many decades, there was a Glasgow to Newhaven car-sleeper express in the mid-1960s, trials with a Portsmouth Harbour to Newhaven Marine service in 1966, and a Newhaven Marine to Manchester Piccadilly service in 1986. Local trains now run to Lewes, Brighton, West Worthing and Littlehampton, together with the frugal daily London service for local commuters.

A variety of early 'Brighton' engines worked the line, including early 2-2-2 types and later 'B1' class 0-4-2 'Gladstones', particularly on the London trains. Just after the turn of the 20th century railmotors were in fashion and were regularly used on the branch, but after what could be regarded as an extensive trial (and in common with other branches) they were deemed to be unsuccessful. Eventually they were replaced with conventional motor trains with a 'Balloon' coach, hauled by 'A1'/'A1X' class 'Terrier' locomotives. Similar trains were later worked by Class D1 and D3 locomotives, in what became standard push-pull mode. After the Grouping 'Chatham' engines sometimes appeared, but LBSCR types dominated, and for many years the handsome Marsh Atlantics ruled on the boat trains. Freight was mostly in the hands

Below:
Headcode '52' denotes that this is a Newhaven (or Seaford) to London Victoria train via the Quarry Line.
In fact, the photograph illustrates a latter-day boat train leaving Newhaven Marine in July 1989. Class 421 4-CIG unit No 1269 heads the train. On the right a Sealink Ferry has just berthed and the bow door of the 'Ro-Ro' can be seen in the raised position for unloading. The line to Bishopstone and Seaford peels off to the left. *JV/TTT*

Top left:
Newhaven Marine now has just a single platform and one passenger train per weekday: the 21.30 Newhaven Marine to Lewes local. When photographed in 1912, there were two lines and three platform faces, with an overall roof above the main track. At the head of a short up Newhaven boat train is LBSCR 'I4' class No 33 (No 2033 in SR days). Note the motley collection of vehicles in the background. *IAL*

Centre left:
The rarely photographed track beyond Newhaven Marine station no longer sees any rail traffic and the weeds and rust are taking over. However, years ago there were large volumes of freight traffic on what was known as the East Quay line. Newhaven Marine station can just be seen on the right, and the cross-Channel ship in the background, *Sardinia Vera*, belongs to Transmanche Ferries Ltd, one of two operators currently using Newhaven. *JV*

Lower left:
The East Quay line once continued along the foreshore parallel with the shingle towards the ghost town of Tide Mills (see text). A collection of buildings with a small population was built around a mill, which ceased grinding in 1883. It was also served by a siding from the original Bishopstone station. In 1940 the town was evacuated and the Royal Navy took over the entire area. Until the 1970s the line was used by incoming spoil trains, and in June 2003 there was just a trace of the transport system of yesteryear. In the right background is the town of Seaford. *JV*

Above:

Since the end of general freight activity at Newhaven and Seaford during the 1960s, there have been several experiments with certain block loads. In addition to the already mentioned aggregates there have been trains of Ford Transit vans from Eastleigh and, in December 1989, Freightliner container traffic made a brief appearance. At the head of a train of Freightliner flats on the rarely used sidings east of Newhaven Marine station is Railfreight Class 47 No 47337 *Herbert Austin. JV/TTT*

Below:

This impressive night study illustrates Newhaven's swansong as an inter-regional destination for long-distance express passenger trains. In the small hours of 18 October 1986 Class 47/4 No 47620 *Windsor Castle* awaits departure from Marine station with the 06.25 service for Manchester Piccadilly. The train had arrived the previous evening as the 16.15 from Manchester and had been stabled overnight at Brighton. *Brian Morrison*

of Craven, Stroudley and Billinton 0-6-0s, but later 'K' class 2-6-0s appeared, and the turntable was replaced by a 60ft example to accommodate them in 1917. Local freights usually had an 'E4' class at the business end. Eventually ex-LSWR 'M7s' and Brighton-built LMS Fairburn tanks worked certain trains, but the variety was remarkable, with 'King Arthurs', 'Schools', Bulleid Light Pacifics and even LMS 'Black Fives' regularly turning up on the branch. As already mentioned, 'A1X' class 'Terriers' exclusively worked the West Quay lines due to weight restrictions on the swingbridge.

The full range of Southern electric units worked the line, from PULs, PANs, NOLs, BILs, HALs, HAPs, CAPs, CORs, CIGs, BIGs and VEPs to the latest sliding-door Class 377s, and there has in the recent past been a handful of workings diagrammed for diesel-electric multiple-units. Class 40s and 45s once worked the Newhaven to Glasgow car-sleeper service, and Class 33s, 47s and 73s were regularly seen on a variety of workings, as shown in the accompanying photographs. Bulleid's early Co-Co electric loco-motives powered some boat trains, and Class 71s were not unknown. Local shunting was taken over by 350hp shunters, which also worked local freight trains. In recent years Class 56 and 60 locomotives worked from Newhaven on regular aggregate trains, and once a year Class 20s traversed the line on the annual weedkilling train.

It could be argued that decline had set in many years ago as feeder lines from Eastwood Cement Works, South Heighton Cement Works and Meeching Quarry closed. Although the line achieved a period of consolidation in the 1950s, there followed the similar pattern that affected all of British Railways' routes at the time: loss of traffic, rationalisation and decline. Also, the cross-Channel services from Newhaven became erratic and, for a time during 1956/57, they ceased altogether. From 1956 to 1964 there were no winter passenger services. However, a roll on/roll off car ferry service was introduced in 1964. The service was run under the 'Sealink' label in 1969, and in 1984 Sea Containers Ltd acquired the company. Since then there have been periods of no service and summer-only service, but at the time of writing Transmanche Ferries Ltd offers a year-round ferry service and Hoverspeed Seacat services also operate from Newhaven, both providing a service to Dieppe for passengers and their cars. The quay lines gradually gave up the ghost, with the West Quay losing all of its sources of traffic, resulting in closure in August 1963. Goods facilities were withdrawn from Seaford in May 1964 and, as if to rub salt in the wound, the Newhaven Harbour to Seaford line reverted to single track in 1975; from that time only the up platform was used at Bishopstone. In 1976 a new road flyover carrying the main A259 coast road replaced the old swingbridge over the River Ouse at Newhaven. Also in 1976 heavy road works at Southerham Junction in connection with a Lewes bypass saw the junction moved further east and the short four-track section at that location abolished. Two platforms and stock sidings were retained at Seaford for a while, but the signalbox closed in 1977, with control of the terminus being exercised by Newhaven via colour lights. Further rationalisation has taken place, and there are but a few sidings connected north of Town station. The signalbox at Seaford has now been demolished and all sidings removed. Newhaven Marine is now used by only one local train per day and the surrounding infrastructure gives the impression of imminent closure.

Although not specifically relevant to the branch, the acres of sidings that once graced Lewes largely disappeared in the 1960s, as did lines running northward to Uckfield and East Grinstead. At Newhaven, after some land reclamation work at the end of the East Quay lines, they too were abandoned. As mentioned earlier, general freight traffic was decimated in the 1960s, but later relatively short-lived container (Freightliner) trains, aggregate trains and van and car transportation loads were using the tracks at Newhaven. There is now a complete absence of freight traffic. Although signalboxes on the line have been rationalised, semaphore signals are still in operation at Newhaven Town and at Harbour. Whether it is the gentle curves that follow the River Ouse through open farmland at the Lewes end of the line, the relatively untidy and industrialised scenery around the Newhaven stations, or the climb over the hill to the compact little terminus of Seaford, the 8-mile branch is full of interest, especially if one is able to spot the key locations of yesteryear. The cliffs at Seaford and the old Fort at Newhaven are on the tourist trail, and a visit to the area is highly recommended. Fortunately this is one of the few branches featured in *Branches and Byways: Sussex and Hampshire* that still boasts a train service, a situation that is unlikely to change.

Left:
Railway map of Newhaven c1960.

Top right:
This Edwardian view of the 1866 swingbridge was the subject of an official LBSCR postcard, and shows the structure from the south-west, looking north-east. The opening 50ft span revolved on a turntable and was opened manually by no fewer than eight men turning a capstan. Opening the bridge normally delayed traffic for 10 minutes, resulting in its replacement in 1976. It carried all of the traffic on the A259 coastal road and the single-track railway line to the West Quay. The bridge was subsequently demolished, but the tiny hut on the right survives to this day.
IAL

Centre right:
The West Quay tramway ran along the west side of the harbour past the base of Newhaven Fort to the 2,800ft breakwater built to protect the harbour from 'south-wester' gales. It also allowed shipping movements irrespective of the state of the tide. Over the years the tramway served a number of sidings, and traffic included chalk, imported ice, tarpaulins, ropes and oil. Here 'Terrier' No 32662, built in 1875, cautiously crosses the swingbridge on 27 April 1958. *S. C. Nash*

Lower right:
The West Quay trains had to be 'red flagged' across several roads, including the main A259. The flagman waves and the little 'A1X' looks to have a good load behind it as the formation travels past the Railway Hotel public house, which served Tamplin's Ales. Only the 28-ton 'A1X' class was permitted to work the West Quay line due to weight restrictions, and one of the class, No 32636 *Fenchurch*, now preserved on the Bluebell Railway, was allocated to Newhaven from 1898 to 1955! The last train over the tramway ran on 10 August 1963.
S. C. Nash

Above:
Newhaven had a four-road engine shed, which opened in 1887 and was latterly a sub-shed of Brighton. In 1917 a new longer turntable was installed to accommodate Billinton's new 'K' class freight locomotives. In 1955 its allocation had dwindled to four steam locomotives and, when it closed in 1963, a solitary Class A1X 'Terrier' was the only permanent resident! On 2 October 1954 local resident No 32632 (once owned by the Newhaven Harbour Company) is dwarfed by stablemate Class E4 0-6-2T No 32513.
Brian Morrison

Upper left:
The entire Newhaven area is worth exploration, and, with a little diligence, railway relics of yesteryear can still be found. The old engine shed survives in commercial use and it was particularly satisfying, 40 years after closure, to find a pair of tracks visible in the concrete. Somebody has taken the trouble to fit a window into the utility hut on the left. *JV*

Lower left:
A fascinating view of the now singled Seaford branch, looking west on the eastern edge of development at Newhaven. In July 1991, and much to the delight of enthusiasts, the surviving 2-BIL and 4-SUB units were specially working a Brighton to Seaford shuttle. On the extreme left is the start of the Newhaven Marine platform, while off-frame on the extreme right is Newhaven Harbour station. The signalbox controlling the junction survives and there are still a handful of semaphore signals in the area. Note the oil tail lamp on No 4732.
JV/TTT

Above:
The Seaford extension from Newhaven to Seaford opened on 1 June 1864. The remains of the original Bishopstone station visible
in this photograph have had an interesting history. The station was originally built to serve the little community at Tide Mills and
was located some way from Bishopstone. A goods yard and a spur to the mill were provided; the mill closed in 1901
and the goods yard in 1922. From 1922 the station was reduced to 'halt' status and renamed Bishopstone Halt.
In 1938 a new Bishopstone station was built nearer the village, and the original station became known as Bishopstone Beach Halt.
The station closed for good in 1942. In June 2003 4-CIG No 1708 is about to pass the old running-in board, heading for Seaford. *JV*

Below:
With freight traffic being withdrawn from Seaford in May 1964 it has only been on rare occasions that locomotives
have traversed the line. In August 1988 a special comprising a Class 33/1 and two 4-TC push-pull units worked the branch
and is seen here climbing the 1 in 100 from Newhaven to Bishopstone. Passing the distant signal is No 33112 *Templecombe*.
Note the caravans on the left, situated between the railway and the beach. *JV/TTT*

Top left:
Another special train, but a quarter of a century earlier: a seven-coach RCTS special passing Bishopstone and descending into Seaford on 7 October 1962. Double-heading the Chartex are 'A1X' No 32636 and 'E6' No 32418. At this time the line was still double track, but rationalisation has since taken its toll. *S. C. Nash*

Centre left:
This very unusual photograph of Seaford station shows steam traction on a local train nearly 20 years after electrification! On 20 March 1954 there was engineering work on the line, affecting the current supply, and in that era on a Sunday there were spare steam locomotives and stock to provide a substitute. Former LSWR 'M7' No 30053 and a two-car push-pull set wait in the bay platform with the 8.1am service to Brighton. In the left background is a 2-NOL unit. *Ian W. Wray*

Lower left:
The picture demonstrates the ultimate exercise in track rationalisation at Seaford terminus in June 2003. The south goods yard, the north goods and coal yard, run-round loop and storage sidings have all been lifted, leaving just a single-line stub from Newhaven Harbour. Slam-door electric unit stock is on its way out after 68 years on the line, as the latest sliding-door product from the railway workshops, in the shape of Class 375 No 375329, waits to leave for Lewes and Brighton. *JV*

Above:
A special visit to the Newhaven and Seaford branch was necessary in April 1990 because the annual weedkilling train
was traversing the line. After the branch had been singled but before the semaphore signals had been removed, there seem to be
trains due in both directions on the single line! In fact the controlling signalbox is 'switched out', so Class 20/9 Nos 20904 and 20901
can proceed safely to the Seaford terminus. The weedkiller is stored in the tanks and spray can be seen coming from
a converted utility van. *JV/TTT*

Below:
A high-powered telephoto lens gives a fascinating perspective of Seaford, nestling beneath the Downs that end in vertical chalk cliffs
on reaching the coast. On 18 September 1993 Network South East Class 421/4 4-CIG No 1835 leaves the terminus with the 16.04
service to Brighton. The signalbox was then still standing, but was out of use. The track in the bay on the left and the storage siding
on the right are now both history (see the previous page). Happily the station building survives. *Brian Morrison*

8. Kemp Town Branch

ALTHOUGH the Kemp Town branch was effectively a suburban branch line catering for the transport needs of the growing population to the east of the hilly town of Brighton, it had a unique character in that, having left the junction with the Brighton to Lewes line, it comprised little more than a viaduct, an embankment, a cutting and a tunnel. From the junction the branch was a mere 1 mile and 32 chains in length, and of that distance more than 46 chains, or 40%, was inside the 1,024yd Kemp Town Tunnel!

In cost-per-mile terms the line was, at £100,000 in 1860 values, hugely expensive to build, but in mid-Victorian times not only was the population of Brighton rapidly increasing, promising a good return on the investment, but there were plans by rival railway companies to access the potentially lucrative watering hole on the Sussex coast. The line was effectively a London, Brighton & South Coast Railway 'wall' around the town to keep others out. Other companies had in 1863 and 1864 proposed a South London to Brighton line via an East Grinstead and Lewes route, and although the adjudicating Parliamentary Committee rejected these plans, the threat remained.

Brighton, located only 50 miles from the capital, had been the nation's primary seaside resort in Georgian and Victorian times following late-18th-century Royal visits by the Prince Regent, which gave aristocratic credentials to an increasingly cosmopolitan conurbation. Kemp Town got its name from one Thomas Read Kemp MP, the son of a former Member of Parliament for Lewes, who saw potential in developing a quality housing estate slightly away from an ever-growing Brighton, originally known as Brighthelmstone. In the early 1820s he attempted to attract the more affluent classes to his Regency-style estate to the east of the town in an area that eventually became known as 'Kemp Town'. By the middle of the 19th century Kemp Town had been almost saturated by housing and stores, and it became famous for the Kemptown (*sic*) Brewery, a producer of fine ales sold from many outlets along the South Coast, and a trading name that has happily been resuscitated in recent years. The LBSCR recognised the traffic potential at a time when street tramcars and motor omnibuses had yet to make an appearance. Accordingly, in 1864 the Brighton company had an Act passed enabling them to construct a branch railway line to Kemp Town.

A railway line had already been opened from Brighton to Lewes (and beyond) via Falmer in June 1846, the London to Brighton main line having been opened throughout in September 1841, and Lewes had been connected to Wivelsfield to give a direct Lewes to London link in October 1847. The most convenient point for the junction for the proposed line to Kemp Town was just beyond the 64yd Ditchling Road Tunnel on the east side, a few chains from Brighton 'London Road' station, opened in 1877, which was a shade under a mile from Brighton. The Mayor of Brighton, Alderman Henry Martin, turned the first sod on 17 February 1866, and slowly but surely the major engineering challenges progressed, including the impressive 14-arch Lewes Road Viaduct. There was a recession during the 1866/68 period, and it would seem that building expenditure was controlled, resulting in slower than expected progress. The line was inspected by the Board of Trade during July 1869, and opened on the following 2 August. The same Alderman Martin who cut the first sod laid a ceremonial 'last brick' with a silver trowel in the eastern pier of the central arch of the curved 180yd Lewes Road Viaduct a few days later, on 6 August 1869.

The rail route from Kemp Town to Brighton station was some 2¼ miles, whereas the distance by road was about a mile. The railway was thus only marginally faster than a horse and carriage, but the LBSCR charged very competitive fares, the Third Class single fare being 2d, and 4d return. Initially three classes of travel were available and there were nine trains per day. Over the years this increased dramatically, and for most of the late Victorian era 17 trains per day ran. Once the road/tram competition hotted up in Edwardian times the service was increased again. Upon the introduction of 'rail motor cars' on 1 January 1906 no fewer than 32 round-trip journeys were scheduled.

The local newspapers were very complimentary about the new line and the facilities that prevailed at Kemp Town terminus, describing it as 'an appropriately handsome building'. They also pointed out that the station was nearer to Brighton racecourse than the main-line terminus, and by travelling to Kemp Town passengers would avoid 'some portion of the hill'. Safety was also dealt with by the newspapers, saying that operations were designed 'never to have but one train on the line [at any one time] going or returning, and that any collision will be impossible'.

In the early 1870s the Kemp Town site was further excavated and additional freight sidings installed. On 1 September 1873 Lewes Road station was opened on the junction side of the viaduct. From the junction, which was controlled by a 19-lever signalbox, to Lewes Road Viaduct the branch was double track, but the viaduct and the tunnel were built for only a single line. The main 268ft-long platform at Lewes Road had some modest buildings on the up side, but a second 293ft-long island platform between the two tracks was also provided, reached by a footbridge. A signalbox was provided at the down end of the station, just before the viaduct. In October 1877 London Road station was opened on the Brighton to Lewes line, and although not on the Kemp Town branch as such, the branch trains called at the station in both directions. The next major development was the opening of a halt at Hartington Road, between the viaduct and the tunnel, on 1 January 1906. Hartington Road had a 150ft-long platform that was 7ft wide and 3ft high. It was provided with a lamp and a nameboard and was accessed by a footpath from the road below.

This event was planned to coincide with the introduction of petrol railcars in an effort to compete with the new electric trams on the road. From that date the service increased to approximately

Above:

The Kemp Town branch in Brighton opened as long ago as 1869, primarily to serve a growing population to the east of the town in an area known as Kemp Town, which had sprung to life in 1823. The problem with providing a railway was the topography, which meant constructing a railway that would entail a 2¼-mile journey from Brighton station, against an 'as the crow flies' distance of just over a mile. With the advent of 'motor trains' in 1905, 'Terriers' Nos 81 and 82 were temporarily converted to a 2-4-0T wheel arrangement and fitted with push-pull apparatus to work with LBSCR 'Balloon' coaches. In this era No 81 and train pose for the cameraman at Kemp Town. *IAL*

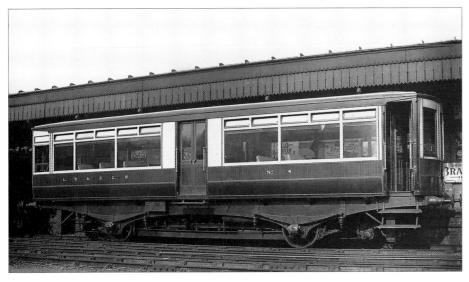

Upper left:

As an economy measure, but also to combat the impact of new street tramcars, a new half-hourly service was introduced on the Kemp Town branch in 1906, utilising new petrol railcars manufactured by Dick Kerr. The vehicles looked very much like trams, and although they worked well initially, one of the petrol engines 'let go' in Kemp Town Tunnel, understandably causing alarm among the passengers. Push-pull steam trains soon replaced the railcars. Here No 4 is seen at Kemp Town terminus in 1906. *IAL*

Lower left:

This photograph from the 1920s shows 'A1X' class No 659 and a 'Balloon' coach at Kemp Town. No 659 was built in 1875 and carried the number 59 until 1901. It was rebuilt in 1922, then carried the numbers 659 and later 2659. In the background a freight train is departing — note the 'off' signal. One of the nails in the coffin of the branch was complete closure between 1 January 1917 and 1 September 1919 as an economy measure during World War 1. This gave passengers a chance to try the new omnibuses that had started to work a network of local services, as well as established street trams. Many never returned to the railway. *IAL*

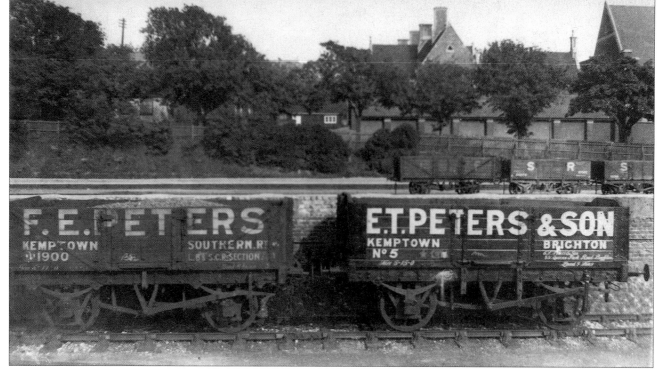

Above:
The author was the beneficiary of a gift of this photograph from the Kemp Town goods office staff just before it closed (the goods 'office' was located in an SR utility van!). The previously unpublished picture shows private owner wagons on the west-side sidings at Kemp Town goods yard during Southern Railway days, probably the 1920s. Was 'F. E. Peters' the son of 'E. T. Peters'? *JV collection*

Upper left:
Although this photograph has been published before, it was the only available view of Kemp Town signalbox, located on the up side of Kemp Town Tunnel. The line comprised little more than a viaduct, a cutting and a 1,024yd tunnel in its length of 1 mile and 32 chains. The next box along the branch was at Lewes Road station, just a short distance from Kemp Town Junction on the Brighton to Lewes line. Both branch boxes closed in July 1933, a few months after passenger services ceased.
IAL

Lower left:
This photograph of a magnificent collection of 1950s raincoats was irresistible, with not an anorak in sight! On both 5 and 19 October 1952 the Railway Correspondence & Travel Society organised special trains from Brighton to Kemp Town in conjunction with the centenary of Brighton Locomotive Works.
The locomotive was the popular 'A1X' No 32636, which had strong associations with Newhaven (see previous chapter). The damp scene is at Kemp Town. *SLS/G. Dendy*

Right:
The typical Kemp Town goods train on 30 June 1951, with an 'E4' class 0-6-2T toying with some coal wagons within the confines of the terminus sidings. After the end of passenger trains on 31 December 1932 either one or two goods trains worked the branch per day; in 1935 22,000 tons of coal were received at Kemp Town, and a total of 6,500 goods wagons were handled, an average throughout the year of 22 wagons per working day. *S. C. Nash*

half-hourly. The 'rail motor cars' were one-class 48-seaters. Unfortunately, one day one of the rail cars was inside Kemp Town Tunnel when the petrol engine 'let go', resulting in the pistons travelling to places they had not been before and terrifying the passengers on board. The noise in such a confined space must have been deafening! The service was soon in the hands of steam push-pull trains hauled by LBSCR 'Terrier' tank locomotives.

The new halt was not a success, and in 1911 the Directors of the LBSCR decided to close it, despite a petition against signed by 96 persons. Kemp Town saw plenty of goods traffic, the income from which was to become increasingly important in the line's continuing viability as a rail route. The branch continued to provide frequent trains for Brighton residents, but the battle with the competition was ever present and as good as lost when, on 1 January 1917, during World War 1, the line was closed for economy

reasons. Although unlike other branches the track was not lifted in 1917, by the time the line reopened in September 1919 the public had become used to doing without it, and branch traffic figures never fully recovered. Trams and buses had gained an even greater foothold in the local transport infrastructure that they would never relinquish. The service remained intense and freight traffic revived, but the motor bus was beginning to make an impression and the LBSCR had been absorbed by the Southern Railway at the Grouping in 1923. The railway responded to what was becoming a lost cause by reducing Lewes Road to an unstaffed halt, and during 1932 no fewer than 36 trains per day were shown in the timetable, but it was all too late. The graph of ticket sales made grim viewing. From more than 66,000 in 1925, it fell to just over 50,000 by 1927, and by 1929 it was a mere 30,000. In 1931, the penultimate year of survival, this further plummeted to just 21,000.

Below:
This wonderful and typical busy scene at Kemp Town yard during the 1950s is well captured by the camera of Les Dench. There is a hive of activity as 'E4' No 32503 shunts mainly coal wagons, although a banana van appears in the bottom right-hand corner. The yard is seen from the eastern side with the tunnel off frame to the right. *L. A. Dench*

The increasingly non-viable circuitous route of the trains combined with the electrification of the main London to Brighton line on 1 January 1933 resulted in the Kemp Town service becoming a loss-maker and something of an anachronism. This would have been especially the case after July 1935 when the Brighton to Lewes line was electrified. The last scheduled passenger train to Kemp Town ran on 31 December 1932, and as early as 29 July 1933 signalboxes at Lewes Road and Kemp Town closed, leaving the branch as a mere freight siding. Sidings were retained at Lewes Road and the old station became a pickle factory, then part of a builder's yard. Coal was the main payload into Kemp Town, and it became something of a concentration depot for Brighton. Most traffic was one-way, incoming loaded wagons outnumbering outgoing loaded wagons by more than 9 to 1. To give some impression of scale, more than 6,500 incoming loaded wagons were handled at Kemp Town during 1935, or more than 20 per working day, which normally arrived in one or two daily trains. Despite the branch not being electrified, the lengthy tunnel was put to good use during World War 2 when long rakes of electric multiple-units were stored therein every night to avoid the real risk of being damaged during Luftwaffe bombing raids. In fact, the nearby London Road Viaduct had two arches destroyed by enemy action on 25 May 1943.

The gradient profile on the Kemp Town branch was very simple. The line was initially downhill at 1 in 100 from the junction to Lewes Road, where it levelled out, then gradually fell away through the tunnel at 1 in 213 until the level Kemp Town station yard was reached. At Kemp Town there were many goods sidings on both the up and down sides, with a large brick-built goods shed on the eastern side. An impressive 481ft-long single platform for passenger trains was provided, with the main station building built at right angles to the platform end. The signalbox was placed almost against the wall of the tunnel mouth on the up side; in later years a ground frame was located in almost the same position. The site was truly 'hollowed out' of a chalk down, giving a sort of amphitheatre impression.

Originally passenger trains comprised of five-coach sets of Stroudley four-wheel coaches, worked by small 'A1X' class 'Terriers' or 'D1s'. After the petrol railcar years the service normally comprised a 'Terrier' and a single 'Balloon' trailer coach, but later push-pull workings were the norm, with the real operational benefit of the locomotive not having to run round its train at both Kemp Town and Brighton. Goods services were normally in the hands of the chunkier Class E4 and E5 locomotives, although others, such as Class E3s, occasionally appeared. From time to time railway enthusiasts' specials would traverse the branch, and these brought 'Terriers', tender types such as the 'Q' class, ex-LMS Ivatt

2-6-2Ts and, in diesel days, even Class 33 'Cromptons' to the branch. When steam ended in the early 1960s, freight traffic was still healthy and Class 08 or 09 diesel shunters took over. The last-day specials comprised a Class 3R 'Tadpole' diesel-electric unit.

When the Kemp Town goods was photographed in the late 1960s it would still comprise about a dozen wagons per day, although one of the photographs reproduced herein shows that only a single wagon made the outward journey. However, bearing in mind that British Railways and the unions self-inflicted most of their freight traffic wounds in the late 1950s and early 1960s, it is perhaps surprising that Kemp Town kept going for so long. During the last years of its life the station was known as Brighton East Goods Depot, but when it was announced that all goods traffic was being transferred to Hove, to the west of the town, the writing was on the wall. The station was already semi-derelict and the land was occupying a valuable site, which Brighton Council subsequently purchased. The author was the only non-railwayman to witness and photograph the freight that worked the line on its centenary in August 1969!

Some enterprise was shown by BR in organising hourly last-day specials on 26 June 1971, with a three-car diesel unit shuttling all day between Brighton and Kemp Town. Commemorative postal covers were issued to aid railway charities, and these were carried on the last train and 'cancelled' by the General Post Office accordingly. The return fare was 25p, but on the very last train the fare was 50p!

After closure the track was lifted and Kemp Town station was demolished. In the ensuing 30 years every trace of the Lewes Road viaduct has been removed, the site of Lewes Road station has been razed, and the site of the junction is now an industrial estate. The cutting from the site of Hartington Road to the tunnel has been partly filled in and now forms William Clarke Park. The northern tunnel entrance is part of the Elm Grove School grounds. At Kemp Town virtually the entire site has become the Freshfield Industrial Estate, and only the old sealed tunnel mouth survives as a testimony to the existence of a railway.

It is hard to believe that more than 30 years have elapsed since those last-day specials, and intriguing to contemplate that a 20-year-old travelling on the last scheduled passenger service from Brighton to Kemp Town in 1932 would now be in his/her 90s! Kemp Town was a fascinating line and it would be interesting to know whether in its lifetime it made a profit for the LBSCR or the SR. Needless to say, the use of Hove Goods Yard as an alternative fizzled out in the early 1990s, when the last loads of coal from South Wales were received, Brighton itself already having been 'freightless' for some time.

Below:
Bradshaw's timetable for April 1910.

BRIGHTON and KEMP TOWN (Motor Cars—3rd class only).

[Timetable: Bradshaw's April 1910 — Brighton and Kemp Town, Down and Up, Week Days and Sundays. Detailed departure/arrival times in columns.]

e Except Saturdays.

Above:

A couple of years before complete closure the line 'celebrated' its centenary, but the author was the only person to photograph the event. The Class 08 0-6-0 shunter has just come to a halt on 4 August 1969 with the customary coal wagons and the driver has just uncoupled the locomotive. The actual centenary was on 2 August, but there was no train working that day, or on the 3rd. The photograph gives a good view of the terminus station buildings, set at right angles to the line. *JV/TTT*

Left:
Some 38 years after the line closed to passengers, the goods traffic was also due to be withdrawn, and BR enterprisingly arranged a last-day hourly shuttle service between Brighton and Kemp Town. The motive power for the occasion was Class 206 'Tadpole' diesel unit No 1205. Here visitors swarm around the scene on 26 June 1971. The fare was 25p, but was doubled to 50p for the very last train! The takings were donated to Woking Homes railway charity. *JV*

Lower left:
After the last-day specials it did not take long before the demolition contractors moved in. It was a sorry sight to see all of the track ripped up and the infrastructure demolished. Even the lovely old station was levelled as the local authority acquired the valuable 7¾-acre plot, which was subsequently covered by commercial buildings, collectively known as the Freshfield Industrial Estate. This view in January 1972 shows the scene of abandonment, looking towards the tunnel mouth. *JV*

9. The Dyke Branch

PROVIDED you were not on the poverty line, the Victorian age was remarkable. Not only was there the Industrial Revolution taking place, but also state-of-the-art technological innovation was changing the face of Britain for ever. Although absolute origins were earlier, the Victorians had seen the birth of the industrial steam engine, the coming of the railways, the evolution of the steamship, and building wonders that spanned rivers and gorges to generally improve transportation systems. The world was becoming a smaller place, and the public was starting to travel more as public transport became affordable, certainly to the upper and middle classes.

In addition to infrastructure items, the public was being entertained by a vast array of engineering novelties, provided for leisure and pleasure, at locations where the Victorians tended to congregate. In many ways Brighton in Sussex (now East Sussex) was something of a magnet for visitors and 'trippers', attracted by the good seaside air and climate, bathing, amusements and, of course, from 1841 the coming of the railway. Later there would be piers, Volk's Electric Railway, opened on 4 August 1883 and said to be the world's first electric railway, and the 'Daddy Long Legs'. The latter was a large elevated platform on 'stilts' that ran along the seashore on rails located below the high-water line, powered by an overhead electric cable, on trolley principles. It gave participants the impression of 'floating' through the air above the sea, particularly at high tide (see the Miscellany chapter).

To reach Brighton from London and the North it was necessary for the main-line railway to penetrate the South Downs through lengthy tunnels. The highest point on the Downs in the immediate Brighton area is the well-known Devil's Dyke, at 700ft above sea level. Devil's Dyke afforded visitors fine views of the surrounding countryside and, on a near perfect day, it was, and still is, possible to view six counties and the Isle of Wight, some 50 miles away, as well as many other topographical features. There are many versions of how Devil's Dyke got its name, and the world is littered with locations employing Satan's other name, but whatever version one accepts, the name is part of local folklore and is of ancient if mythical origin. Nevertheless, the name 'clicked' with the Victorians and they visited this hill in their thousands. In fact, as early as 1818 there was a wooden shack providing refreshments, including alcoholic beverages, at the top of Devil's Dyke.

As soon as horse-drawn charabancs started to make the 5½-mile journey up from Brighton, the tourist industry expanded, especially in the summer months, and by 1831 an inn had been built at the top of the hill, which later became a hotel. In her younger days Queen Victoria visited Devil's Dyke with Prince Albert, so it is a wonder that the hill did not become 'Royal Devil's Dyke'! It was almost inevitable that during the railway age somebody would consider the viability of building a railway to the top, even if it would involve a fairly steep climb on to the South Downs. As explained later, various schemes were proposed, but on 1 September 1887 a standard gauge branch line from the main Brighton to Worthing and Portsmouth 'Coastway' route was opened to a point near to the summit but about 200ft below the hotel.

What had become the Dyke Park Estate under the ownership, from 1892, of James Henry Hubbard, expanded hugely and almost became the Victorian equivalent of Alton Towers! In addition to the railway and the enlarged, luxurious hotel, the estate included swings, roundabouts, rocking-horses, coconut shies, shooting galleries, penny machines, a bicycle railway and a host of 'funfair'-style entertainments. However, an air of sophistication was retained by the quality of the hotel, which included a main bar, a large-capacity coffee room, a smoking lounge and an extravagant dining room adorned with oil paintings and fine furnishings. To cater for cultural needs the Dyke Park Estate Brass & Reed Band played a wide selection of music every Sunday. In 1893 a total of 1 million visitors made their way up to Devil's Dyke!

If all this was not enough, in 1893 the first major transport novelty was proposed — the building of an aerial cableway across a small 230ft-deep ravine in the folds of the South Downs. The cableway would be 1,200ft long with small stations at either end of the run. The 'track' cables would be suspended from a catenary cable by a number of metal supports, two of which would extend outwards with one vertical rod. The cars moved on an endless cable powered by a Crossley patent oil engine. Two small cars, each holding four people, were employed, and the journey time was about 2¼ minutes. The span between the two major iron support columns, which were embedded in concrete, was 650ft. The grand opening missed the 1894 summer season, but the cableway was ready for service on 13 October that year. The fare was 6d in each direction. The cableway was backed by Mr Hubbard, and after some £5,000 had been consumed on construction, the first car across the ravine contained the Mayor and Mayoress of Brighton, who formally opened the 'line'. There were many speeches and the group retired to the pavilion of the Dyke Estate for a slap-up luncheon. The line was marketed as 'The Great Cable Railway'.

There was some criticism of the venture and the pylons and cables were, to some purists, a blot on the landscape. However, the smoothness of the ride was legendary, and passengers talked about the ride providing a unique sensation. The aerial cableway made a promising start and by the turn of the 20th century was a 'must' for many visitors. The economics of the venture were based on about one in four visitors travelling across the ravine. Whether the novelty of the ride wore off is anybody's guess, but in early Edwardian times traffic declined. By 1907 Mr Hubbard ran into financial difficulties, and later that year he emigrated to Canada. Without his enthusiasm and support, the fate of the cableway was inevitable and it seems that the last journey across the dip in the Downs occurred in 1909. Apparently the remains were used as target practice during World War 1 and, except for a concrete

As mentioned in the Kemp Town chapter, 'A1X' class Nos 81 and 82 were fitted with push-pull apparatus in 1905, converted for motor train usage and temporarily run as 2-4-0Ts. This photograph at Hove West signalbox shows an immaculate No 82 *Boxhill* leaving for Devil's Dyke with a 'Balloon' coach, all in LBSCR livery. The motor trains were soon withdrawn from the Dyke branch because the coaches did not have a hand brake and were considered unsafe on a line that was 1 in 40 for most of its length. *IAL*

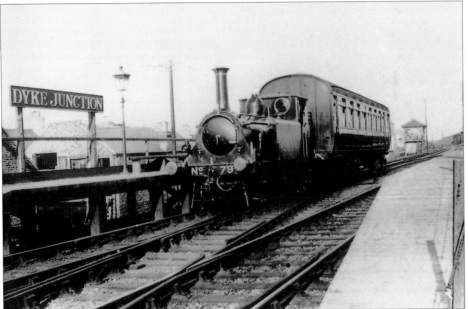

Centre left:
Dyke Junction was located just east of the junction with the Dyke branch on the Brighton to Portsmouth coastal route. The halt was opened in the age of the motor train, on 3 September 1905, and was served by both Dyke and local trains along the coast. Originally comprising two wooden platforms, the halt later received the SR concrete treatment and in June 1932 became known as Aldrington Halt. Looking very much like the branch train, but in fact a motor train bound for Worthing, is 'Terrier' No 79 *Minories*. Note the junction signalbox. *IAL*

Lower left:
From December 1933 a small station called Rowan Halt was opened to serve new housing estates, in an attempt to boost sagging takings. It comprised a single wooden platform on the up side of the line. The only other intermediate stopping place was Golf Club Halt, located just 62 chains short of The Dyke terminus, and used primarily by golfers; it never appeared in the public timetable. The author visited the site in March 1972 and the remains of the single brick-faced platform were very obvious. This was the view looking north. *JV*

support base, nothing now remains. However, for well over a decade the cableway added to the attractions of Devil's Dyke.

About the same time as the cableway was proposed it was also proposed to build a sort of cliff railway from the top of Devil's Dyke down towards the village of Poynings at the bottom of the escarpment slope on the north side of the Downs. Cliff tramways at Scarborough, Hastings and Folkestone were cited as having been successful, with a useful dividend being paid to investors. In the usual rosy prospectus terms it was said that there would be utility, novelty and exhilaration in partaking of the journey on the envisaged line, which was to become known as the Steep Grade Railway. Effectively it was a double-track narrow gauge funicular where one car ascended as the other descended.

Although this railway was to be another novelty item designed to continue to attract the crowds to Devil's Dyke, Mr Hubbard thought there might be a practical application in carrying farm produce from the farms below up to the hotel, so he granted a lease on the land necessary to build the railway to the Brighton Dyke Steep Grade Railway Limited. The capital sum required was £10,000. To engineer the line Mr Hubbard employed Charles O. Blaber, who was also the engineer of the Brighton & Dyke Railway Company (the standard gauge railway line). The gauge was 3ft and 35lb per yard flanged rails were used. The track was ballasted and there were three gradients along the 840ft line: 1 in 2.9 at lower levels, 1 in 1.5 in the middle section, and 1 in 1.8 at the upper section. The driving machinery in the form of a Hornsby-Ackroyd oil engine was housed in a small brick building at the top of the incline.

The same building doubled as a station. Slightly below the station were open platforms supported on wooded stilts. The cables had a 34-ton breaking strain and the cars travelled at a pedestrian 3mph. Each car could seat 12 passengers, and although there were level platforms at both ends, the floor of the main car was at an angle of 30 degrees. The cars were roofed to give some protection in inclement weather, but open-sided, and the underframes were steel, as were the 2ft-diameter wheels. The station platform at the lower end was brick-built, and an advertising poster shows a grand, ornate but fictitious station on the lower site, which was never built. Construction went smoothly and Sir Henry Howorth MP formally opened the line on 24 July 1897. Perhaps more was expected from the ride because a local paper said that the run was smooth, controlled and curious, but that was all! Again the local dignitaries and shareholders retired to the Dyke Hotel for luncheon in rather splendid weather.

The fares on the line were 2d single and 3d return, the imbalance being explained by the natural inclination of visitors to walk down to Poynings and to take the Steep Grade Railway back up! As with the cableway it seems that the Steep Grade line performed successfully, and on one summer day takings were as much as £5 per hour. However, there seemed to be a combination of the aforementioned financial problems experienced by the promoter Hubbard and a slight change in the type of visitor whereby the hotel was increasingly catering for day trippers, with, consequently, fewer people descending to Poynings for a cream tea in the village. The line seems to have ceased operation at about the same time as the cableway in 1909. The equipment was all removed about 1913, and all that remains today is the base of the top station and a slight scar in the Downs. One can conclude from all this that the halcyon days of transport novelties on Devil's Dyke lasted little more than a decade, but the standard gauge railway line was to survive for almost another 30 years.

With increasing visitors to Devil's Dyke and the expansion of the railway system all about, it was hardly surprising that thought would be given to serving the location by rail. A company called the Brighton & Devil's Dyke Railway drew up plans in 1872 to provide such a line, which would run from the Old Shoreham Road in the Parish of Preston to a point 130yd from the summit to the north-west of the hotel. The resulting Bill never got as far as a second reading, scheduled for February 1873. Two other schemes emerged, this time proposed by the same company but, most importantly, connecting with other railway lines. One scheme would leave the coastal route to the west of Hove (formerly West Brighton) station, ending to the south of the hotel, and the other would deviate from the London to Brighton main line just south of Patcham Tunnel, terminating at the same location as the very first proposal. The lines were options and neither was intended to compete with the other. The second of the lines would have involved a 369yd tunnel and a steeper gradient than the alternative; 1 in 37 versus 1 in 40. Eventually the second alternative was abandoned.

In March 1874 the Bill was thrown out because there was a dispute between the railway company and two prominent landowners. However, the Brighton & Dyke Railway Act of 2 August 1877 was passed by Parliament. The junction would be from the coastal line, 1 mile and 69 chains from the Brighton terminus, and the line would be 3 miles and 45 chains in length. The Act provided that the works should be completed within five years, but the promoters were slow in getting work under way and subsequently, in 1881, new promoters obtained an extension for completion until August 1885. A most important development was an agreement reached with the London, Brighton & South Coast Railway to provide all locomotives and rolling stock and to maintain the railway for 55% of gross receipts. The overall journey time from Brighton to the Dyke would be less than half an hour, whereas the ponderous horse-drawn journey by road was at least an hour in each direction. It was estimated that the line would carry some 273,000 passengers per annum.

The first sod was cut with an oak and silver spade by the Deputy Mayoress, Mrs Davey, just south-west of the Dyke Hotel on 2 June 1883, but there were more delays as the promoters sold out to a new Board of Directors. Further extensions to the time limit were sought and granted, and by June 1887 a locomotive was at last able to traverse all but the last few yards of track. The track was to LBSCR standard, being 84lb steel rail laid on 40lb chairs. The line climbed at 1 in 40 for most of the distance, rising 415ft from the junction to reach a height of 501ft at The Dyke terminus, which was about 200ft below the hotel on the summit. The line formally opened on Thursday 1 September 1887, and the first timetabled train left Brighton at 8am, arriving at The Dyke at 8.20am and, after running round, arrived back in Brighton at 9.5am. A special train to 'officially' open the line left Brighton at noon behind a gaily decorated 'E' class 0-6-0T called *Orleans*. The train contained local and civic dignitaries, officers of the LBSCR and shareholders, and they all enjoyed lunch in a large marquee near the station while the heavens opened 'greatly militating against everyone's pleasure'. A band provided the music and there were a number of speeches. The only regret expressed was that the line did not terminate even nearer to the Devil's Dyke summit. Initially there were eight trains in each direction and five on Sundays, and all three classes of travel were available on every train.

The final location of the junction was 2 miles and 2 chains from Brighton. From the junction the line curved away towards Hangleton, passing underneath the Old Shoreham Road, the A27. There were 13-chain curves to avoid additional embankments. Cuttings varied from 20 to 40ft in depth, and as the line crossed Hangleton Farm there were three overbridges and three under-bridges, built to double-track standards. Later, the southerly part of the line would become enveloped by housing estates and, as mentioned later, within 46 years or so a halt would be provided to cater for an increasing population. The line then continued to climb in a northerly direction at a steady 1 in 40 up on to the South Downs, passing Brighton & Hove Golf Club, where, from 1891, a

halt was provided, just 62 chains from the Devil's Dyke terminus. After a series of gentle curves, a final cutting scarred the Downs just before the terminus.

When opened, the terminus was far from its eventual state of development. There was a single 300ft-long platform which was some 15ft wide, a run-round loop, a galvanised iron and match-board station building, ticket office and ladies' and general waiting rooms. Saxby & Farmer provided the signalling equipment, with a 21-lever signalbox at the junction and one with 15 levers at the terminus. Early slotted signals gave way to standard LBSCR lower-quadrant semaphore signals. The main platform was later extended, and from 1892 a single goods siding was provided. Also by then an old railway carriage had been placed on the platform for use as a station buffet. Locomotive watering facilities were never provided. The first train of the day in each direction tended to be a 'mixed' train, but in general terms freight volumes were never heavy. An adjacent footpath was used by passengers to walk to the hotel and the summit.

The line was an immediate success and in the first six months of 1888 nearly 50,000 passengers were carried, and in the following three 'peak' summer months of July, August and September more than 77,000 were carried. The annual total of just under 160,000 fell short of the original annual estimate of 273,000, but apparently the weather had been unkind during the year. By 1893 this figure had improved, but was still short of 200,000. The creation of so many attractions at the summit increased the popularity of the Dyke, and on Whit Monday 1893 a total of some 30,000 people travelled up by rail, road and on foot! The Directors anticipated that this volume of traffic, together with income from goods, would soon boost funds, but the net income, after the LBSCR had been paid (including the agreed 55% and other debts amounting to 70% in total), together with liabilities to other suppliers and creditors, saw the financial situation deteriorate. In October 1895 a petition was submitted to the High Court for the Brighton & Dyke Railway Company to be put into Receivership. An order was granted and a Receiver appointed, and the company was to continue to operate in this status until absorbed by the Southern Railway in 1923. This did not directly affect the day-to-day operation of the branch.

In 1891 a halt was opened just 50yd from the Brighton & Hove Golf Club clubhouse. The brick-faced platform on the up side of the line never had a shelter, although the golf club had been informed that if members donated the sum of £100, one would be provided by the LBSCR. There was no platform lighting, but from

BRIGHTON and THE DYKE (Motor Cars—One class only).—L. B. and S. C.																					
Miles		**Week Days.**											**Sundays.**								
		a	mrn	mrn	aft	aft		aft	aft	aft	aft	mrn	mrn	aft	aft	aft	aft				
Central Station, Brighton ¶....dep.	10 0	11 3	1158	1250	1 45		2 35	2 40	4 40	5 50	10 0	1115	2 40	3 35	4 30	6 25					
1½	Hove ¶	10 9	11 9	12 4	1256	1 51		2 41	2 46	4 46	5 56	10 6	1121	2 46	3 41	4 36	6 31				
5½	The Dyke....arr.	1025	1123	1218	1 10	2 5		2 55	3 0	5 0	6 10	1020	1135	3 0	3 55	4 50	6 45				

Miles		**Week Days.**									**Sundays.**						
		a	mrn	aft	aft	aft	aft	aft	aft		mrn	aft	aft	aft	aft	aft
	The Dyke ¶....dep.	1045	1128	1225	1 20	2 10	4 15	5 10	6 15		930	1 53	5 4	0 5	15	7 0
4	Hove ¶	11 1	1141	1238	1 33	2 23	4 28	5 23	6 28		1043	18 3	18 4	13 5	28	7 13
5½	Brighton (C.)....arr.	11 6	1147	1244	1 39	2 29	4 34	5 29	6 34		1049	1 24	3 24	4 19	5 31	7 19

a 1, 2, and 3 class Trains; not stopping at the Halts.
¶ "Halts" at Holland Road, between Brighton and Hove; and Dyke Junction, between Hove and The Dyke,

BRIGHTON and THE DYKE (Motor Cars—3rd class only).													
Miles	**Down.**		**Week Days.**					**Sundays.**					
		mrn	mrn		aft	aft	aft		mrn		aft		
	Brighton (Central)......dep.	9 57	1112	..	1235	2 25	3 45	..	10 5	..	3 45	..	
1	Holland Road Halt	....	1114	..	1237	2 27	3 47	..	10 7	..	3 47	..	
1½	Hove	10 5	1118	..	1240	2 30	3 50	..	10 9	..	3 50	..	
2	Dyke Junction Halt	....	1121	..	1243	2 33	3 53	..	1012	..	3 53	..	
5½	The Dyke	.....arr.	1023	1134	..	1256	2 46	4 6	..	1026	..	4 6	..

Miles	**Up.**		**Week Days.**					**Sundays.**			
		mrn	mrn		aft	aft	aft		mrn		aft
	The Dyke.........dep.	11 8	1157	..	1 5	3 0	4 19	..	11 0	..	4 20
2½	Dyke Junction Halt	....	12 8	..	1 16	3 11	4 30	..	1111	..	4 31
4	Hove	1126	1211	..	1 19	3 14	4 33	..	1113	..	4 33
4½	Holland Road Halt	....	1214	..	1 22	3 17	4 36	..	1115	..	4 35
5½	Brighton (Central)...arr.	1131	1218	..	1 26	3 21	4 40	..	1120	..	4 40

☞ For other Trains

BETWEEN PAGE
Brighton and Dyke Junction Halt 250

Bradshaw's timetables for April 1910 (*above*) and January 1927 (*below*).

Top right:
When passengers arrived at
The Dyke station they had a steep
climb in order to reach the summit
200ft above the railway terminus.
In the early days this was not a
particular problem, but once
omnibuses started to run up from
Brighton they delivered their
passengers right to the hotel at the
summit. In 1933 a Sentinel steam
railbus was tried on the line (see
overleaf), and it is seen here leaving
the terminus with a good head of
steam. *J. Hicks collection*

Centre right:
The loadings on the railway
in the early days were considerable,
especially in the summer season.
However, usage never met the
original optimistic estimates, and
once motorised road transport
started to serve the Dyke, passenger
journeys diminished. Moreover,
services were suspended during
World War 1, which caused the
public to focus on other means
of transport. The line finally
succumbed on 31 December 1938,
and this view shows a much
strengthened four-coach train on the
very last day of service. 'E4' class
No 2480 had just arrived with the
2.10pm from Brighton.
SLS/O. J. Morris

Lower right:
This view shows the Colonel
Stephens-type terminus building
comprising a wooden frame and
corrugated iron cladding.
In Southern Railway days the
building is beginning to look in need
of some 'TLC' as a crew member
removes the headcode disc
of 'I3' class No 2089.
The normal train length on the
branch was either one or two
coaches. *Lens of Sutton*

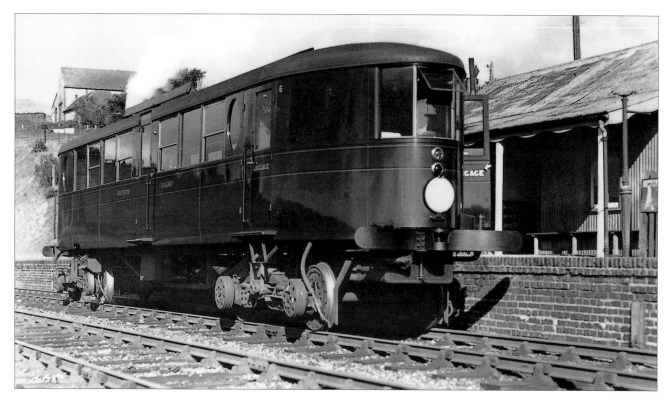

Above:
In 1932 a steam railbus was built by the Sentinel Wagon Works in Shrewsbury and sent to the Metropolitan Cammell Company Works in Birmingham to have a streamlined body fitted. R. E. L. Maunsell, the CME of the Southern Railway, had an influence on the design, and after trials the vehicle arrived on the branch in May 1933. It worked well but its capacity was limited, and after two years of service it was transferred away. The smart-looking unit is seen at The Dyke. *J. Hicks collection*

1895 an electric bell sounded in the clubhouse whenever The Dyke starting signal was lowered, so that members could rush down the hill to catch the train. There were a number of rules relating to train operations at Golf Club Halt — for example, which part of the train was to be stopped at the platform, and that drivers and guards should keep a good look out for passengers standing on the platform.

In September 1905 a halt was opened on the LBSCR line along the coast just on the Brighton side of Dyke Junction, which rejoiced in the name of Dyke Junction Halt, although the SR changed this to Aldrington Halt in June 1932, prior to electrification. The LBSCR was opening a number of new halts at the time, which would be served by single-coach 'Motor Trains', introduced to head off competition from the growing street tram networks and later motor omnibuses. The coaches were 54ft long, weighed just over 23 tons and were nicknamed 'Balloons'. These 'Balloons', normally hauled by 'Terrier' 0-6-0Ts, soon found themselves working Dyke branch trains, especially off-peak. World War 1 saw the line closed completely between January 1917 and July 1920, although unlike some minor lines the track was not lifted. Services continued, but the main worry to the railway was the ever-increasing use of motorised omnibuses that reached the summit from the seafront in far less time than the old horse-drawn charabancs, and which were in direct competition with the railway. In fact, in 1933 only a little over 20,000 passengers were carried on the branch, a mere 10th of the traffic carried in the line's late-Victorian heyday.

On 12 January 1934 Rowan Halt was opened, just half a mile from Aldrington Halt; boasting a 70ft-long wooden platform, it was built by the Southern Railway to serve the new Aldrington Manor Estate. A corrugated iron shelter and a footbridge across the single line were provided. It was hoped that the halt would generate much traffic and in 1938 a total of nine motor trains per day terminated at Rowan Halt. However, the writing was on the wall for the

Devil's Dyke branch, and while some summer trains were still well patronised, others in winter ran completely devoid of passengers. The buses, some of them 'open top' in summer, took passengers directly to Devil's Dyke and its hotel, whereas train passengers had to face the quite steep hike to the summit from the station. Economics deteriorated and the by then loss-making branch closed on 31 December 1938.

'E4' class No 2505 hauled the last train from Brighton to Devil's Dyke at 5.7pm. It received a tremendous send-off, including the attendance of the Brighton station master in top-hat, who took with him the destination boards for the last up train, which read 'Journey's End 1887–1938'. There was a great celebration, with many hundreds of people along the way waving to the last train. Fog signals were detonated and other locomotives sounded their whistles (had this been noted by the film-makers for the final scenes in the Ealing comedy *The Titfield Thunderbolt*?). The five-coach train, including one saloon (complete with crates of beer!), carried 400 passengers, who were all grasping their farewell tickets. There were some remarkable scenes at The Dyke as musicians played, the crowds sang 'Auld Lang Syne' and some 50 detonators sounded as the 5.37pm steamed out a mere 10 minutes late. A couple of golfers got in on the act as, dressed in their plus-fours, they attained brief fame by being the last ever passengers to board a train at the halt. The rowdy company made its way to Brighton, and although there were crowds on Rowan Halt platform, there would be three more terminating motor trains that day, the last being hauled by 'D1' class No 2699, which departed at 8.31pm. Thus ended 51 years of fascinating railway history.

The most common steam locomotives to work the Devil's Dyke branch were Brighton tanks of the 'E4', 'E5', 'D1', 'A1X', 'I1X' and 'I2' classes. Between 1933 and 1935 a 97bhp Sentinel-Cammell steam railbus was used on the branch, although due to limited seating capacity the approximately 17-ton 44-seater was

Left:
This splendid landscape shows a single-carriage train at The Dyke. Despite the single 'Balloon' coach, the train is not working in push-pull mode. Of particular interest is the solitary goods siding with a single wagon thereon. Goods traffic was so light that facilities were withdrawn from 2 January 1933. The line can be seen disappearing across the South Downs towards Golf Club Halt. The locomotive is 1876-built 'D1' class No B627. *O. J. Morris*

not used at weekends during the peak season. The machine was a prototype, and although it was capable of speeds in excess of 60mph, its brakes were weak and a large number of other, mainly minor, modifications were necessary before it settled down in almost everyday service. The railbus had no conventional couplings and a trailer coach could not be hauled, resulting in passengers having to stand on many occasions. It was transferred away to Tonbridge in October 1936, where it terminally failed in 1937, was withdrawn from storage in 1942, and scrapped in 1946.

Today little is left of the Devil's Dyke branch. At the southern end housing has covered much of the line, overbridges and under-bridges have been demolished and abandoned, and most of the cuttings were filled in long ago. The site of Rowan Halt can be detected behind Rowan Avenue, and the remains of the overgrown Golf Club Halt can be found a short distance from a nearby footpath. Part of the old line has been converted into 'The Dyke Railway Trail' (see photograph), and the old trackbed still forms a scar on the South Downs landscape in places. At The Dyke, the buildings were all removed at the outbreak of World War 2 and now just a trace of brick platform edging remains, albeit on private farmland. At the summit the Dyke Hotel burned down in 1945, but it was rebuilt as a restaurant in 1954 and continues to serve the public, who still visit the Dyke in some numbers, for the view, to walk their dogs or to watch the hang-gliders take off and drift down towards Poynings at the foot of the escarpment slope. But the excitement of the Victorian era with its numerous mechanical attractions has gone for ever, and the sight of a branch train steaming into the terminus is for history books such as this!

Below:
Seen in October 2003, the line of the old Dyke branch and the cutting into the terminus can be clearly seen 65 years after closure. With the old terminus site located just behind the farmhouse in the middle foreground, the Sussex coastline is visible in the far distance, giving a good topographical appreciation of the branch, from an elevation of about 700ft. *JV*

Right:

In Victorian and Edwardian times there was plenty to attract visitors to Devil's Dyke including the Steep Grade Railway and the Great Cable Railway. The former took the form of a funicular that ran down the escarpment slope for 840ft towards the village of Poynings, 480ft below the summit, while the latter ran across the Devil's Dyke ravine for 1,100ft and some 230ft above the ground. The Steep Grade Railway opened in 1897, and although initially popular the novelty wore off and it closed in 1909. This locally produced postcard was posted in 1904 and shows the upper station and engine house and one of the cars. *JV collection*

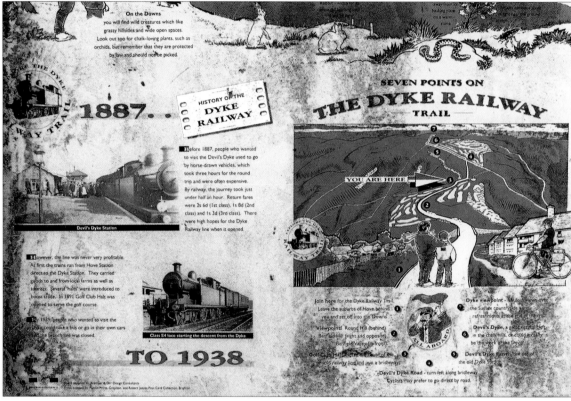

Above:

Part of the old trackbed, including a section near Golf Club Halt, has now been converted into a footpath appropriately called 'The Dyke Railway Trail'. Although a useful facility, the notice board contains errors including the caption to the bottom picture, which states 'Class E4 starting the descent from the Dyke', whereas the locomotive is an 'I3' class 4-4-2T that has just arrived from Brighton! Also, according to the notice, 'several halts were introduced to boost trade'. In fact, only two halts opened, although the opening and closing years are correct. *JV*

Right:

There are few remains of the various railways and attractions at Devil's Dyke, but the brick base of the 1897 Steep Grade Railway has survived the ravages of time, although the building and the equipment were removed in 1913. Visitors were encouraged to descend to Poynings, visible in the middle distance of this 2003 shot, for afternoon cream teas. The line descended at a maximum gradient of 1 in 1.5, and the maximum speed of the cars was 3mph. *JV*

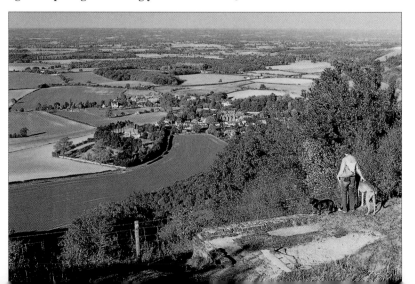

10. Shoreham by Sea to Itchingfield Junction

THE eastern end of the coastal line from Brighton to Shoreham was an early addition to the rapidly growing railway network. Under an Act of Parliament passed on 15 July 1837, a line between London and Brighton throughout with branches to Newhaven and Shoreham was authorised. Some of the materials for construction of the main Brighton line were landed at Shoreham Harbour, and in order to transport such materials a railway was constructed between there and Brighton. This 'branch' opened on 12 May 1840 with about half a dozen round trip workings between the towns. The population of Shoreham at this time was just over 2,000, and intermediate stations at West Brighton (Hove), Portslade, Southwick and Kingston were provided. The main Brighton line finally opened on 21 September 1841, and the coastal line was extended beyond Shoreham towards Worthing in November 1845.

Shoreham was a well-established port, and for many years had been a boat-building centre as well as a place of import and export for a wide range of produce and materials. Just as the London & Brighton Railway had used the port when constructing the Brighton main line, the London & South Western Railway had also been eyeing the Sussex coast, and in 1844 a line was proposed from the Dorking area, which was already served by routes from London. The LSWR also proposed a branch leaving the proposed line near Horsham, which would run in a southerly direction through the River Adur gap to Shoreham. When this news leaked out, the London & Brighton Railway greeted it with alarm as it represented a risk to its potential South Coast monopoly. Accordingly a Bill was hastily prepared, and on 18 June 1846 it received Royal Assent, allowing the London & Brighton to proceed with a Shoreham to Steyning branch.

Unfortunately about this time there was a nationwide recession and a large number of railway expansion plans were deferred or abandoned. As a result the LSWR abandoned its plans and the (by then) London, Brighton & South Coast Railway suspended its Steyning line proposals. During 1856 and 1857 there were moves by, initially, some local dignitaries at Steyning for a branch from their town to Shoreham, then by some landowners to promote a line from Dorking to Shoreham via Horsham, similar to the old LSWR

Below:

It is now hard to believe that when the author occasionally made the 11-mile journey to Brighton as a youngster, in the mid-1950s, such visits were an adventure and full of expectation. However, with such quaint sights as this almost guaranteed, it was perhaps understandable! Before its withdrawal I managed to 'cop' this elderly 'D3', No 32390 of 1894, which was the last surviving example of Billinton's design. Looking something of an anachronism in the EMU-infested station, the locomotive and its two push-pull coaches wait to leave for Horsham on 21 June 1955. *E. R. Wethersett*

Left:
The Shoreham by Sea to Itchingfield Junction and Horsham line closed to passengers in March 1966, but a short section of singled track between Shoreham and Beeding Cement Works remained open for freight traffic. However, this petered out in 1981, but the track was left in place. In 1986 the line was used for trials and for stabling of track maintenance vehicles such as No DB979511/611 seen here. This was almost certainly the last 'train' on the branch. In the background a Class 421 4-CIG unit crosses the River Adur and heads west on the 'Coastway', while on the right the good ship *Estelle* seems to have had its day. *JV/TTT*

Below:
To some, Beeding Cement Works was a blot on the landscape, but for decades it provided welcome jobs in an otherwise non-industrial area. For 15 years it was the only reason for a small remnant of the Shoreham by Sea to Itchingfield Junction line to remain open. Class 33s, but normally Class 73s (working on their 600hp auxiliary diesel engine), worked up to Beeding, usually on a daily basis. In 1966 No E6039 (later 73132) leaves the works with coal empties. *JV/TTT*

scheme. This spurred the LBSCR into action, and, following discussion of a branch from Shoreham that connected with the 'Mid-Sussex' line at Billingshurst and the rejection by a Parliamentary Committee of the landowners' plan, the LBSCR surveyed a route that would join the Mid-Sussex line (opened in part in 1859) at Itchingfield, near Christ's Hospital, south of Horsham. The Act for the route received Royal Assent on 12 July 1858.

Construction commenced in the summer of 1859 and the first section from Shoreham to Partridge Green opened to all traffic on 1 July 1861. All the guests on the inaugural train alighted at Steyning and headed off to the White Horse Inn for a champagne party. The initial timetable allowed for three round-trip workings per day, including Sundays. Without any significant obstacles,

other than river crossings, the line through to Christ's Hospital was opened to passengers and goods just weeks later on 16 September 1861, with three classes of passenger accommodation on offer. The stations had not been built by the time of opening, and huts were provided on the platforms for the sale of tickets etc. At this stage the line was single track, but during the 1877 to 1879 period it was doubled throughout. With the exception of Bramber, all stations had signalboxes at this stage, to control the double track and the many goods yards and sidings. The line was 17 miles long, although most of the passenger services ran from Brighton to Horsham, a distance of some 26 miles. By 1910 there were about a dozen trains per day in each direction, with Saturday extras and some 'short' workings between Brighton and Steyning.

Right:
Back in 1952 'H' class locomotives were still 'shopped' for works overhaul, and it must have been refreshing to see and photograph a truly immaculate example in BR lined black livery. No 31265 is south of Bramber station with a Horsham to Brighton service on 27 August 1952. Push-pull set No 656 also looks to be in good fettle for its age. *E. R. Wethersett*

Below:
In contrast to the 'H' class in the last photograph, 'I3' class No 32080 looks decidedly tired as it accelerates away from Bramber station with a Brighton-bound train on 1 September 1950. Although the locomotive carries the full BR number, the side tanks still bear the legend 'Southern' and it probably had not been repainted since before World War 2. The driver and the motorman seem anxious to be captured on film for posterity. *E. R. Wethersett*

The Steyning and Horsham line left the 'Coastway' route at Shoreham Junction just to the west of Shoreham by Sea station. The line initially followed the course of the River Adur, and about ¾ mile from the junction crossed the main A27 road, which crossed the river on an old 1740-built wooden toll bridge. The railway owned the bridge and tolls were collected until a substantial new flyover was built to cope with modern traffic flows. A crossing-keeper's box was provided on the up side, where the protecting signals were operated. As the river, the railway and the road made their way through a gap in the line of the South Downs, the massive Beeding Cement Works was reached. For some nine decades this works was a rich source for freight traffic, with clay, coal and gypsum being imported and substantial volumes of cement and some general

goods being exported. Wagon tippling facilities were available and for some time the works had its own resident shunting locomotive to reposition wagons on the extensive sidings. Beeding Sidings signalbox was located on the western side of the 'branch' opposite a complex of sidings that diverged into the cement works.

Immediately beyond the works the line made the first of three crossings of the River Adur. After crossing some water meadows the station of Bramber was reached, just under 4 miles from the junction. The station was at the western extremity of the village, almost beneath the shadow of the famous but ruined Bramber Castle. In 1901 Bramber had but 162 inhabitants. Within a mile of Bramber was Steyning station, the most important on the line. The population of 1,752 in 1901 has now more than doubled! There was

Above:
When the 'Hampshire' three-car DEMUs arrived on the line, a comprehensive regular-interval timetable was introduced, but the economies arising were insufficient to save the line. With only weeks to go before the line closed, from 7 March 1966, 3H No 1112 in green livery pauses at Bramber station, but there are no passengers to pick up. Bramber was the only station on the line to be lit by electricity! Much of the trackbed either side of the station was later converted into a road that bypassed both Bramber and Steyning villages. *JV/TTT*

Upper left:
By 1969 the track had been lifted and the station buildings had been demolished. This photograph was deliberately taken from exactly the same spot as the previous plate. Even the platforms and overbridge were later levelled and no trace now remains of the old line at this point. The totem sign that was affixed to the lamp-post on the right would now be worth £1,000 at auction!
JV/TTT

Lower left:
This unusual and previously unpublished view shows the east or works end of Beeding Cement Works sidings. This particular configuration was completed in 1951 and is seen here in 1969. The works had a wagon tippler, and coal and gypsum were the main payloads in later years (see text). The main branch can be seen crossing the River Adur in the background. *JV/TTT*

plenty of agricultural traffic at Steyning and the weekly market was held beside the goods yard. In the early days grain, oil cake, stone, marble, coal and, later, coke, beer (and its ingredients barley, malt and hops), bricks, groceries, spirits, wood, flour and lime, all amounting to more than 10,000 tons per annum, were carried by rail. Before the coming of the railway some 12,000 farm animals were 'driven' into Brighton for slaughter and the railway took much of this traffic. A fair-sized goods yard was provided on the up side and there was once a narrow gauge railway in the adjacent east-side timber yard.

After passing through pleasant but low-lying farmland the town of Henfield was reached, 8½ miles from Shoreham Junction. The station was on the western outskirts of the town, which in 1901 had a slightly higher population than Steyning, but the numbers included in Henfield's census were more dispersed. The goods shed and associated sidings were on the down side of the line. Beyond Henfield the countryside became hillier and more wooded. This section of line generated much less traffic because Partridge Green served only a small village (with a delightful pub just at the start of the station approach road!), and West Grinstead, just under 13 miles from the junction, was over a mile away from the village that it purported to serve. West Grinstead had been the terminus of the old Adur Navigation & Baybridge Canal. Both of these stations had goods yards and small cranes, although traffic receipts were never great.

Southwater, just 1½ miles from Itchingfield Junction and 42 miles from London, was the busiest station towards the northern end of the line, and once boasted a private siding to an adjacent brickworks, which added to the takings of the LBSCR/SR/BR(SR) — it was all a matter of coal in and bricks out. The station was significant in being the only one on the line without a footbridge; however, there was a road overbridge at the Horsham end of the station and a foot crossing. Itchingfield Junction signalbox was in the 'V' of the junction with the Mid-Sussex line some ¾ mile south of Christ's Hospital (effectively the junction station). The original station building was a grand affair, built to serve a substantial new housing development that never materialised, but which was nevertheless somehow in keeping with the nearby and famous Christ's Hospital School, where students still wear a very distinctive school uniform. The station was also the junction with the Guildford branch, which ran through Slinfold, Rudgwick, Baynards, Cranleigh and Bramley & Wonersh, opening in October 1865 and closing just short of its centenary in June 1965. The station, which is still open for Mid-Sussex line trains, was briefly renamed 'Longhampton' in 1965 for the filming of the movie *Rotten to the Core*. The route then continued to Horsham, 2¼ miles from Christ's Hospital. None of the ex-Brighton services started or ended their journeys at Christ's Hospital. As mentioned earlier, nearly all ran from Brighton to Horsham and vice versa, except the Brighton to Steyning 'shorts' and the occasional Shoreham starter.

Services on the line varied only slightly over the years, with 12 or 13 through workings. There was an increase just before World War 2 and the service peaked in about 1960 when up to 17 weekday departures left Brighton for Horsham. In 1961 the centenary of the opening of the line was celebrated with a special train and the Brighton Works 'A1X' class 'Terrier' performing in the goods yard at Steyning. Even though some preliminary work was done before World War 2, the line was never electrified, which almost certainly would have been its salvation. It was used as a diversionary route, and during the season excursions for Brighton would trundle through the pastures to get them off the busy Brighton main line. There was at least a daily goods that ran between Hove and Horsham to Three Bridges, but as with virtually the whole BR system this traffic gradually dwindled, resulting in the withdrawal of all freight facilities in 1962, except for the Beeding Cement Works traffic.

Over the years most types of 'Brighton' tank engine worked the line, from Class D1s to D3s, E4s and LBSCR cousins, I3s, M7s, 'H' class, Ivatt and Standard tanks, and 3H and 3R diesel-electric units. Over the years motor trains and push-pull trains regularly featured, and a variety of Moguls from the

Left:
With Itchingfield Junction at the foot of the map, and the Shoreham line branching south-east, the focus is Christ's Hospital station. Top left is the branch to Guildford, which closed in 1965, and the long-abandoned west-to-south spur. Horsham is off the map top right. In the centre is Christ's Hospital public school. *Crown Copyright*

Top right:
Steyning was the most important station on the line, and for many years a large amount of goods traffic was handled. As regards passenger services, in addition to Horsham trains some worked from Brighton to Steyning only. In this 1966 view an Austin A55 stands outside the LBSCR up-side station building. After closure everything except the goods shed was demolished to make way for the aforementioned bypass. *JV/TTT*

Centre right:
A visit on the bleak last day of service in March 1966 found 'Hampshire' unit No 1113 working a busier than usual Brighton to Horsham service. In terms of illumination the yellow 'V' on the front of the DEMU contrasts with the lovely old platform gas lamps. In the days of steam most tank locomotives stopped at Steyning to take on water. *JV/TTT*

Lower right:
Another fascinating comparison is this post-closure shot of Steyning station after it had been smashed to oblivion.
A way of life had gone for ever. Although a welcome improvement to the grossly inadequate road system of West Sussex, motor cars now speed along the road bypass, between what would have been the platforms, at 60mph-plus! *JV/TTT*

Top left:
This vintage view shows Henfield station, looking north. The signalman is keeping an eagle eye on the photographer, who is obviously trespassing. Note the delightful LBSCR lower-quadrant semaphore signals and the milk churns on both the up and down platforms. The whole of this area is now covered by a modern housing estate. *IAL*

Centre left:
The LBSCR did not do things by half and all of the stations on the line were substantial. Rather than the main buildings being on either the up or down side, they were built on whatever side of the line the approach road was located. Henfield's goods shed had a permanent look about it, but it too was swept away. The last train has long since departed in this 1969 view, and the platforms that served the local community for 105 years would never see passengers again. Initially the line was single track but it was doubled throughout in 1880. *JV/TTT*

Lower left:
This view of Partridge Green in SR days shows all the main buildings to advantage. For the last years of the line's life the only station signalling on the branch was at Steyning, the wooden signalbox here having been abolished. The goods yard was at the end of the down platform and the shed is visible just above the Brighton-bound 'D3' class, which is propelling a utility van and two coaches. *IAL*

Above:
During the 1960s the line was traversed by a number of railway enthusiasts' special trains.
On 13 June 1965 heavy power was brought to the branch in the shape of 'Battle of Britain' class No 34050 *Royal Observer Corps*
with the LCGB 'The Wealdsman' railtour. There was a photographic stop at Steyning, allowing photographers 'two bites
of the cherry'. Here the gleaming Pacific leaves Steyning and makes for Horsham. *JV/TTT*

LBSCR 'K' class to SR 'N' class all worked special excursion trains. In 1965 a Bulleid 'Battle of Britain' Pacific appeared. Most freight services in the latter days of steam were worked by members of the 'C2X' class, and in the last days of the line Classes 33 and 73 diesels and electro-diesels worked up to Beeding. The line saw much extra traffic during the war years and a greater variety of motive power. Sir Winston Churchill used Wiston House near Steyning to plan part of his campaign against the Germans (see also Droxford in the Meon Valley chapter).

As regards infrastructure, the stations were all of a standard LBSCR pattern, varying mainly in size: Steyning and Henfield had larger two-storey buildings whereas Bramber, Partridge Green and Southwater had two-storey houses for accommodation purposes with single-storey extensions for station offices and waiting rooms. West Grinstead station was different in that the platforms were in a cutting and the buildings were located above at approximately road level. The station platforms were always backed by immaculately maintained shrubbery. Stations were not specifically located on the up or down sides, but reflected the side of the line where the main approach road was situated. Sadly all the stations were demolished after closure. There were significant goods sheds at some stations, particularly Steyning. The only station without a goods yard or signalbox was Bramber. Throughout the life of the line no new stations were opened and none of the intermediate stations were closed. Overall the gradients and curves on the line were gentle and the quality of the track maintenance won prizes in railway competitions.

Of all those featured in this book the case for closure of the Itchingfield Junction (Christ's Hospital) to Shoreham line was arguably the flimsiest. The double-track line served rural communities, but communities that were growing. In fact, since closure in March 1966 population increases at Southwater, Henfield and Steyning have been significant. Southwater has become an overspill town for Horsham and large new estates have been developed. At Henfield housing has sprawled, ironically to cover the whole of the old railway station site! Steyning has become an

even more 'des res' postcode to show on one's letterhead, and there has been building on the outskirts of the old town. There have also been property developments at West Grinstead, Partridge Green and Bramber, but on a smaller scale. Of one thing there is no doubt, that the railway would today have been better used than it ever was, and would provide at least some relief to the poor and out-of-date road system in the county of West Sussex.

One of the great problems with measuring the viability in 'profit and loss' terms in the so-called 'Beeching era' was the lack of public visibility of the basis for assessment and costing. It was extremely difficult for pressure groups to challenge official figures, especially on items such as infrastructure write-down values, as distinct from, say, staff wages. However, even based on the railways' own calculations, the cost of running the line with diesel motive power exceeded passenger receipts by a mere £43,000 per annum, chicken feed when compared with today's yardsticks in railway finance, which seem to be based on how many billions of pounds are needed to upgrade a line or to provide safety equipment.

Also there is little doubt that at the time of closure passenger numbers were increasing, 120,000 tickets being sold during 1965, twice the number of the 1951/52 period. While that 1965 figure would appear to be impressive, it represented only about 25 passengers per train. On the other hand, little value seems to have been placed on the line being used as a diversionary route from the main Brighton line, and no value was placed on its usefulness for occasional excursion trains or for incoming passengers who purchased tickets at distant stations.

It is also surprising that no serious attempts were made to rationalise the line. Although this would have involved initial costs, there could have been significant long-term savings from singling most of the line, abolishing conventional signalling (all but Steyning signalbox had closed in 1964, nearly two years after the withdrawal of most goods traffic), withdrawing railway station and crossing staff, and using diesel units on a reduced but regular-interval service throughout the day. As it was, a full-blown double-track railway was maintained to the end of passenger services.

Above:
This picture at West Grinstead just had to be included in the selection due to its unconventional formation. Although by no means an isolated occasion, there are few photographs of the train engine sandwiched between rolling-stock on the line. On 7 June 1951 LSWR 'M7' class No 30049 propels a normal formation in push-pull mode, but an extra coach has been added. The photographer was very precise, and notes that the train was the 5.19pm ex-Horsham and the shutter was pressed at 5.36pm. *E. C. Griffiths*

Upper right:
Once most of the LBSCR and LSWR tank locomotives had been withdrawn, but before English Electric DEMUs were employed full time, trains were in the hands of the purposeful Ivatt 2-6-2Ts, which also worked the Horsham to Guildford branch. West Grinstead station was located in a cutting and the station building was at street level. On 30 April 1964 No 41301 heads the 1.30pm Brighton to Horsham service. *J. Scrace*

Lower right:
This view, looking south, shows West Grinstead in April 2003, 37 years after closure. The trackbed is now part of the Downs Link footpath and the scene is now somewhat sylvan. A station running-in board and an upper-quadrant signal have been added, perhaps showing those too young to remember the line what purpose the site once served. In a goods siding to the north, coach No S25823 serves as a seasonal information office. *JV*

Top left:
Southwater station in Victorian times finds one lady passenger who has arrived early to catch the train. On the far right is the brickworks, which had its own dedicated siding. The small goods yard with the luxury of a crane is at the end of the up platform. There was no footbridge at this station and passengers had to use the board crossing by the signalbox or the nearby road overbridge. *IAL*

Lower left:
Southwater station, looking towards Horsham on 10 October 1965, finds the board crossing intact but the signalbox long removed. The old sidings have been lifted and the oil lamp standards are lamp-less! With the early 'V' yellow warning 'panel' standing out, No 1113, with the correct '66' headcode, forms the 10.30 Horsham to Brighton service. *J. Scrace*

Below:
How pleasant to see one of Billinton's 'K' class freight locomotives in full cry on a ten-coach passenger train. Approaching Itchingfield Junction, just south of Christ's Hospital, with the road clear for the branch, an Easter Monday Reading to Brighton 'Adex' (advertised excursion) is headed by No 32344, one of 17 locomotives built from 1913. Bearing in mind that the locomotives lasted until the 1960s, it is a tragedy that none of these Moguls was preserved. *Derek Cross*

HORSHAM, SHOREHAM-BY-SEA, and BRIGHTON.

London, Brighton, and South Coast.

Miles	Down.	Week Days. mrn	mrn	mrn	mrn	aft	aft	aft	aft	m	aft	aft	Sundays. mrn	aft
	Horsham ....dep.	7 20	8 14	1018	1147	1 41	3 10	5 36	6 50	7 26	8 47	Weds. only.	8 55	8 20
2½	Christ's Hospital, West	7 24	....	1022	....	1 45	3 15	....	6 54	7 31	8 51		8 59	8 24
4½	Southwater ..[Horsham	7 29	8 22	1027	1156	1 51	3 20	5 44	6 59	7 37	8 57		9 5	8 30
7½	West Grinstead	7 35	8 28	1033	12 2	1 57	3 26	5 50	7 5	7 44	9 4		9 12	8 37
9¾	Partridge Green	7 41	8 34	1039	12 8	2 3	3 31	5 55	7 11	7 52	9 10		9 19	8 44
11½	Henfield..............	7 46	8 39	1044	1213	2 8	3 36	6 0	7 16	7 57	9 15	11 0	9 24	8 49
15½	Steyning	7 53	8 47	1052	1220	2 16	3 43	6 8	7 23	8 4	9 23	11 7	9 32	8 57
16	Bramber ......[176,184	7 56	8 49	1054	1223	2 19	3 46	6 12	7 26	8 6	9 25	1110	9 35	9 0
20	Shoreham-by-Sea †	8 6	8 59	11 3	1232	2 29	3 56	6 21	7 36	8 15	9 35	1120	9 46	9 11
21½	Southwick..............	8 10	9 4	11 7	1236	2 34	4 1	6 25	7 41	8 19	9 39	....	9 51	9 16
23	Portslade..............	8 16	9 9	1112	1241	2 38	4 5	6 29	7 45	8 23	9 44	1127	9 55	9 20
24½	Hove 226..........[198	8 20	9 14	1116	1245	2 43	4 9	6 34	7 49	8 27	9 48	1131	9 59	9 24
26	Brighton 194, 197, arr.	8 25	9 20	1121	1250	2 48	4 14	6 39	7 54	8 33	9 53	1136	10 4	9 29

Miles	Up. Central Station,	Week Days. mrn	mrn	mrn	mrn	aft	aft	aft	aft	aft	aft	aft	Sundays. mrn	aft
	Brighton ....dep.	6 30	8 10	9 40	1155	1 55	3 43	5 5	6 45	7 53	1015	11 0	7 30	6 10
1½	Hove	6 34	8 14	9 45	1159	1 59	3 47	5 9	6 49	7 57	1019	11 4	7 34	6 15
3	Portslade	6 39	8 19	9 49	12 4	2 3	3 51	5 14	6 53	8 2	1023	11 8	7 38	6 20
4½	Southwick ...[176,184	6 43	8 23	9 53	12 8	2 7	3 55	5 18	....	8 6	1028	1113	7 42	6 24
6	Shoreham-by-Sea †	6 50	8 29	9 58	1214	2 14	4 0	5 23	7 0	8 10	1033	1118	7 48	6 30
10	Bramber	6 59	8 38	10 6	1222	2 22	4 10	5 32	7 9	8 19	1042	1127	7 57	6 40
10½	Steyning................	7 3	8 42	1010	1225	2 25	4 13	5 35	7 12	8 22	1045	1130	8 1	6 44
14½	Henfield................	7 12	8 51	1017	1232	2 33	4 21	5 44	7 21	8 30	h		8 9	6 53
16½	Partridge Green	7 18	8 56	1022	1237	2 38	4 25	5 49	7 26	8 35	Except Sats.	Sats. only.	8 14	6 58
18½	West Grinstead	7 24	9 3	1027	1242	2 43	4 32	5 56	7 33	8 42			8 21	7 5
21½	Southwater	7 32	9 11	1034	1249	2 50	4 39	6 4	7 40	8 48			8 28	7 12
23½	Christ's Hospital ¶ 184	....	....	1040	1254	....	4 45	....	7 46	....			8 35	7 19
26	Horsham 184, 187 arr.	7 42	9 21	1045	1259	3 2	4 50	6 15	7 51	8 58			8 40	7 25

h Arrives at 10 53 aft. on Wednesdays.

m Motor Car, one class only; "Halts" at Fishergate, between Southwick and Portslade; Dyke Junction, between Portslade and Hove; and Holland Road, between Hove and Brighton.

† Station for Lancing College (2 miles). ¶ Christ's Hospital, West Horsham.

☞ For LOCAL TRAINS between Shoreham-by-Sea and Brighton, see page 195.

HORSHAM, SHOREHAM-BY-SEA, and BRIGHTON.

Miles	Down.	Week Days. mrn	mrn	mrn	mrn		aft	aft	aft S	aft	aft	aft	aft	aft E	aft	aft		Sundays. mrn	mrn	aft	aft	aft
	Horsham..............dep.	7 20	8 10	1030	1130	..	..	1 33	..	3 10	4 35	5 42	6 52	7 29	8 25	9 0	..	8 0	9 6	2 5	4 20	8 22
2½	Christ's Hospital, West Hors-	7 25	8 14	1035	1135	..	..	1 37	..	3 14	4 39	5 48	6 56	7 33	8 29	9 4	..	8 4	9 11	2 9	4 25	8 26
4½	Southwater ....[ham	7 31	8 20	1041	1140	..	..	1 43	..	3 19	4 44	5 53	7 2	7 39	8 34	9 9	..	8 10	9 16	2 14	4 30	8 32
7½	West Grinstead..........	7 37	8 27	1047	1146	..	..	1 49	..	3 26	4 50	6 0	7 8	7 45	8 40	9 15	..	8 18	9 22	2 20	4 38	8 39
9¾	Partridge Green	7 42	8 33	1053	1151	..	..	1 54	..	3 31	4 55	6 6	7 13	7 50	8 45	9 20	..	8 25	9 29	2 25	4 44	8 46
11½	Henfield	7 48	8 39	1059	1156	..	..	2 0	..	3 36	5 1	6 13	7 19	7 56	8 50	9 26	..	8 32	9 35	2 31	4 52	8 52
15½	Steyning	7 56	8 47	11 6	12 4	..	1 43	2 7	3 35	3 44	5 9	6 21	7 27	8 4	8 58	9 34	..	8 40	9 42	2 38	5 0	9 1
16	Bramber	7 58	8 50	11 9	12 7	..	1 45	2 10	3 37	3 47	5 12	6 24	7 30	8 7	9 1	9 37	..	8 44	9 46	2 41	5 4	9 6
20	Shoreham-by-Sea A 250...	8 7	8 59	1119	1216	..	1 51	2 19	3 46	3 56	5 21	6 33	7 38	8 14	9 9	9 46	..	8 53	9 55	2 50	5 13	9 16
21½	Southwick	8 11	9 3	1123	1220	..	1 58	2 23	3 50	4 0	5 25	6 38	7 42	..	..	9 51	..	8 58	10 0	2 55	5 18	9 21
23	Portslade................	8 16	9 9	1127	1224	..	2 3	2 28	3 54	4 5	5 29	6 42	7 46	..	..	9 55	..	9 3	10 5	3 0	5 22	9 25
24½	Hove ....(258	8 20	9 15	1131	1229	..	2 8	2 33	3 59	4 10	5 33	6 47	7 51	8 24	..	10 1	..	9 9	1010	3 5	5 27	9 30
26	Brighton (C.) 229, 245, arr.	8 25	9 21	1136	1234	..	2 13	2 38	4 4	4 15	5 38	6 52	7 56	8 29	..	10 6	..	9 14	1015	3 10	5 32	9 35

Miles	Up.	Week Days. mrn	mrn	mrn	mrn	aft	aft	aft S	aft	aft	aft E	aft S	aft	aft	aft	aft		Sundays. mrn	mrn	aft	aft	aft
	Brighton (Central) ......dep.	6 27	8 0	9 52	1146	1 4	1 50	..	3 40	5 3	6 5	6 7	..	7 10	8 10	9 10	..	7 20	1010	2 15	6 15	8 55
1½	Hove	6 31	8 4	9 56	1150	1 8	1 54	2 38	3 45	5 7	6k17	6H19	..	7 14	8 14	9 14	..	7 26	1014	2 19	6 19	8 59
3	Portslade	6 35	8 9	10 0	1154	1 12	1 58	2 42	3 49	5 11	6 23	6 25	..	7 18	..	9 18	..	7 30	1018	2 23	6 23	9 3
4½	Southwick	6 39	8 13	10 5	1158	1 16	2 2	2 46	3 53	5 15	6 27	6 29	..	7 23	..	9 22	..	7 34	1022	2 27	6 27	9 7
6	Shoreham-by-Sea A........	6 44	8 20	1010	12 3	1 21	2 8	2 50	3 59	5 21	6 31	6 33	6 36	7 28	8 22	9 27	..	7 40	1028	2 33	6 31	9 12
10	Bramber	6 52	8 28	1018	1211	1 29	2 16	2 58	4 9	5 29	..	..	6 44	7 36	8 30	9 36	..	7 48	1036	2 41	6 40	9 20
10½	Steyning	6 56	8 31	1022	1214	1 32	2 20	3 1	4 12	5 33	..	..	6 47	7 40	8 35	9 39	..	7 52	1039	2 45	6 44	9 23
14½	Henfield..................	7 4	8 39	1029	1221	..	2 26	..	4 19	5 41	..	..	6 54	7 47	8 41	9K46	..	8 1	1046	2 53	6 52	9 30
16½	Partridge Green	7 10	8 43	1033	1226	..	2 31	..	4 24	5 46	..	..	6 58	7 51	8 45	..	..	8 7	1051	2 59	6 58	9 35
18½	West Grinstead............	7 17	8 53	1039	1232	..	2 37	..	4 30	5 52	..	..	7 4	7 56	8 50	..	..	8 16	1058	3 6	7 5	9 41
21½	Southwater	7 24	9 2	1046	1238	..	2 44	..	4 37	5 59	..	..	7 10	8 3	8 56	..	..	8 24	11 5	3 12	7 12	9 48
23½	Christ's Hospital B 218	..	9 10	1052	1245	..	..	..	4 43	..	..	..	7 16	8 9	9 2	..	..	8 32	1112	3 19	7 18	9 54
26	Horsham 229, 266 ....arr.	7 34	9 15	1057	1250	..	2 54	..	4 49	6 10	..	..	7 22	8 14	9 7	..	..	8 37	1117	3 24	7 23	10 0

A Station for Lancing College (2 miles).
B Christ's Hospital, West Horsham.
E Except Saturdays.
H Arrives at 6 11 aft.
K Wednesdays and Saturdays.
k Arrives at 6 9 aft.
S Saturdays only.

☞ For Local Trains and intermediate Halts
BETWEEN PAGE
Shoreham-on-Sea and Brighton 258

*** For other Trains
BETWEEN PAGE
Horsham & Christ's Hospital 218
Hove and Brighton 268

The branch timetables from 1910 (*left*) and 1927 (*below*) show little difference; in fact, the first down train from Horsham on both timetables is at 7.20am! However, the Sunday service in the later year has significantly improved.

Also, little was made in advertising the line as a through route from Brighton to Guildford via the now closed Horsham to Guildford line, which despite varying connection waiting times at Christ's Hospital was a perfectly viable proposition, if one had any faith whatsoever in the integrated railway network.

The case for closure of this particular line may have been flimsy but close it did, much to the concern of local residents. It had remained under threat for some two years before finally succumbing from 7 March 1966, by chance the same weekend as the famous Somerset & Dorset line. As the final train, comprised of 'Oxted' diesel unit No 1306, left Steyning for the last time at 11.15pm on Sunday 6 March, the 'Last Post' was sounded on a bugle and 'Auld Lang Syne' was heartily sung by the gathered crowd as the throb of the diesel disappeared towards Bramber for the final time. The line was lifted with indecent haste, as if BR was scared that the decision to close might somehow be reversed. The only section of line to remain open was that from Shoreham up to Beeding Sidings, where the cement works was served by a daily train. However, this working became infrequent as production slowed, and the remaining stub also closed in 1981. In that year the works employed 335 people, and 330,000 tonnes of cement clinker were produced. The single-line stub was mothballed, but in September 1986 it was used to trial and stable some permanent way vehicles (see photograph), which was probably the last 'train' to use the line. The remaining track was subsequently lifted.

There was the usual brief talk of some form of railway preservation on the line, but this came to nothing. There is a railway carriage positioned in the old goods yard at West Grinstead to provide refreshment in summer months for those using the pedestrian/cycle trail that runs along part of the old line. Although the magnificent Lancing College School and Chapel still looks down on the Adur Valley, the massive Beeding Cement Works now stands as a silent sentinel to the industrial past of the area. There is still some track set in concrete within the works, but little remains otherwise. Rows of workers' cottages still survive on the Shoreham to Bramber road near Upper Beeding, and the old railway alignment in the area was eventually used for a much-needed A283 Upper Breeding, Bramber and Steyning bypass, albeit some 15 years after closure. Although it could be argued that the Shoreham to Christ's Hospital line was a through route, in practice its operation and atmosphere was very much akin to a branch line, and its fate was certainly that of other branch lines of the era!

11. Selsey Tramway

WHEN viewing photographs of one of the old Shefflex railcars working towards the end of its career on the Selsey Tramway, with the sparsely populated unit negotiating the grass-covered track with rattles, oily smells and, no doubt, the entire episode resembling a bizarre novelty, there is now an overwhelming desire to have experienced the quaint old show. But if one had been a local Selsey resident or visitor in the late 1920s there is little doubt that the shiny new Southdown bus would have been the chosen mode of transport into Chichester, especially if the journey was going to be smoother, quicker, more frequent, no more expensive and took you fractionally nearer your actual destination point.

This is of course all far removed from the early plans for a successful railway that seems to have first come to light in The Selsey Railway and Pier Act of 1888. The plan included a railway running down the peninsula from Chichester and ending at Selsey on a 100yd-long pier. As with many early schemes it came to nothing. Another scheme was put forward in 1895 whereby Chichester Council was asked to approve a light railway of standard gauge linking Chichester with Selsey. With a population of 1,258 in 1901, Selsey was hardly a heavily populated area and, except for the beach, there was little in the area of special or architectural note to attract visitors. All of the other villages on the 'Hundred of Manhood' peninsula such as the Witterings, Birdham (1901 population 389), Pagham (717), West Itchenor (121), Sidlesham (799), Hunston (217), etc, were all very small indeed, with only a bit of fishing and some agriculture as income or employment generators. Also, no railway could serve all of the scattered villages. As if to demonstrate what a lost cause it thought the venture might be, there was no objection to the 1895 plan from the London, Brighton & South Coast Railway.

Yet again, these plans seemed to fizzle out, possibly because agreement could not be reached with all the landowners. However, an influential meeting was held at the Dolphin Hotel on 23 March 1896 where, possibly aided by the impact of the local ale, the full Council, chaired by the Mayor, listened to Mr Powell of Lewes, who explained that it was planned to form a limited company, the Hundred of Manhood & Selsey Tramways Company Limited, to build a standard gauge line to Selsey. It was hoped that most of the money would be raised locally and that the flat terrain and lack of any significant earthworks (except an embankment across Pagham Harbour and a lifting bridge over the Chichester Canal) would result in capital of only £12,000 being required. The problem with the canal was that, although nearing the end of its days of practical heavy use, there were still some small craft using it for commercial purposes, so a lifting drawbridge had to be incorporated in the design for the line. The local authority paid for the bridge to be constructed, then rented it back to the railway at a peppercorn rent of £2 per annum. As an aside, the provisions of the then forthcoming Light Railway Act were not relevant at that time. It was

decided to proceed and the company was duly set up on 29 April 1896; however, it was January 1897 before contracts were signed and work was ready to proceed.

The engineer for the line was Holman F. (Colonel) Stephens, and, as was the case with the Rye & Camber Tramway that had opened in 1895, the contractors were Messrs Mancktelow of Horsmonden. Messrs Peckett & Co supplied a contractor's locomotive and a second locomotive, and the Falcon Engine Company built the passenger carriages. Land acquisition took some considerable time to execute, but once completed some 100 navvies soon got to work. An additional £7,000 needed to be raised to pay for the land required for the trackbed, which had clearly been underestimated when the original proposals had been drawn up. The line was completed in August 1897, by which time the popularity of Selsey as a place to spend a day by the seaside was growing. Also, especially in later years, many hundreds of redundant railway coaches were positioned on non-railway land on the Selsey peninsula for use as seaside summer homes, with many becoming permanent residences.

Although the line was now more or less ready for service, the enthusiasm of the Directors slightly outstripped their patience, because on the sunny opening day of 27 August the line was a few hundred yards short of Selsey, where a road overbridge had still not been completed. This was to be the site of the platform that became known as Selsey Bridge Halt. Even the finishing touches at the Chichester terminus, which was located just to the south of the LBSCR main-line station, had not been completed, but the event still took place and the crowds congregated to watch an 0-4-2T called *Chichester* and three smartly decorated coaches enter the station from Selsey, where it had been to collect a number of important dignitaries for the formal opening. The Mayor of Chichester gave the opening speech, which, as usual on such occasions, forecast growth and prosperity for the entire area. The Mayor apparently announced that he was going to drive the train, but there must have been a failure in communication, as his footplate career comprised jumping on the footplate, sounding the whistle, then being ushered back into the train! The train moved off to the sound of detonators and all along the way there was considerable interest from the public, who waved, cheered and hung out flags. There were more speeches at Beacon House, Selsey, where the aristocracy gathered, but the local MP, Lord Edmund Talbot, was late and was therefore unable to attend, so a message from him had to be read out.

The line was extended to Selsey when all the trackwork and buildings had been completed. In August 1898 the line was further extended ½ mile to Selsey Beach station, which was opened only in the summer months. It had a single platform and station building with a run-round loop. However, it was closed and the track lifted during World War 1, and never reopened. Along the single line from Chichester there were stations at Hunston (2 miles 6 chains),

Top left:
The Selsey Tramway was a quaint old railway that struggled to make a living for much of its life. The engineer for the line, which opened in 1897, was the famous Colonel (from 1914) Holman Fred Stephens. The full name of the line in the early days was the Hundred of Manhood & Selsey Tramways Company Limited. Acquired by the tramway in 1907, *Sidlesham* dated back to 1861, although Messrs Hawthorn Leslie had later rebuilt the Manning Wardle locomotive. Seen at the Chichester terminus in the early days, the train will soon depart for Selsey. The man on the roof is filling the oil lamps in the carriages. *JV collection*

Lower left:
This photograph of the sad remains of the railway at Chichester after closure in 1935 finds some of the motive power and rolling-stock already reduced to scrap status. In the foreground are the frames of the Shefflex railcars and the Manning Wardle 0-6-0T *Ringing Rock*. In the right background wagons in the SR goods yard and two signal gantries on the main line can be seen. The land here remained undeveloped until recent years when new offices were built. The nearby road is still called Terminus Road. *JV collection*

Below:
In happier times, when *Ringing Rock* was not only in steam but helping the railway earn a frugal living, it has just collected from the interchange sidings three open wagons and one box van together with an old compartment coach for, at best, a handful of passengers, and is approaching Chichester terminus. The ancient locomotive will run round its train before proceeding to the first station at Hunston, then all stations and halts to Selsey. *Lens of Sutton*

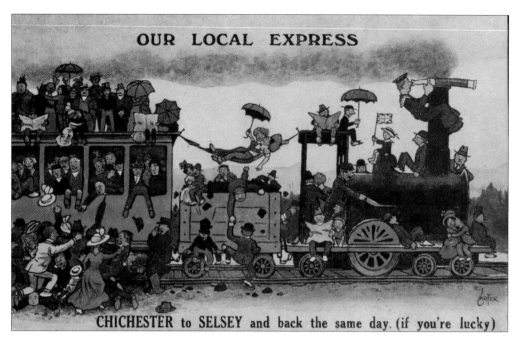

OUR LOCAL EXPRESS

CHICHESTER to SELSEY and back the same day. (if you're lucky)

Above:
The line was ridiculed locally for many years because of its slow speeds, rough ride and at times unreliable service.
It inevitably became the subject of comical postcards, and this Carter example refers to the tramway as 'our local express'
and suggests that there was an element of chance in successfully making the return journey.
The card was posted in 1920, from Bognor Regis to Leytonstone. *JV collection*

where there was a short siding in the early days and a short loop serving a nearby brickworks, a private station without a building called Hoe Farm (2 miles 65 chains), and Chalder (3 miles 50 chains), effectively north Sidlesham, which had short sidings north and south of the station. There were further stations at Mill Pond Halt (4 miles 30 chains) and Sidlesham (4 miles 75 chains), where there was a loop for goods wagons, but where the track configuration changed after some disastrous floods in 1910 (when the station building was moved to be at right-angles to the track). The next station was Ferry (5 miles 54 chains), where there was a goods siding, Golf Club Halt (6 miles 53 chains), another private station but one that crept into the timetable in later years, Selsey Bridge Halt (7 miles 7 chains), where in later years there was a thriving brickworks, Selsey (7 miles 27 chains), where the head-quarters was located as well as the engine shed and various sidings, and finally, but for a few years only (see above), Selsey Beach (7 miles and 40 chains).

Of the stations that had buildings (primarily waiting shelters, as all tickets were issued on the trains), all were of the Colonel Stephens type, being single-storey, wooden-framed and clad in corrugated iron. There were no signals and therefore no signal-boxes on the line. Weighted point levers were used to throw the switches. Although Holman Fred Stephens was the line's engineer, and the engineer of very many other lines, it would be quite wrong to think that he was on the Hundred of Manhood & Selsey Tramway every other day supervising movements or repairs. In fact, when giving evidence to the court after a fatal accident on the line in 1923 (when a locomotive and all three coaches left the line near Golf Club Halt), 'Lieutenant-Colonel Stephens as Engineer and Chairman of the Directors', when called upon to give evidence, said that 'he had not personally visited the line for 18 months as he was responsible for 12 different lines, but the track [on the tramway] was the original one.' Colonel Stephens supported the evidence of the platelayer and gave his opinion that some

Left:
To reduce running costs and to rival the growing number of omnibuses, the railway acquired its first pair of Ford-powered railcars and a luggage/light goods trailer in 1923. Edmunds of Thetford built the bodies on Ford Model T chassis. In 1928 another pair of cars from the Shefflex Motor Company of Sheffield arrived on the line. In this quite delightful study the Ford railcars pause at Chalder station, while milk churns wait to be loaded through the lowered door of the trailer. There was a single goods siding behind the platform. *JV collection*

Top right:
Between Sidlesham station and Ferry the line ran beside Pagham Harbour, and at the southern end an embankment was only a few feet above the water line. In new condition the Shefflex cars approach Ferry with only one or two passengers visible, but unusually with the trailer car coupled behind. The journey time for the 7¾-mile run was half an hour, but mixed trains could take up to 50 minutes, partly due to all trains having to slow at the many road crossings. *Maurice Dart collection*

Centre right:
Morous, a Manning Wardle 0-6-0ST of 1866 vintage, did not arrive on the railway until 1924, by which time much of the original motive power was out of service. The locomotive came from the Colonel's Shropshire & Montgomeryshire line, and was employed on the daily mixed train; the other four service trains were worked by the railcars. The fascinating formation seen here comprises a couple of goods wagons, a vintage coach and five more wagons. *JV collection*

Lower right:
This third photograph taken beside the harbour is one of the author's all-time favourites, and was purchased at a local postcard show for a whopping £15! The poor old Selsey Tramway was on its 'last knockings' as the infrastructure deteriorated, with no prospect of finding the money to repair anything. The grass is beginning to cover the tracks as the weathered Shefflex unit makes for Selsey, with just two passengers visible. It would not be long before services were suspended. *JV collection*

obstruction on the line had caused the derailment. It took more than 4½ hours for the jury to return a verdict of accidental death (the fireman had been crushed against the boiler by the buffer of the leading coach), but they added the caveat that they thought the Chief Engineer of the Company was indirectly to blame, as there was evidence of neglect in the upkeep of the track. A police constable said he could not find one completely sound sleeper at the scene of the mishap, and one juryman said that at a point within 200yd of the accident it was possible to lift out the bolts that were supposed to hold the rails to the sleepers. Without making a personal judgement, I think perhaps the Colonel and the railway officials were extremely fortunate not to be living in today's world of 'sue first and ask questions later', because the subject of corporate manslaughter would have no doubt reared its ugly head, and there is no doubt that finances dictated that these light railway operations were run on a shoestring, thereby making corporate culpability a distinct possibility! This is all of course the less romantic side of quaint old railway lines and byways!

Within the 8 miles of railway there were no fewer than 11 stations and halts, including the private ones. As already mentioned, the stations were all modest in size and standard in construction, but at Selsey there was a booking office and a Superintendent's office. Hunston was the only intermediate station that was staffed, partly because it was a coaling and watering point. At Chichester there was a link with the LBSCR, and most of the freight was carried in the wagons of various other railway companies, the Selsey Tramway having just a few 'domestic' wagons. There was an interchange siding, but the LBSCR/SR were not keen to have the Hundred of Manhood's museum pieces on its tracks, although as a concession they were sometimes allowed to use the larger company's turntable. The locomotive shed was of course at Selsey, and it was capable of housing six small tank locomotives. It became unsafe in later years and large beams literally propped up the structure. It housed some of the most remarkable locomotives imaginable, and most had complex histories and had travelled on several of the Colonel's lines. Only one of the locomotives was built in the 20th century (in 1903), and the original, *Chichester*, was built in 1847! The motive power fleet, showing basic data, is shown in the table below.

It should be stated that while some of these locomotives had had four or five previous owners, and some had come from Colonel Stephens's other lines, *Selsey* was the only locomotive to arrive

Name	Wheel arrangement	Builder	Date	Acquired	Scrapped
Chichester (1)	0-4-2T	Longbottom	1847	1897	1913
Selsey	2-4-2T	Peckett	1897	1897	1935
Sidlesham	0-6-0ST	Manning Wardle	1861	1907	1932
Hesperus	0-4-2ST	Neilson	1872	1912	1931
Ringing Rock	0-6-0ST	Manning Wardle	1883	1917	1935
Chichester (2)	0-6-0ST	Hudswell Clarke	1903	1919	1932
Morous	0-6-0ST	Manning Wardle	1866	1924	1936

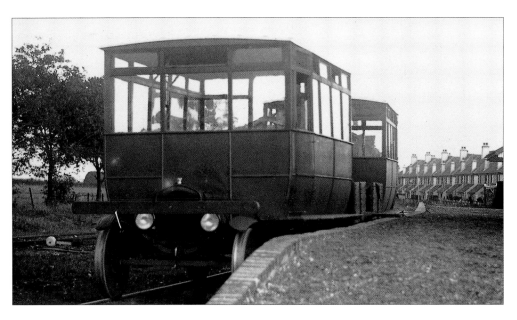

SELSEY and CHICHESTER.—Selsey.
Sec. and Man., H. C. Phillips.   Eng., H. F. Stephens, Tonbridge.

Miles	Up.	Week Days.											Sundays.
		mrn	mrn	mrn	mrn	mrn	aft	aft	aft	aft			mrn	aft	aft
	Selsey Town .....dep.	7 0	7 40	8 36	9 18	9 50	1130	1 25	5 5	50 7 5			8 50 1 20 7 0
2	Ferry Siding........	7 4	7 44	8 34	9 22	9 54	1135	1 29	9 5	54 7 9			8 54 1 24 7 4
2½	Sidlesham	7 6	7 46	8 36	9 24	9 56	1137	1 31	11 5	56 7 11			8 56 1 26 7 6
4	Chalder...........	7 10	7 50	8 40	9 28	10 0	1147	1 35	15 6	0 7 15			9 0 1 30 7 10
5½	Hunston ....[187.203	7 15	7 55	8 45	9 33	10 5	1157	1 40	20 6	5 7 20			9 5 1 35 7 15
7½	Chichester 184. arr.	7 30	8 10	9 0	9 48	1020	1212	1 55	35 6	20 7 35			9 20 1 50 7 30

Miles	Down.	Week Days.									Sundays.
		mrn	mrn	mrn	mrn	aft	aft	aft	aft	aft	mrn	aft	aft
	Chichester ....dep.	7 45	8 38	9 15	1035	1248	2 20	4 25	6 32	8 0	1120 2 0 8 15
2½	Hunston...........	7 50	8 43	9 20	1045	1253	2 25	4 30		8 5	1125 2 5 8 20
3½	Chalder...........	7 55	8 48		1050	1258	2 30	4 35		8 10	1130 2 10 8 25
5	Sidlesham	8 0	8 53	9 35	1055	1 3	2 35	4 40	6 43	8 15	1135 2 15 8 30
5½	Ferry Siding.......	8 5	8 58		11 5	1 8	2 40	4 45		8 20	1140 2 20 8 35
7½	Selsey Town......arr.	8 15	9 8	9 45	1115	1 18	2 50	4 55	7 0	8 30	1150 2 30 8 45

SELSEY and CHICHESTER.—Selsey.
Sec. and Man., H. C. Phillips.   Eng., H. F. Stephens, Tonbridge.

Miles	Up.	Week Days.											Sundays.
		mrn	mrn	mrn	mrn	mrn	aft	aft	aft	aft			mrn	aft	aft
	Selsey Town .....dep.	7 0	7 40	8 36	9 18	9 50	1130	1 25	5 5	50 7 5			8 50 1 20 7 0
2	Ferry Siding........	7 4	7 44	8 34	9 22	9 54	1135	1 29	9 5	54 7 9			8 54 1 24 7 4
2½	Sidlesham	7 6	7 46	8 36	9 24	9 56	1137	1 31	11 5	56 7 11			8 56 1 26 7 6
4	Chalder...........	7 10	7 50	8 40	9 28	10 0	1147	1 35	15 6	0 7 15			9 0 1 30 7 10
5½	Hunston ....[187.203	7 15	7 55	8 45	9 33	10 5	1157	1 40	20 6	5 7 20			9 5 1 35 7 15
7½	Chichester 184. arr.	7 30	8 10	9 0	9 48	1020	1212	1 55	35 6	20 7 35			9 20 1 50 7 30

Miles	Down.	Week Days.									Sundays.
		mrn	mrn	mrn	mrn	aft	aft	aft	aft	aft	mrn	aft	aft
	Chichester ....dep.	7 45	8 38	9 15	1035	1248	2 20	4 25	6 32	8 0	1120 2 0 8 15
2½	Hunston...........	7 50	8 43	9 20	1045	1253	2 25	4 30		8 5	1125 2 5 8 20
3½	Chalder...........	7 55	8 48		1050	1258	2 30	4 35		8 10	1130 2 10 8 25
5	Sidlesham	8 0	8 53	9 35	1055	1 3	2 35	4 40	6 43	8 15	1135 2 15 8 30
5½	Ferry Siding.......	8 5	8 58		11 5	1 8	2 40	4 45		8 20	1140 2 20 8 35
7½	Selsey Town......arr.	8 15	9 8	9 45	1115	1 18	2 50	4 55	7 0	8 30	1150 2 30 8 45

Top left:
Although Selsey, 7 miles and 27 chains from Chichester, was the terminus of the line, and where the locomotive and goods sheds were located, a ½-mile extension to Selsey Beach was in operation for a few years at the start of the 20th century. Apparently the railcars were noisy, smelly (from the exhaust fumes) and the ride over the rough track was appalling. Nevertheless they must not be underestimated, because in the year 1933 they notched up no less than 20,861 miles! The Ford cars are seen here at Selsey. *Maurice Dart collection*

Centre left:
These timetables show the service in 1910 (*above*) and 1927 (*below*). The former mentions Colonel Stephens of Tonbridge as Engineer and the latter shows that the service is run by 'Motor Cars — 3rd class only'. The main difference is in the Sunday service.

Lower left:
Another old postcard view shows Selsey station, a typical Colonel Stephens style of building, with corrugated iron cladding, a modest awning and an oil lamp. The locomotive shed is on the extreme left. The train has just arrived from Chichester and comprises the three bogie coaches by Falcon Works of Loughborough, which were purchased new in 1897 for the opening of the line. *JV collection*

new on the line, and although slightly modified at a later date, it proved to be one of the best.

In addition to the locomotives, a four-wheeled Wolseley-Siddeley petrol railcar was tried about 1921. This was the precursor of a pair of Ford-powered petrol railcars that were acquired in 1923 as an operational economy measure. These interesting vehicles with Edmunds bodies fixed to Model T Ford bus chassis worked the line for many years. Two Shefflex petrol railcars that arrived on the line in about 1928, also used as an economy measure, shared some of the duties, although it was reported that Colonel Stephens rather than the railway owned the cars. These four-wheeled cars normally worked back-to-back but sometimes with an open four-wheeled wagon coupled between them. Each car had a four-cylinder petrol engine with power delivered via a three-speed gearbox. Each car held 23 passengers with a 14-gallon petrol tank situated under the driver's seat They had some disadvantages in terms of loading capacity and they obviously had no place on mixed trains or any goods train workings; however, their total running costs, including driver's wages, fuel, insurance and repairs, was just 3.12d (1.3p) per mile.

The Hundred of Manhood & Selsey Tramways rolling stock was as varied as its motive power. Three smart new vehicles were delivered from Falcon in 1897, and another new bogie coach arrived from Hurst Nelson in about 1900. Three ex-Lambourn Valley four-wheeled coaches arrived on the tramway in 1910, then a whole list of very tired and withdrawn ex-London, Chatham & Dover Railway four- and six-wheelers arrived between about 1916 and 1931. These were followed by the abovementioned four-wheeled petrol railcars. In total it was a rag-bag of vehicles that were maintained at Selsey, but the ravages of the weather and a limited maintenance budget soon found some of the coaches looking very shabby indeed. At its peak the railway had 18 goods vehicles.

From the start the timetable reflected the seasons of the year. Generally there were about half a dozen trains in each direction off season and about twice as many during the summer months. The almost 8-mile journey took about half an hour when things were going well. In the summer of 1913 there were 11 trains per day each way and even half a dozen round trips on Sundays. The Edwardian era really was a promising time for the tramway. Cheap day excursion tickets on to the LBSCR were available and vice versa, although arrival times and connections off the Selsey line were never guaranteed! The trains were new, the crowds wanted to travel, the previously unfinished details, such as the full-length platform at the Chichester terminus, were complete, and for a few years the line really prospered. However, Mother Nature was unkind to the tramway in 1910 when there was the most tremendous storm that flooded much of the Selsey peninsula and totally immersed Pagham Harbour under several feet of water. The tramway was badly affected, but it eventually managed to run a service from Chichester down to Mill Pond Halt and up from Selsey to Ferry. The 'missing link' was filled by horse-bus until the railway could be partly rebuilt, with the entire Pagham Harbour stretch being raised to about 15ft. It was perhaps fortunate that the storm occurred in 1910 when the railway had the money to repair the permanent way, because in later years, in terms of finances and infrastructure, circumstances had deteriorated to such an extent that it would have finished the railway for good.

In 1913 there were plans to extend the tramway to West Itchenor and East Wittering under the provisions of a Light Railway Order, but World War 1 intervened and the plans never came to fruition. Immediately after the war, circumstances recovered and in 1919 the tramway carried more than 102,000 passengers. However, increasing bus competition, private motoring and a rundown in its condition caused a serious downturn for the tramway. By 1922 passengers had plummeted to only 60,000, and unbelievably by

1926 the total was just 17,000, only 16% of (and 85,000 people fewer than) the 1919 figure! From 1924 the long tramway title was formally changed, and it became the West Sussex Railway, with the redundant addition 'Selsey Tramway Section'! Also about this time road crossing rules changed, whereby the fireman or the guard had to stand in the centre of every road crossing and wave a red flag at any road traffic to signify that a train was about to cross. This new process hardly speeded up the already ponderous journey. In Bradshaw's timetable for January 1927 there were just five trains in each direction with one extra on Saturdays, but no Sunday service. The railway tried a price war, but even by 1933, when it reduced the fare to a mere 8d compared with the bus fare of 11d, passengers would still take the bus.

Sadly the railway became something of a joke because of bad timekeeping, weed-covered tracks, unreliability, road crossing accidents and, of course, reduced patronage. On some petrol railcar workings, photographs show just a couple of passengers on the trains. Passengers were also generally discouraged from travelling on the mixed trains as the railway announced that they would not hold themselves responsible for any loss, accident or delay. In fact, many workings were mixed, even if it came down to milk churns in the trailer between the petrol railcars, so the distinction between timetabled passenger workings and mixed trains became foggy at times! The railway had a contract to transport GPO parcels until about 1930.

Although in the past the railway had made a reasonable profit, by 1926 costs exceeded income by some £550. By 1929 passenger train mileage had dropped to 22,542 miles, goods traffic was down to 1,785 miles, and the financial position was dire. The High Court became involved when debenture interest could not be paid, and it appointed a local Receiver on 8 May 1931. The story from this point on was one of gradual but inexorable decline, with no money available to repair any item of railway equipment and with patronage falling away to almost nothing. By November 1934 there was just a single train working in each direction, leaving Selsey at 10am, arriving at Chichester at 11am, returning at 11.30am to arrive back at Selsey at 12.15pm. The West Sussex Railway tried to get the Southern Railway interested in the line, but the cost of providing crossings and of completely rebuilding the railway would have been prohibitive. Accordingly a notice appeared on all stations that as from 19 January 1935 services would be suspended 'until further notice'. At the end there were only 12 employees and the railway had lasted just 38 years. An old driver recalled that in its heyday he had carried some 300 passengers on one train, and he also claimed the speed record by covering the 8-mile route in 18 minutes!

A Mr F. Watkins from Gloucestershire had his tender of £3,610 accepted for the railway 'lock, stock and barrel', almost all of it merely scrap value. The final report shows just how hopeless it all was: for example, 2-4-2T *Selsey* was 'beyond repair', the Ford twin railcar 'in poor condition', original bogie tram (coach) 'hopeless condition', four-wheeled carriage 'bad condition', etc. Colonel Stephens had died in 1931, so he did not witness the end of the tramway.

It is now difficult to realise the hand-to-mouth existence on the railway. At times no locomotive was available to steam. On another occasion *Ringing Rock* ran for three weeks on only one cylinder. At one time re-railing was such a frequent occurrence that a re-railing jack was carried on the footplate of the locomotive. However, speeds were generally low and danger levels were not high, with the notable exception of the fatality referred to earlier. Passengers were sometimes carried in the four-wheeled wagon located between the railcars, and in 1917 a young schoolgirl fell from a train and lost a leg. She was given a free pass for life, not a particularly valuable gift as things turned out.

The old line ignored many conventions for the whole of its life.

None of the road crossings was completely in accordance with regulations. Goods trains never worked with a brake-van; in fact, the company never owned one! At no point did the flat terrain exceed the 50ft contour line. There were few facing point locks on sidings. The average speed of the mixed trains was 10mph. One surprising statistic relates to goods traffic carried over the line in 1933, which was 4,464 tons of general goods, 2,260 tons of minerals and 5,224 tons of coal and coke. However, broken down this equates to about 46 tons, or perhaps four or five wagons, per day; clearly not enough to survive. Ninety-two per cent of all passengers on the West Sussex Railway originated on the line, a truly local line serving mainly the local community! At the end of the line's existence the Superintendent of the Line received about £3 per week, whereas the conductor/guard was paid £1 per week. Staff worked a 54-hour week.

Today little remains of the old Hundred of Manhood & Selsey Tramway. At Chichester the road near the old station site is still called Terminus Road. A local pub on the Selsey Road south of Chichester is named the 'Selsey Tram', with an appropriate pub sign. Although now buried in undergrowth and foliage, the old canal bridge abutment survives, as does the embankment across part of Pagham Harbour. Happily there are traces of platform at Hunston and Chalder, but a fragment of foundation at the old Selsey Beach site has been removed. The nameplate of *Ringing Rock* is on display at a museum in Chichester. Otherwise there is little to view other than the subjects in the photographs contained within these pages. Thank goodness for photography!

Finally, a locally composed song that should have been performed at a concert at Sidlesham in 1934 was, at the request of the West Sussex Railway's station master at Chichester, not performed, because it was very uncomplimentary. Nevertheless the words reflected the amusement, one might almost say ridicule, that had been directed at the line in those final years. The chorus went:

The Sidlesham snail, The Sidlesham snail
Her boiler's burst, She's off the rail!

Above:
One of the saddest sights in this miserable scene, taken at Selsey in June 1935, five months after the line had closed, is the old Ford railcars rotting away together with a box van and a cattle truck. From a 1916 peak of 105,000 passengers, numbers fell to 13,416 in 1931, producing an annual income of just £280. Although numbers increased in the following two years, most locals travelled by comfortable Southdown double-deck bus, which was cheaper and more convenient. *J. Hicks collection*

Above left:
A public house just south of Chichester on the road to the Witterings is near to the alignment of the Selsey Tramway,
and Brickwoods Brewery (absorbed long ago) named the establishment 'The Selsey Tram'. The company also had the imagination
to produce a humorous pub sign featuring one of the old railcars. This has been removed since pictured in March 1973. *JV*

Above right:
Adjacent to the site of Sidlesham station the trackbed now forms a footpath known as 'The Selsey Tram Way'.
The delightful etched sign shows the original 1897 Peckett 2-4-2T *Selsey*. As the years have passed, evidence of the tramway
has disappeared, but there is a section in Chichester Museum dedicated to the line that is well worth visiting. *JV*

Right:
This turn-of-the-20th-century map
shows the position of the tramway
terminus in relation to the
LBSCR/SR/BR main-line station.
The large scale shows the precise
track layout at the fairly cramped
site. The road to the south of the
station is still called Terminus
Road, but the gasworks opposite
the station has long gone.
Crown Copyright

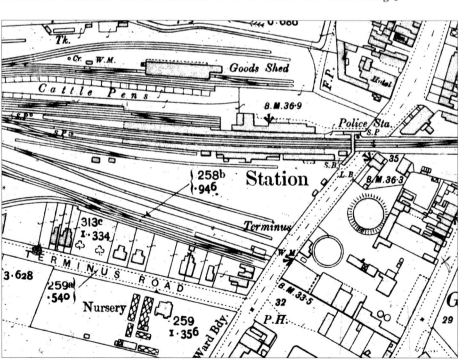

12. Pulborough to Midhurst

IN the mid-1840s the most significant towns along the Sussex and Hampshire coastline, certainly in population terms, were Brighton, Portsmouth and Southampton. However, Portsmouth, with its great naval traditions and a population that was 50% higher than any other coastal town, was something of a jewel in the crown when it came to traffic potential and therefore receipts for a railway company. Just as there had been rivalry between the LBSCR and the SER, the former attempting to 'head off' the latter from reaching Brighton, Eastbourne and Hastings, so the LBSCR also tried to keep the London & South Western Railway away from Portsmouth (and Shoreham and Brighton — see Chapter 10).

By reaching Brighton from London in 1841, and having connected Brighton and Shoreham a year earlier, the LBSCR drove its coastal line westward, Worthing being reached in November 1845, Chichester in June 1846 and through to Portsmouth in June 1847. By 1857 the partly single-track route had been doubled throughout. Unfortunately the total route mileage from London to Portsmouth via Brighton was 95½ miles. The LSWR had opened its line from Bishopstoke (Eastleigh) to Gosport via Fareham back in November 1841, giving London travellers an 89½-mile journey, albeit with a ferry crossing necessary to reach Portsmouth. Although not the subject of this chapter, the LSWR built a line from Fareham to join the Brighton to Portsmouth line, which opened on 1 October 1848. After various schemes were considered, the LSWR had an Act of Parliament passed in 1853, which resulted in the building of the 'Portsmouth Direct' line from Waterloo,

Guildford and Havant to Portsmouth, which was ready for service at the end of 1858. In fact, there was already a line from Guildford to Godalming, and the Act effectively bridged the gap down to the coast. Agreements were eventually reached between the LSWR and the LBSCR regarding sharing receipts or 'pooling' income over certain sections of the routes and various running rights over what turned out to be jointly owned tracks.

The longer Brighton route from London to Portsmouth could not compete with the 'Portsmouth Direct', although the LSWR was running only four passenger trains per day each way over the route in 1865. In 1878 the partly single-track line was doubled throughout and services increased. In the meantime the Brighton company had done some head-scratching. It had opened its line from Three Bridges on the London to Brighton main line to Horsham on 14 February 1848, and although some of the planning had occurred some years before, all of the necessary formalities had been completed and the navvies had done their work, enabling the 17½-mile line from Horsham to the important town of Petworth, at a spot known as Coultershaw Mill, to be opened under the auspices of the Mid-Sussex Railway Company on 10 October 1859. In fact, Petworth station was more than 1½ miles from the town, and a connecting horse and carriage service was provided for those who could afford it. This was the first phase of the Mid-Sussex line. However, just four years later, in August 1863, the line from Hardham Junction, south of Pulborough, to Arundel and Arundel Junction, near Ford on the coastal line, was opened,

Left:
Originally, from October 1859, the line down from Horsham ran via Pulborough to Petworth, and the publicity encouraged passengers to alight at Petworth for Midhurst, some 6 miles distant.
The 'Mid-Sussex' line from Pulborough through Arundel to the coastal line was not opened until 1863, from which time the Petworth line became a branch. Midhurst was reached by rail from Petworth in 1866, two years after the line from Petersfield, to the west, arrived in 1864. With the sign proclaiming 'Pulborough for Petworth, Midhurst &c', 'I3' class No 2091 takes water with a down 'Mid-Sussex' line train on 16 April 1938, just weeks before electric trains took over all passenger services. *IAL*

Below:
Fittleworth, with a population of about 650, was deserving of a small station, especially as the branch to Petworth and Midhurst passed just south of the village. However, it was not until September 1889, 30 years after the opening of the branch, that a station was provided. No doubt proud of their station, the staff of four pose for the Victorian photographer.
The signalbox was an early casualty, being replaced by a ground frame in 1930. *JV collection*

thereby giving the LBSCR a direct but 87-mile-long route to Portsmouth. As mentioned in Chapter 10, the line up from Shoreham to Itchingfield Junction on the Mid-Sussex line had opened in September 1861. Although powers had been extended to the Mid-Sussex & Midhurst Junction Railway to extend the line by 5½ miles to Midhurst, it took no less than seven years to complete the extension, which finally opened on 15 October 1866. There had been problems in the railway company acquiring all of the necessary land, and finances were also stretched at that time.

The Act of Parliament authorising the extension had stipulated the building of an intermediate station at Selham, but although the Act was eventually complied with, Selham station did not open until July 1872. There were howls of protest from the villagers of Fittleworth, between Hardham Junction and Petworth, that they were not directly served by the railway, even though the line ran just a few hundred yards south of village. The local MP, Sir Walter Barttelot, pressurised the railway and in September 1889 Fittleworth station was opened. As mentioned in the next two chapters, the LSWR reached Midhurst from the Petersfield direction in 1864, and in 1881 a line from Chichester also reached Midhurst, making the market town more of a railway centre than perhaps its modest population deserved.

The station at Pulborough had a main down platform and an up island platform, Midhurst trains normally using the outer face of the island. Pulborough also boasted sidings, a down-side goods yard and shed, a turntable and a signalbox. The platforms were (and still are) connected by subway. After leaving Pulborough the line to Midhurst and the 1863 Mid-Sussex line crossed the River Arun, which at that point was very susceptible to flooding. At Hardham Junction, where the lines separated, the LBSCR signalbox gave the impression of being 'on stilts'. Train crews would take the single-line token from the signalman at this point. The Midhurst line then veered west and crossed the Arun Navigation canal that had once carried produce down through Amberley to the coast. After passing through a cutting and beneath a road overbridge, Fittleworth station was reached, 2½ miles from Pulborough. At the turn of the 20th century the village had a population of just over 650 inhabitants. A single-faced platform on the down side served trains running along the single track — a passing loop was never provided. A signalbox was located opposite the platform on the up side of the track, but it was not a block post, the only surprise being that it did

not close before 1930! There was a small two-track goods yard at the down end of the platform and a loading dock. In addition to goods traffic (especially coal and agricultural traffic) substantial quantities of milk were handled. In 1938 319 loaded wagons arrived at the yard and 145 loaded wagons were despatched. Fittleworth was something of a backwater, and even in 1965 the local coalman still delivered coal from the goods yard by horse (even though by then the coal was brought in by road), the local streets were still repaired by the last West Sussex County Council steam-roller, and the small telephone exchange had an old manual 'doll's eye' switchboard with pre-payment button-less call boxes in the village. Perhaps the redeeming feature was the fact that almost the first building encountered by rail passengers on their walk to the village was the Swan Inn! The station comprised a modest single-storey wooden building with booking office and waiting room. An awning was provided for passenger comfort. In 1938 1,415 tickets were issued at the little station, only four or five per working day. It cost £1,000 to build and survives as a private dwelling. On opening, the station had a station master, booking clerk and three porters.

The line then ran across rolling farmland for some 2¾ miles to Petworth, the original terminus of the line and, as it transpired, the terminus at the very end of the line's existence. The original Petworth station was broadly similar to Fittleworth, but in 1889 it was demolished and replaced by a larger and more substantial building. In 1938 the booking clerk was selling 2,709 tickets per annum, hardly an onerous task. In addition, however, there were 38 season ticket holders! Again only a single platform was provided on the up side, but there was a 'goods' passing loop, until removed in about 1957. The signalbox was again on the opposite side of the line to the platform. The 18-lever box was operational until December 1957, more than two years after passenger services were withdrawn. There was a busy goods yard on the up side with a goods shed and both internal and external goods cranes. In later years the two primary commodities were coal and imported grain for use in the nearby Coultershaw flour mill; a grain silo was also part of the infrastructure. In 1938 1,706 loaded wagons (six or seven per working day) were received and 209 loaded wagons were despatched, many of which conveyed seasonal produce. The station master's house was located at a higher level than the track on the south side.

Left:
In the mid-1960s, at the tender age of 23, the author was the GPO caretaker telephonist at the tiny Fittleworth telephone exchange, and occasionally, while travelling home from work, the thrice weekly Petworth goods was glimpsed. Goods facilities at Fittleworth were withdrawn in May 1963, but coal continued to be delivered to the station yard by road. From there it was delivered to the villagers by horse and cart, owned by Mr J. Strudwick, the local coal merchant. A bridge over the line can be seen in the background in this 1966 view. *JV/TTT*

Left:
By the winter of 1966 the demolition contractors had moved in on Fittleworth and the track was being ripped up from the Petworth direction, cut into small lengths and deposited with the redundant sleepers into old wooden four-wheeled goods wagons. This was the depressing scene on 9 December 1966. The station had seen its last passenger in February 1955, long before the so-called 'Beeching era'.
JV/TTT

Below:
The old wooden station remained derelict for many years. Last used by passengers in 1955 and having stood silent until the last freight ran in 1966, it looked as though the building would be lost. However, in July 1987 planning permission was granted, on appeal, for the building to be converted into a dwelling. In March 2003 the building looked to be in excellent condition. A couple of nearby railway cottages also survive. *JV*

Top right:
Eight Petworth station staff pose for the photographer in about 1900. A single-faced platform was provided and in the foreground is the goods loop. On the left the roof of the small signalbox can just be seen. This is the second, 1890, station building, which is listed and has been preserved. Once upon a time the sizeable goods yard saw much traffic, particularly coal, timber, grain (for the nearby Coultershaw flour mill) and sugar beet. *IAL*

Centre right:
The last scheduled goods train from Horsham to Petworth ran on 20 May 1966 behind a Class 08 350hp shunter. The train comprised two wagons and two brake-vans, one for the guard and the Area Manager and the other for the author and two fellow enthusiasts. The train shunted some wagons at Petworth and the station's furnishings were loaded into one of the wagons. The ensemble is seen waiting to return towards Pulborough, and a line of detonators would soon commemorate the event. The signalbox on the left had not been used since 1957 and the goods loop had, by then, long gone. *JV/TTT*

Lower right:
Petworth station was some 2 miles south of the small town it served and it is little wonder that there were few passengers, especially after car ownership became commonplace. After closure and a period of abandonment, a local coal merchant took over the site, but in the fullness of time the listed building was renovated as a residence. More recently some restored Pullman cars, providing overnight accommodation in a unique setting (see text), were sited at the old station. This was the westward view in March 2003. *JV*

Above:
After closure to passengers in 1955, goods traffic to Midhurst and the intermediate stations of Fittleworth and Selham continued. The frequency of goods trains gradually declined, and when 'C2X' class No 32523 was photographed on 23 March 1960 it was down to thrice weekly. Having shunted at Selham, the freight, comprising five box vans and seven open wagons, makes for Hardham Junction and Horsham. The ninth and tenth open wagons contain chestnut fencing, 750 tons of which were shipped from Selham in 1937. *Derek Cross*

The next station was Selham, 7¾ miles from Pulborough, which opened 13 years after Petworth but 17 years before Fittleworth. The single-storey wooden building did not provide living accommodation and no awning was provided. In common with Fittleworth the building was in stark contrast to the substantial buildings that the LBSCR was constructing on other branch lines. There was a diminutive signalbox at the west end of the single platform, located on the up side. The box was abolished in 1933 and two ground frames then controlled the points to the general goods yard and down cattle siding. By 1938 the cattle sidings handled only 12 wagons in the entire year. Again, agricultural produce, cattle and milk were important sources of traffic, but unusually at this location more than twice as many loaded wagons were despatched than received, 712 being loaded in 1938. There were only a few buildings in the immediate vicinity of the station, but at the end of the railway approach was, and still is, the Three Moles public house. In 1901 Selham had a population of 60 souls, but by 1938 the booking clerk did manage to sell nearly five railway tickets per working day!

The line continued to Midhurst, 11 miles from Pulborough, but not before passing through a 276-yard tunnel situated just a couple of hundred yards east of the LBSCR station. The latter, and the LSWR station beyond, were on the southern outskirts of the market town. Immediately beyond the tunnel entrance on the down side was a sand quarry with a dedicated siding. A new substantial station replaced the much smaller original one in 1881, and at the same time it was resited about ¼ mile to the east, with the junction of the new line from Chichester providing the prospect of operating the Chichester to Pulborough line as a through route. Midhurst had lengthy through platforms and generous awnings graced both up and down sides. There was also a bay platform at the western end on the up side that was used by terminating trains from Petersfield after 1925 when, under the auspices of the Southern Railway, the old LSWR station closed to passengers. Signalboxes were located at the east end of the 'Brighton' station (Midhurst South) and at the west end (Midhurst West). The latter was a 47-lever box, located at a point where the line to Chichester branched off and beside the single-track connection to the LSWR lines. After closure of the South box in 1925, it was used as the station master's office.

Midhurst LBSCR had a sizeable goods yard with a brick-built goods shed. There were numerous sidings and for many years there was goods traffic over all three lines radiating from Midhurst. The LBSCR built a small wooden locomotive shed and a wooden goods shed. After listing at an alarming angle, the locomotive shed was replaced in 1907 by a new single-track shed, and a more substantial brick-built goods shed was added to the facilities at a later date. Goods cranes and the usual cattle dock were provided. There was also an LSWR engine shed, described in Chapter 14. The LBSCR locomotive shed was closed shortly after the Grouping when Horsham provided the motive power (see the train services paragraph below).

The population of Midhurst in 1901 was 1,650, but that belies the fact that the market town was the most important in that part of West Sussex, with a considerable 'catchment area' for merchants and farmers. For example, coal distribution was greatly enhanced by the arrival of the railway. However, unlike many other towns, despite the population eventually having the choice to travel west, south or east, the railway did not cause an overnight population explosion. This might have been a different story if a line to Haslemere had been built, offering faster times to London (see below). Also, although most towns had their share of local aristocrats and a 'lord of the manor', Midhurst was heavily influenced by the Cowdray Estate, which owned huge tracts of land in and around the town. In later years the name became synonymous with the rich and famous who rubbed shoulders with Royalty as they indulged in the exclusive sport of polo at Cowdray Park. However, few participants would have travelled by rail once the age of the motor car arrived.

In the past there had been a number of abortive railway schemes that would have affected Midhurst. At one time it was to have been on a through route to Portsmouth, as the Directors of the Chichester & Midhurst Railway secured authority to build an extension from Midhurst to Haslemere, to the north, to join the LSWR's 'Portsmouth Direct' line that had already opened between London, Guildford and Portsmouth. In 1902 no lesser person than Colonel Stephens (see Chapter 1) proposed a Surrey & Sussex Light Railway. The 17-mile-long light railway would have run from

Selham to Cranleigh and Ockley, where it would have linked with the LBSCR lines serving those villages. The proposal failed to materialise. Midhurst was also important as a regional boundary between the LBSCR and LSWR, where by agreement the companies agreed not to extend their railway lines west or east from the town, a situation that was only resolved by the formation of the Southern Railway at the Grouping in 1923.

The train service between Pulborough and Midhurst was never intensive. In 1888 there were eight trains in each direction on weekdays and two on Sundays. Of the weekday trains five worked down through Midhurst to Chichester and six worked up from Chichester to Pulborough via Midhurst. There were no 'through' trains on Sundays. The LBSCR locomotive for the first working of the day came off Midhurst shed and worked the 7.35am to Pulborough, returning at 8.15am. Late-night revellers had to content themselves with the 9.6pm from Pulborough to Midhurst. By 1927, after the Grouping, there were nine down trains, with all but one working through to Chichester, and 10 up trains, the last being the 10pm from Midhurst to Pulborough, in order for the locomotive to return to its by then Horsham base. The 1937 timetable shows that some trains worked through from Midhurst to Horsham and even Dorking North. Another curiosity was the 9.58pm from Midhurst, the last train of the day, which called at Selham (10.5½pm to 10.6½pm!) on Saturdays only. By 1950 there were nine trains in each direction on weekdays, but the Chichester line had long since closed, and by then some trains were running through from Pulborough to Petersfield and vice versa. There were four round-trip workings on Sundays. In addition to this traffic there was the daily goods that shunted all intermediate stations and yards on its round trip from Horsham to Midhurst. A public timetable footnote added that only Third Class travel was available between Pulborough and Petersfield; presumably by then the gentry and polo-players had found alternative modes of transport!

When one considers the population of the town, and the villages served by the Pulborough to Midhurst railway, and for that matter the associated lines to Petersfield and Chichester, it is perhaps a wonder that any railways were built in the area. In the era before the motor car and motor lorry, there was clearly a role for railways, but it was unfortunate for most branch lines that the technological development of the railways was followed so closely in time by the development of road transport. With part of the Midhurst rail complex closing to passengers in 1935 (the line to Chichester — see Chapter 13), there was clearly not much cash being generated by the branch lines in the area. A number of economies were made, such as running LSWR trains into the LBSCR Midhurst station after the Grouping, and the closing of various signalboxes between 1927 and 1933. Also by then push-pull trains dominated the scene, but after World War 2 the line was clearly making a loss, and it was the Southern Region of British Railways rather than Dr Beeching that decided that the passenger service should be withdrawn.

The notices of closure of the line to passengers (and that from Midhurst to Petersfield) were posted and announced that the last day of normal passenger services would be 5 February 1955. Some of the trains during the last few days of the line's operation were strengthened by an extra coach, but farewell visits were never going to provide sufficient regular income to save the line. The day after closure to passengers, an enthusiasts' special, filled to capacity, traversed the entire remaining route. For a while freight traffic continued between Pulborough and Midhurst, but the line beyond to Petersfield was to close completely from 7 February 1955. Goods trains continued to run to Midhurst but services were withdrawn from the intermediate stations of Selham and Fittleworth in May 1963. The freight rundown continued, and although the line still saw occasional use by ramblers' and railway enthusiasts' specials, Midhurst finally succumbed when freight facilities were withdrawn in October 1964. Towards the end of

steam no water was available at Midhurst and BR had to supply a tender locomotive for the Midhurst goods. From that month the line was cut back to Petworth, and the frequency of the freight diminished to thrice weekly, as required, with the train continuing to work out of Horsham yard. After the end of steam, diesel locomotives took over, but the writing was on the wall and in May 1966 even the Petworth goods facility was withdrawn.

The author and his old friend John Frith were two of only three enthusiasts who travelled on the last train, on 20 May 1966. A Class 08 shunter worked the train of two wagons and two brake-vans, and as it had come from Horsham it used the down main line platform at Pulborough, then briefly ran 'wrong line' at Hardham Junction to gain access to the single-line branch. The signalman handed the single-line token to the train crew. The old Fittleworth station was still standing but the awning was sinking into the ground as the timbers rotted. At Petworth many of the station fixtures and fittings were loaded into one of the wagons and some coal wagon shunting was completed. After posing for photographs the final scheduled service left Petworth for the last time and, to mark the occasion, detonators were placed on the line. Thus 106 years of history came to an end, except for a final unscheduled train to pick up the last wagons, and the demolition train, which traversed the route in the November 1966 to January 1967 period. An amusing aside, spotted from the brake-van on the last train, was the sight of two lineside workers cutting back the undergrowth on embankments with scythes! Clearly nobody had told them that the line was closing. Nowadays such a sight cannot be observed, even on a main line.

The Pulborough to Midhurst branch had remarkably little variety in motive power. After miscellaneous early types were tried on the line, from the 1880s LBSCR 'Terriers' appeared. They were in turn replaced by Class D1s and, later still, D3s. From the end of the 1940s the Southern used mainly the ex-LSWR 'M7' class, which continued as the staple motive power until passenger services were withdrawn in 1955. There was more variety on freight services. In addition to LBSCR 'E4' and 'E5x' tanks, tender locomotives of the 'C2x', 'C3', 'Q' and 'Q1' classes normally worked the goods, depending on the era. 'E4s', 'E5Xs' and even 'E6' tanks worked enthusiasts' specials. Once steam ended, the only classes of motive power noted were Class 33 Bo-Bos and Class 08 shunters.

Other than odd traces of track alignment and a handful of minor overbridges, the main survivors on the line are the station buildings and railway houses/cottages. After spending some time derelict, Fittleworth station was completely refurbished, and at the end of the minor approach road the building survives as a well-preserved private residence. Petworth, a Grade II listed building, has also undergone complete restoration, whereas for some time after closure it too became quite dilapidated — see the photograph. It was then used as a craft and antique furniture business. Now it has developed into a remarkable establishment where the public can spend a luxurious evening dining in one of four superbly restored Pullman coaches, which date back to World War 1. Two former First Class parlour cars were the first to arrive in 1998. Named *Alicante* and *Mimosa*, they were built in 1912 and 1914 respectively, and stood on an old siding at Marazion in Cornwall for 35 years before being rescued. Thus after all these years Petworth still has a railway flavour, even though Pullman car specials never traversed the line! Selham station also survives, but mainly for storage, whereas Midhurst's LBSCR station was completely obliterated many years ago to make way for a housing estate, although the old tunnel mouth is still visible behind a block of flats. The brick goods shed was demolished in 1986 to make way for yet more housing. It is now almost half a century since the passenger trains ceased, and it is hard to believe that 38 years have gone by since the last freight. However, the line holds special memories and happily the photographs herein are testimony to those days when the pace of life was just a little slower.

Above:
Although the line closed to passengers in 1955, it continued to be used by ramblers' excursions and, from time to time, enthusiasts' specials. In October 1964 the line from Petworth through Selham to Midhurst closed completely. Long before there was talk of closure, on 15 October 1950, a 10-coach ramblers' excursion from Victoria to Selham, headed by 'Q' class No 30531, climbs away from Selham for berthing at Midhurst. *S. C. Nash*

Upper left:
This wonderful view of the Selham station track layout shows the goods yard on the left or up side, the main branch in the centre and the siding built to serve the cattle dock on the right. The signalbox here was abolished in 1933 and replaced by two ground frames. At the time of railway nationalisation in 1948 a Pulborough-bound push-pull working comprising set No 731 calls briefly at the station. *IAL*

Lower left:
In a remarkable 'then and now' comparison, Selham station looks relatively unchanged in this 2003 view, nearly 50 years after the end of passenger trains and 40 years after the end of goods traffic. The line to the east of the station is completely overgrown by substantial trees and undergrowth, but the platform and the trackbed in the immediate vicinity have been well maintained. Opened in 1872, the wooden station looks to be in relatively good shape. *JV*

Above:
This photograph was taken at a sunny Midhurst on the penultimate day of service, 4 February 1955. 'M7' class No 30028 has just arrived with the 10.40am Petersfield to Midhurst train, while at the down platform sister locomotive No 30049 has also just arrived with the 10.33am Pulborough to Midhurst service. On the left is the 61 milepost (from London), while under the awning can be seen two British motorcycles, one being a Velocette. Note the oil tail lamp on the locomotive of the down push-pull train. *S. C. Nash*

Upper right:
This truly magnificent example of an LBSCR lower-quadrant signal, also photographed on 4 February 1955, stands just outside the 276yd Midhurst Tunnel as the 12.33pm Pulborough to Midhurst emerges, being propelled by No 30049. The motorman in the driving trailer is clearly visible, and he will be controlling the train brake. It is hard to believe that a major market town that had railways arriving from three directions is now completely rail-less. *S. C. Nash*

Lower right:
A startling comparison shows the March 2003 scene with a three-storey block of flats erected immediately to the west of the tunnel mouth. To the right of the picture was once a sand quarry, which was served by its own siding. As built, the first LBSCR station was some distance from the town, and the second, 1881, station was even further away, but as Midhurst grew the station area became enveloped in housing. *JV*

Left:
This somewhat amusing 1897 view shows the original
LBSCR locomotive shed at Midhurst; constructed
in 1864, it suffered from considerable settlement.
The shed was not replaced until 1907. *IAL*

The Chichester to Pulborough via Midhurst timetable,
in 1888 (*top*) and 1927 (*below*).

PULBOROUGH, MIDHURST, and CHICHESTER.

Miles from Pulboro'	Down.			Week Days.									Sundays.		
		mrn	mrn	mrn	mrn	aft		aft	aft		aft	aft		mrn	aft
	218 VICTORIA ....dep.	..	8 50	..	12A5	..	1 40	4e20	..	4 53	7 25	..	..	6 55	..	7 0	..
	218 LONDON BRIDGE ...... ''	6 33	7 20	..	1015	..	1 50	..	..	5 e 0	..	..	..	6 55	..	..
	Pulborough ....dep.	8 17	9 50	11 0	1210	2 3	..	3 33	5 59	..	7 11	9 23	..	9 30	..	4 17	9 4
2½	Fittleworth	8 25	9 56	11 6	1217	2 9	..	3 39	6 5	..	7 18	9 30	..	9 37	..	4 25	9 12
5½	Petworth	8 32	10 2	1112	1223	2 15	..	3 47	6 11	..	7 25	9 36	..	9 43	..	4 31	9 18
7½	Selham	8 39	10 8	1118	1229	2 21	..	3 56	6 18	..	7 32	9 42	..	9 49	..	4 37	9 29
11	Midhurst 182 ...... { arr.	8 47	1015	1125	1236	2 28	..	4 5	6 26	..	7 41	9 49	..	9 53	..	4 45	9 41
	{ dep.	8 56	1017	1127	1256	2 34	..	4 32	6 28	..	7 55	..	..	..	..	..
13½	Cocking	9 3	1024	1134	1 3	2 41	..	4 38	6 36	..	8 3	..	..	..	..	..
16½	Singleton	9 10	1031	1141	1 10	2 48	..	4 46	6 43	..	8 10	..	..	..	..	..
19½	Lavant 1086	9 17	1037	1147	1 17	2 54	..	4 52	6 49	..	8 16	..	..	..	..	..
23	Chichester 250. 258, arr.	9 25	1044	1155	1 25	3 1	..	5 0	6 57	..	8 24	..	..	..	..	..
02½	229 LONDON BRIDGE ...... arr.	..	..	..	4 14	..	..	..	..	..	..	..	..	..	..	..
92½	229 VICTORIA .... ''	12 21	..	..	..	..	7 33	10 1	..	..	..	..	..	..	..	..

Miles.	Up.				Week Days.								Sundays.		
		mrn	mrn	mrn	mrn		aft	mrn	aft		aft	aft	aft		mrn	mrn	aft
	218 VICTORIA ....dep.	..	..	..	..	..	11s30	..	..	3 20	4 53	..	..	..	..	..	..
	218 LONDON BRIDGE ''	..	..	..	..	..	..	..	..	..	4e50	..	..	..	..	..	..
	Chichester ....dep.	..	8 15	9 40	10 55	..	1210	1 56	3 55	..	5 45	7 25	..	..	..	..	..
3½	Lavant	..	8 22	9 46	11 2	..	1216	2 2	4 1	..	5 52	7 32	..	..	..	..	..
6½	Singleton	..	8 31	9 54	11 10	..	1224	2 11	4 9	..	6 1	7 40	..	..	..	..	..
9½	Cocking	..	8 39	10 1	11 17	..	1231	2 19	4 16	..	6 8	7 47	..	..	..	..	..
12	Midhurst 182 ...... { arr.	..	8 47	10 7	11 23	..	1237	2 26	4 23	..	6 15	7 53	..	..	..	..	..
	{ dep.	7 23	9 16	1017	11 28	..	1239	2 30	4 35	..	6 28	7 55	10 0	..	6 50	1010	4 55
15½	Selham	7 30	9 25	1025	11 36	..	1246	2 38	4 44	..	6 37	2 10 s 6	..	..	6 57	1017	5 2
17½	Petworth	7 38	9 31	1031	11 42	..	1252	2 44	4 53	..	6 43	8 10 12	..	..	7 6	1023	5 11
20½	Fittleworth	7 45	9 39	1037	11 48	..	1258	2 51	5 1	..	6 49	8 14	..	..	7 14	1029	5 17
23	Pulborough C 218, 229. arr.	7 55	9 50	1046	11 55	..	1 5	2 59	5 11	..	6 57	8 22 10 24	..	..	7 24	1037	5 29
73	229 LONDON BRIDGE ...... arr.	9 58	..	..	..	..	3s31	..	..	..	..	..	..	..	7 58	..	..
73½	229 VICTORIA .... ''	1028	1153	1221	..	..	4 46	7 33	..	..	10 1	..	..	..	9 30	..	7 50

A Change at Three Bridges and Horsham.

a Arrives at 3 36 aft. on Saturdays.

C Station for Storrington (5 miles).

e Except Saturdays.

s Saturdays only.

☞ **For other Trains**

BETWEEN .... PAGE

Pulborough and Chichester 218

130

13. Chichester to Midhurst

THE last of the three railway lines to reach Midhurst was the Chichester & Midhurst Railway. That such a relatively small market town should be the focal point of three railways was not only remarkable but was testimony to the fact that its position was adjacent to the boundary between the London, Brighton & South Coast Railway and the London & South Western Railway.

Way back in 1845 Midhurst could have been an important point on the proposed Guildford, Godalming, Chichester, Portsmouth and Fareham line, but that railway never materialised. In terms of land ownership, in the general Midhurst area and in the key surrounding towns, there were numerous country houses of note and large estates, owned by the upper echelons of society. These landowners were extremely powerful and this resulted in the railway seeking their support and assuring them that their affluence would be enhanced by more efficient transportation systems.

Also, it would be this very aristocracy that would be approached as potential shareholders of any railway company. Accordingly it would have been unwise for the railway company to ride roughshod over them, even though some of their demands were pompous in the extreme, such as insisting that the railway tunnelled beneath their land to keep it from their view.

Included in this roll of aristocracy were the Duke of Richmond and Gordon (Goodwood), the Montague family (Cowdray House), the Earls of Egmont (Cowdray Park), Lord Leconfield (Drove House) and Lord Selsey (West Dean House), to name but a few. The surrounding towns were ancient, with Chichester Cathedral having been founded in 1075. The LBSCR first reached Chichester as part of its drive along the coast from Brighton to Portsmouth in 1846. Having secured the growing town of Brighton, the LBSCR wanted to reach Portsmouth before any other railway, even though

Below:
The line from Brighton to Portsmouth reached Chichester in 1846. There had been calls for a rail connection from the City of Chichester to Midhurst for many years, but it was 1881 before a line via Lavant, Singleton and Cocking was opened. At Chichester the Midhurst trains normally used the up bay platform (see the map on page 120). At the end of the line's life only a section from Fishbourne Junction, Chichester, to Lavant was open, mainly for coal and sugar beet, but at the very end for gravel trains. Backlit by the February sunshine, a Class 73 working on diesel power leaves Chichester and makes for Lavant with empty hoppers in 1988. *JV/TTT*

the LSWR had reached nearby Gosport as early as 1841. In the process the City of Chichester would be served and this was a welcome bonus for the area.

The Duke of Richmond was especially keen on the Guildford, Chichester, Portsmouth and Fareham railway proposal because its route would pass though his lands and serve the famous Goodwood racecourse. However, the line was not free from opposition in respect of other proposals. This was the height of railway mania, when numerous schemes were tabled linking places such as Redhill and Godalming with Midhurst and Chichester. Gradually the recession of the mid-1860s took its toll and many of the schemes, some of which were unlikely ever to be profitable, were abandoned.

As mentioned in Chapter 12, the main proposal potentially affecting Midhurst and Chichester was the Mid-Sussex Railway, authorised by an Act in 1857 and completed as far as Petworth in 1859. The Mayor of Chichester and his cronies then got together to propose an extension from Petworth (Coultershaw Mill) to Chichester, although, at least temporarily, the short-term terminus might have been near Cocking Causeway. However, the Mid-Sussex Railway already had a much easier rail route to the coast on the stocks, via Amberley and Arundel, so for it to put serious effort into a much more costly alternative was at that stage wishful thinking. Mention should be made of one Henry Bird, an engineer who, year after year, tried to promote a line from Bognor to Midhurst, but each year his plans, which were slightly altered annually, were rejected through lack of interest. Finally, when the LBSCR plan for a branch from Bognor to Barnham was approved, he reluctantly had to give up his proposals.

However, Bird was tenacious and one of his plans, to link Chichester with Midhurst, found particular favour with 80% of affected landowners. Typical of those imposing their individuality on the situation was one Colonel Wyndham, dubbed Lord Leconfield in 1859, who insisted that as the railway, due to pass near his Drove House near Singleton, would be an eyesore, it would have to be submerged in a tunnel. It seems extraordinary in this day and age that established aristocrats should have been able to exercise a veto of this magnitude. In today's world the land would have been compulsorily purchased and unreasonable objections summarily dismissed. Eventually an LBSCR route won the day, with strong links to the original Mid-Sussex & Midhurst Junction Railway. Originally the junctions at Midhurst were to serve the line to Petworth and Pulborough and that to Petersfield, which had been completed in 1864 and 1866 respectively. In the Act it did not specify where Lavant station, on the Duke of Richmond's land, should be built, but it was to be 'agreed with the Duke' and 'all trains shall stop at such station for the purpose of taking up and setting down passengers'. An extension had been planned north of Midhurst whereby the new line would terminate near Haslemere station, and although both the LBSCR and the LSWR objected to the extension, all objections were later withdrawn and the Chichester & Midhurst (Extension) Act was passed on 5 July 1865. The total length of the new railway was 20 miles. A first sod was cut on Cocking Causeway, about 2 miles south of Midhurst, to great merriment with all the usual celebrations and a crowd of dignitaries, who would rival a Goodwood horse race meeting!

A surprise move by the South Eastern Railway for a line from Dorking to Midhurst resulted in the LBSCR almost panicking into the purchase of the necessary Chichester to Midhurst land, while the great recession of 1866 resulted in the abandonment of the Haslemere extension, which was never built, and the suspension of all work on the Midhurst to Chichester extension, as there was simply no venture capital to be spared. After long delays, when no work was undertaken and powers had lapsed, the LBSCR received Royal Assent in 1876 for its 'LBSCR (Chichester & Midhurst Railway) Act', the old 1864 Act being effectively dissolved. A deviation

Act followed in 1877 and the company was given four years to complete the line. The LSWR was upset by the fact that the junction of the new line at Midhurst would face Pulborough and therefore favour the Brighton company in terms of through-running potential. The new line would be 11 miles and 16 chains in length. Most of the works were built, somewhat optimistically, to accommodate double track, but other works, including tunnels, were single track only. The line was very expensive to build and, with three tunnels and deep cuttings, as well as the multitude of requirements demanded by the various landowners, the total bill was a staggering £291,546, twice the cost per mile of the average railway.

There was a rush to have the line opened in time for the Goodwood race season in 1881, but there were a number of serious deficiencies and permission was declined. Also, the Inspector was most unhappy about the location of the respective Midhurst stations. The LSWR and LBSCR stations were already more than 130yd apart, and after the 1881 changes, when the LBSCR station was moved to accommodate the new line from Chichester, they were no less than 450yd apart. The line from Chichester to Midhurst was opened to both passenger and goods traffic from Monday 11 July 1881. A total of 57 passengers travelled on the first train, and the locomotive, Craven single-driver No 222, was decorated by a wreath of flowers, but the grand opening did not compare with other lines in the area. This may have been because the LBSCR had publicly expressed misgivings about capital expenditure on the line. The service trains for the rest of the day were reported as being 'well patronised'.

In the early years the line from Midhurst did not form an actual junction with the LBSCR Brighton to Portsmouth line at Fishbourne (located some distance east of the much later Fishbourne Halt), but used a third line especially built for the exclusive use of Midhurst line trains, which ran into their own bay platform at Chichester; this was not the same bay as was used in later years after the station was rebuilt. Chichester was a busy place, not only because it had a population of over 12,000 people, but because it was also the junction for the Hundred of Manhood & Selsey Tramway and the gateway for the whole of the Selsey peninsula (see Chapter 11). Chichester had a large goods yard and, slightly unusual for this country, a 'Y' for turning locomotives. There were several local industries, many with their own sidings, and just to the north of the town was the famous Goodwood racecourse (and in later years the Goodwood motor-racing circuit). Nowadays there is the bizarre situation at Goodwood of the German BMW Corporation building Rolls-Royce cars in the Sussex countryside, near Westhampnett, a wartime fighter station where Rolls-Royce engines had powered the Hurricanes and Spitfires that had fought against the Luftwaffe some 60 years earlier! As they say, 'it's a funny old world', but the employment opportunities are welcome and World War 2 is now a very long time ago.

From the junction at Fishbourne, 59 chains from Chichester, the line climbed at 1 in 76 to reach Lavant, 3 miles and 31 chains from Fishbourne. Lavant was never a passing place as such, but a second line, without a platform, was later installed to assist with goods train movements and run-rounds. Also, many years later a siding over half a mile long south-east of Lavant was laid by the LBSCR to a gravel pit, and there was a further siding, where the goods yard eventually became established, to the north-west. The station was substantial, built on the lines and scale of the 'Cuckoo line' structures, and a 16-lever signalbox stood opposite the station on the down side. In the last years of the line's life Lavant became the sole source of income, and we will return to those activities later.

North of Lavant the line travelled through pleasant country and, after passing under the Chichester to Midhurst road, entered the 445yd West Dean Tunnel, still climbing at 1 in 75 to reach Singleton station. Singleton was to have the great distinction of being the station associated with the horse-race meetings at Goodwood.

Above:
A busy scene at Fishbourne in July 1988 finds a named Class 73/1 coming off the Lavant branch (formerly the Midhurst line) with an 880-ton trailing load. The train is destined for Drayton to the east of Chichester, where the hopper doors will be activated during the unloading process. About four trains per weekday worked the service. At this date the infrastructure included manual crossing gates and semaphore signalling. The road crossing is now used only by pedestrians. *JV/TTT*

Right:
On 3 October 1965 the LCGB ran its 'Vectis Farewell Rail Tour', which incorporated the Lavant branch in its itinerary before continuing to Portsmouth Harbour for a visit to the remaining railways on the Isle of Wight. A pair of Bulleid 'Q1' class locomotives, including No 33020, were diagrammed over the branch to 'top and tail' the special. The trackbed here is now a foot and cycle path. *Gavin Morrison*

As mentioned earlier, the West Sussex aristocracy had enormous influence, and with its tree-lined station approach, long twin island platforms, commodious sidings, waiting rooms with stained glass windows, and extensive 25ft-long buffet with marble bar, for many years Singleton was a special place that was regularly visited by Royalty. The platforms were connected by subway and long awnings protected the VIPs from the inclement climatic conditions that can sometimes affect the South Downs. There were two signalboxes, a turntable, water tank, goods yard, loading dock and no less than ¾ miles of siding to accommodate the many race-day specials.

North of Singleton the summit of the line was reached at the beginning of the 741yd Singleton or Drove Tunnel. After the summit the line dropped at a sharp 1 in 60, the steepest gradient on the line, through the 738yd Cocking Tunnel to the substantial Cocking station, some ½ mile north and 9 miles and 51 chains from Chichester. The fine station building boasted a 16-lever signalbox

and there was a small goods yard on the down side to the east of the line. There was also an adjacent siding that the railway had to provide as a condition of the land being sold by Lord Egmont. North of Cocking the line descended more gradually to Midhurst, at 12 miles 3 chains. The whole of the route was rural and picturesque, and ended on a tight 10-chain-radius curve, which carried a 20mph limit. A description of the new 1881 Midhurst station is included in Chapter 12. As mentioned elsewhere, there were complaints that passengers had too long a journey between the LSWR station and the new LBSCR one, especially after 1881, and only a partially covered walkway was ever provided until 1925 when, under the auspices of the SR, the LSWR station closed.

In 1901 it was proposed to build a station at Brandyhole Lane Bridge between Fishbourne and Lavant, but this came to nothing. In 1888 there were six trains per day in each direction between Chichester and Midhurst with one extra up train on Wednesdays.

Above:

Class 33 and 73 locomotives worked the gravel trains from Lavant to Drayton, and a new section of line that sharply descended from the old branch alignment to the loading mechanism had to be built just south of Lavant station. The conveyor transported the gravel a considerable distance from the quarry to the loader, which on this November day in 1984 was being visited by Class 73/1 No 73112. Note the overbridge, top right, spanning the original trackbed. *JV/TTT*

Below:

Prior to the gravel traffic, Lavant was the freight terminus of the line from 1953 until formal closure took place in January 1970. Although some sugar beet was loaded at Lavant at the end of the 1969 season, the very last *scheduled* freight train ran on 3 August 1968; until that date small amounts of coal had been delivered to Lavant. Having motorcycled to Lavant, the author recorded the last train — a single coal empty and the mandatory brake-van — leaving the site behind Class 08 No D3226 (later No 08158). There are at least five people on the footplate and others on the brake-van veranda! *JV/TTT*

Right:
Although passenger trains between Chichester and Midhurst succumbed to bus competition as long ago as 6 July 1935, freight continued to run. However, this was cut back to Cocking when the line to Midhurst was severed in 1951. This wonderful picture, which dates back to 23 April 1937, captures 'C2X' class No 2548 powering the 9.25am Chichester to Midhurst goods through Lavant. A run-round loop was later installed in the foreground. Lavant station survives in extended form and is now surrounded by other houses. *IAL*

There was no Sunday service. Market days and Goodwood race days were the busiest, and at times there were so many trains and horseboxes at Singleton that some had to be unloaded at nearby Lavant. There were plenty of staff on the line and all stations had a full complement, including station masters, leading porters, signalmen/porters, and booking office clerks. In 1896 the Prince and Princess of Wales visited Singleton with their family, together with some of the Danish aristocracy. They again visited Singleton in race week during 1899, but did not return on the train with the Royal party as they went on to Cowes Regatta. In November 1900 the pheasant population had a lucky break when King Edward VII was unwell and did not attend a local shoot; he did not take part in a further Sussex shoot until 1904. Security seemed to be a problem even in those far-off days, as no member of the public was allowed on the platform when Royalty was about! In 1906 the King visited Midhurst to open the new, large sanatorium. It was hard-hat time for the poor old pheasants again in 1906 and 1909 when King Edward VII and a large entourage visited the West Dean estate at Singleton for another shoot. It must have been reassuring for the locals that there was nothing happening on the international scene to divert participants from these Sussex junkets.

The Chichester to Midhurst line continued in existence as a rural branch with many trains working through to and from Pulborough. There were general goods, but the main volumes were associated with seasonal produce, especially sugar beet. A regular daily load included large numbers of milk churns from most stations. Most other loads were common to a rural agricultural community and included incoming coal, fertilisers and animal foodstuffs, together with outgoing farm produce, livestock and timber. Some of the race-day traffic did not touch the branch line at all, as passengers were encouraged to embark at Chichester and Drayton for a road transport connection to Goodwood.

Passenger loadings on the line were never heavy and, despite the grand stations on the line (especially compared with the Pulborough to Midhurst intermediate stations), the connections with Goodwood, the races, Royalty and average goods loadings, the line could never be called a success. It had to some extent always been a strategic line that was heavily influenced by the 'Brighton', but even at an early date loadings were light. In 1927 there were eight trains in each direction, all running broadly between the hours of 8am and 8pm. There was still no Sunday service. Under the newly formed Southern Railway in 1923

economies started to be made. The age-old nonsense of passengers having to walk between the stations at Midhurst ceased when the LSWR station was closed and the short link line between the former rival railways was strengthened to carry locomotives. A number of signalboxes were closed, especially where they did not perform the role of block post, and the complete staff was withdrawn from a number of intermediate stations, such as Cocking, in 1932. The largest ballast pit at Lavant was worked out and had closed by 1932, and the private siding was removed from Cocking. The decline continued, with all station master posts being abolished in the early 1930s except for that at Midhurst, who then assumed responsibility for all stations. From June 1932 booking offices were permanently closed and all tickets were issued on the trains, which were mostly two-car push-pull units.

Gradually horsebox specials and race-goers' specials ceased to run to Singleton, and although it remained a special place, by the late Edwardian era most of the aristocracy had limousines and chauffeurs and the railway's glory days declined. The turntable was removed in the 1920s. Although an accommodation coach continued to be provided for the extra staff needed during race week (more than 20 were required for the week), in about 1930 the large refreshment rooms finally closed. Everywhere that the keen observer looked, the line was in decline. The block section was now Chichester to Midhurst, although goods trains could be 'put away' at a couple of locations. One Lavant employee recalled that while goods continued to raise revenue for the railway, he took only about £5 per month in passenger takings. Bus competition was taking a great toll, with Southdown Motor Services providing a reliable service and running through the centre of the towns and villages on the line. To eliminate the large losses there was no alternative but to close the Chichester to Midhurst line to passengers, and the last train ran on 6 July 1935.

Goods continued to thrive, however, and a daily goods train ran from Chichester to Horsham. Inward and outward commodities included fodder, hay, straw, sand, sugar beet, parcels, pit props (from Singleton), bricks and horseboxes (for polo ponies at Midhurst rather than racehorses at Singleton). The line struggled on to World War 2, when the long tunnels on the line were used for storing ammunition trains; naval guards were always present at the tunnel mouths when trains were hiding from the Luftwaffe. At this time metal doors were fitted to each end of Singleton and Cocking tunnels, and these were left *in situ*, in the open position, after the war.

Top right:
There is absolutely no doubt that this is the Royal Train. Adorned with special lamps and headcode discs, together with a magnificent coat of arms — note the orb in front of the chimney! — LBSCR 'B4' Class No 60 *Kimberley* poses by the running-in board at Singleton. The occasion was the visit by King Edward VII to West Dean House, near Singleton; the usual reason for such a visit was to have a day at the races at nearby Goodwood. *IAL*

Centre right:
Singleton was a lavish station that was riddled with excesses compared with any other country station. There were two long island platforms, providing four platform faces, sufficient siding space to accommodate no fewer than 14 trains, an ornate goods shed, two signalboxes and a splendid tile-hung station building.
There was even a refreshment room with a marble-topped counter. The track was at a much higher level than the station buildings, and grand subways, which survive to this day, gave access to the platforms. This view, looking south towards West Dean Tunnel, shows the station stripped of its finery in 1947. *IAL*

Lower right:
In this tremendous panorama from the north end of Singleton station, the signal in the distance is in the 'off' position for a down train, while the daily freight is indulging in a little shunting activity on the right. The signalboxes closed in 1933, when the lovely 'Brighton' lower-quadrant signals seen here were removed. The station staff have had the time to plant rose bushes beneath the running-in board. *IAL*

Top right:
There seem to be sleepers across the line to the north of Cocking station, and this would date the photograph to 1952, a year after the line to the north was closed but before the goods service to Cocking finished. By this time the signalbox, which was located at the down end of the platform on the right, had been dismantled. The goods yard was to the right of this view. *IAL*

Centre right:
The old expression 'getting yourself into a hole' would seem to apply here. On 19 November 1951 heavy rain and a blocked culvert conspired to wash away a railway embankment about ½ mile south of Midhurst station. As 'C2X' class No 32522 trundled along the line the crew jumped clear before the locomotive plunged into the cavernous pit. The coal wagon behind the locomotive was reduced to matchwood, as can be seen in this graphic picture.
The locomotive was not recovered until 25 February 1952. Sid Nash recorded the scene on 2 December 1951.
S. C. Nash

Lower right:
This panorama shows the west end of the LBSCR station at Midhurst to great effect. From left to right, a two-coach 'D3' class-hauled train from Chichester is arriving and has the road to enter the station, the LSWR station is just to the right of the splitting signals, then come the LBSCR goods shed, yard, engine shed and water tank, on the extreme right. This undated photograph was probably taken in the mid-1920s because the locomotive is in a fresh coat of paint in SR (post-1923) livery. *IAL*

After the end of hostilities the freight service continued. One new development was track and loading dock modifications at Lavant to cater for the burgeoning sugar beet business. This was at its busiest between September and December, but the Midhurst goods was always regarded as something of a day out, with much freedom afforded to the train crew, who had complete possession of the line (no mobile phones in those far-off days!). However, the tranquillity of this working was to come to an abrupt end when on a stormy night in November 1951 floods washed away the trackbed near Midhurst, leaving the line suspended 20ft in the air. The next morning, the 9.30am goods from Chichester was approaching Midhurst with eight wagons and a brake-van in tow when the footplate crew saw the gap and jumped clear, leaving the locomotive to plummet into the chasm followed by one of its wagons containing 10 tons of coal, which piled up around the firebox and ignited. Although the damaged wagons were recovered easily by breakdown crane, it was February 1952, some three months later, before the locomotive and tender were rescued. Surprisingly, by May 1952 the 'C2X', No 32522, had been repaired, although attached to something of a hybrid tender. It was not finally withdrawn until 1962.

However, much damage had been done to the trackbed and it was simply impracticable in both engineering and financial terms to repair the line. The annual deficit spiralled to £19,000, and from 28 August 1957 both Cocking and Singleton station (sites) closed, leaving Lavant as the railhead. With just the Lavant freight to contend with, the third parallel 'Midhurst' line across Fishbourne crossing was lifted. As mentioned in earlier chapters, all goods had gone from the other Midhurst lines by 1966, and Lavant became the sugar beet concentration depot for the whole of this part of Sussex following the cessation of loading at Chichester, Barnham and Drayton. During the season some 40 wagons forming two trains per day became a regular feature.

There was also some regular freight traffic to Lavant, but this became very sporadic and sometimes more than a week could pass without any traffic. The track became very weed-covered, but nevertheless the remaining stub from Chichester was in demand for railway enthusiasts' specials. By this time much of the sugar beet was being conveyed by lorry without transhipment to rail. Also there had been one or two disastrous industrial disputes when the train drivers' union, ASLEF, had pressed the self-destruct button, especially in respect of marginal activities such as local sugar beet, where the customer really did have a choice. Accordingly, the last scheduled goods train to Lavant station ran on 3 August 1968, the unscheduled sugar beet trains finished in January 1970, and the line was mothballed.

This should have been the end of the old Chichester & Midhurst Railway story, but like the phoenix rising from the ashes in 1972 the Parker Concrete Group started to excavate gravel from a site west-south-west of Lavant. The gravel was to be conveyed by a ½-mile-long conveyor belt system to a site immediately adjacent to the old branch line, south of Lavant station. The gravel was to be conveyed by train to Drayton, but at Lavant a siding at a much lower level than the old branch was required, necessitating a steep gradient for loaded trains to regain the alignment of the branch. The entire site would be over 500 acres. The trains, of 900 to 1,000 tons, would carry as much as 30 loaded lorries. Despite these advantages, the usual crop of 'nimbys' ('not in my back yard') appeared, but their selfish objections were dismissed and work on the revitalised branch continued apace. A run-round loop was created between Brandyhole Lane Bridge and Snakes Lane Bridge (now Hunters Race), and in 1978 more than half a million tons of aggregate was carried along the 6-mile route to Drayton on the east side of Chichester. Due to supply and demand variations in the local area, the operation ceased in 1981, but recommenced in 1983. On 11 July 1981 Middleton Press sponsored a series of centenary specials using a three-car English Electric diesel-electric

multiple-unit, which travelled as far as the Brandyhole Lane run-round loop.

The aggregate trains continued to work from Lavant to Drayton until the end of the 1980s, when gravel extraction and transportation became an uneconomic operation and it duly succumbed. This really was the end of the Chichester to Midhurst branch, and the remnant of trackbed was converted to a splendid paved nature trail where pedestrians, cyclists and the equestrian community can remove themselves completely from the local traffic and enjoy a run along the old trackbed to Lavant and beyond.

As with the other lines working to Midhurst, dealt with in the last chapter, other than for very early LBSCR types such as 2-2-2s and 4-4-0s and the 'B4s' that worked race-day specials, there was not a huge variety of motive power on the line. Locomotives of the 'D' class and its derivatives performed sterling work for many years, together with 'E4' tank engines. By chance, two of the 'D' class locomotives carried local names, *Singleton* and *Lavant*. LSWR 'M7s' were more regularly seen on the Petersfield to Midhurst line, and later the Midhurst to Pulborough section, due simply to the early parentage of the lines and the early demise of the Chichester section. Freight traffic seemed to be the preserve of the LBSCR 'C2X' class, although in later years both 'Q' and 'Q1' classes appeared. An English Electric 3H diesel-electric multiple-unit worked the centenary train, and the Lavant freights in later years were worked by a Class 08 shunter, but once the aggregate trains ran to the new loading terminal Class 73 electro-diesel and Class 33 diesels were the regular source of power.

There had been many changes at Chichester over the years and, needless to say, the track layout has reflected the changing scene. As mentioned in Chapter 11, the Selsey Tramway occupied most of the site south of Chichester station. There were three important industrial sidings to the west of the city: Drayton aggregates, Portfield Oil and Bartholomew's Animal Feedstuffs. There was a large goods yard on the north side of the line west of the station, and a large 'Y' for turning locomotives. At the station there were down bays for Midhurst trains on the north side, and a bay for Portsmouth 'shorts' on the south side. Even in the late 1980s part of the old goods yard was being used for loading timber, which had become available on the estates after the great storm of 1987. Sadly, most of the land has now been sold off and supermarkets and other retail outlets now cover the space once occupied by goods wagons. There are still sidings to the west of Chichester, but these are unused, except for occasionally berthing engineering trains. The sidings to the east of the city are now all disused, with the aggregate traffic having finished the same day as Lavant workings, while other commodities are either distributed from elsewhere or are road-hauled.

Although a tiny piece of the old Lavant branch track remains at Fishbourne Junction, and there is a telegraph pole or two along the way, the cycle path to Lavant is a pleasant and rural journey. North of Lavant one gains the impression of what a heavily engineered line the old Midhurst route was. With tunnels, embankments and cuttings, it is easy to see how the line cost so much to construct, but more difficult to see how even the LBSCR's boundary delineation efforts justified the expenditure involved. The tunnels have seen commercial use since closure, including the growing of mushrooms in West Dean Tunnel. The awning at Lavant was removed to the Bluebell Railway and preserved. A very popular tourist attraction near to the line is the Singleton Open Air Museum, where a variety of ancient rural buildings ranging from everyday homes to small mills, factories and outbuildings have been preserved. It is strange to relate that, with the sole exception of Midhurst, all the LBSCR stations are still standing, and most are well-cared-for private residences. I personally travelled only from Chichester to Lavant in the brake-van of the thrice weekly sugar beet freight, together with the centenary special to Lavant, but the line provides many happy memories for a photographer of railways.

14. Petersfield to Midhurst

BY way of background, the LSWR's 'Portsmouth Direct' line, which connected London and Guildford with Havant and Portsmouth, via Petersfield, opened at the end of 1858. By a previous agreement that emerged from LBSCR and LSWR negotiations over access to Portsmouth in the 1840s, Midhurst (or more accurately a line from Godalming to Midhurst and Chichester) became the westerly limit of the LBSCR in the area and also the easterly limit of the LSWR. Neither company was permitted to extend its lines beyond the market town of Midhurst.

In 1860 a Petersfield Railway Company was authorised with the objective of building a standard gauge railway from the LSWR at Petersfield to Midhurst. The progress made by the company, with the full backing of the LSWR, was faster than the Mid-Sussex & Midhurst Junction Railway's efforts to extend the line from Petworth to Midhurst. From the LBSCR's Mid-Sussex line, the line had reached Petworth in 1859, but it was to be a full seven years before the formalities and the finance were completed and the line to Midhurst was constructed and opened. As it was, the LSWR

absorbed the Petersfield Railway Company in 1863, and when the 9¾-mile line finally opened on 1 September 1864 it was wholly owned and operated by the LSWR. Due to the LSWR/LBSCR boundary issue, the LSWR built its own station, goods yard, goods shed and engine shed at Midhurst. These were quite separate from the LBSCR facilities, although an 11-chain connection for the interchange of goods was provided. This connection ran over a weak bridge and locomotives were not allowed over the line, so goods wagons were either horse-drawn or fly-shunted between the railways. When the line was first opened, Midhurst was described as being the station for Petworth, some 5¾ miles distant, but then the limit of the LBSCR line!

The branch junction at Petersfield trailed in to join the down main line. At Petersfield there was a substantial station building on the down side and an adjacent down platform, while on the up side was a large island platform with commodious awning, waiting rooms, etc. The main road to Winchester crossed the railway immediately north of the station and Petersfield Junction signalbox

Below:
The third route to Midhurst featured here — but the first to arrive at the town — was the LSWR line from Petersfield. In the early days the branch trains used the main Portsmouth Direct line station, but eventually a bay platform north of the road crossing, seen in the foreground, was constructed. In this view, looking north, the push-pull branch train pauses at the bay and will shortly depart under the distant right-hand overbridge. Note the dozen milk churns in the shadows on the platform. *IAL*

141

controlled the crossing gates over the road. There was a second signalbox at the south-west end of the station where access to both up and down sidings and the goods yard was gained. In the early days the Midhurst branch trains used the outer face of the island platform, but at a later date a very basic wooden and shelter-less bay platform, north-west of the crossing and therefore detached from the main station complex, was provided for the use of Midhurst trains. This had the advantage of branch trains operating without interruption to road traffic or to trains on the main line. However, particularly during the 1920s and 1930s, some branch trains used the main-line platforms on Sundays because they ran to and from Portsmouth; for example, in 1927 the 2pm from Portsmouth & Southsea arrived at Petersfield at 2.43pm, departing for Midhurst at 2.47pm, where it arrived at 3.9pm. This practice ended with the electrification of the 'Portsmouth Direct' line in 1937. Partly behind the bay platform there was a short siding that served a dairy, while running parallel to the branch and curving towards Midhurst was another siding that served a rubber works.

On leaving Petersfield it was not long before trains found themselves in open farmland. In the early days the branch skirted the north of Petersfield, but inevitably housing development spread along each side of the trackbed. The branch had two intermediate stations, at Rogate — at various times known as Rogate & Harting and Rogate for Harting — and, further east, Elsted. The stations could not have been more inconveniently located for the villages shown on the running-in boards. Rogate, which including the surrounding area had a population of 940 in 1901, was 1¼ miles from the station, while Harting, with a population of 1,238, was

approximately 1¾ miles distant. However, Harting included a village and two hamlets: South, East and West Harting. The station had up and down platforms and was a passing place on the single-track branch until the signalbox closed in 1932; however, the second road was retained to facilitate shunting operations. The signalbox was located at the east end of the down platform and after closure was used as a ground frame for the small goods yard. The station, which was 4¼ miles from Petersfield, had no awning, but on the up side there was a small shelter with a roof that covered part of the platform. The cluster of houses and other buildings by the station formed the hamlet of Nyewood. At the west end of the station, beyond a road overbridge, was a private siding to the Nyewood Brick & Tile Works. Nyewood is now best known as the home of Ballard's Brewery.

About 2 miles down the track towards Midhurst was Elsted station. The station building was identical to Rogate except it was built on the north side of the line. Again, the village was 1½ miles from the railway and the population in 1901 was a paltry 191 inhabitants. There was a small goods yard and adjacent brickworks, but there was never a passing loop and a signalbox was never provided, the points for the goods yard being controlled by a ground frame. The goods yard was at the east end of the site on the north side of the line. There was a small goods shed clad entirely in corrugated iron and a loading bay. Nearby was a small terrace of railway cottages that had their own wind pump and water tower.

Two miles further on, 9¼ miles from Petersfield, was the LSWR terminus at Midhurst. The LSWR route was the first to arrive at Midhurst, beating the LBSCR line by two years. The station

Below:
The signalbox that controls the busy road crossing was still in action in February 1987 as a 'large logo'-liveried Class 47 thundered past with a southbound inter-regional train that had worked via Reading and was bound for Portsmouth Harbour. The bridge is still intact but the branch track was removed after complete closure on 5 February 1955. *JV/TTT*

Upper right:
The first station out of Petersfield was Rogate, which was actually in the village of Nyewood even though it was variously known as Rogate for Harting, Rogate & Harting and just plain Rogate. The villages of both Rogate and Harting were well over a mile from the station. There was a brickworks siding here and a small goods yard. The signalbox had been reduced to ground frame status in 1932, but when photographed on 25 April 1953 it was still intact. This general view is looking towards Petersfield. In the early days both up and down platforms were used.
S. C. Nash

Lower right:
This view of Elsted station is also dated 25 April 1953. The station was identical to Rogate, but was located on the opposite, north, side of the track. Again the village was a mile from the station, which hardly encouraged passengers, especially once alternatives became available. On the north side of the line was a two-road goods yard and a loading dock stub. Only a single platform face was provided here. *S. C. Nash*

Below:
In this March 2003 view looking towards Midhurst, the old goods yard was still a hive of industry, but it had nothing to do with the railway. The old loading dock was still extant and the old railway cottages survive, but the branch on the right, with the trackbed disappearing into the distance, has long gone. *JV*

building was larger than those provided at the intermediate stations because it housed the station master and his family. Unlike the other two stations, a large canopy was added in 1881 for the protection of passengers, but there was merely a single, slightly curved, platform face. There were two cottages for railway employees just a few yards from the station. Just outside the station was a siding serving Midhurst Whites Brickworks, and a brick-built single-road locomotive shed with an integral water tank located on the roof, which was in use until 1937. In the early days locomotives could be turned on a turntable but this was removed in the 1920s. An LSWR signalbox was located at the point where the LSWR goods yard fanned out into a number of sidings, on the north side of the line. A large brick goods shed was provided, as was a yard crane and a cattle pen.

By a directive of the Southern Railway the LSWR station and signalbox were taken out of use in 1925, when all services used the LBSCR station. For years passengers had complained that the journey between the stations was too long, especially in inclement weather and particularly after 1881, when the LBSCR moved its station some ¼ mile further east, so that it could be used by trains from the then new line to Chichester. For the convenience of passengers a new road was built in 1895 and adopted by Midhurst

Rural District Council in 1899, but even that failed to compare with a single station for all, which was available from 1925. After 1925 Petersfield trains worked into and out of the bay platform at the former LBSCR station, although after the Chichester line closed to passengers in 1935 Petersfield to Pulborough through trains obviously used the main platforms. In order to provide through running the weak bridge on the 11-chain connection between the former rival companies was rebuilt. From 1925 the platform road at the LSWR station was removed and the track slightly skewed on to the connecting line.

When the line opened there were five return journeys between Petersfield and Midhurst. By 1888 there were eight or nine trains in each direction on weekdays and three trains on Sundays. The journey time in that era for the 9¼-mile journey was precisely half an hour. By 1927 there were 10 or 11 trains in each direction except for Saturdays when an extra late-night revellers' train ran, leaving Petersfield at 9.30pm and arriving at Midhurst at 9.52pm. The train returned from Midhurst at 10pm, arriving at Petersfield at 10.22pm. The trains of the 1920s gained 8 minutes in journey time over their Victorian predecessors, and by then the journey to the LBSCR station was slightly longer, at 9¾ miles! A delightful touch in the 1937 timetable shows the 8.45am from Petersfield to Midhurst

Upper left:
After the 1923 Grouping the Southern Railway saw no merit in having two Midhurst stations and consolidated activities on the LBSCR site. This made sense bearing in mind that the junction from Chichester directionally ran into the Brighton company's platforms. The LSWR station and signalbox closed on 4 April 1925, from which time Petersfield trains used the bay platform at the former rival station. Here the old abandoned station looks forlorn. The station canopy was added in 1881.
IAL

Lower left:
For many years locomotives were not allowed over the track that linked the LSWR and LBSCR lines. However, there were no such problems for 'M7' class No 30048 on 25 April 1953 as push-pull set No 731 was propelled up the climb from the ex-LBSCR station towards Petersfield. The old LSWR station can be seen on the extreme left. At this time there were nine trains per day over the line.
S. C. Nash

Above:
Once the line from Midhurst to Chichester closed to passengers, the majority of trains worked through from Pulborough to
Petersfield (rather than Chichester). This train is the 10.40am from Petersfield and the signals are 'off' for the through platform
road to Pulborough rather than the bay platform. Although by 4 February 1955, when the photograph was taken,
the Chichester line in the foreground had closed completely, the track was still *in situ*. *S. C. Nash*

running as a mixed train. It must have infuriated some passengers
on that train to arrive at Midhurst at 9.11am only to find that the
connection to Pulborough (and beyond) had left Midhurst at 9.5am,
and the next up train was at 10.10am. By 1950 there were either
eight or nine trains in each direction and four or five on Sundays. In
later years only Third Class accommodation was available on the
trains, which invariably comprised one- or two-coach push-pull
units, the latter starting to work the line from 1926. By 1951
Sunday trains had been withdrawn, a significant downturn for the
line and perhaps the sign of things to come. There was also a goods
working over the line once per day Mondays to Fridays.

Although it is possible to get the impression that the LSWR line
was a rather sleepy affair, a few statistics put a slightly different
complexion on the situation. In 1938, for example, 2,660 tickets
were issued at Elsted and 3,995 at Rogate. Elsted had 295 loaded
goods wagons arriving and 67 loaded wagons being despatched,
while Rogate received 467 loaded wagons and sent away 109 loaded.
Elsted received 842 parcels and sent 121, whereas Rogate received
1,738 and despatched 379. The problem with statistics is that,
divided by just weekdays, the 2,660 tickets issued at Elsted equates
to just nine per day, and 295 wagons received is only about one per
working day, Rogate's figures on the same basis being 13 tickets
per day and between one and two wagons per working day. Even
the seemingly impressive incoming parcels totals amounted to only
between two and five parcels per day. In these terms Elsted and
Rogate together issued 22 tickets per day and, based on an average
of 18 trains per day, this equates to only about one passenger per
train, although in reality peak periods probably saw several
passengers boarding, and off-peak services must, on occasions,
have stopped at the intermediate stations for no reason, hardly a
way to make money!

It became clear that the railways of Midhurst were losing money,
and by the mid-1950s the Southern Region of British Railways
decided to close the remaining routes from Petersfield to Midhurst
and from Midhurst to Pulborough. The important difference
between the lines was that the former LSWR section would close
completely from 7 May 1955, whereas the remaining LBSCR route
would lose its passenger trains but remain open for freight (see

Chapter 12). Freight on the LSWR section had been light for some
time and there are photographs showing just a locomotive and
brake-van traversing the route, presumably having taken just a
handful of wagons in one direction only. The last service trains ran
to Petersfield on 5 May 1955, and on 6 May a railway enthusiasts'
special, the 'Hampshireman' organised by the RCTS, with two
Class E5X locomotives working bunker to bunker, formed the last
train. The locomotives were removed at Petersfield and worked
back to Horsham over the route 'light engine'. The line remained *in
situ* for a short while and the District Engineer travelled over it on a
permanent way vehicle in 1956, after which the track was lifted.

The LSWR line to Midhurst had even less variety of motive
power than the LBSCR section. LSWR Beattie tanks and Adams
'T1' class worked the line in the early years, but for the majority of
the time passenger services were totally dominated by the 'M7'
class. The LSWR locomotive depot was originally a sub-shed of
Fratton, near Portsmouth, but from the date of electrification of the
'Portsmouth Direct' line the steam locomotive for the branch was
supplied by Guildford, and Midhurst shed closed. Various LSWR
types worked goods trains, but ex-LSWR 'Jubilee' class 'A12s'
were regulars. In later years, after the Grouping, LBSCR classes
such as 'E4', 'E5X' and 'C2X' worked over the line on goods, and
the Southern Railway 'Q' class also popped up from time to time.
As the line closed in 1955, diesels never featured in the motive
power roll-call.

Nearly 50 years after closure there is very little to show that the
line from Petersfield to Midhurst ever existed. The site of the old
branch platform at Petersfield is obvious and one of the arches in a
road bridge to the north-east of the crossing clearly spanned the
branch track alignment (see photograph). The intermediate stations
have been demolished and most of the trackbed has truly gone back
to nature, although at Elsted the goods yard area is in commercial
use. The odd hedgerow and a shallow embankment here and there
delineate the alignment, but only the old LSWR terminus at
Midhurst remains. The station was near derelict for some time, but
it has been completely refurbished and enlarged, and is now used
as the headquarters offices of a civil and structural consulting
engineering company.

Upper left:
This view shows the general layout at the west end of Midhurst station. On the far right is the bay platform, just in front of the 47-lever signalbox, while in the foreground are the through lines. By this time the down starting signals were of the later upper-quadrant variety. The first train to reach Midhurst was in 1864, and the last train to leave was in 1964! *IAL*

Lower left:
Map showing the Petersfield to Midhurst line, and connecting lines.

Below:
This fascinating working timetable for down trains dates back to the summer of 1909.

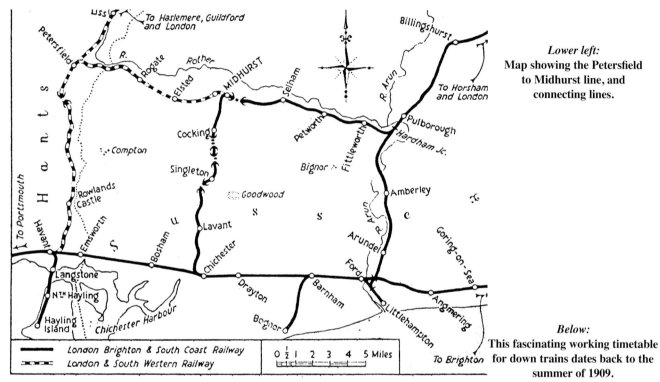

MIDHURST BRANCH.

FOR SPEED RESTRICTIONS SEE PAGES A, B, C, D, E, F & G.

This is a Single Line, and is worked under the Regulations for Working Single Lines by the Electric Train Tablet Block System.

Distance from Petersfield.		Nos.	1 Engine Weds. when required.	2 Goods & Pass.	3 Pass.	4	5 Pass.	6 Pass.	7 Goods.	8 Pass.	9 Pass.	10	11	12
		DOWN TRAINS. WEEK-DAYS.		B										
M.	C.		arr. dep. a.m. a.m.	arr. dep. a.m. a.m.	arr. dep. a.m. a.m.	arr. dep. a.m. a.m.	arr. dep. a.m. a.m.	arr. dep. a.m. p.m.	arr. dep. a.m. p.m.	arr. dep. p.m. p.m.	arr. dep. p.m. p.m.	arr. dep. p.m. p.m.	arr. dep. p.m. p.m.	
—	—	Waterloo..........	... ...	... 5 20	... 6 20	... ...	... 9A5	... 1114	... ...	... 1 20	... 3 45	... ...	... ...	
—	—	Petersfield........	... 6 25	... 8 3	... 9 12	... ...	11 12	11 28 1 28	... 1 40	... 3 55	... 5 21	... ...	... ...	
4	23	Rogate............	6 35	8 14 8 18	9 20 9 21	... ...	11 20 11 22	1 36 1 37	1 50 2 15	3 4	5 29 5 30	... ...	... ...	
6	22	Elsted	6 41	8 23 8 25	9 25 9 27	... ...	11 26 11 28	1 41 1 43	2 20 2 35	4	5 34 5 36	... ...	... ...	
9	27	Midhurst..........	6 48 ...	8 33 ...	9 33 ...	... ...	11 34 ...	1 49 ...	2 45 ...	4 16 ...	5 42 ...	... ...	... ...	

		Nos.	13 Pass.	14 Pass. and Milk Vans. June only.	15 Pass. and Milk Vans. Com. July.	16 Pass.	17		1 Pass.	2	3 Pass. & Milk Vans.	4 Pass.	5 Pass. & Milk Vans.	6	7
		DOWN TRAINS. WEEK-DAYS.						SUNDAYS.							
			arr. dep. p.m. p.m.	arr. dep. p.m. p.m.	arr. dep. p.m. p.m.	arr. dep. p.m. p.m.	arr. dep. p.m. p.m.		arr. dep. a.m. a.m.	arr. dep. a.m. a.m.	arr. dep. a.m. a.m.	arr. dep. p.m. p.m.	arr. dep. p.m. p.m.	arr. dep. p.m. p.m.	
		Waterloo..........	... 4 55	... 5 52	... 5 52	... 7 10	... ...		... ...	... 9 40	... 5 25	... 6 10	... ...	... ...	
		Petersfield......	... 6 34	... 7 55	... 8 0	... 9 38	... ...		... 8 45	... 1125	... 7 19	... 8 24	... ...	... ...	
		Rogate............	6 42 6 43	8 3 8 6	8 8 8 11	9 46 9 47	... ...		8 53 8 54	1133 1136	7 27 7 28	8 32 8 34	... ...	... ...	
		Elsted	6 47 6 49	8 10 8 13	8 15 8 18	9 51 9 53	... ...		8 58 9 0	1140 1143	7 32 7 33	8 38 8 41	... ...	... ...	
		Midhurst..........	6 55 ...	8 19 ...	8 24 ...	9 59 ...	... ...		9 6 ...	1149 ...	7 39 ...	8 47 ...	... ...	... ...	

15. Hayling Island Branch

HAYLING ISLAND on the Hampshire coastline is an 'island' only by virtue of a strip of water, which, even at high tide, required a railway bridge only 1,000ft in length to cross it. The road builders were first to arrive when, in 1824, the Duke of Norfolk sponsored the building of a road bridge 24ft wide and 960ft long that stood 10ft above the high tide mark. Provision was made for shipping, which comprised small wooden sailing ships, by an opening section. He recovered his investment by the charging of road tolls. However, despite this link, Hayling was little more than an agricultural community for many decades.

Due north of the island is the town of Havant, and by 1847 the LBSCR had reached the town from the Brighton direction as part of its London-Brighton-Portsmouth route. In 1859 the LSWR had also reached the town, and eventually the two companies came to an agreement regarding running powers into the City of Portsmouth. In 1851 an Act of Parliament was approved to form the Hayling Bridge & Causeway Company, which planned to build a horse-drawn tramway from the new railway at Havant down to the waterside at Langstone Quay on the shore of Langstone Harbour. The company already operated the original road bridge. Activity around the quay there was growing and in the railway age the potential of better connections between the island and the mainland both for goods and for tourism was being explored. The tramway proposal failed, however, as it proved impossible to raise the necessary capital.

By 1860 the locals at Langstone and on Hayling Island were becoming frustrated at being left out of the Victorian transport boom, and in the absence of any interest from the major railway companies local businessmen formed the Hayling Railway Company in 1860. The alignment of the route would be from the established Havant railway station to Langstone, across the water

by bridge, and along an embankment on the western side of the island to Sinah Point at its south-western corner. The area between the island and the embankment would then be infilled, thus re-claiming some 1,000 acres of land. Also, it would not be necessary to purchase land, theoretically reducing the cost of the overall project. Work commenced in 1863, but the sea continually battered the part-built embankment and by 1865 only a mile of single track from Havant down to Langstone, on the waterfront, had been built and opened for freight traffic.

Although an alternative route had been mooted in 1864, the scheme stalled and a knight in shining armour was required to regenerate activity in establishing a railway link to Hayling Island. One duly arrived in the shape of Francis Fuller from London. This wealthy land agent had a vision for the future of Hayling Island and he acquired a large amount of building land, which would be better served by any railway if there was a deviation from the original route. His influence and cash resulted in such a deviation, the new alignment along the western shoreline being approved in an Act dated 12 August 1866. He intended to create a resort to the south of the island that would rival Brighton and Bognor, which would include not only villas and hotels but also a racecourse. He became Chairman of the Hayling Railway Company in 1866.

Construction proceeded at a great pace and as early as June 1867 officials were able to travel from Havant to South Hayling, the terminus of the 4½-mile branch line. The Board of Trade Inspector insisted that certain modifications were carried out, but on 17 July 1867 the first passenger-carrying train left Havant, albeit with the stipulation of a 20mph speed limit. The track was single throughout, but there was a third-of-a-mile spur that ran down to Langstone Quay. The bridge across the shipping channel was the major feature of the line, and weight restrictions on the bridge

Left:
The Hayling Island branch train stands at its dedicated bay platform at Havant. The formation of this 'height of the season' train includes a utility van for holiday luggage and perhaps a few prams and bicycles. The leading carriage is an all-Third Class affair with a large '3' painted on each compartment door. At the head of the train, still in its Southern Railway livery with pre-nationalisation number, is No (3)2659 on 17 August 1949. *S. C. Nash*

were to influence the choice of motive power for the entire life of the line. There were two intermediate stations, at Langston(e) and North Hayling. The 'stations' were effectively halts, but this was never reflected in station signs. Initially Hayling Island was known as South Hayling, but the name was changed in 1892. It was the LBSCR that dropped the 'e' from Langstone, but for consistency the original name will be used in this chapter.

There had been plans for many years to run through trains from South Hayling to London and other destinations, and a triangular junction with the main line was envisaged at one stage, although such grandiose plans never came to fruition. There was also a plan authorised in 1886 to link the 1885-opened Fratton to Southsea branch with the Hayling Island branch by a road/rail bridge across Langstone Harbour, with a circular railway service running from Havant to Fratton and on to Southsea before continuing via the new bridge to South Hayling and returning to Havant. However, this project also failed to get off the ground. At the beginning of 1872 the LBSCR took over operation of the branch and later signed a 999-year lease on the line, from which time the Brighton company was in full control of all services. The Hayling company survived until the Grouping in 1923, when it was formally absorbed by the Southern Railway.

Over the years there have been three stations at Havant, including two rebuilds in 1889 and 1938. During the 20th century all branch trains used a bay platform at the eastern or up end of the down platform on the south side. The line curved sharply at an 8-chain radius from an easterly to a south-westerly direction and, after negotiating a gated road crossing just outside the station, passed beneath East Street bridge, the only road overbridge on the line. Prior to 1874 there was a small engine shed and a water tank located in this area. Within about a mile Langstone was reached, where the station comprised a single low wooden platform and a wooden station building. There was a small signal cabin and an important gated road crossing just north of the station. The platform was replaced by a typical SR-style concrete example in the early days of BR.

Beyond the station and near the water's edge were some interesting sidings. One was the original 1865 siding down to Langstone Quay, on the east side of the branch, which was originally used for coal traffic for the Isle of Wight and for road-building materials; the track went on to the Old Coal Wharf. In later years part of the siding was used by the military, and finally by the permanent way department. Adjacent to the 'main' branch line, but on the western side, was a line that dropped down on to the Old Wharf, effectively a 700yd-long embankment with a timber jetty at its end that contained a special loading mechanism. A Langstone to Brading train ferry run by the Isle of Wight Marine Transit Company between the years 1885 and 1888 used this interesting single-line siding, which changed to a pair of tracks on the wharf. The small ferry was a 243-ton vessel that had two parallel tracks on the deck, and could accommodate about a dozen four-wheeled wagons. The ship, loaded with railway freight wagons, ran between Langstone and St Helens Quay at Brading on the Isle of Wight, a journey of 11 miles. A novel loading system featuring ramps was utilised so that wagons could be loaded and unloaded at varying levels of the tide without disturbing their payload. The marine company subsequently experienced financial problems and after a year of operation it entered into an agreement with the LBSCR whereby the railway company effectively hired the ship and the quays from the marine company. However, in 1888 the service was withdrawn for good, resulting in a loss of traffic for the Hayling Island branch.

The branch then crossed the 1,000ft-long Langstone Bridge, about 1½ miles from Havant. The bridge was built on wooden piles, strengthened by being encased in concrete in the late 1920s. A 30ft swingbridge, which opened to allow vessels to pass, was incorporated in its design. There was also a signal cabin on the bridge, but this ceased to be manned on a full-time basis in 1938. After World War 2 the bridge was rarely opened for boat traffic — a total of only nine openings was recorded in 1949. By this time the bridge was opened only by prior arrangement with the railway company. Fishplates had to be removed in order to open

Below:
A remarkable photograph that underlines the seasonal nature of traffic on the Hayling Island branch is this shot of 'A1X' class No 32646 arriving at Havant with an absolutely wedged train on 25 June 1961. The four-coach train is signalled for the bay platform and the fireman is adopting an 'action man' pose before his gloved hand uncouples the locomotive in order to run round for the next down working. *R. S. Greenwood*

Above:
The Hayling Island branch opened to passengers in July 1867, but back in 1865 a line down to the shoreline at Langstone was opened for goods traffic. The LBSCR took over operation of the branch in 1872, and dropped the 'e' from the name Langstone, the first station on the branch. Pausing at Langstone with four splendid four-wheeled coaches in tow is one of the many 'Terriers' that worked the line, No 78 *Knowle* in LBSCR livery. It is hard to believe that such primitive coaching stock worked some branch trains until World War 1. *O. J. Morris*

Left:
Between 1885 and 1888 a ferry for the conveyance of goods wagons between Langstone and Brading on the Isle of Wight was in operation and a separate siding was built from the Hayling Island branch line down to a wharf, just to the west of Langstone Bridge. To the east was another siding to the Old Coal Wharf, which until about 1890 was used to ship coal supplies to the Isle of Wight. Just north of the bridge was this engineer's siding, visible on the left of this August 1952 scene, as No 32655 works an up train towards Langstone station. *S. C. Nash*

the bridge, a signal wire disconnected and locking bolts activated, hardly a casual operation! The bridge had severe speed and weight restrictions and for this reason only very small locomotives could be used on the line during its entire 96-year history. The speed limit was 20mph.

Alongside the railway bridge was the only road bridge connecting the mainland with the island. This was always a toll bridge; a situation that continued until April 1960, nearly four years after a new bridge was built. The old bridge was a wooden structure that was owned by the railway company, and it too was heavily weight restricted. By 1954 the restriction was reduced to 5 tons and bus passengers, except the infirm and pregnant, had to disembark and walk across, even though a specially adapted 1930s Leyland Club single-decker was pressed into use. The author remembers leaving the Southdown bus and walking across the bridge in July 1956 — see the photograph.

The line curved towards the south-west at the Hayling end of Langstone Bridge to the second intermediate station on the line, North Hayling. This station was located in a remote and windswept location on the western coast of the island about 2½ miles from Havant. The platform, on the down side of the line, was constructed from old railway sleepers, with a tiny wooden hut, a backless bench seat and a single oil lamp! The station was connected to the nearest

road by a rough path. Just south of the station was a short siding on the up side, which from 1870 served some ancient oyster beds that once added to railway revenues. As if to avoid the population of the island, the branch continued to run along the western coast to Hayling Island station (originally South Hayling), the terminus of the line.

Hayling Island station comprised a single 420ft platform with the main platform face and station building being on the western side of the line. A 330ft bay platform was also provided in later years, effectively elevating the main platform to 'island' status. There was a nine-lever signal cabin, a small mess room, a goods shed (built in 1900), and sidings, run-round loop, a small wooden coaling stage and a loading dock by the headshunt. For many years there was a thriving goods business, with coal, milk, produce, fertiliser and cement heading a varied list of payload items. One curiosity was the fact that locomotives took on water only at Havant and coal only at Hayling. The station building, which was later extended, was very attractive, with a herringbone brick pattern and exposed timber framing. There was once a small old wooden second-hand engine shed that had been transferred from another LBSCR site. In SR days the station platform canopy was extended, but during the war the original station canopy was bomb-damaged and demolished. Hayling Island was an incredibly busy place during the summer months when a half-hourly service was provided and two trains were in the environs of the station at the same time.

Although in 1867 the railway served a rural community, the popularity of Hayling Island as a holiday destination grew, and by the turn of the 20th century a considerable influx of visitors in the summer months was a regular feature. Over the years caravan sites and holiday camps popped up, but many of these were served by the frequent bus service. Electrification of the main line had an impact, but the advent of World War 2 put a brake on holiday traffic. The railway was a very seasonal undertaking and, while trains ran all year round, the summer loadings were exceptional, leading to chronic peaks and troughs in activity. For example, in March 1961 just over 2,000 tickets were collected, but in August of the same year over 32,000 were collected, a 16-fold increase! From one or two coaches in the winter months, operating approximately hourly, the service grew to half-hourly using two rakes of four coaches in the summer months, an eightfold increase in capacity. At the height of summer a van was included on many trains to accommodate perambulators, bicycles and holiday luggage. Loadings were so heavy that on one May Bank Holiday no fewer than 598 passengers disgorged from a three-coach train! Although there were no appreciable gradients on the line, loadings were limited to four coaches and a van (eight coaches in the days of the old Victorian four-wheelers) due to the employment of the diminutive 'A1X' class tank engines, popularly known as 'Terriers'. Right up to closure in 1963 mixed trains were a feature of the line, but unfitted loose-coupled wagons had to be located behind the braked passenger coaches in the consist.

In the very early days, before the LBSCR was in full control, there was a timetable of between four and six round trips over the branch per day. Bradshaw's timetable for 1888 shows nine services each way, which gradually increased to 10 trains at the turn of the century. In the early days of the SR the summer service increased to 15 trains per day, and by the late 1930s this had grown again to 17 trains, with as many as 15 working the Sunday service.

Ironically the absolute peak of activity occurred on Saturdays in 1963, the last summer of operation, when a staggering 24 trains made the return journey between Havant and Hayling, and all this without the facility of an intermediate passing loop. The journey time was about 13 minutes. Manpower was increased at the busy road crossing at Langstone and at Hayling during peak periods.

From the railway enthusiast's perspective one of the great attractions of the Hayling Island branch was the restriction on the use of motive power. Weight restrictions on Langstone Bridge resulted in small engines being used throughout the life of the line. In the very early years small 2-4-0Ts and 0-4-2Ts from the Sharp Stewart and Kitson stables worked the line, but for the majority of its life it was the LBSCR Stroudley 'A1X' class, a development of the 'A1' class, that worked the line. Turning the scales at a modest 28 tons 5 cwt, these six-coupled locomotives were ideally suited to the line and were in operation on the Hayling Island branch for more than 68 years. Their diminutive size contrasted with the size of the average coach end, making them look even smaller than they were. They became a real magnet for railway photographers during their later years. A 'P' class 0-6-0T was once tried on the line, but it was unsuccessful and the 'Terriers' reigned supreme. The line was never push-pull worked and the locomotives always ran round at Havant and Hayling Island. The locomotives were serviced and shedded at nearby Fratton, but when that shed closed in 1959 they had to simply stand there overnight with all maintenance work being carried out at Eastleigh. On busy summer Saturdays three locomotives were required to operate the timetable.

Despite fierce opposition in the shape of omnibuses there was sufficient rail-borne traffic to justify the survival of the line, even with some grant-aid assistance. As already mentioned, the problem was that the level of traffic experienced in the summer months tailed off severely in the winter, which resulted in a situation where annual takings were only half the sum needed to meet the full costs of operating the line. A number of circumstances contributed to the final demise of the line: the coaching stock was near the end of

Branch timetables (*from top to bottom*) 1888, 1910 and 1927. None compares with the final 1963 summer timetable, when there were 15 round trips Monday to Friday and no fewer than 24 trains each way on Summer Saturdays!

Right:
This absolutely cracking shot shows that most fascinating of workings, the 'mixed' train. With snow on the ground, 'A1X' No 32667 livens up proceedings between Langstone and Havant on 14 January 1955 with the 2.53pm mixed train from Hayling Island to Havant. The ancient compartment brake coach is followed by five wagons and a brake-van. Regulations required that loose-coupled wagons had to be positioned behind any passenger coaches. *IAL*

Below:
Langstone Bridge had a significant impact on the Hayling Island branch. In the first place, its 1,000ft length was the distance from Hayling Island to the 'mainland'. In the second place, it was the reason why throughout the 96 years of the branch's life motive power was limited in variety due to weight restrictions on the bridge. In the third place, although the line was one of the few branches that ever made a profit, by the 1960s the bridge was in need of replacement at a cost of £400,000 (probably in excess of £10m in today's values), a cost that could never be justified, especially as a new road bridge had been opened in 1956. Note the signalbox by the opening span half way across, and the unsightly pylon, which was erected in 1946. On the last day of regular service, 2 November 1963, No 32650 leaves the bridge (and a number of photographers in those much missed, less formal, times) with the 1.35pm train to Hayling Island. *Brian Stephenson*

its days, the days of steam were rapidly coming to an end, a brand new non-weight-restricted road bridge had been opened in 1956, and the entire infrastructure of crossing gates and semaphore signals was becoming an anachronism, but above all else Langstone Bridge needed replacement or substantial rebuilding and the cost was put at some £400,000 in 1963 prices. The cost could not be justified under any circumstances, and the decision to close the line was made. Many objections to the closure were voiced at a meeting at Havant Town Hall in December 1962, but these were overruled and a closure date of 4 November 1963 was set. The last service train ran on Saturday 2 November 1963 and the very last train, in the form of an enthusiasts' special, ran the following day.

After closure the line was dormant for some time. As usual with line closures of the era, there were the usual bands of optimists who hoped to preserve the line. One organisation, calling itself the Hayling Light Railway Society, came up with a novel plan of using an ex-Blackpool Corporation tramcar on the line, which would have complied with weight restrictions but would have involved the provision of an overhead electric current supply. The plan was

serious enough for tramcar No 11 to be deposited in the up goods yard at Havant in 1965; the author photographed it on 1 October of that year and, as it transpired, it was only the second photograph of the author's to be published in the railway press! The scheme failed to come to fruition, partly because of the complexities and costs emerging with the construction of the A27 Havant bypass. Much of the line was lifted in 1966 and I visited and photographed the trackless terminus during that year. By the beginning of 1967 the branch track was being lifted at Havant station. When the local authority tried to demolish Langstone Bridge, a process that included the use of explosives, they failed to budge some of the piers and as a result the remains can still be seen today.

At Havant the old bay platform face is visible but the track area is now a car park. At Hayling Island only the goods shed remains and the site has industrial buildings thereon and could never be recognised as an old railway terminus. The trackbed from Havant down to Langstone is now a footpath/cycle path and some of the low-lying embankment in the North Hayling area can be traversed on foot. The 'Hayling Billy', as it was colloquially known, has now been dead for over 40 years, but many fondly remember it. For those interested in the line, a visit to Havant Museum is rewarding and highly recommended.

Above:
A model-maker's delight is this excellent record of the Hayling Island terminus, looking south towards the buffer stops. There was a bay platform on the right and the main platform, with run-round loop, was on the left. The large goods shed, with a couple of wagons outside, is now the only surviving structure. Curiously, locomotives were coaled at Hayling Island but not watered, and at Havant they were watered but not coaled. No 32661 is being manually coaled from the wooden dock, but there is nobody on the bench seats to watch the process! *IAL*

Upper right:
A student of railway coaches would be interested in this arrival at Hayling Island on 25 July 1959, which includes a Bulleid example. The date of the photograph could be determined by the clothing of the large crowd of children on the platform, especially the boy in short flannel trousers! No 32640 has just arrived with the 10.35am train, and judging by the member of the train crew with heavy-duty gloves on some uncoupling/coupling is imminent.
J. H. Aston

Lower right:
When the author visited the abandoned terminus in mid-1969 this sad scene was encountered, with the track ripped up, the station boarded up and the entire area derelict. The lovely old terminus building at Hayling Island had timber framing with herringbone brickwork to set off its Gothic architectural design, but it was soon pulled down. The canopy was, however, saved and re-erected at the Hollycombe Steam Collection near Liphook. It was sobering to think that the swarms of holidaymakers that had once graced the platforms had gone for ever, and that the hundreds of thousands of passengers who had arrived on the island by train since the first passenger stepped on to the platform in 1867 were now confined to the pages of local history books. *JV/TTT*

Top right:
The author is almost ashamed to admit that when he visited Hayling Island for the first time, on 7 July 1956, it was by bus! At this time the Southdown Company was operating old 1937 Leyland Cubs, with Park Royal bodies, on the Hayling route from Havant railway station. In common with the railway bridge, the old road bridge had severe weight restrictions and all but the pregnant and the very elderly had to alight from the bus, walk across the bridge, and rejoin on the other side. Just two months later a new road bridge opened allowing larger, more modern buses to be used. Here No 9, registration DUF 9, has just returned to Havant station. Within seven years the bus company would enjoy a transport monopoly. *JV*

Centre right:
After the closure proposals were announced, a preservation society was, almost predictably, established. Known as the Hayling Light Railway Society, the organisation planned to run lightweight ex-Blackpool tramcars on the line, thus obviating the need for Langstone Bridge to be replaced. An overhead electricity supply would be required. In 1965 the first tram had actually arrived in Havant goods yard and was photographed from a passing train. However, the project never got off the ground partly because of local authority plans to build a much needed road bypass. *JV/TTT*

Lower right:
Here we pay our last respects to the old Hayling Island branch at Havant on 1 February 1967, more than three years after the departure of the last train. With the main 'Coastway' line on the left, the demolition contractors set about their onerous task of track removal. The tractor is lifting redundant sleepers on to the Leyland lorry, the branch starting signal has been removed and some oxy-acetylene cylinders for track cutting can be seen behind the workers. *JV/TTT*

16. Bordon Branch

Left:
The branch line from Bentley to Bordon, just under 4¾ miles long, was opened in December 1905. Although the railway would serve the village of Bordon, its real *raison d'être* was to link the growing Army camp conurbation at Longmoor with a main line. The logistical advantages of having a through running capability for locomotives, stock and supplies, as well as military and civilian personnel, were overwhelming. Built under the provisions of a Light Railway Order, it took just 18 months to complete the line. In this very early view, horse-drawn carriages and goods carts wait for trade in the Bordon terminus railway approach. *JV collection*

WITHOUT the British Army the Bordon branch would probably never have existed. The Army was rather slow in recognising the full potential of the transportation of troops, armaments and equipment by rail even in specific war areas. In order to have railway expertise, including every aspect of operations, from driving to permanent way building and maintenance to various aspects of signalling, it would be necessary to have a military railway training school. Any such school site would obviously have to incorporate a real working railway.

Way back in 1865 the Engineer & Railway Volunteer Staff Corps had been formed to advise the Government of the day on how to make the most effective use of the civil railways within the UK, if there was to ever be a real or threatened invasion. It was not until 1889 that a *Manual of Military Railways* was published, which proved to be most useful in the South African War. After various campaigns it was realised that the Army had gradually increased in size to such a degree that upon its return to the UK there was insufficient accommodation to house all of the troops. Accordingly it was decided that in addition to enlarging existing sites it would be necessary to construct a number of 'hutted' camps. One of the largest sites selected was in Woolmer Forest, north of Liss, the camp becoming known as Longmoor Camp.

There was already an existing Army camp at Bordon, about 3 miles to the north of Longmoor, and once Longmoor started to become heavily populated by troops between 1900 and 1903, there were complaints about the damp ground in the area, and as a result, part of the Longmoor Camp was removed to Bordon. This was a massive task, as no fewer that 68 30/40-ton huts had to be removed. This gave the Army the opportunity for some real-life railway practice, and two parallel 4½-mile 1ft 6in gauge lines were built for

the purpose. This background is simply to explain why Longmoor and Bordon were synonymous with railways, and how it came about that Bordon was greatly developed and enlarged.

At the time that Bordon and what was to become the Longmoor Military Railway were being developed, it was vital that the military railway had access to the national rail network. Moreover, although small in population, there was also the village of Bordon, which could usefully be served by a railway. Coincidentally, towards the end of Queen Victoria's reign legislation was passed promoting 'Light Railways'. This was a streamlined process for gaining approval for the building of railways, and it allowed level crossings without gates, a permanent way that could be less substantial than a standard railway, gradients that could be steeper and curves tighter, so that costs could be reduced. The primary penalty for these concessions was a 25mph speed restriction. The London & South Western Railway had been involved in the very first railway to make use of this legislation, the nearby Basingstoke & Alton Light Railway (see Chapter 18), and therefore there was little surprise when in 1902 'The Bordon Light Railway' was approved, especially as the proposal had the backing of the War Department. The 4½-mile branch would leave the LSWR Farnham to Alton line at Bentley, which in 1901 had a population of 645; the station was about a mile from the village. This busy but secondary line had been opened as early as 1854 and was well established. The down platform had to be extended in 1905 to make provision for a Bordon bay platform at the down end.

The countryside was almost entirely given over to agriculture and the terrain was, at worst, gently undulating. Construction of the line was thus relatively straightforward, and once all of the necessary land had been acquired, construction was completed in

Top left:
For much of the line's life, but particularly after World War 2, the LSWR Drummond 'M7' class dominated passenger services on the branch. This shows a typical view from the 1950s, when on 14 September 1957, the last ever Saturday of service, No 30110 arrived at Bordon with the 3.9pm from Bentley. The formation was, as usual, operating in push-pull mode, and there would be no need to use the run-round loop in the foreground. Note that the tail lamp has already been attached to the locomotive in readiness for the return journey. *SLS/R. F. Roberts*

Centre left:
Looking north towards Bentley on 2 February 1952, the large water tank can be seen on the left, while the little signalbox by the board crossing had 20 levers, but looked like a ground frame in a hut. In the centre is the single-road engine shed, which became very second-hand-looking when a locomotive ran through the back of it. On the right are a number of signals that are opposite the exchange sidings with the Longmoor Military Railway. *SLS/R. F. Roberts*

Lower left:
After the Bordon branch closed to passengers in 1957 it remained open for freight traffic until 4 April 1966, when it closed completely. However, on 16 and 30 April 1966 special dispensation was given for two RCTS specials, which had visited the Longmoor Military Railway, to traverse the line. This afforded the author the only opportunity he had to photograph a train in action on the Bordon branch. In truly appalling weather, and with the shutter set at 1/125th sec, instead of the usual 1/500th or 1/1000th, LMR WD 2-10-0 No 600 *Gordon* was photographed crossing a minor ungated road just outside Bordon terminus, heading off into the mist for Bentley. *JV/TTT*

just 18 months at a cost of £30,000. The LSWR anticipated that the standard gauge line would be used for both passenger and freight traffic, and to accommodate the likely passenger traffic and to provide a service of reasonable frequency eight trains in each direction on weekdays with two round-trip workings on the Sabbath were deemed sufficient. The LSWR had also purchased some land in the area of what was to become the line's only intermediate station, Kingsley Halt, to cater for what was anticipated would be a growing population to the west of the village of Kingsley and also for a possible railhead for local farmers. At Bordon developments occurred on quite a grand scale, because while the Bordon Light Railway was being built the War Department had decided in 1905 to build a standard gauge railway, along the route of the old 'hut-removing' narrow gauge line. Therefore interchange facilities would be necessary at Bordon, as described below.

Without special celebration the LSWR branch opened on 11 December 1905. It seems slightly strange that the company did not provide a dedicated line from the bay platform at Bentley on to the branch, avoiding the necessity for branch trains to use part of the main line from Farnham to Alton. The down platform was wide enough for the branch bay to be delineated by a line of metal railings, which somehow emphasised the existence of a separate railway line. However, up branch trains had to run into the main up platform, discharge their passengers then shunt back to the down bay via the down main line. The actual junction for Bordon was a

mere 17 chains from the bay platform, but as stated, the branch trains had to join the main line for this short distance before passing Bentley signalbox. The main line had been doubled in 1901, and before that date there had been three other Bentley signalboxes at various locations. The box contained the single-line signalling apparatus for the branch.

The single-line branch headed south on a slightly rising gradient, and after 1 mile and 10 chains the first of three ungated road crossings was encountered, Blacknest Road. The line ran on a fairly straight route to the site of Kingsley Halt, 2 miles and 57 chains, which was opened on 7 March 1906. The single-platform halt comprised a running-in board, a notice board, a lamp and a single station seat.

South of Kingsley Halt the line crossed Binsted Road level crossing, then ascended at 1 in 358 and descended at 1 in 145, hardly dramatic or challenging countryside! On the approach to Bordon the line crossed the third of the ungated crossings at White Hill Road before entering the terminus station 4 miles and 58 chains from Bentley. There were two platforms at Bordon with a locomotive release/run-round facility from the down platform. On the up, or west, side of the station was a signalbox (at the end of the up platform), engine shed and coal stage, with a water tank beyond. There was also a selection of railway cottages built adjacent to Bordon station for railway employees. On the down, or east, side was the main single-storey station building, a goods shed and goods sidings (with crane), but beyond that there was the whole

Below:
In its heyday the branch saw a colossal amount of military traffic ranging from lengthy freight trains with supplies and equipment to troop train specials. There was some local 'domestic' freight, but most was handled in the exchange yard, which was often congested during the war years. On 31 August 1964 'Q' class No 30542 arrives at Bordon with a long freight. The exchange sidings are on the right of the signal-less gantry. *Maurice Dart collection*

LONDON, WOKING, ALDERSHOT, FARNHAM, BENTLEY, BORDON, and ALTON.

Miles.	Down.	Week Days.																					
		mrn	mrn	mrn	mrn	mrn	mrn	mrn	mrn	mrn	mrn	mrn	aft	mrn		aft E	aft S	aft	aft	aft	aft	aft S	aft E
	London (W.) 194 ... dep.	4 50	5 40	..	..	6 55	..	..	8 10	..	9 10	10 4	..	1124	..	1 0	1 4	..	2 0	3 5	4 20	5 0	5 10
24½	Woking 194 .... arr.	5 58	6 18	...	...	7 55	...	...	9 2	...	9 43	1059	...	1218	...	1 31	1 38	...	2 33	3 37	4 51	5 31	5 43
—	Woking .... dep.	6 3	6 33	..	..	7 57	..	..	9 7	..	9 45	11 6	..	1226	..	1 39	1 39	..	2 35	3 39	4 52	5 45	5 45
28	Brookwood	6 14	6 41	...	...	8 7	...	...	9 17	...	...	1116	...	1236	...	1 48	1 48	...	2 44	3 48	5 1	5 54	5 54
32½	Ash Vale A 169	6 26	6 53	..	..	8 18	..	..	9 28	..	..	1127	..	1247	..	1 59	1 59	..	2 55	3 59	5 12	6 5	6 5
35¼	Aldershot B	6 35	7 1	...	...	8 27	...	...	9 36	...	10 6	1135	...	1256	...	2 7	2 7	...	3 4	4 8	5 20	6 13	6 13
38¼	Farnham. 169 .... arr.	6 43	7 8	..	..	8 34	..	..	9 43	..	1013	1142	..	1 4	..	2 14	2 14	..	3 11	4 15	5 27	6 20	6 20
	Farnham. 169 .... dep.	6 45	7 10	7 45	8 11	8 37	9 7	...	9 44	9 59	1014	1143	1255	1 5	...	2 15	2 15	2 31	3 13	4 17	5 28	6 21	6 21
42	Bentley .... arr.	6 54	7 20	7 53	8 20	8 47	9 15	..	9 53	10 8	1023	1152	1 3	1 14	..	2 24	2 24	2 38	3 23	4 26	5 37	6 30	6 30
—	Bentley .... dep.	...	...	...	8 23	...	...	9 41	...	...	1030	...	...	1 19	...	...	...	2 39	3 30	4 41	5 41	6 33	6 33
44¾	Kingsley Halt	..	..	..	8 31	..	..	9 49	..	..	1038	..	..	1 27	..	..	..	2 48	3 38	4 49	5 49	6 41	6 41
46¾	Bordon .... arr.	...	...	...	8 38	...	...	9 56	...	...	1045	...	...	1 34	...	...	...	2 55	3 45	4 56	5 56	6 48	6 48
—	Bentley .... dep.	6 55	7 22	..	..	8 48	9 16	..	9 54	..	1024	1153	..	1 15	..	2 25	2 25	..	3 24	4 27	5 38	6 31	6 31
47	Alton C 168 .... arr.	7 4	7 31	...	...	8 57	9 25	...	10 2	...	1032	12 1	...	1 24	...	2 33	2 33	...	3 32	4 36	5 46	6 39	6 39

Down.	Week Days—*Continued.*											Sundays.											
	aft	aft	aft S	aft E	aft S	aft	aft S	aft	ngt.			mrn	mrn	mrn	mrn	mrn		aft	aft	aft	aft	aft	aft
London (W.) 194 ... dep.	5 47	6 38	6 42	7 0	..	8 10	..	9 50	12 5	..	..	..	..	8 30	..	1110	..	1 20	..	6 10	6 40	9 52	1045
Woking 194 .... arr.	6 19	7 11	7 24	7 33	...	8 48	...	1024	1244	...	...	...	...	9 14	...	1150	...	2 20	...	6 49	7 33	1047	1121
Woking .... dep.	6 22	7 12	7 48	7 48	..	8 55	..	1030	1246	..	..	7 25	..	9 16	..	12 3	..	2 22	..	6 51	7 36	1049	1123
Brookwood	6 32	...	7 56	7 56	...	9 5	...	1040	1255	...	...	7 33	...	9 26	...	1211	...	2 32	...	7 1	7 45	1059	1133
Ash Vale A 169	6 43	7 28	8 7	8 7	..	9 16	..	1051	1 6	..	..	7 44	..	9 37	..	1222	..	2 43	..	7 12	7 56	1111	1145
Aldershot B	6 50	7 37	8 15	8 15	8 25	9 26	1040	11 0	1 14	...	...	7 52	8 19	9 46	1010	1230	...	2 52	7 10	7 21	8 8	1120	1154
Farnham 169 .... arr.	6 57	7 45	8 22	8 22	8 31	9 34	1045	11 7	1 21	..	..	7 59	8 26	9 54	1016	1237	..	2 59	7 17	7 28	8 15	1127	12 1
Farnham 169 .... dep.	...	7 46	8 24	8 24	8 32	9 35	1046	11 9	...	...	...	8 0	8 27	9 56	1017	1238	...	3 0	7 18	7 30	8 17	...	12 2
Bentley .... arr.	..	7 55	8 33	8 33	8 41	9 44	1054	1118	..	..	..	8 8	8 36	10 5	1026	1247	..	3 9	7 26	7 39	8 26	..	1211
Bentley .... dep.	...	7 58	...	8 43	8 43	9 49	1055	...	...	...	...	...	8 37	10 6	...	1248	...	3 10	...	...	8 36	...	1212
Kingsley Halt	..	8 6	..	8 51	8 51	9 57	..	..	..	..	..	..	..	..	..	..	..	..	..	..	..	..	..
Bordon .... arr.	...	8 13	...	8 58	8 58	10 4	1111	...	...	...	...	...	8 52	1021	...	1 3	...	3 25	...	...	8 53	...	1227
Bentley .... dep.	..	7 56	8 34	8 34	..	9 45	..	1119	..	..	..	8 9	..	..	1027	..	..	..	7 27	7 40	..	..	..
Alton C 168 .... arr.	...	8 4	8 43	8 43	...	9 54	...	1128	...	...	...	8 17	...	...	1036	...	...	...	7 36	7 49	...	...	...

Miles.	Up.	Week Days.																					
		mrn	mrn	mrn	mrn	mrn	mrn	mrn	mrn	mrn	mrn	mrn E	mrn S	mrn	mrn	aft	aft	aft	aft	aft	aft	aft	aft
	Alton .... dep.	...	...	7 35	...	8 5	...	...	9 6	9 46	...	1040	1040	11 7	...	1222	1 5	...	1 56	2 58	...	4 2	4 29
5	Bentley .... arr.	..	..	7 43	..	8 14	..	..	9 16	9 54	..	..	..	1116	..	1230	1 13	..	2 5	3 6	..	4 10	4 37
—	Mls Bordon .... dep.	...	...	...	7 45	...	...	8 42	...	...	10 5	...	...	...	1155	...	...	1 41	...	...	3 2	...	4 10
—	2 Kingsley Halt	..	..	..	7 51	..	..	8 48	..	..	1011	..	..	..	12 1	..	..	1 47	..	..	3 8	..	4 16
—	4¾ Bentley .... arr.	...	...	...	8 0	...	...	8 57	...	...	1020	...	...	...	1210	...	...	1 56	...	...	3 17	...	4 25
—	Bentley .... dep.	..	..	7 44	8 5	8 15	..	9 0	9 18	9 56	1025	..	..	1117	1211	1231	1 14	1 57	2 6	3 7	..	4 11	4 38
8¾	Farnham 169 ..... arr.	...	...	7 52	8 13	8 23	...	9 8	9 27	10 5	1033	1056	1056	1126	1219	1240	1 23	2 5	2 14	3 16	...	4 20	4 46
	Farnham 169 ..... dep.	6 27	7 12	7 53	..	8 24	8 43	..	9 28	10 6	..	1057	1057	1127	1225	1242	1 24	..	2 15	3 17	..	4 21	4 47
11¾	Aldershot B	6 34	7 20	8 3	...	8 34	8 50	...	9 38	1016	...	11 6	11 6	1137	1232	1252	1 34	...	2 25	3 27	...	4 31	4 56
14¾	Ash Vale A	6 40	7 26	8 10	..	8 40	8 56	..	..	1022	..	..	..	1143	..	1 1	1 40	..	2 32	3 34	..	4 37	5 2
19	Brookwood 195	6 50	7 37	8 21	...	8 50	9 6	...	...	1032	...	1119	1119	1154	...	1 11	1 50	...	2 42	3 44	...	4 47	5 12
22½	Woking H 180, 195 arr.	6 58	7 45	8 29	..	8 57	9 13	..	..	1040	..	..	1126	12 2	..	1 19	1 58	..	2 49	3 52	..	4 55	5 19
—	Woking 196 .... dep.	7 1	8 2	8 30	...	9 0	9 15	...	...	1048	...	...	1133	12 4	...	1 22	2 1	...	2 51	4 4	...	4F58	5 27
47	London (W.) 196 ... arr.	7 49	8 39	9 7	..	9 35	1011	..	1029	1124	..	1159	12 9	1239	..	2 5	3 0	..	3 30	5 1	..	5F54	6 19

Up.	Week Days—*Continued.*											Sundays.											
	aft	aft	aft	aft	aft E	aft	aft	aft	aft			mrn	mrn	mrn	mrn		aft	aft	aft		aft	aft	
Alton .... dep.	...	5 21	5 50	...	...	7 30	8 14	...	1020	...	...	8 51	...	9 24	...	...	...	...	7 54	...	8 26	...	...
Bentley .... arr.	..	5 31	5 58	..	..	7 38	8 24	..	1028	..	..	9 1	..	9 33	..	..	..	..	8 4	..	8 36	..	..
Bordon .... dep.	...	5 10	...	6 10	...	7 15	...	8 18	9 15	...	...	...	9 8	...	1120	...	1 20	5 26	...	...	...	9 18	...
Kingsley Halt	..	5 16	..	6 16	..	7 21	..	8 24	9 22	..	..	..	9 14	..	..	..	..	..	..	..	..	..	..
Bentley .... arr.	...	5 25	...	6 25	...	7 30	...	8 33	9 30	...	...	...	9 22	...	1135	...	1 35	5 41	...	...	...	9 33	...
Bentley .... dep.	5 21	5 32	5 59	..	..	7 40	8 25	..	1029	..	..	9 2	9 23	9 34	1136	..	1 36	5 42	8 5	..	8 38	9 34	..
Farnham 169 .... arr.	5 29	5 40	6 8	...	...	7 49	8 34	...	1037	...	...	9 11	9 32	9 42	1144	...	1 44	5 50	8 13	...	8 47	9 43	...
Farnham 169 .... dep.	..	5 41	6 9	..	7 10	7 50	8 36	..	1038	..	..	9 12	..	9 44	1145	..	1 45	5 51	..	..	8 48	9 45	..
Aldershot B	...	5 50	6 19	...	7 17	7 59	8 46	...	1045	...	...	9 20	...	9 54	1154	...	1 53	6 1	...	...	8 57	9 56	...
Ash Vale A	..	5 56	6 26	..	7 23	8 5	8 53	..	1051	..	..	..	..	10 1	12 0	..	1 59	6 7	..	..	9 3	10 3	..
Brookwood 195	...	6 6	6 36	...	7 33	8 15	9 4	...	11 1	...	...	...	...	1011	1210	...	2 9	6 17	...	...	9 13	1013	...
Woking H 180, 195 arr.	..	6 14	6 44	..	7 40	8 23	9 12	..	11 8	..	..	..	..	1019	1218	..	2 17	6 25	..	..	9 21	1021	..
Woking 196 .... dep.	...	6 16	6 53	...	8 0	8 37	9 16	...	1121	...	...	...	...	1021	1234	...	2 28	6 41	...	...	9 24	1023	...
London (W.) 196 ... arr.	..	6 49	7 51	..	8 40	9 25	1014	..	1226	..	..	..	..	1116	1 28	..	3 12	7 43	..	..	9 58	1126	..

A Station for North Camp and South Farnborough.
B Station for South Camp.
C Station for Selborne (4½ miles).
E or *e* Except Saturdays.

F Passengers can depart Woking at 5 7 and arrive London (Waterloo) at 5 41 aft.
H Station for Chobham (3¼ miles); to Woking Village (1½ miles).
S Saturdays only.

*** **For other Trains**

BETWEEN	PAGE
Woking and Brookwood	154, 195
London and Farnham	169
Aldershot and Farnham	169
London and Aldershot	290

Longmoor Military Railway complex, which included military platforms, various roads and sidings, together with a double-track lead on to the military branch to Longmoor (and a number of other more obscure destinations, camps, fuel and supply depots). The Longmoor railway system became a significant network and, as described in the Miscellany chapter, its 'vital statistics' were impressive.

The station building was enlarged during World War 1 and a larger awning was added. During World War 2 white bands were painted around the awning supports as part of the blackout system, when exposed lighting was banned, lest enemy aircraft should see it. It may sound strange that the weather protection facility was on the down side, but as the years passed by the up platform became disused for passenger train departures and its length was subsequently halved. The small single-road engine shed comprised little more than a metal frame and corrugated iron cladding. It was later enlarged slightly, but after being ravaged by the weather, then run through by a locomotive, in later years it gave the impression of almost total disintegration! Subsequently motive power was provided by Guildford shed. The small ground-level signalbox contained just 20 levers. From 1927 the line was run on the 'one engine in steam' principle, although its status could be changed if there was heavy military

***Left* is the public timetable for 1927, while *below* is the LSWR working timetable for the year 1909.**

BENTLEY AND BORDON LIGHT RAILWAY.

FOR SPEED RESTRICTIONS SEE PAGES A, B, C, D, E, F & G.

This s a Single Line between Bordon and Bentley Junction and is worked under the Regulations for working Single Lines by the Electric Train Tablet Block System.

No Engine, Carriage, or Truck bringing a weight of more than 16 tons upon the rails, by any one pair of wheels, must be allowed to run on this Line. The Motors on this Line are 1st and 3rd Classes only.

Distance from Bordon.	UP TRAINS. WEEK-DAYS	Empty Ald'rsh't Mons.c'y		Motor.		Motor.		Motor. F'rnhm.				Motor.		Goods. Guildfrd		Motor.		Pass. Watrloo. SO		Motor.		Motor.		Motor.		Motor.	
		arr.	dep.	arr.	dep.	arr.	dep.	arr.	dep.			arr.	dep.	arr.	dep.	arr.	dep.	arr.	dep.	arr.	dep.	arr.	dep.	arr.	dep.	arr.	dep.
M. C.		a.m.	a.m.	a.m.	a.m.	a.m.	a.m.	a.m.	a.m.			a.m.	a.m.	p.m.	p.m.	p.m.	p.m.	p.m.	p.m.	p.m.	p.m.	p.m.	p.m.	p.m.	p.m.	p.m.	p.m.
— —	Bordon	...	1210	...	7 8	...	8 12	...	9 20	...	...	...	1117	...	12 5	...	1252	...	1 15	...	2 15	...	3 17	...	4 10	...	5 10
1 75	Kingsley Halt ...	...	...	7 14	7 15	8 18	8 19	9 26	9 27	...	...	1123	1124	...	...	1258	1259	...	...	2 21	2 22	3 23	3 24	4 16	4 17	5 16	5 17
4 42	Bentley Junction	12 23		7 21		8 25		9 33		...	...	11 30		12 19		1 5		1 28		2 28		3 30		4 23		5 23	
4 59	Bentley	12 25		7 22	...	8 26	...	9 34	9 35	...	...	1131	...	12 20		1 6	...	1 29	1 30	2 29	...	3 31	...	4 24	...	5 24	...

UP TRAINS. WEEK-DAYS	Goods. F'rnhm.		Motor.		Pass. Guildfrd		Motor.		Motor.		Motor.				SUNDAYS.	Motor.		Motor.		Motor.		Motor.		Motor.			
	arr.	dep.	arr.	dep.	arr.	dep.	arr.	dep.	arr.	dep.	arr.	dep.				arr.	dep.	arr.	dep.	arr.	dep.	arr.	dep.	arr.	dep.		
	p.m.	p.m.	p.m.	p.m.	p.m.	p.m.	p.m.	p.m.	p.m.	p.m.	p.m.	p.m.				a.m.	a.m.	a.m.	a.m.	p.m.	p.m.	p.m.	p.m.	p.m.	p.m.		
Bordon	...	6 0	...	6 20	...	7 37	...	8 35	...	9 18	...	1130	...	...		...	8 20	...	1015	...	4 24	...	7 20	...	8 10	...	...
Kingsley Halt ...	...	..	6 26	6 27	...	...	8 41	8 42	9 24	9 25	1136	1137	...	...		8 26	8 27	1021	1022	4 30	4 31	7 26	7 27	8 16	8 17	...	...
Bentley Junction	6 14		6 33		7 49		8 48		9 31		11 43		...	...		8 33		10 28		4 37		7 33		8 23		...	...
Bentley	6 15		6 34	...	7 50	7 51	8 49	...	9 32	...	1144	...	...	...		8 34	...	1029	...	4 38	...	7 34	...	8 24	...	...	...

Distance from Bentley.	DOWN TRAINS. WEEK-DAYS	Motor.		8.0 a.m. Goods. F'rnhm.		Motor.		Motor. F'rnhm.				Motor.		Empty. Watrloo. SO		Motor. SE		Motor. SO		Goods. Guildfrd		Motor.		Motor.		Motor.	
		arr.	dep.	arr.	dep.	arr.	dep.	arr.	dep.			arr.	dep.	arr.	dep.	arr.	dep.	arr.	dep.	arr.	dep.	arr.	dep.	arr.	dep.	arr.	dep.
M. C.		a.m.	a.m.	a.m.	a.m.	a.m.	a.m.	a.m.	a.m.			a.m.	a.m.	p.m.	p.m.	p.m.	p.m.	p.m.	p.m.	p.m.	p.m.	p.m.	p.m.	p.m.	p.m.	p.m.	p.m.
— —	Bentley	...	7 44	8 10	8 55	...	8 40	10 8	1053	...	...	..	1146	12 32		...	1 22	...	1 30	1 40	2 35	...	2 55	...	3 50	...	4 52
— 17	Bentley Junction	7 45		8 57		8 41		10 54		...	...	11 47		12 33		1 23		1 31		2 37		2 56		3 51		4 53	
2 64	Kingsley Halt ...	7 51	7 52	...	...	8 47	8 48	11 0	11 1	...	...	1153	1154	...	...	1 29	1 30	1 37	1 38	...	...	3 2	3 3	3 57	3 58	4 59	5 0
4 59	Bordon	7 57	...	9 12	...	8 53	...	11 6	...	...	...	1159	...	1245	...	1 35	...	1 43	...	2 50	...	3 8	...	4 3	...	5 5	...

DOWN TRAINS. WEEK-DAYS	Motor.		Motor.		Pass. Watrloo.		Motor.		Motor.		Motor.				SUNDAYS.	Motor.		Motor.		Motor.		Motor.		Motor.		Pass. Watrloo.	
	arr.	dep.	arr.	dep.	arr.	dep.	arr.	dep.	arr.	dep.	arr.	dep.	arr.	dep.		arr.	dep.	arr.	dep	arr.	dep.	arr.	dep.	arr.	dep.	arr.	dep.
	p.m.	p.m.	p.m.	p.m.	p.m.	p.m.	p.m.	p.m.	p.m.	p.m.	a.m.	a.m.	a.m.	a.m.		a.m.	a.m.	a.m.	a.m.	p.m.	p.m.	p.m.	p.m.	p.m.	p.m.	p.m.	p.m.
Bentley	...	5 44	...	6 50	7 13	7 14	...	9 3	...	9 43	...	12 3	...	...		...	8 50	...	11 3	...	4 50	...	7 50	...	8 40	1148	1149
entley Junction	5 45		6 51		7 15		9 4		9 44		12 4		...	...		8 51		11 4		4 51		7 51		8 41		11 50	
Kingsley Halt ...	5 51	5 52	6 57	6 58	...	...	9 10	9 11	9 50	9 51	1210	1211	...	...		8 57	8 58	1110	1111	4 57	4 58	7 57	7 58	8 47	8 48	...	...
Bordon	5 57	...	7 3	...	7 26	...	9 16	...	9 56	...	1216	...	...	...		9 3	...	1116	...	5 3	...	8 3	...	8 53	...	12 2	...

S O Saturdays only. S E Saturdays excepted.

traffic in an emergency or if there was an exceptional situation to manage. No turntable was ever provided.

As already mentioned, the initial weekday service was eight round-trip workings per day. By 1910 the number totalled 14 each way, and in 1927 it was 12, with 13 trains on Saturdays. It was still 13 just before World War 2, with 11 round trips in 1950. A Sunday service seems to have been maintained throughout, presumably because of the military implications with soldiers returning from leave etc. Photographs show that the normal branch train loading was two coaches with a range from one to three coaches. However, on occasions the line really came to life when there was heavy military traffic following one world crisis or another. Over the years there was little variety in passenger train motive power, with the LSWR using 0-4-4Ts from the ranks of its 'O2', 'T1' and 'M7' classes. 'M7s' were more associated with the line than any other class during its last decade or two, when trains normally ran in push-pull mode. For a short period during the 1930s some LBSCR 'D1' class tanks were allocated to Guildford and consequently worked the line. Also in the early years some LSWR Drummond 'H13' class steam railcars were used, but they were all converted to trailer coaches from 1916. In the Great War an Adams 4-4-2 Radial tank was used. On the goods front a range of 0-6-0 locomotives were employed on the daily goods; '700' class 'Black Motors', ex-SECR 'C' class, SR 'Q' class and Bulleid's 'Q1' class, as well as 'N' and 'U' class Moguls, were all on the roster at one time or another. Military specials could bring an infinite selection of locomotives and stock to the line — LSWR Classes T9, L12 and S11 all put in appearances. Railway enthusiasts' specials visited the line in post-World War 2 years, headed by a variety of motive power.

Like many branch lines in this country, there were not too many passengers on board an early afternoon branch train on a wet day in February, and like so many other branches Bordon slowly succumbed to the influences of road transport; local buses ran direct to Farnham, whereas train passengers had to walk to the station and change trains at Bentley. The A325 connected Bordon with the likes of Aldershot, and more potential door-to-door goods traffic disappeared from the railway. Even the Army had huge and growing fleets of road vehicles. The line was so obviously a loss-maker, and not even the strategic value of the military connection could save it from closure, especially as the Longmoor Military Railway could be accessed, if necessary, from the southern end of the complex at Liss. Also, as mentioned in Chapter 26, the military

still ran a regular branch-line service from its Liss platform to Longmoor, so Longmoor would still be accessible by rail.

Accordingly, during 1957 the closure notices were posted, and from 16 September Bordon and Kingsley Halt were to close to passengers. Bordon would remain open for freight traffic, although the withdrawal of passenger trains from a branch line never gave any of the freight customers a feeling of confidence! They were more likely to be looking to see what contingency plans they might make if the goods services were to be withdrawn as well. In fact, customers were right to think along those lines, for during 1966 all freight services, which by then were but a trickle, were discontinued, and the line was officially closed to all traffic on 4 April. However, during that month the Railway Correspondence & Travel Society received authority to run the last train through from London to Liss, then to Longmoor, for a tour of LMR lines, with the special returning to London by travelling north to Oakhanger and Bordon and on to Bentley and Waterloo via the just closed 'Bordon Light Railway'. The train was so oversubscribed that it ran on both 16 and 30 April 1966. I must confess that the sight of LMR 2-10-0 *Gordon* leaving Bordon for Bentley was the only train I ever witnessed on the original light railway. Information exchange was so bad in those days that I never realised the whole tour was going to be repeated two weeks later. Needless to say, I got soaked on 16 April and those covering the 30 April tour got sunburnt!

There is practically nothing left of the Bordon Light Railway nowadays. The alignment of the branch can be detected at the road crossings, there is a small mound of earth where Kingsley Halt once stood, and there are brambles aplenty at the old Bordon bay platform at Bentley. At Bordon the terminus and transfer yard sites are now covered by a modern industrial estate, and only a couple of concrete fence-posts in the bushes remain. Much of the trackbed has been ploughed up and is indistinguishable from the surrounding fields. In a life of only 50-60 years the branch served a useful purpose for a while, and there is no doubt that many military personnel will have lasting memories of Bordon, but otherwise the line has truly been returned to nature. Ultimately the entire Longmoor Military Railway would close as the British Empire dwindled and the cost of maintaining specially trained troops spiralled — the entire network closed on 31 October 1969. Over the years the LMR had became a familiar location for film-makers, and between 1938 and 1972 no fewer than 14 movies were part made on location. The LMR was also well known for its spectacular public open days.

Right:
For many years LSWR 'O2' and 'T1' class 0-4-4Ts worked the Bordon branch, and in Edwardian times steam railmotors were the preferred motive power. However, on the last Saturday of service, 14 September 1957, the usual 'M7' was in charge at Bentley. Although there was a small crowd paying their last respects to the doomed branch line, the numbers paled into insignificance compared with many of the closures in the 1960s 'Beeching era'. *S. C. Nash*

Upper right:
There was only one intermediate station on the Bordon Light Railway, at Kingsley Halt, 2 miles and 64 chains from Bentley station. The single platform was located on the down side of the line and no shelter was ever provided; just a notice board, a lamp and a bench seat comprised the total facilities made available for passengers. Most trains stopped at the halt except on Sundays, when it appears to have been closed (see the 1927 timetable reproduced on p. 158). *SLS/R. F. Roberts*

Lower right:
With one door open on the second compartment coach, one wonders whether the photographer had leapt off the train, grabbed this photograph and reboarded. Whatever the circumstances, an excellent view of 'M7' class No 30027 on the Bentley to Bordon branch train at Kingsley Halt was recorded for posterity. Note the height of the vandal-proof platform light. *Norman Simmons*

Below:
Both 0-6-0 and 2-6-0 tender locomotives usually worked freight services, although an LSWR '700' class would have been more usual than the SECR 'C' class seen here. Classically framed by a mature oak tree, the 9.40am Farnham to Bordon goods trundles down the branch on 28 June 1948 behind No 1294 (later BR No 31294), still sporting its SR livery. It should be noted from the 1909 WTT that there were then two goods trains per day. *E. C. Griffith*

17. Mid-Hants Railway

BY 1849 the LSWR had opened its line from Guildford to the ancient Surrey market town of Farnham. This situation prevailed until 1852 when the temptation of extending the line to the important town of Alton became irresistible. The 8¾ mile extension was opened in July of that year, giving the Hampshire town access to the growing national rail system, which was to the benefit of the local population in terms of both freight and passenger traffic. The main line from London to Southampton had been opened in part by 1839 and throughout by 1840. Once rail traffic had become established at Alton, thoughts turned to the potential for continuing the railway line west of Alton to join the main London to Southampton line, some 17 miles distant, to the north of Winchester.

Accordingly, in June 1861, the Alton, Alresford & Winchester Railway was formed, a number of prominent and wealthy landowners being the principal subscribers. These astute individuals not only wanted to bridge the 17-mile 'gap' but they were also aware of a further LSWR plan to link the established main line to the Alton branch via a new line that would leave the main line west of Woking at Pirbright Junction and travel to Farnham Junction, just east of Farnham, via Aldershot. However, due to the recession in the mid-1860s the finance to complete the line was deferred,

completion not taking place until 1870, five years after the opening of the Mid-Hants Railway (see below).

Although there were some relatively small centres of population between Alton and Winchester that would benefit from a railway (such as Medstead with about 500 inhabitants, Ropley with 1,000, Alresford with a population of 1,500 and Itchen Abbas with a mere 250), the initial thoughts were first to create an alternative main line from London to Southampton, and second to facilitate the rapidly growing military traffic from Aldershot to establishments at Winchester, Dorchester and a military hospital near Southampton, as well as the Channel ports of Southampton, Gosport, Portsmouth and even the Isle of Wight. The link to Portsmouth was to be via a branch line from Ropley to a proposed line (that was never built) from Petersfield to Bishops Waltham; the link would then continue via Botley and Fareham on established LSWR lines.

In January 1865 the company had changed its name to the 'Mid-Hants Railway' and, just one month later, an important 10-year agreement was reached with the LSWR, whereby it would work the line for approximately half the takings. Work on the Alton to Winchester line thus commenced, even though public financial support had been less than anticipated. The exercise was costly because the LSWR had insisted that the line be completed to

Left:
This photograph was taken in 1954, when even Brian Morrison was a young man! The Mid-Hants Railway Company opened its line from Alton to Winchester on 2 October 1865, although even at that early date the LSWR operated the line. For many years the typical branch train formation was a former LSWR tank locomotive and a couple of coaches. On 2 July 1954 No 30480 and two Bulleid coaches form the 8.55am from Alton to Southampton. Note the electrified line at Platform 1, used by trains to Farnham and beyond. *Brian Morrison*

double-track main-line standards. Earthworks were heavy, with 1.3 million cubic yards of material being handled, including ¼ million cubic yards of chalk that was removed from a deep cutting near Four Marks. There was also a multitude of arches, culverts and bridges included in the building work. Funds were so stretched that compensation to many landowners was made in the form of shares in the railway company. Nevertheless, the line was inspected and pronounced fit for purpose from 2 October 1865.

Although built to double-track standards, the line was single with passing places. From the date of opening there were three intermediate stations, which all had substantial brick-built station buildings. These were located at Ropley, Alresford and Itchen Abbas. Medstead (& Four Marks) was not opened until August 1868 and, by contrast to the original stations, was the 'poor relation', with only single-storey buildings on the up side. The station was located in the village of Four Marks, more than a mile away from the more important village of Medstead. However, over the years the station generated an income that was second only to Alresford.

Just over a mile west of Alton the line passed what was to become known as Butts Junction, an important site where, in later years, the Basingstoke & Alton Light Railway and the Meon Valley line joined the Mid-Hants Railway. From Butts Junction all the way to Medstead the line climbed sharply, with more than 2 miles at 1 in 60, entering the station via a chalk cutting. A passing loop was provided, which was controlled by a signalbox at the up end of the up platform. There was a substantial station master's house on the up side behind the station buildings and a small goods yard. The name Four Marks was added to the station name in October 1937, the hamlet having grown to become a village between World Wars 1 and 2. The remains of an old siding, abandoned before World War 2, ran across the station approach and was visible for many years.

Beyond the summit at Medstead, 4¼ miles from Alton, the line descended at 1 in 60/80 all of the way to the curved platforms of Ropley, 7½ miles from Alton. For many decades the platforms were graced with ornate shrubs and hedges as staff exercised their topiary skills, a tradition that was happily resurrected in the preservation years. The main station building was on the down side, and

for many years passing facilities were provided. The southern aspects of the brick building were rendered to reduce the risk of water ingress from the direction of prevailing winds. A small platform awning afforded a modicum of passenger protection from the elements. In addition to a signalbox there was an active goods yard at the up end of the down platform. The yard contained a small goods platform.

Alresford station, 10 miles from Alton, served a small town rather than a village and was the busiest station on the line. Also, being roughly half way between Alton and Winchester, it had a good catchment area from the surrounding rural communities. In the down direction the station was approached via a deep chalk cutting, reflecting the gradients on the line. In fact, during the days of steam the expression 'over the Alps' became popular to describe, albeit in exaggerated terms, the undulating nature of the line. Alresford had its main buildings located on the up platform and was an important passing place; indeed, from 1967 it became the only passing place! Awnings were provided on both up and down platforms. The station was the only one on the Mid-Hants with a substantial brick goods shed, and the yard, located at the down end of the up platform, could handle a wider range of produce and payloads than the smaller stations. The signalbox was located at the up end of the up platform, and beyond a private siding served a warehouse, adjacent to the station approach road. Freight traffic at Alresford became synonymous with watercress, and for decades large volumes were transported by rail all over the UK. Loads ranged from a few punnets being loaded on to passenger trains to the bulk loading of up to 14 tons into dedicated vans in a single day during the peak season. This resulted in the adoption of the epithet 'Watercress Line' for marketing purposes in the preservation years.

Beyond Alresford the line passed through agricultural land for a further 3¾ miles and crossed the Rivers Alre and Itchen and some watercress beds before reaching the rural station of Itchen Abbas. This was the quietest station on the line in terms of general activity and, consequently, takings. The large station building was constructed on the down-side platform and, as with Ropley, the exterior facing the direction of the prevailing wind and therefore the

Below:
This map from the 1970s shows the track re-laying task that faced the Mid-Hants Preservation Society, as well as the track configuration at Butts Junction, Alton.

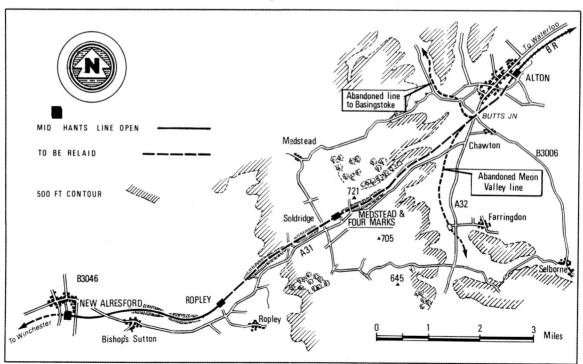

Above:

Not only was the Mid-Hants line a branch line but it was also regularly used by trains diverted from the Waterloo to Southampton main line, especially when engineering work was being carried out. The line was also in demand for railway enthusiasts' specials long before closure plans were confirmed. On 18 September 1960 SER Wainwright 'L' class No 31768, introduced in 1914, was unusual power over the line with the LCGB's 'The South Western Limited' railtour. The train is leaving Alton. *Bryan H. Kimber*

Below:

It was perhaps ironic that the most comprehensive use of the line for diversionary purposes was when the main London to Bournemouth main line was being electrified during 1966/67, when steam was about to give way to diesel and electric traction throughout the Southern Region. In this cracking study the motive power of the famous 'Bournemouth Belle' fully reflects the changing times. With its Sulzer eight-cylinder 1550hp diesel engine working hard, Class 33 No D6556 (later No 33038) has a significant boost from 'West Country' class No 34017 *Ilfracombe* with the down train, seen here west of Alton on 24 April 1966.
M. Pope

Above:
During the last years of the Mid-Hants line, but before freight services were withdrawn completely, one goods train worked up the branch as far as Alresford (from Eastleigh), while another worked down the line as far as Ropley. On 26 July 1961 the diesels have not yet arrived as seasoned campaigner No 30698, one of the '700' class 'Black Motors', approaches Alton with the 9.45am goods from Ropley. *C. Small*

Right:
Contrary to first impressions, this is not a diverted main-line train and it is not a short version of the down 'Bournemouth Belle'. The five resplendent Pullman cars had been chartered for a wedding special in association with the marriage of Sir Anthony Tichborne's daughter. Bulleid 'WC' class Pacific No 34010 *Sidmouth* is seen near Butts Junction on 19 September 1959. *S. C. Nash*

Left:
On the bleakest February day imaginable, a DEMU formation up from Winchester approaches Butts Junction in 1973. To the left the Meon Valley line once curved away to the south towards Wickham and Fareham, while on the right the old Basingstoke & Alton line once headed north. The remains of the signalbox can be seen on the right. *JV*

Above:
Some time after the closure of the Mid-Hants line in 1973 the track between Ropley and Alton was lifted, presenting the preservation effort with a formidable and expensive re-laying task. Replacing the track to Medstead & Four Marks commenced at Ropley in 1982 using the Boyer-Schwarz track-laying gantry seen here, which, running on the 10ft-gauge rails on either side of the standard gauge track, lifted track panels into position. Nevertheless, such activities were still labour-intensive — witness the three dozen volunteers in this cheery shot. *MHPS*

Left:
Medstead station had the most modest station buildings on the line. It did not open until 1868 and was renamed Medstead & Four Marks in October 1937, by which time a community had grown up around the station site.
In this charming everyday scene in the mid-1950s a down train from Alton, headed by 'M7' No 30029, enters the passing loop at the down platform and prepares for its stop. The signalman is ready to exchange tokens with the driver, who will then be able to proceed safely to Ropley. *Norman Simmons*

Right:
By the time the author recorded this scene at Medstead & Four Marks on a frosty day in November 1969, the down passing loop had been disconnected. Goods facilities had been withdrawn from 1964, and in 1967 the signalbox had closed and all station staff had been withdrawn. One of the faithful 'Hampshire' 3H Class 205 DEMUs, No 1133, arrives at the station with an Alton to Southampton train. The running-in board (left) used '&', but the totems used the word 'and' between the two place names in the title. *JV/TTT*

elements was rendered in cement. The station originally boasted a passing loop and signalbox, with a goods bay at the up end of the down platform, and one other long siding that comprised the 'yard'. The station approach was noted for a splendid avenue of beech trees. Although there were no other stations on the Mid-Hants line between Itchen Abbas and Winchester Junction, towards the end of the line's life in BR ownership there were plans to construct a halt not far from Kings Worthy, to the north of Winchester, to serve a new housing estate, but nothing came of the plan.

The single line joined the main London to Southampton line at Winchester Junction. As can be seen from the interesting map of the junction herein, the Newbury, Didcot & Southampton Railway passed under the main line at this location, and there was once a connecting spur linking the two. All Mid-Hants trains either collected or surrendered the single-line token at Winchester Junction, and, as there was no junction station, all trains over the line ran to Winchester and beyond.

Back in 1865 there were four trains per day in each direction, running mainly from Guildford to Southampton Terminus, but including two up trains and one down train to and from Waterloo. In this context the Mid-Hants line was indeed an alternative route to the main line, but not in a competitive sense. A single Sunday train was soon withdrawn. By November 1888 a total of eight trains were running in each direction together with two each way on Sundays; these included some workings to and from the capital. By 1927 there were six weekday services and two on Sundays. In that year the 19-mile journey from Alton to Winchester took about 48 minutes, at an average of less than 24mph — hardly express timings!

In 1937 the SR pushed its electrified network as far as Alton, and some 30 years later the London to Bournemouth main line was electrified, both modernisation schemes emphasising the exclusion of the Mid-Hants line from major capital investment. Electrification to Alton resulted in fewer Mid-Hants services working beyond Alton in the up direction. By 1938 there were seven round trips over the line, but in addition there was a wonderful curio: a through train in each direction between Bournemouth West and Folkestone/ Dover and Deal. Respect for the Sabbath had diminished with four round trips on Sundays, all running between Southampton and Alton. By then the Alton to Winchester element took 41 minutes to accomplish. During World War 2 the line was busy with military traffic and troop trains. In 1950, some five years after the war, there were nine round-trip workings, serving all stations on the line. Throughout the years there were slightly eccentric workings over the line including, by way of example, trains to Romsey, Portsmouth and even Fawley! Until the early 1960s there was normally a weekday goods train in each direction over the route, which picked up and set down as necessary.

Thus the railway served a useful purpose to the Mid-Hants community for over a century, although it never provided a viable alternative route to the main line and the potential double-track option was never taken up. Often there were main-line diversions over the Mid-Hants, for example when there were engineering works or a landslip or line blockage. But ironically it was towards the end of the line's life when, during the electrification of the LSWR main line to Southampton and Bournemouth, there were regular diversions, including the famous 'Bournemouth Belle'.

In November 1957 diesel-electric units started to replace steam traction and a regular-interval hourly service was introduced. This resulted in the most active Mid-Hants timetable ever, with no fewer than 16 round-trip workings. Journey times immediately decreased, and although this was a period when car ownership was rapidly increasing, passenger receipts grew substantially. In the first six months of 1960 more than 30,000 tickets were issued on the Mid-Hants line, excluding Alton. Even though the story of contraction goes back to the 1930s, when in 1931 the passing loops and signalboxes at both Ropley and Itchen Abbas closed, it was the

coming of the BR modernisation scheme and the subsequent exercise conducted by Dr Beeching in the early 1960s, to identify loss-making lines, that resulted in the 'beginning of the end'.

Although the introduction of diesel services had been beneficial, expenditure still exceeded income. Ropley and Itchen Abbas yards closed to goods traffic in 1962, followed in 1964 by those at Medstead and Alresford. The watercress traffic was diverted to the roads from 1963. Latterly, two goods workings operated over the line: a down freight from Woking working only as far as Ropley, and an up goods from Eastleigh working to Alresford and back. In 1965 Itchen Abbas lost its single member of staff, and in 1967 Medstead & Four Marks lost its passing loop and signalbox. In the same year all station staff were withdrawn, except at Alresford, which, from 1967, provided the only passing place on the line. Conductors issued most tickets on the trains, but because of problems caused by a lack of corridor connections many trains were double-manned, thereby adding to costs. With the completion of the Bournemouth electrification scheme in 1967, closure notices were posted along the Mid-Hants line, giving 6 May 1968 as the final day of services.

There was fierce local reaction to these proposals and a 'save the line' campaign was launched. However, BR embarked on a familiar pattern of closure by stealth, so effectively used on the Somerset & Dorset Railway. A new timetable resulted in poor Mid-Hants line connections at Alton. The line ceased to be used for diversions, even though it was readily available, and there were some highly suspect censuses of passenger traffic over the line. Certain speed restrictions were introduced, possibly caused by a lack of maintenance. However, the anti-closure campaign gained momentum and there were numerous hearings over five long years in an effort to save the line. A number of civic dignitaries and even Members of Parliament were enlisted, and some very robust anti-closure arguments were put forward. For example, it was demonstrated that buses could not cope in terms of providing a viable train replacement service, especially in terms of journey times; the train took 23 minutes from Alresford to Eastleigh, whereas the bus would take 2 hours (presumably via a devious 'all-villages' route)!

At the eleventh hour BR agreed to keep the line open, but only if an annual subsidy of £100,000 could be guaranteed by local authorities. Only £58,000 was immediately forthcoming, and consequently closure notices were again posted, with the last day of service being scheduled for 4 February 1973. The last train, with the author on board, was hauled up from Eastleigh behind a Class 33 locomotive, No 6511 (formerly D6511 and later 33011) and eight coaches, comprising two 4-TC units. There was a great send-off by the locals and detonators cracked along the line.

Although a wide variety of LSWR/SR/BR motive power operated over the Mid-Hants route in pre-preservation days, the main recollection of the majority of readers will be former LSWR 'M7' class locomotives hauling two ancient coaches in push-pull mode, a formation that comprised the mainstay of services for many decades. Also worthy of mention are the venerable 3H two-car and three-car Class 205 diesel-electric units that operated services for the last 16 years of the line's existence. In earlier days through trains were in the hands of tender locomotives, such as the graceful Class T9s, and locals were powered by a variety of 0-4-4Ts, including Class T1s. Latterly freight traffic was powered by 0-6-0 locomotives, particularly the '700' class. These Drummond locomotives were built at the same time as the 'M7' tank engines, and both their boilers and cylinders were similar and interchangeable. However, during 108 years of railway history a more detailed analysis of Mid-Hants motive power would resemble an LSWR/SR/BR stock book, especially when diverted trains are added to the variety!

During 1972 the first moves to preserve the line were mooted. Two groups were involved, and although they had slightly different

objectives, such as whether to run only east of Alresford or through to Winchester Junction, they later merged. As was the fashion with potential preservation schemes at the time, it was anticipated that the line would continue to provide a local service, by running daily diesel railcars, with steam trains operating on summer weekends. Following the merger, a parent company, the Winchester & Alton Railway Ltd, went public in May 1975, supported by the Mid-Hants Railway Preservation Society Ltd. There followed a protracted series of negotiations between the railway company, District and County Councils and BR. Much discussion concerned buying the trackbed and/or the actual track. All forms of analysis were carried out, from overall feasibility to legal and commercial considerations. An initial share offer failed to meet its targets by a considerable margin, but after abandoning the idea of a daily diesel service and the aspiration to run trains west of Alresford, a second attempt at raising the minimum (and much reduced) capital necessary was successful.

Eventually the track and land between Ropley and Alresford was purchased, but the track between Alton and Ropley was lifted, even though the land and buildings between those locations were purchased for posterity. The first train services provided by the preservationists were in 1977 between Alresford and Ropley, where a locomotive depot was established in the old goods yard.

The re-laying of the line between Ropley and Alton was completed in 1985, a huge project requiring 25,000 tons of ballast, 16,000 sleepers, 14 miles of rail and 1,300 pairs of fishplates. Gradually, over the years, the entire line to Alton was reopened, attracting large numbers of visitors. It is not possible in the space available here to record a 30-year history of the preservation era, suffice to say that the 'Watercress Line' has gone from strength to strength with a large roster of interesting steam and diesel locomotives and stock, operating a seasonal service over a demanding line. It has all the usual trappings of special events, 'Thomas' Days, footplate experience sessions, visiting locomotives and various galas. From time to time there have been disagreements between various parties, with a multitude of vested interests causing occasional conflicts, but these are irrelevant compared with the overall objective of successfully running an important preserved railway in a pleasant part of central Hampshire.

There is much of interest along the line, ranging from the locomotive depot, the topiary and the former LSWR Netley signal-box at Ropley, to the beautifully restored station at Alresford. Signs of the old Basingstoke and Meon Valley lines have all but gone, but the remains of Butts Junction signalbox can still be made out. Sadly the beech trees at the closed Itchen Abbas station have been reduced to stumps. A visit to the Mid-Hants is highly recommended.

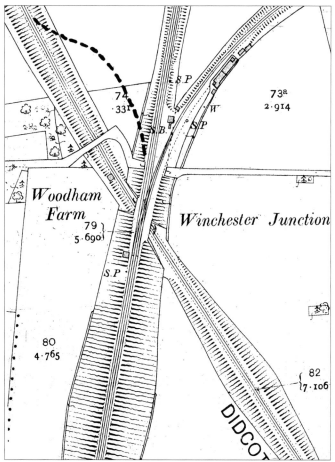

Above:
The preservationists have done a great job to revive the Mid-Hants line. Having closed in February 1973, it was as early as 30 April 1977 that the reopening steam special worked from Ropley to Alresford (a section that had not been lifted) behind 'N' class No 31874. Although plans to extend the line beyond Alresford were abandoned, during the first 17 years the 10-mile line from Alton to Alresford has been transformed as the reborn 'Watercress Line', and has become firmly established. Many fine steam and diesel locomotives have appeared on the line, typified by this shot of 'West Country' class No 34016 *Bodmin* blasting away from Alresford on 30 April 1988, adorned with the 'Pines Express' headboard. *J. Bennett*

Left:
This *circa* 1900 map shows the position of the signalbox at Winchester Junction. The single-track Mid-Hants line veers off the London to Southampton double-track main line to the north-west, while beneath is the GWR's Didcot, Newbury & Southampton Railway. The dotted line relates to a 1943 spur connecting the two lines, which saw little use after World War 2. It was disused by about 1950 and removed entirely in 1962. *Crown Copyright*

LONDON, ALTON, DROXFORD, FAREHAM, EASTLEIGH, and SOUTHAMPTON.

Down — Week Days / Sundays

Miles	Station	
	London (Waterloo) 167 ..dep.	
47	Alton A 167 ..arr.	
	Alton ....dep.	
52	Tisted	
55¼	Privett	
59	West Meon	
63¾	Droxford B	
68½	Wickham	
70½	Knowle Platform	
72¼	Fareham 184, 187 ..arr.	
	Fareham ....dep.	
76¼	Fort Brockhurst 199b	
77	Gosport ....arr.	
	Alton ....dep.	
51½	Medstead	
54½	Ropley	
57	Alresford	
60¾	Itchen Abbas	
65	Winchester C	
69	Shawford D 49	
73	Eastleigh F 184, 187 {arr. / dep.}	
75¾	Swaythling	
76½	St. Denys 184	
77¾	Northam	
78¾	Southampton G 1132 ..arr.	

Up — Week Days / Sundays

Miles	Station	
	Southampton Ter ....dep.	
—	Northam	
2	St. Denys	
3	Swaythling	
5¼	Eastleigh F 184, 187 {arr. / dep.}	
9½	Shawford D 49	
12¾	Winchester C	
17¾	Itchen Abbas	
21½	Alresford	
24	Ropley	
27	Medstead	
31½	Alton A 167 (below) ..arr.	
—	Gosport ....dep.	
¾	Fort Brockhurst 199b	
4¾	Fareham 184, 187 ..arr.	
—	Fareham ....dep.	
2	Wickham	
9¾	Droxford B	
13½	West Meon	
17½	Privett	
20¾	Tisted	
25¼	Alton A 167 (below) arr.	
—	Alton 167 ..	
78½	London (Waterloo) 167 ..arr.	

Legend:

A Station for Selborne (4½ miles).
a Arrives Waterloo at 12 9 aft. on Sats.
B Station for Hambledon (3½ miles).
C 1 mile from Cheesehill Station.
D Station for Twyford.
F Station for Bishopstoke.
F Southampton West.
G Southampton Terminus, for Docks.

☞ **For Local Trains** BETWEEN Winchester and Southampton...203 Fareham and Gosport...200

☞ **For other Trains** BETWEEN London and Southampton...154

☞ For Steamers from Southampton to Havre, see page iv; for Jersey, Guernsey, and St. Malo, see page iii.

BASINGSTOKE, HERRIARD, and ALTON.

Week Days only.

Miles	Station	
	London (Waterloo) 154 dep.	
	Basingstoke 154 ..arr.	
—	Basingstoke ....dep.	
3	Cliddesden	
6¼	Herriard	
9¼	Bentworth and Lasham	
14¼	Alton A 167 (above) arr.	
	Alton 167 ....dep.	
61¼	London (Waterloo) 167 arr.	

Miles	Station	
	London (Waterloo) 167 dep.	
	Alton A 167 ..arr.	
—	Alton ....dep.	
5	Bentworth and Lasham	
11	Cliddesden 159, 179	
14¼	Basingstoke 47, 154 ..arr.	
—	Basingstoke 159 ....dep.	
62¼	London (Waterloo) 159 arr.	

A Station for Selborne (4½ miles). a Arrives Waterloo at 12 9 aft. on Saturdays. b Departs at 5 aft. on Saturdays.

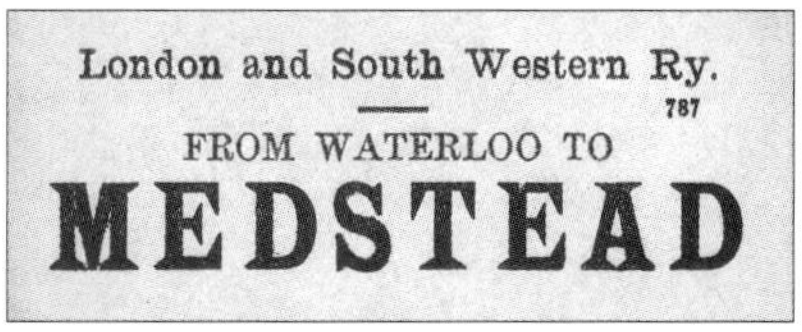

Above:
Itchen Abbas was the quietest station
on the line, even though the station
buildings were on a par with Alresford
and Ropley. As with other stations,
there were two distinct periods of
decline: the 1930s, when the passing loop
and signalbox were dispensed with, and
the 1960s, when all goods services
and all staff were withdrawn.
The station approach road was
distinctive because it was lined with
beech trees, now all pruned to stumps.
Class 205 No 1122 pauses at the
surviving grass-covered platform
in November 1969 with a down train.
JV/TTT

Left:
It's all action at Winchester Junction
as the driver of an up 'Hampshire'
three-car DEMU keeps his hat on as he
successfully collects the single-line token
from the signalman for the single-track
section to Alresford. The signalman's
typical BR silver-buttoned waistcoat
dates the scene. The signalbox closed
on 25 March 1979, more than six years
after the closure of the Mid-Hants line.
JV/TTT

WINCHESTER–ALTON LINE
CLOSURE
SPECIAL LAST RUN
4th February, 1973
Alton to
WINCHESTER OR EASTLEIGH
AND BACK
0041
0041
(S) For conditions see over

18. Basingstoke & Alton Light Railway

THE Basingstoke & Alton Light Railway was certainly not built to satisfy the army of 'film buffs' who have become so addicted over the years by the classic movie *Oh! Mr Porter* starring the redoubtable Will Hay, Graham Moffatt and Moore Marriott, that they regard the line as a monument and a point of pilgrimage. There is no doubt that the June 1937 comedy contains a number of one-liners that have become immortal, and the vintage motive power and rolling stock, not to mention the fictional 'Buggleskelly' station, with its goods sidings, the non-functional crossing gates and the signalbox-cum-greenhouse, produces some hilarious scenes. Moore Marriott's response of 'Next train's gone!' to Will Hay, alias new station master William Porter, tapping at the closed booking office window, is memorable, and the nosy postman repeatedly telling Will Hay that he is 'wastin' yer time' in planting lobelia is highly amusing. Perhaps the funniest scene is when they are working out how to perform a simple shunting move when resident vintage shunting engine *Gladstone* builds up steam and, without anybody on the footplate, starts to move and crushes their precious timepieces that had been placed on the track to represent goods wagons. A mix-up over the 'daylight saving hour' adds to the chaos, and there is a hilarious scene when a jumped-up uniformed Will Hay stops the express at his 'halt' only for the chimney of the locomotive to stop beneath Moore Marriott's 'long-johns' that are on a washing line over the track! *Gladstone* was in fact an 1899-built Hawthorne Leslie 2-4-0T, hired from the Kent & East Sussex Railway, and the other two tender locomotives used were an 1895 LSWR Adams 'X6' class 4-4-0 and an Adams '395' class 0-6-0 of 1885 vintage. All

Below:
The railway line from London to Basingstoke was opened as long ago as June 1839, but it was 62 years later, in June 1901, that a line was built from Basingstoke to Alton under the new regulations contained in the 1896 Light Railway Act. A 'nice little earner' for the branch was Thornycroft's Works, where, over the years, thousands of motor lorries were built. The original siding was on the 'up' (to Alton) side, but a further siding was later added on the down side of the line. There was also a BP oil siding nearer to Basingstoke. In the last years of the line's life there were freight-only stubs at either end, but these both succumbed in 1967. On 23 March 1963 'The Rambling Rose' railtour visited the northern stub powered by 'M7' class No 30108, the last passenger train on the line. *Trevor Owen*

of the locomotives had slight modifications, while *Gladstone* (alias *Northiam*) was dramatically changed, especially by the application of a tall comical chimney.

By the time *Oh! Mr Porter* was made the line was already in the process of demolition. However, back in August 1928 Gainsborough Pictures had already used the line to create a very realistic crash in a film called *The Wrecker*, when an ex-SER 'F1' class 4-4-0 and six early SECR bogie coaches hit a Foden steam lorry on a crossing at Salter's Ash Crossing, Hill Farm, Lasham. The track had been seriously undermined to create the desired effect, which was completely successful. Many of the cameras were concealed in 'hides', some of which were dummy haystacks, and in total 22 cameras were assembled to film the event from every angle. The train was travelling at 45mph at the point of impact. The wreck was then set on fire for effect, and as the petrol ignited, the scene became extremely realistic. Although two breakdown cranes cleared up the wreck, pieces of metal could be found in the adjoining field for years after the event. At a time when the line was losing money at a rapid rate, the £6-7,000 of income from the film company was most welcome.

The idea for building a railway from Basingstoke to Alton goes back more than 100 years, yet even today, despite the substantial growth of Basingstoke, once the M3 motorway to the south of the town has been passed, there is practically nothing in population terms until one reaches the outskirts of Alton. Along the line that was eventually built (see below), none of the intermediate stations were located anywhere near the villages they were supposed to serve, and but for a little intermediate coal and agricultural freight traffic, one could not imagine an investment less likely to succeed in terms of profitability. It was 1795 before even a turnpike road connected Alton with Basingstoke, and that was difficult to negotiate with its many hills.

The first proposal for a railway joining the two towns dates back to 1884, when there was a rather grand proposal to link the two towns with Petersfield, also in Hampshire, which was located on the 'Portsmouth Direct' line — there were all sorts of 'running rights' implications. However, the 22-mile, £450,000 line was rejected at committee, as was a later modified version in 1888. In 1895 a group of wealthy landowners and businessmen planned to build a staggeringly expensive £2 million railway line from the Great Western Railway at Basingstoke to Portsmouth via Alton, with a branch to Guildford.

Served firstly by the Basingstoke Canal of 1794, Basingstoke grew steadily but was really put on the map when the London & Southampton Railway reached the town in 1839. By 1848 the Great Western Railway had opened its branch from Reading to Basingstoke, and there was to be plenty of future rivalry. The GWR reached Salisbury in 1856 with its eye on the increasingly important ports of Portsmouth and Southampton, but in this area the LSWR was pushing outward and reached Alton via Farnham in 1852. However, the abovementioned 1895 plan really put the cat amongst the pigeons, and both the LSWR and the LBSCR put forward their case that Portsmouth was already well served by the two railway companies, and, as if to try and put a lid on expansionist plans, the LSWR also offered (subject to the rejection of the 1895 plan) to build a railway line from Basingstoke to Portsmouth via Fareham (effectively the Meon Valley line).

This all happened about the time that the Light Railway Act of 1896 was passed. As if to justify the Act, the LSWR proposed to cover part of its proposed route by a 12½-mile standard gauge light railway from Basingstoke to Butts Bridge, Alton, where a junction with the 1865-built Mid-Hants line would be formed. On 9 December 1897 the Light Railway Commissioners granted powers to the LSWR to build the line, subject to the rules and stipulations contained in the Act. This was to be the first railway to be sanctioned under the new Act. The first sod was cut in a field called Sixteen Acres near Basingstoke by the Right Honourable C. T. Ritchie, President of the Board of Trade, on 22 July 1898.

Although the word 'light' referred to aspects of operation on such a line, such as maximum speed, and construction, for example at crossings, there was nothing whatsoever 'light' about the construction of the Basingstoke & Alton. Significant cuttings had to be cut through clay and chalk, and the 230,000 cubic yards of material removed was used to form the many large embankments. The countryside was undulating and gradients of up to 1 in 50 were encountered. Construction work included a house for the station master and four terraced cottages for the staff at each of the stations! Everything else, from culverts to fencing, produced a cost estimate amounting in total to £67,000 for just under 13 miles of railway. There was only one fatality during construction, when a chalk fall crushed a labourer. In terms of land purchase and some permanent way construction, provision was made for any future double track requirement. There would be a 20mph speed limit over the route and 10mph on the tighter curves. A contractor's train travelled over the complete line in July 1900, just two years after the cutting of the first sod, but further lengthy wrangles meant that it would be nearer three years before the line opened. There were no fewer than 40 crossings of the railway: 20 were occupational, 11 were parish or road crossings, and nine were footpath crossings! A siding to Thornycroft's Works near Basingstoke, where lorries were constructed, was part of the original specification.

Initially there were just three stations on the line: from Basingstoke they were Cliddesden (3 miles 2 chains), Herriard (6 miles 46 chains) and Bentworth & Lasham (9 miles 19 chains). Not only was the population of these villages tiny, at 321, 351 and 571/144 respectively (1901 census), but the stations were hopelessly situated to usefully serve the villages whose names they carried. There was also a mighty dispute with the Cliddesden Parish Council about the remoteness of its station from the village centre. The stations had modest wooden-framed buildings with corrugated iron outer skins and a couple of goods sidings. All of the platforms were 3ft above the ground.

The *Hampshire Herald and Alton Gazette* of 8 June 1901, describing the opening of the line on 1 June, was less than complimentary. The report stated that 'the villages bearing the names of the stations are a long way from the stations and not a glimpse of them can be seen from the train . . . The village of Cliddesden is about a mile and a half from the station and in fact is almost as near to Basingstoke station' (in fact it was about a mile). It went on to say that 'the only houses near any of the stations are the cottages which the railway company have put up for their own employees.' The paper stated that 'the station buildings proper are most primitive. They consist of little galvanised iron shanties divided into "booking office" and "waiting rooms" in neither of which was there room to swing a cat.' The *Gazette* went on to say that the most imposing structures at the stations were the windmills built for the purposes of water supply. Having recently revisited Bentworth & Lasham station, the sole survivor, I can confirm that the newspaper's description of the stations was accurate. However, construction of the station cannot have been all that bad bearing in mind that my inspection was more than 102 years after the opening of the line. The floor is now rotten and, although it is firmly perched on the still extant concrete platform, its doors and windows are open to the elements. One end is sagging badly and the other has no cover, and the owner of the coal yard/lorry park complex confirmed that this ancient and rare survivor could be taken down shortly. It now serves no useful purpose, but it does seem a shame to lose a century-old landmark.

Trains strangely worked 'up' from Basingstoke to Alton. At Basingstoke they used the Alton branch bay platform and ran west on an independent line parallel to the main one, although trains had to pause for the single-line tablet. After about ½ mile the light

Above:

The Basingstoke & Alton Light Railway became famous in the annals of railway film-making when Gainsborough Pictures filmed *Oh! Mr Porter* on the line, particularly at Cliddesden (alias 'Buggleskelly'), in 1937. Here the principal characters in the film, Will Hay (William Porter), Graham Moffatt (Albert) and Moore Marriott (Jeremiah Harbottle), are seen in the cab of *Gladstone*, a Hawthorne Leslie 2-4-0T from the Kent & East Sussex Railway, previously named *Northiam*, which had the rear of its cab cut off just for the movie. *J. Hicks collection*

Below:

This remarkable extract from the LSWR working timetable shows the possible movements over the Basingstoke & Alton Light Railway in 1909. While it is reassuring that passenger trains could load to five coaches and freight trains to 25 empty wagons, no photographs survive that suggest these limits were ever approached by normal service trains.

BASINGSTOKE AND ALTON LIGHT RAILWAY.

This is a Single Line between Basingstoke West Box and Butts Jc. and is worked under the Regulations for working Single Lines by the Electric Train Tablet Block System.

The maximum load of Trains on the Basingstoke and Alton Line is as follows :—Goods Trains, 15 Loaded Wagons or 18 Mixed Wagons, or 25 Empty Wagons. A load of Coal, Sand, or Bricks to be counted as 1½ Wagons. Passenger Trains, 5 Bogie Vehicles. (V. 19,748.)

A—On Week-days when required (Mondays excepted).—Cattle Traffic, Great Western Railway to Aldershot, via Basingstoke.—When Wagons with Cattle for Aldershot are handed over at Basingstoke too late to go forward, via Woking, by the 3.20 a.m. Goods from Southampton, Mr. Prince, Basingstoke, to arrange to send the Wagons forward by the 7.55 a.m. Goods to Alton. The latter Train will be extended to Aldershot, when necessary, the Engine to return from Aldershot to Alton Pilot to the 10.6 a.m. Train from Woking. Basingstoke and Alton to arrange and advise all concerned. (S.D 2/18,964.) (T.R. 40,250.)

B—Cliddesden to call over the 10.30 a.m. Train from Alton daily and advise Basingstoke when there are Passengers for London.

C—When No. 7 Up Train runs the 5.30 p.m. Goods from Alton will start at 5.58 p.m. and arrive Bentworth at 8.18 p.m.

D—Bentworth to call over the 6.10 p.m. Train from Basingstoke daily, and advise Alton when there are Passengers for Medstead and below.

E—2 minutes earlier, commencing 12th July.

THORNEYCROFT'S SIDING BETWEEN BASINGSTOKE AND CLIDDESDEN.—Basingstoke to arrange to work Traffic to and from this Siding as may be necessary at the following Speed Table :—

Basingstoke	0 0	0 0
Thorneycroft's Siding	0 4	0 16
Basingstoke	0 20	

Right:
Cliddesden was the first intermediate station out of Basingstoke. The station was some way from the village, which resulted in protests at the time of construction. A single platform was provided and the small station building was like something from the world of Colonel Stephens, being wooden-framed with corrugated iron cladding.
There were two goods sidings on the up side. On the village side of the line there was a large water tower fed by an enormous wind pump. The pump was felled decades ago, but when the author visited in May 1972 the tank was still *in situ* **and a telephoto lens picked out the original works plate, a remarkable survivor.** *JV*

railway turned southward. Here a waterworks siding was built in 1906 and, at a later date, but on the other side of the track, a fairly busy oil terminal opened. Further to the south was Thornycroft's Works, which provided revenue for the line for many years, long after the railway closed to passengers. Indeed, it continued to be a customer of the railway after World War 2 and into the 1960s. There were alterations to the track alignment south of Basingstoke after the bypass opened in 1930/32. The line then climbed for a considerable distance, passing Cliddesden but on such a gradient that the village station could not be located at this point. The line ran around a long 80-chain-radius curve to the station, which was about a mile from the village. In addition to the sidings the station boasted a huge water tower and adjacent wind pump. This was the station known as 'Buggleskelly' in the film *Oh! Mr Porter*.

Again, steep gradients were encountered south of Cliddesden and the line included climbs of 1 in 50 combined with 12- and 15-chain-radius curves. The countryside continued to be attractive with small copses to the right and left with the settlement of Winslade and its church in the distance. Eventually the station of Herriard was reached, 3 miles and 44 chains beyond Cliddesden. Until the line was temporarily closed and lifted during World War

1, Herriard had the only passing loop, and hence the only fixed signals. As at Cliddesden there was a small two-road goods yard to the east of the station on the 'up' side, with one of the two roads having a loading bank and livestock pen. Beyond Herriard the line climbed again to reach its summit at 596ft above sea level. Not far from this point is Lasham airfield, which opened in 1943, and nearby was the crash site of *The Wrecker* motion picture, referred to earlier. The line now generally descended for some 6 miles. Eventually Bentworth & Lasham station was reached. Although there was a goods loop, built beyond the north end of the platform in 1904, and a two-road yard, this was not signalled and not a recognised passing loop. As with the other stations the site had four cottages, the station master's detached house and a water tank with windmill as basic infrastructure.

The line ran down the edge of a valley approaching Alton, turning right then left on many occasions before crossing what is now the main A339/A32 road and encountering substantial earthworks before reaching a small platform at Treloar's Hospital (originally an old military hospital). A small platform, opened to cater for patients and visitors, was provided in 1908 at a cost of £170. The platform, known as 'Alton Park', was for those using

Left:
The light railway opened in 1901, was closed and lifted in 1916/17, relaid and reopened in 1924, and finally closed to passengers in 1932, and goods in 1936. By 1972 the platform at Cliddesden, where the actor Will Hay was stationmaster of the fictitious 'Buggleskelly', was heavily overgrown, and by 2002 it was obscured beneath ground level by a manicured garden and copse. This last glimpse of the platform edge should be compared with the following photographs. *JV*

Right:
This classic photograph shows the very first scheduled train at Cliddesden station on 1 June 1901. The gleaming LSWR Class O2 No 203 (which was still active in the West Country 50 years later!) heads a guard's van, two four-wheeled coaches and four wagons, including two wagons of coal and two road boxes. Standing to attention in the centre of the posing group is the bearded stationmaster, Mr Bushnell, with his hat reflecting his rank. Note the wind pump referred to earlier.
JV collection

Left:
There are half a dozen local children befriending the redoubtable Mr Bushnell, his assistant and a platelayer at Cliddesden in this undated photograph.
In view of the relative isolation of the station from the village, the youngsters must have come from the row of railway cottages that were built adjacent to the station. Initially there were only three trains per day in each direction, leaving Basingstoke at 9.15am, 12.20pm and 5.45pm.
JV collection

Right:
Even specialist books on just the Basingstoke & Alton contain very few photographs of trains in action on the line. Possibly the early closure of the line and the infrequent service discouraged the photographers of the age. Accordingly, photographs such as Henry Casserley's study at Cliddesden on 13 June 1931 have become classics and have been published several times.
Here the crew of a Basingstoke-bound train headed by 'O2' class No 234 (BR No 30234) have ample time for a picture and to pose for the cameraman, just over a year before services were withdrawn for ever.
SLS/H. C. Casserley

Top left:
Other than the delightful
Bentworth & Lasham station
building, the main relics of the old
Basingstoke & Alton Light Railway
are the cottages built for
employees. This group,
photographed in January 2003,
are adjacent to the next station
down the line at Herriard.
The heavily overgrown platforms
are nearby and just discernible.
It is possible to drive between
the platforms. *JV*

Centre left:
Until 1916 Herriard was the only
passing place between Basingstoke
and Alton, and two signals were
controlled from the station,
but when the track was reinstated
in 1924 the branch was single
throughout, except for the goods
sidings and access thereto.
The former 'down' platform
can be seen here on the right.
As with Cliddesden, the small
goods yard was on the up side
behind the platform, and a wagon
can just be glimpsed through
the fence on the left. Note the milk
churns on the platform.
SLS/H. C. Casserley

Lower left:
Another shot of No 234,
this time entering Herriard,
also on 13 June 1931. Herriard was
the most important station on the
line, even though the population
of the village at the time of opening
was only 350. This was because
freight volumes — incoming coal,
fertiliser and seeds, together with
outgoing timber products, hay,
straw, livestock and, above all,
milk produced plenty of
income for the railway.
SLS/H. C. Casserley

Above:
A truly magnificent survivor, at least at the time of writing, is the station and platform at Bentworth & Lasham.
For many years it has been used as a coal yard and commercial vehicle storage area, so more than 100 years after the opening
of the line it is still possible to walk inside an original light railway station building (with permission of the site owners/occupiers).
However, the building is now in a poor state of repair and in 2003 the author was told it could soon be demolished. Located between
the villages incorporated in its name, the station also had a two-road goods yard, loading dock and cattle pen.
In 1931 745 tickets were issued at the station, just over two per working day! *JV*

and visiting the 'Lord Mayor Treloar Cripples Hospital'. Originally wooden, the halt was rebuilt in concrete at a later date. It did not appear in public timetables, as only one train each way served it, on Thursdays. Sir William Treloar was the Lord Mayor of London, and the hospital specialised in treating children who were crippled and those who were infected by tuberculosis, then a serious but common complaint.

Beyond the Alton end of the platform there was a coal siding to feed the hospital power plant. The siding was connected when the hospital reopened in 1908 and the establishment was renamed 'Lord Mayor Treloar's Hospital'. Locomotives could not access the siding, which was worked by a reversible steam winch that allowed coal wagons to be lowered to the hospital power plant. The siding was worked by a new ground frame that was controlled by the electric tablet for the Butts Junction to Herriard section. About 1,500 tons of coal were delivered to the siding each year. Originally delivered by the daily pick-up goods, the coal was later 'tripped' from Alton.

At Butts Junction (13 miles 4 chains) the Basingstoke & Alton Light Railway joined the Mid-Hants line from Alton to Winchester and also, from June 1903, the Meon Valley Railway from Alton to Fareham. Butts Junction had a fairly complex track layout because just yards before the junction all three single-track routes changed to double track. The entire line, encompassing all three routes, was doubled to Alton in 1901 in anticipation of the additional traffic from the (then) new lines. The 40-lever Butts Junction signalbox was located right on the junction but high above the main road. It is said that on rare occasions a careless single-line token change could see the token ending up in the road below! Alton station was

remodelled in 1903 and trains from Basingstoke used either the up main or outer face of the newly created island platform.

The initial service in June 1901 was three trains in each direction, the first not leaving Basingstoke until 9.15am and the last leaving Alton as early as 7pm. An opening fireworks display was declined by the LSWR because the service for the day finished before darkness fell! The opening was therefore a low-key affair and the *Hampshire Herald and Alton Gazette* said that there were just 19 people on each of the first two trains leaving Basingstoke, many of who were 'free trippers'. The paper conceded that the first train, comprising the locomotive ('O2' class No 203), two coaches, a guard's van, two trucks of coal and two road boxes, did at least have fresh-painted and upholstered coaches and guard's van. It stated that merely a score of people gathered on the platform at Basingstoke to see the first train off, and 'there was not the least excitement'. A road box was put off at Cliddesden, but no passengers left the train and only three boarded. The two coal wagons and the remaining road box were put off at Herriard, but the order of the vehicles necessitated much shunting. Apparently just a few locals along the way waved flags or handkerchiefs. The newspaper estimated that a dozen locals were at Bentworth & Lasham station to see the first train, and about four passengers alighted with as many boarding. The paper sarcastically noted that the train had taken 3 minutes under the hour for its 13-mile (in fact 14-mile) journey. It said that there were only about 20 people to see off the return departure from Alton at 10.25am, and again it suggested that there was little cheer or celebration. The return journey was faster than the outward because the only unscheduled

177

stop was to pick up an old coach from a siding at Bentworth & Lasham. About a dozen passengers joined the train at Herriard. The second departure from Basingstoke had no more general passengers than the first, but a 'saloon' coach was added for VIPs.

The train service soon increased to four trains per day. Each could work as a mixed train, depending on demand. Normally an 'O2' class off Basingstoke shed worked the train, but occasionally a 'Jumbo' 0-6-0 was used, in which case it always had to travel chimney-first (and be turned at Alton). A series of cheap day return tickets were available to encourage travel. In 1903 there was an experiment by the LSWR and LBSCR on the Southsea branch using 'railmotors', which effectively comprised a railway carriage with a small integral steam engine contained within, built for use on lightly used railways. The units cost nearly £1,400 to build, even though they were built 'in house' at Nine Elms. They contained a First Class saloon for eight passengers and another compartment for 32 Third Class. They were quite cramped within, and although they used less fuel than a conventional steam locomotive, their lack of power meant that they were of little use on a steeply graded branch, especially when a limited amount of goods traffic had to be handled. Two cars entered service on the branch on 1 July 1904, but by 12 August both were transferred away to shorter, flatter branches, after a stay of just six weeks!

Once the railmotors had been transferred away, the service improved to five passenger trains in each direction with a separate single goods train per day. From 1906 the service again improved to six round-trip workings, a frequency that did not change for a decade. In addition, a special cattle train for Basingstoke market worked the line on Wednesdays. With the line speed increasing in places to 25mph and with the abolition of mixed trains, overall journey times tumbled to 44 minutes in 1905.

As we have seen with many minor branches and byways, the coming of World War 1 had a serious impact, with either services being severely curtailed or, in extreme cases, lines being lifted altogether. Sadly, after services were reduced to just four trains in each direction during 1916, the Basingstoke & Alton Light Railway, which had been a loss-making line since its opening, was to suffer the ultimate fate, and the last train ran on 30 December 1916 'until further notice'. Apparently this was a good deal for the LSWR, because not only did it fulfil its obligation to Government (all companies had a mileage quota) but the company was paid for the value of the recovered assets and even for the cost of the line being lifted, the total cheque amounting to a whopping £26,000-plus. After closure it seems that the stations were still manned, at least initially, and a motor lorry freight service was still provided to get produce to town from the station goods yards. The sidings at both Thornycroft's and Treloar's were retained, as both were needed, the former contributing to the war effort.

After the war many lines were reinstated, but there seemed to be little action on the Basingstoke & Alton, and as early as January 1919 the LSWR received a petition from local residents asking when the 'temporarily' closed line would be reopened both for passenger and goods services. They may not have realised just how much of a loss-maker the line had been, or what the LSWR had received by way of compensation for its removal. Questions 'were asked in the House'. It then came to light that pre-war receipts from the line had been £1,232 per annum, while operating costs had been £5,400, and except for the track-lifting 'deal' the full capital cost of the line of nearly £108,000 had not been (and as likely as not would never be) recovered. Also, it was observed that traffic had been lost to road competition, probably for ever. Thus the decision not to reopen was taken. The LSWR also wanted to close Butts Junction signalbox and to run the surviving Mid-Hants and Meon Valley lines into Alton as single lines. However, despite the railway's intention to abandon the line permanently, the 1923 Grouping was on the horizon and the LSWR had not scheduled legislative time

for the abandonment process to take place. Then the petitioning locals of 1919 found new and influential strength and started what amounted to a campaign to have the line reinstated. However, despite their efforts the House of Commons approved the closure Bill. The House of Lords then became involved and a Select Committee was appointed to adjudicate.

What was by then the Southern Railway under Sir Herbert Walker made a robust case for closure, saying (I would think realistically) that the line would cost £35,000 to reinstate and that the maximum forecast receipts of about £5,000 would compare with annual running costs of more than £11,000. The objectors then seemed to let every man have his say, and all of these influential gentlemen said how much they intended to use the railway, and those that had nothing to say referred to various promises made by the railway back in 1895! At one point the SR became so exasperated that it offered to give the railway trackbed to the objectors so they could fund it and make the alleged forecast profits! The wrangling went on and on, and the newly created SR eventually caved in by getting agreement that the company would have the right to review the entire situation in 10 years' time if the line was working at a loss. Accordingly, in 1923, the process of track clearing and re-laying commenced. The passing loop at Herriard was not reinstated and the Butts Junction to Basingstoke West box became the longest single-line section on the new SR.

All works having been completed, and the customary inspections having been made, the 12 mile 72 chain line (the distance between the respective junctions) reopened from Monday 18 August 1924. In addition, a new oil terminal siding was opened for BP at the Basingstoke end of the line. Just three trains in each direction were to be provided, the same as back in 1901, with the middle of the three being mixed. The station master at Basingstoke was given an allowance for overseeing the line, in other words for becoming 'station master' of all three intermediate stations.

Although trains were well patronised during the early weeks of reinstatement, the line was still losing money. Timings were inconvenient because the SR was getting all three timetabled workings from the same train crew. Connections were poor and the first train was too late to pick up the milk traffic. In 1925 a fourth train was introduced to cure the latter problem, but this resulted in a huge gap in services in the middle of the day. The line struggled on, but a real knockout punch was delivered in 1927 when the Venture Bus Company introduced a competing service between Alton and Basingstoke, calling at the intermediate villages. The railway cut back its services to three trains per day — in 1928 Cliddesden station on average sold only three full price tickets *per week*! In that same year the railway was even able to accommodate the filming of *The Wrecker* referred to earlier. Within a couple of years there was also an efficient local motor lorry carrier. Bus fares were competitive and by 1931 Venture claimed that nearly 40,000 passengers were using its services. Accordingly, in April 1932 the SR wrote to local authorities and landowners informing them of its intention to close the line to passengers inside the 10-year review period mentioned at the time of the House of Lords Select Committee review. The SR observed that in the heaviest month of usage in August 1931 loadings averaged just five passengers per train. The last train duly left Alton on Saturday 10 September 1932 with only one passenger on board, a Mrs Eliza Bowman, who had travelled on the very first train!

The daily goods train continued to run, but only from Alton to the Hospital siding, with stop blocks placed just beyond the north end of Alton Park platform, and from Basingstoke to Bentworth & Lasham station site, with the stop blocks on the north side of the crossing, which consequently was no longer used. Butts Junction signalbox was abandoned in February 1935. The goods service from Basingstoke to Bentworth & Lasham was withdrawn on 31 May 1936 and the line remained open only to Thornycroft's

Works at the Basingstoke end. There were no objections! The track was lifted from the Bentworth & Lasham section, and while this was in progress Gainsborough Pictures again contacted the SR about using one of its lines for the film *Oh! Mr Porter*, as mentioned earlier. The total of about 50 film crew were in the vicinity of 'Buggleskelly' (alias Cliddesden) for nearly two months, producing much local excitement. Shortly after filming ceased the remainder of the line was lifted.

The stubs at each end of the line continued to operate for another 30 years, and its was thus possible to travel over small sections of the Basingstoke & Alton Light Railway, a fact not lost on the popular railway societies who ran 'specials' from time to time over the last few hundred yards of track. The first of the remaining three sidings to be lost was the BP siding at Basingstoke, in 1964. The other sidings had been busy with coal and lorry parts and materials, but both the Treloar Hospital siding and the Thornycroft sidings were given notice of closure in an era when most of BR's wagonload freight was being lost to road. Both sidings saw their last trains in 1967.

The line had been through a number of very different eras during its lifetime, but of one thing there was no doubt — over the years the railway had lost a great deal of money. It is amazing that by and large the area has retained its rural nature even though more than a century has elapsed since the line opened. Today, some 70 years after closure, much of the trackbed has been ploughed back into the fields, and in many places it is only just possible to make out where the line ran. However, the cottages and station master's house around each of the stations survive. At Cliddesden the platform was visible in a small copse some 30 years ago, but the land between the platforms has now been filled in and, while the site is now tidy, there is no trace of the old station. At Herriard there is a muddy track between the platforms, which are still quite visible albeit covered in trees, ivy and undergrowth. There are a handful of brick bridge abutments and an embankment or two, but the highlight is undoubtedly the survival of Bentworth & Lasham station building on the original platform, as mentioned earlier.

I wonder what Will Hay would have made of it all today.

19. Meon Valley

EVEN in the 21st century a drive from Alton to the outskirts of Fareham takes the driver through some remarkably rural countryside. The attractive scenery and the idyllic small villages are a delight, but, with the exception of the former market town of Wickham, population is still sparse and clearly agriculture remains 'king'. The trained eye can still see plenty of evidence that a railway line once ran along the route, which for most of the southern section follows the alignment of the valley of the River Meon. But what is more difficult to understand is how any passenger train service could ever be made to pay in an area with such a small population, and how any return could ever be secured on the huge amount of capital needed to meet the truly massive construction effort. This included tunnels, deep cuttings, heavy embankments, main-line standards at stations and even a large metal viaduct. It is necessary to look at railway company rivalry and transport politics in an attempt to answer the viability question.

Although removed from the Meon Valley, the area around Portsmouth and Gosport holds a clue to the development of the railway. From Napoleonic times the naval bases facing the Solent had become strategically important; logically, where there were ships there was industry, and where there was industry there were jobs, and where there were jobs there were people and houses. Consequently the Portsmouth and Gosport areas grew rapidly, with almost 70,000 residents by 1840. Steam replaced sail, there was increasing industrialisation, and nearby Southsea was becoming an established resort beside the sea. Within 20 years the 70,000 population became nearly 120,000. As soon as railway technology developed it was a natural progression to link cities, and a link from Portsmouth and Gosport to London was of course vital.

The LSWR linked 'Portsmouth' to London in 1841 by building a branch line from its London & Southampton Railway — the problem was that it ended on the other side of the harbour at Gosport! In the meantime the LBSCR had been making its way along the Sussex coastline, and in 1847 crossed into Hampshire and opened a line into the City of Portsmouth. The LSWR reacted in 1848 by building a branch from Fareham (where its Gosport line branched off) to join the LBSCR line, although passengers still had to travel from London via Winchester to reach Portsmouth. It was not for another 11 years, in 1859, that the 'Portsmouth Direct' line opened, affording LSWR passengers the service they reckoned they deserved.

Returning to the Meon Valley, there had been a number of plans over the years for railway lines in this area. As usual, some plans were ill thought out and highly speculative, but others had some strategic value. For example, the LSWR and LBSCR were both anxious that the Great Western Railway (and other potential competitors) should not gain access to the lucrative traffic generated in the area between Eastbourne and Southampton, where a combination of ports, docks and growing resorts had enormous potential. The GWR had reached Basingstoke way back in 1848 and clearly must have considered the possibilities of using its route as part of a South Coast to the Midlands and North link. In fact, the GWR did get as far as Winchester in 1885 when it operated the nominally independent Didcot, Newbury & Southampton Railway. The LSWR was always worried about possible incursions by the GWR.

There were many schemes for various lines in the Meon Valley area, too numerous to mention here, but one of the more serious

Left:
To head off opposition, mainly from the GWR, the LSWR opened a line from Alton to Fareham with the objective of shortening its route from London to Gosport on 1 June 1903. The first location for earning revenue was at Farringdon, where there were a number of sidings that were mainly used for agricultural produce. A small halt was opened in May 1931, and until 1934 the nameboard featured just one 'r' in the spelling of Farringdon. The tiny 65ft platform is seen in the 1950s.
Norman Simmons

ones, proposed in 1884, was to link Basingstoke with Alton and Petersfield, then, via the 'Portsmouth Direct', to Portsmouth. In fact, the GWR was against this private (but serious) proposal, which reached the Bill stage in Parliament. The same backers tried again with a second scheme, the Basingstoke, East Hampshire & Portsmouth Railway, which was to run from Basingstoke GWR to Alton, then via the Meon Valley to end a short distance from Southsea Pier, but the scheme failed to attract sufficient financial support. In the mid-1890s there was another scheme, the Portsmouth, Meon Valley & Alton Railway Company, backed by influential Portsmouth businessmen who were dissatisfied with the railway service afforded to their city. This and other schemes also did not come to fruition, but by 1896 the LSWR was sufficiently rattled by a seemingly never-ending list of proposals, which could not all be simply ignored, to propose that a light railway be built along the Meon Valley route. However, because the LSWR could see scope for the Meon Valley as part of a through, shorter and faster route to Gosport, the 'light' railway idea was replaced by its South Western (Meon Valley) Railway Act, which was passed in June 1897. The primary line was to be routed from Waterloo to Alton and Fareham as part of a through route to Gosport and Stokes Bay. The LSWR also saw limited scope for the line as an alternative route to Portsmouth.

Although casting one's mind back well over 100 years, it is possible to see why the LSWR would want to build the Meon Valley line to main-line standards, with curves and gradients suitable for express train running, especially if the Stokes Bay route to the Isle of Wight had become well established, but it is almost impossible to understand why the intermediate stations at the tiny villages served by the line had 600ft platforms. Even if the line had become a well-established through route, the express trains would not presumably have called at the villages en route. Also, further evidence of corporate indecision related to the permanent way, whereby all land acquisitions and embankment, bridge and tunnel tolerances were for double track, even though the permanent way provided was for single track with passing loops. In addition to the primary route, much building work was necessary widening the line from Alton to Butts Junction in the north and for avoiding the original 1841 tunnel at Fareham by building a 2-mile 'bypass' from Knowle to Fareham in the south.

Work on the line started in 1898 with an estimated total building cost of £400,000. With more than 24 route miles of track, albeit not all of it starting from scratch, construction commenced at a number of points on the line. At many locations it was a case of using the

spoil from cuttings, in this area mostly chalk, as the base material for nearby embankments. The line was well engineered and the maximum ruling gradient was 1 in 100. Compared with, say, the Basingstoke & Alton Light Railway, the station buildings were palaces. They were brick-built with Portland stone facings, partly tile-hung and of generous proportions and attractive design. The area was invaded by large numbers of navvies and their families, whose work was not without danger, and several met their deaths in a variety of accidents during the long five or six years of construction. In some of the large camps the navvies could get a dinner of meat, 'two veg' and bread for 6d and wash it all down with some decent beer, which cost 2d a pint.

In addition to the entire general building work there were several items of special note on the Meon Valley line. One of the obstacles to rapid progress was Privett Tunnel, which was curved and some 1,056 yards in length. There were huge volumes of excavated chalk used in a massive embankment that spanned the main Petersfield to Winchester Road, now the A272. The 64ft-high embankment was so large that the road itself ran, as it still does, through a 167ft 'tunnel'. The works here were, allegedly, the largest on the railway, which is why one of the main navvy encampments was located nearby. Three navvies lost their lives in separate incidents while the tunnel was under construction, one buried by chalk when a ventilation tunnel caved in, another crushed by a spoil wagon and a third fell between two wagons and was run over in a candle-lit tunnel working.

The third feature of note was West Meon Viaduct, which spanned the River Meon at West Meon and was 62ft above the ground. Although an eight-arch concrete viaduct had been considered, the subsoil and rock conditions resulted in a four-arch metal viaduct being built at a cost of £10,000, although it should be pointed out that the cost was reasonable considering the structure contained 725 tons of iron! Needless to say, the bridge abutments were enormous and great interest was generated locally when no fewer than four locomotives were placed on the viaduct to test architectural deflections etc.

From Alton to Butts Junction the line was double track, but once on the Meon Valley line 'proper' it was single track. The first location of note was Farringdon, where a siding was built primarily for the conveyance of agricultural produce. In later years additional sidings were in use and a ground frame 50 miles and 37 chains from London gave access to a goods shed and loading dock. After the Grouping an additional siding known as Aylward's was brought into use, and in the same area a Ministry of Food siding came into

Top left:
The first station down the line at the time of opening was Tisted. The Meon Valley line was built to main-line standards, but although provision was made for double track the line was single throughout, with passing loops at the stations. The main stations had full-length 650ft platforms and substantial station buildings. Signalboxes and goods sidings were provided and, indeed, goods traffic produced a greater income than passenger receipts. In this northbound view in 1948 we see the main building on the up side and the box and goods sidings on the down side. *IAL*

Centre left:
This view of Tisted station, looking north from the road bridge seen in the previous picture, is dated January 2003. Housing now covers the track towards Alton and the goods yard, which was once in the top right of this view, now serves another purpose. It was a pleasure to see the building in everyday use and surprising to see a Mark 1 coach at the up platform, which unfortunately could travel no further than its own length. *JV*

Lower left:
Three miles further down the track was Privett station. It was located about a mile from the village it served, although another village, West Tisted, was also only just over a mile away. Privett station was on a slight curve and had a busy goods yard at the south end. On 18 December 1954 '700' class 'Black Motor' No 30325 is shunting the yard. The goods train has been left at the down platform and a total of 13 goods wagons are in the sidings. *S. C. Nash*

Upper right:
The sun finally set on the Meon Valley line as a through route on Sunday 6 February 1955 when the RCTS ran its 'Hampshireman' special over the line, the day after service trains ceased. With the setting sun illuminating 'T9' class Nos 30301 and 30732, and with the driver giving the photographer a wave, locomotives and coaches pass Privett station for the very last time. Note the abandoned up platform, the old signalbox that had been closed for conventional use in 1922, and the loop line, latterly used only by occasional goods trains. *S. C. Nash*

Lower right:
For a considerable time after closure, Privett station was abandoned, rapidly becoming derelict. However, unlike West Meon station further down the line, the fine building was saved and is now in use as a private residence. This January 2003 view was taken from the site of the old goods yard, which is now fallow grassland. *JV*

Left:
South of Privett station were the 1,056yd Privett Tunnel, the summit of the line, and the 538yd West Meon Tunnel. The line then descended to West Meon village, but just before the station site, and standing 62ft above the road and the river valley, was the unusual metal West Meon Viaduct. Comprising more than 700 tons of iron, it was removed in March 1957 and this shot shows demolition taking place. *Hugh Davies*

use during World War 2. However, the main development for members of the public was when Farringdon Halt was opened in May 1931. The wooden platform was only 65ft long, so stopping was something of an art! Until 1934 the nameboards spelled the location 'Faringdon', with just one 'r'.

At 52 miles and 16 chains was Tisted station. The station had two full-length platforms, signalbox, goods yard and goods shed, yet there were a mere 52 inhabitants in the vicinity of the station. East and West Tisted each had about 250 inhabitants at the time of the opening of the line, but of course West Tisted's nearest station was Privett, albeit some 1¼ miles distant. More than 3 miles nearer Fareham was Privett. There had been a dispute over the naming of the station because the LSWR wanted to call the station West Tisted, the parish in which the station was located, but the landowner insisted that Privett should be the name because he wanted it that way and because it would be confusing to have both an East and West Tisted station on the same railway line. The landowner won the battle and, to be fair, Privett, at about a mile from the station, was nearer than West Tisted and it did, at 315 souls, have a larger population. Privett station was on a slight curve and again the double track ran between long platforms. At the south end of the station there were sidings on both sides of the main line, but the goods yard, cattle pen and goods shed were all on the east side of the track. The signalbox, located on the up platform, was closed as early as June 1922 and converted to a ground frame, and at the same time the former up loop ceased to be used as such and became a siding for goods train shunting.

After Privett the line climbed to its 510ft summit and entered the 1,056yd Privett Tunnel. On exiting the tunnel the line ran through particularly undulating countryside and on to the large embankment that ran across the A272 road, previously referred to. The next item of note was the curved West Meon Tunnel; at the completion of boring, when work from each end duly met, the two sections were within a mere ½ inch of each other! The line dropped away at 1 in 100 through the 538yd West Meon Tunnel, and just ½ mile beyond the tunnel was West Meon Viaduct, 62ft above the river and the first location where the line actually joined the river forming the valley in its name. A deep cutting took the line on to West Meon station at 59 miles 42 chains. With a population of 956 in 1901, the inhabitants were among the best served by the railway because the station was just ¼ mile from the village. Again, long curved platforms graced the cutting, with a multi-road goods yard on the up, or west, side, and a goods shed, loading dock and signalbox on the down-side platform. As elsewhere, the station provided the opportunity for trains to pass, and as at Tisted and Privett there was a large station building, at this location on the up side. All the building materials were brought to the site by horse and cart or by traction engines hauling up to three wagons.

The line then passed the hamlet of Meonstoke, where the water meadows are still susceptible to flooding, but on the whole the going here was a little easier. A deep cutting took the line on to Droxford, which eventually attracted some notoriety. In the first place skeletons were discovered when the station site was being excavated. The police became involved and work was temporarily suspended, but it turned out to be a Saxon burial ground and not the bodies of locals murdered by a yokel serial killer! In the second place, during June 1944 the final preparations for the World War 2 D-Day invasion were made at Droxford with a special train containing the War Cabinet stabled in a long siding at the station. Sir Winston Churchill, General Eisenhower, Mackenzie King, Anthony Eden, Ernest Bevin, General de Gaulle and General Smuts were among the international 'hall of fame' attendees. Droxford had a population of just 500 at the time of the line's opening, and for many years the running-in board read 'Droxford for Hambledon' (Hambledon being 3½ miles away). The goods yard containing cattle pens and a goods shed was at the southern

end of the up platform. The signalbox was on the up platform, but the main station building was on the down side.

The line continued along the valley beside the River Meon and chalk gave way to clay. A ground frame at 66 miles 42 chains controlled some goods sidings at Mislingford, and this freight-only site was important enough to have a goods shed. The ancient market town of Wickham had a four-figure population at the end of Queen Victoria's reign and the LSWR provided a full-sized station that was only a stone's throw from the town. In common with the other stations there was a goods shed, a two-road goods yard and a goods bay. The signalbox was on the down-side platform. The river had to be crossed twice in the environs of the station and the viaducts were more substantial than up country because the river was wider at Wickham. The Meon Valley line joined the 1841 Bishopstoke (Eastleigh) to Fareham and Gosport line at Knowle Junction. Initially Meon Valley line trains had to run through a single-bore tunnel into Fareham, which had been troublesome for many years, but in 1904 a deviation line was completed avoiding the tunnels. Nevertheless, after refurbishment, one might say almost rebuild, both up and down Meon Valley line trains used the old tunnel and there was no connection with the deviation line. At Fareham there was a bay platform that was used by most Meon Valley trains in later years.

The railway opened on 1 June 1903. The initial service over the 22¼-mile route provided for six round-trip workings from Monday to Saturday and two on Sundays. There was also a late-evening train on Saturday evenings for revellers. There were some through trains from Waterloo to Gosport that were normally in the hands of LSWR Adams 'Jubilee' 0-4-2 tender engines. On Alton to Fareham/Gosport workings LSWR Adams 4-4-2T locomotives were the preferred traction. It was clear from the start that in terms of total railway revenue goods traffic was far outstripping passenger revenues. There were coal merchants at all of the stations, milk was despatched in large quantities, there were 'in season' strawberry specials, large volumes of seasonal sugar beet, and cattle travelled to both Fareham and Alton markets. The railway responded by selling cheap market day tickets.

The line settled down and while neither traffic nor earnings were spectacular, the Meon Valley Railway served a useful purpose. In fact, during World War 1 additional use was made of the line for troop movements etc, but never enough to warrant the provision of the double track potential incorporated in the original design. However, during the war, in November 1915, the Stokes Bay line closed, and consequently the grand plans for a premier route to the Isle of Wight never materialised. This was a blow to the Meon Valley line, and after World War 1 the through Waterloo to Gosport trains were only partially reinstated. The January 1927 Bradshaw shows that there were seven through trains in each direction on weekdays plus a Saturdays-only 'short' working to Wickham; there continued to be two trains each way on Sundays. Subsequently most trains worked just to Fareham, whereas hitherto many had worked to Gosport. By 1938 there were seven round trips on weekdays over the entire line and three on Sundays; all the latter operated to and from Portsmouth & Southsea. By 1954 the rot had truly set in, and services had dwindled to just four weekday trains in each direction with no Sunday service at all.

It has again to be stated that World War 1 seemed to be something of a milestone for the railway. Shortly after the end of the war the line increasingly developed a branch-line feel and with the usual story of personal motor vehicles, motor buses and especially motor lorries increasing in numbers, there was going to be an almost inevitable decline in both passenger and freight traffic. The direct farm-to-market potential of the motor lorry with no transhipment requirement became an overwhelming temptation to many rural farms and businesses, especially over short distances, and road transport companies also began to emerge. During 1922

Upper right:
A delightful scene for the
railway romantic but not
one to cheer the Chief
Finance Office is this view
of the daily goods up from
Fareham. With just a single
wagon and a brake-van in
tow, the driver of '700' class
No 30350 prepares to
surrender the token to the
West Meon signalman in
the early 1950s. There was
a large goods yard at this
location and, unusually,
the village was within
a few hundred yards
of the station.
R. K. Blencowe collection

Lower right:
It is hard to believe that
this entire scene is now
in a heavily wooded area.
On this day in the 1950s
West Meon was a busy
place as the up goods
crossed with a down
passenger working, the
latter comprising the usual
'M7' and two coaches.
Note the unusual break in
the line of the platform,
used by both passengers
and signalmen to cross the
running lines. The main
station here did not survive
and was reduced to rubble.
R. K. Blencowe collection

Left:
By the time the author
visited West Meon, some
17 years after closure in
June 1972, to make this
pleasant pastoral record
of the abandoned station
and goods yard (on the left),
the station building was
abandoned but still standing
at that time. It was only just
possible to walk the length of
the long platforms towards
the distant road bridge (see
the previous plate), and in
2003 it was impossible. *JV*

the up platform at Privett ceased to be used by passenger trains and the signalbox was reduced to ground frame status. In 1926 the footbridges at Tisted, West Meon and Wickham were removed. A positive move was the opening of the halt at Farringdon in May 1931, named Farringdon Platform in May 1932 and just plain Farringdon in July 1934. However, the counter to any thoughts of a revival was when plans were made to electrify the SR line from Waterloo only as far as Alton. World War 2 again saw the line used for special additional traffic, but other than for the famous Droxford episode and a few bombings there was no lasting impact on the line. The line was still being maintained to a high standard and in 1950 the permanent way gang at Privett received a special 'best kept section of line' diploma. The route was still the quickest way of getting from Fareham to London, but by the early 1950s the writing was truly 'on the wall'.

The last train down the route to Fareham from the early 1950s was the 4.30pm from Alton, which did an awful lot of good for day return tickets to London! For some time the services had comprised just two-coach push-pull sets that looked rather strange at the 600ft-long platforms. Other than the motive power from the early days already mentioned, passenger trains were for many years in the hands of the purposeful 'M7' class. Occasionally veteran 'T9s'

would appear, but the only real variety came on the freight trains, and even that was limited. 'T9', 'L12' and '700' classes worked most of the goods services. In later years both the 'Q' and 'Q1' class emerged from Guildford shed from time to time, and once the main central part of the branch closed, 'C2Xs', 'U' class and BR Standards all put in appearances, mostly at the southern end of the line. Long before Dr Beeching could be blamed for any closures, BR (SR) calculated that it could save almost £40,000 per annum if the line was closed, and public subsidies were not exactly falling into its hands at that time. The inevitable announcement soon came and notice was given of the withdrawal of all passenger services and freight from the yards at Tisted, Privett and West Meon.

There were of course the usual round of objections, but the case for closure was overwhelming and all the pleas were ignored. Freight would continue to run to Farringdon in the north and to Droxford in the south. The last day of normal scheduled services was 5 February 1955, but on Sunday 6 February the RCTS ran its 10-coach 'Hampshireman' railtour (also covering the Pulborough to Petersfield via Midhurst line), which over the Meon Valley line was double-headed by a brace of 'T9s' (see photograph). 'M7' No 30055 had worked the last scheduled down train and Drummond '700' class 'Black Motor' No 30326 worked the last

MEON VALLEY (ALTON AND FAREHAM) LINE.

FOR SPEED RESTRICTIONS SEE PAGES A, B, C, D, E, F & G.

This is a Single Line from Butts Junction to Fareham Junction and is worked under the Regulation Single Lines by the Electric Train Tablet Block System.

UP TRAINS.—WEEK DAYS.

Distance from Gosport.	Nos.	1 Pass.		2 Pass.		3 Pass. Eastleigh. B		4 Special Discharged Soldiers when req'd.		5 Pass. F		6 Pass.		7 Goods. D		8 Pass.		9 Pass.	
		arr.	dep.	arr.	dep.	arr.	dep.	arr.	dep.	arr.	dep.	arr.	dep.	arr.	dep.	arr.	dep.	arr.	dep.
M. C.		a.m.	a.m.	a.m.	a.m.	a.m.	a.m.	a.m.	a.m.	p.m.	p.m.	p.m.	p.m.	p.m.	p.m.	p.m.	p.m.	p.m.	dep.
—	Gosport ...	...	725	...	...	...	...	...	...	...	...	...	...	...	...	...	...	...	...
1 36	Fort Brockhurst ...	7 28	7 29	...	...	...	...	...	11 38	...	...	...	...	...	...	5 8	5 9	...	...
5 0	Fareham ...	735	740	...	1039	...	1130	11 15	...	...	1 37	...	430	...	5 5	515	526	...	6 47
7 6	Knowle Platf'rm	...	...	Aft. No.1 Dn 10 44	10 44	Aft. No.1 Dn 11 34	11B38	Aft.No.1 Dn		Aft.No.4 Dn		Aft.No.6 Dn		Aft.No.6 Dn		Aft.No6 Dn		Aft. No.7 Dn 6 51	6 52
7 33	Knowle Box ...	...	7 45	...	10 45	...	11 39	11 50		1 42		4 35		5 13 D		5 31		6 53	
9 13	Wickham ...	7 48	7 49	10 46	1049	11B42		11 53		1 45	1 46	4 38	4 39	5 18	5 46	5 34	5 35	6 56	6 57
								Cross Nos. 2 & 3 Down.						Fol.No. 8 Up		Precede No. 7 Up			
11 8	Mislingford Gds.	...	...	...	...	...	...	...	...	...	...	...	...	5 51	6 5				
14 23	Droxford ...	7 58	7 59	10 58	10 59	...	...	12 2		1 55	1 56	4 48	4 49	6 14	6 35	5 44	5 45	7 6	7 7
				Cross No. 2 Down.										Cross No. 7 Down.					
18 11	West Meon ...	8 6	8 7	11 6	11 7	...	...	12 9		2 3	2 4	4 56	4 58	6 45	7 34	5 52	5 53	7 14	7 15
														Cross No.8 Dwn. & Fol. No. 9 Up.					
22 19	Privett ...	8 16	8 17	11 16	11 17	...	...	12 18		2 13	2 14	5 7	5 8	7 46	8 2	6 26	6 5	7 24	7 25
25 32	Tisted ...	8 22	8 23	11 22	11 23	...	...	12 22		2 19	2 20	5 13	5 14	8 10	8 20	Crs.No.7 Dn 6 10	6 11	Crs.No.8 Dn 7 30	7 31
				Crs.No 3 Dn.				Crs.No.4 Dn.											
27 12	Faringdon Gds.	...	...	...	...	...	...	...	...	...	...	...	...	8 25	8 35	...	...	...	...
29 53	Butts Junction ...	8 29	...	...	11 29	...	...	12 27		2 26		5 20		8 40		6 17		7 37	
30 61	Alton ...	8 31	8 48	11 31	1136	...	...	12 39		2 28	2 31	5 22	5 32	8 45	...	6 19	657	7 39	7 58
77 56	Waterloo	1021	...	1 0	...	...	...	2 3		4 13		7 1		...		846	...	9 29	...

LEE ON THE SOLENT RAILWAY.

		WEEK DAYS.																						SUNDAYS.		
M.C.			a.m.	a.m.	p.m.	p.m.	p.m.	p.m.	p.m.	p.m.	p.m.													p.m.	p.m.	p.m.
—	Fort Brockhurst Jct.	...	1015	1130	1250	2 30	3 35	4 55	7 5	8 5	...	...	...	...	...	...	...	...	...	...	...	...	...	4 10	4 55	7 0
1 10	Privett ...	} Stops by Signal										...	...	...	...	...	...	...	...	...	...	...	...	...	...	...
1 77	Browndown ...		...	...	...	...	...	...	...	...																
3 0	Lee on the Solent	...	1030	1145	1 5	2 45	3 50	5 10	7 20	8 20	...	...	...	...	...	...	...	...	...	...	...	...	...	4 25	5 10	7 15

		WEEK DAYS.																						SUNDAYS.		
M.C.			a.m.	a.m.	a.m.	p.m.	p.m.	p.m.	p.m.	p.m.														p.m.	p.m.	p.m.
—	Lee on the Solent	...	9 20	1035	1150	2 10	3 0	4 10	6 30	7 30	...	...	...	...	...	...	...	...	...	...	...	...	...	3 0	4 35	6 40
1 3	Browndown ...	} Stops by Signal										...	...	...	...	...	...	...	...	...	...	...	...	...	...	...
1 70	Privett ...																										
3 0	Fort Brockhurst Jct.	...	9 35	1050	12 5	2 25	3 15	4 25	6 45	7 45	...	...	...	...	...	...	...	...	...	...	...	...	...	3 15	4 50	6 55

Left and below:
These interesting 1909 LSWR working timetables give precise mileages and full details of all trains traversing the Lee-on-the-Solent and Meon Valley branches (up trains).

Below:
The Meon Valley line joined the Eastleigh to Fareham line at Knowle Junction, which was adjacent to Knowle Halt (before 1942, Knowle Asylum Halt). Knowle Junction was 2 miles and 32 chains northwest of Fareham, an important junction where lines to Portsmouth, Gosport, Eastleigh and Southampton radiated. This 1984 view, looking north-west, shows a train from the West Country to Brighton double-headed by Class 33s entering the station from the Southampton direction. The line behind the ninth coach goes through the Fareham/Funtley Tunnels to Eastleigh (and previously the Meon Valley). The stone terminal on the right is still open but now 100-tonne wagons, rather than these small four-wheelers, are hauled to and from Somerset behind American-built Class 59 and 66 locomotives. *JV/TTT*

up train, both being formed of four coaches, with wreath and headboard suitably applied and detonators duly exploded! From 7 February the line between Farringdon and Droxford was closed completely. After the crowded scenes of the last few days, when public and enthusiasts came in their hundreds from all over the South East to witness the last rites, it seemed strange that everything had fallen silent.

Demolition started very quickly indeed, and through the latter part of 1955 and 1956 piece by piece the railway was dismantled. For some time the two remaining stubs were worked by daily freights, but after being reduced to three trains per week the Droxford/Wickham goods finally succumbed on 30 April 1962. During the freight-only period Wickham and Droxford signalboxes were demolished. For some time parts of this section of line were used for the storage of withdrawn goods wagons. In the north the Farringdon freight lingered on until 13 August 1968, but it too had out-served its usefulness and, to be honest, BR was at that time not encouraging wagonload freight — it was block loads or nothing. Combine that situation with increasing costs and seemingly perpetual strikes being called by railway trade unions, which prevented customers getting their goods and produce on time, and you have a recipe for disaster, in this case complete closure of the Meon Valley Railway.

For a time the 'closed' line from Droxford station to Knowle Junction was used by Mr Charles Ashby, who had designed the Sadler 'Pacerailer' railbus and was using the line for testing it. It was also tested on the Isle of Wight, but sadly its ultimate fate was to be destroyed by vandals, the scourge of recent generations. An LBSCR 'A1X' class 'Terrier' was located at Droxford for a short period of time before being transferred to a plinth outside a public house at Hayling Island. The Southern Locomotive Preservation Company moved some stock to Droxford, including a USA tank and a diesel shunter, because there was, at that time, a slim chance of the line becoming a preservation centre. However, a site at Liss on the closed Longmoor Military Railway was another possibility, and once BR decided to close Knowle Junction the preservation effort came to an end (as did the Liss plan at a later date). The entire track was subsequently lifted.

The stations at Tisted, Privett and Droxford continue to survive as private residences, and the old tunnels can be found with difficulty. The amazing 'road tunnel' on the A272, under the huge railway embankment, remains as a reminder of the Meon Valley

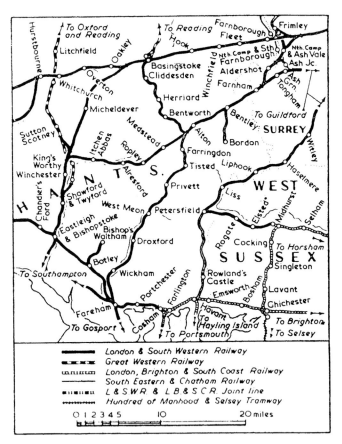

Above:

Map of the Meon Valley line and connecting lines.

line, and a Mark 1 railway carriage resides at the old up station platform at Tisted. There is a piece of platform edging at Wickham, and an industrial estate covers much of the old Farringdon site, but a fine road overbridge survives. However, it is now almost half a century since the line closed and, whatever relics may survive, the remarkable line has gone for ever. Discovering an old coping stone hardly compares with the sight of a black, lined 'M7' trundling through the splendid Hampshire countryside with a pair of red push-pull coaches and a wisp of steam!

Left:

Wickham was the largest place on the line and an important market town in the area. In addition to the two-platform station, with a station building similar to others on the line, a goods yard was provided on the up side with all the usual facilities. After closure to passengers in 1955, Wickham station understandably developed a rather forlorn appearance, even though it continued to be visited by freight trains until April 1962. The down siding, down loop, up headshunt and signalbox were all removed in 1957. Pausing at the station with a Branch Line Society tour in March 1959 is 'M7' No 30111, with a good crop of 'gricers' inspecting the remains.

David Lawrence

20. Gosport and Lee-on-the-Solent Branches

THE railway line from Bishopstoke (now Eastleigh) to Gosport was the earliest route in the area to open and the first branch line in the county of Hampshire, the first train running along the route in November 1841. It is interesting to note that in formulating the relevant Act of 1839, the London & South Western Railway (formerly the London & Southampton Railway) described its plans as serving the 'Port of Portsmouth'. However, under the terms of the 1839 Act the line ran only from Eastleigh to Gosport via Fareham, and for the next five years the citizens of Portsmouth had to cross the water to Gosport in order to gain access to the railway, a situation they were far from happy about. They wanted rail access to the capital by a direct route.

The importance of Gosport must not be underestimated. Although completely overshadowed by its larger neighbour in later years, in the mid-19th century Gosport was well established and had important connections with the Royal Navy. This importance was reflected in a very impressive terminus building at Gosport, which although now rail-less, survives to the present day. Sir William Tite designed the grand building and it boasted fine arches and a magnificent colonnade comprising 14 bays. There were buildings

on the down and up side, but the southern 'departure' side was more impressive, with an all-over roof and a centre road between the platform lines. The fine building had to be built to dimensions specified by the military, such was their influence in the area. Sadly the station suffered from bomb damage during World War 2, but on the bright side, part of the fine listed building is preserved, albeit in a state of 'arrested decay'.

The line down to Gosport was extended beyond the 'terminus' across a main road to reach the fortified Clarence Yard in 1845. For the exclusive use of the Royal Family on their visits to Osborne House on the Isle of Wight, a unique station was built within the confines of the yard, known as Royal Victoria Station and boasting a 520ft platform covered by an overall roof supported by iron columns. From this station the Royal party normally walked a short distance to board the Royal Yacht *Alberta*. Thus, while Royalty may well have used the ornate 'public' station at Gosport for a short time in the early 1840s, from 1845 they 'crossed the road' to Clarence Yard out of the public gaze.

Another important factor in the railway development of the area was the focus on services to the Isle of Wight. There was also the

Below:
The tight curve at the south-east end of Fareham is testimony to the fact that the straight line down to Gosport, seen just above the locomotive's cab, was the original route, opening as early as November 1841. The line to the left is the 1848 route to Cosham and Portsmouth, at that time the LSWR's main line to Portsmouth, the 'Portsmouth Direct' line through Guildford and Petersfield not opening until the end of 1858. In October 1990 Class 33/0 No 33057 in 'Dutch' engineer's livery arrives from Brighton with an Exeter-bound train comprising Network South East Mark 2a/b stock. *JV/TTT*

growing Victorian activity of 'taking the sea air' to consider, whereby city dwellers got away from factory smoke for a breather by the seaside. Queen Victoria and Albert, the Prince Consort, purchased Osborne House on the Isle of Wight in 1845, and this really put the island on the map. In future years this 'publicity' would be a catalyst in the development of seaside resorts such as Sandown and Shanklin, which became popular destinations. From 1863 a line would veer off southward just ¼ mile from the Gosport terminus to Stokes Bay, making good use of the short distance from the Gosport area to the Isle of Wight (see below). A triangular junction was also established.

In the meantime, in June 1847 the LBSCR had driven its route from Brighton into the heart of Portsmouth, an event celebrated by the large and growing city. In 1848 the LSWR's line from Fareham to Portsmouth via Cosham was built, joining the LBSCR line at

Below:
The normal passenger train service from Fareham to Gosport ceased as long ago as June 1953, by which time there were only two trains per day. Goods trains continued to run to Gosport, but in 1969 these were cut back to Bedenham sidings. All traffic finally ceased in 1995, but the rails were left *in situ* pending decisions on a possible comprehensive tramway system for the Portsmouth and Gosport area which might incorporate parts of the old branch. At the end of 2003 the Government failed to approve the *circa* £250 million scheme. This view shows part of the old Gosport branch in 2003, which is popular with local dog-owners and fly-tippers! *JV*

Portcreek Junction, to the northeast of the city. The opening of this line had an immediate effect on the traffic handled at Gosport, and of course no longer did passengers have to cross the harbour to gain access to the railway. However, there was an abundance of general freight traffic at Gosport, and military and admiralty stores were voluminous. Not only was Gosport growing, but the area further west, along the coastline at Lee-on-the-Solent, was also increasing in population. As mentioned above, there was also a possibility of exploiting the potential of the land south of Gosport around Stokes Bay to lead the competition to reach the Isle of Wight by the quickest route.

The 5-mile double-track line from Fareham Junction to Gosport was well used in the early days and Bradshaw's Guide of 1888 shows that there were 11 trains per day to and from Fareham, with seven arrivals and departures from both Gosport and Stokes Bay (some trains called at one or other of the stations while some called at both). There was but one other intermediate station on the original line, at Brockhurst. Opened in 1865, it stood at a point where a military road connecting a line of forts was crossed by the railway line to Gosport (and later Stokes Bay). From 1893 the station name was changed to Fort Brockhurst to avoid confusion with Brockenhurst, located on the main line from Southampton to Bournemouth. Brockhurst had long platforms to accommodate a growing traffic in troop trains and there are journals referring to such traffic as long ago as 1871. The station also handled large quantities of military stores, but they were mostly dealt with at the adjacent Government sidings. A signalbox controlled the road crossing and the sidings. The line was originally built without road crossings, but as the Gosport area grew there were eventually a total of four, one of which was replaced by an overbridge in the 1930s.

As viewed from the station overbridge at Fareham there is no doubt, judging from the straight alignment beyond the station, that the original double-track line was the line to Gosport. In fact, the route runs in almost a straight line to Fort Brockhurst. Some 2¾ miles from Fareham was a sizeable Admiralty depot and stores area called Bedenham. Eventually this site became the only reason for the line's existence. Fort Brockhurst was 3½ miles from Fareham, and from 1894 was the junction for Lee-on-the-Solent, and, as already mentioned, some Government sidings were located adjacent to the station. Just before reaching Gosport terminus, 5 miles from Fareham, was the junction that headed south to Stokes Bay. This was constructed in 1863. An additional spur constructed in 1865 created a triangular junction, enabling Stokes Bay trains to call at Gosport, albeit with a reversal at the original terminus. A small engine shed and watering facilities were located adjacent to the north chord. At Gosport there was a down-side goods yard, the extension to Clarence Yard and up-side sidings.

The Stokes Bay Railway & Pier Company was formed in 1855 with the objective of building a double-track 1¾-mile line from the junction with the Gosport line down to a pier on the foreshore where passengers would transfer from train to ship for the short journey to the Isle of Wight. It would be necessary for the railway to cross two significant creeks in the area and to build a pier to facilitate a rail-to-ship interchange. There were delays while negotiations were conducted with the Admiralty and the War Office, as well as problematical fund-raising to provide the capital for the grand plan. Finally the line opened on 6 April 1863. To accommodate Gosport passengers on those trains not calling at the original branch terminus, a new station called Stokes Road was opened just south of the triangle in 1865. The name was changed to Gosport Road in 1866 and to Gosport Road & Alverstoke in 1893.

At the triangle there were three signalboxes, one at each apex: Lees Lane to the west, Stokes Bay Junction to the south and Gosport to the east. Although the Stokes Bay line closed in 1915, Stokes Bay Junction signalbox did not close until 1924! Lees Lane closed in 1934, when the branch to Fareham was singled.

Above:
The Army had an extensive railway system and a large stores and equipment depot at Bedenham, about 2¾ miles from Fareham, and worked wagons to and from exchange sidings on the Gosport branch. Latterly small Hunslet diesel locomotives were used, and once they left the secure confines of the MOD they crossed a road into a two-road loop. Due to security sensitivities one had to be inconspicuous with a camera, so a powerful telephoto lens was used for this shot; note the MOD police constable just to the left of the right-hand 'Stop' sign! The little Hunslet hauls four ammunition and two other vans through the secure fencing into the loop during May 1991.
JV/TTT

Left:
Having picked up the six-wagon load featured in the above photograph from the exchange sidings, hence its reverse order, Railfreight Class 47 No 47354 heads up the Gosport branch on its way to Fareham. Note that the old 'bullhead' rail is attached to concrete sleepers. These military freight trains ran as and when required, and without inside information there was little likelihood of securing photographs.
This traffic ended in 1995, effectively closing the Gosport line and ending an incredible 154 years of railway history.
JV/TTT

The triangle was disused from 1965 and closed with the rest of the branch south of Bedenham in 1969.

The track on the actual pier was single, and in order to run round its train the locomotive had to propel its coaches out of the station and on to an embankment where there was double track and a signalbox. There were no freight facilities at either Gosport Road or Stokes Bay, other than for the movement of passengers' luggage from train to ship at the pier. In the early 1870s the best time from London to Ryde IOW via Bishopstoke (Eastleigh) and Stokes Bay was 2hrs 45min. Sadly, despite early success, the dreams of the railway company never came fully to fruition and passenger volumes never reached forecast levels. Once the LBSCR/LSWR line had reached Portsmouth Harbour in 1876, decline set in, and although the original pier was replaced in 1896 to facilitate berthing in bad weather, the decline continued. By 1914, with the advent of World War 1, which reduced public travel and increased naval activity, the steamers serving Stokes Bay ceased. Train services staggered on until November 1915 when all traffic was withdrawn. The Admiralty took over the pier and the railway land, which in the late 1930s was sold off for development. However, a stub of track south of the junction was retained so that the junction triangle could continue to be used for turning locomotives.

It was hoped that Lee-on-the-Solent would become a major resort and early plans allowed for an up-market establishment where there would be a parade along the coastline over a mile in length and a greensward some 150yd in width between the wide parade and the sea. Plots of land were sold off by auction and some fine houses began to appear. A 750ft-long pier was built in 1885 and a steamer service started between Lee-on-the-Solent and Clarence Pier at Southsea, with six journeys a day in the summer months. The plans for a railway finally came to fruition when, in 1890, a Board of Trade certificate under the Railways Construction

Facilities Act of 1864 was granted to a local company. The standard gauge line would be just over 3 miles in length.

Work started in 1891, but due to a defaulting contractor the line was not completed and ready for service until 12 May 1894. There were halts at Privett (1 mile 3 chains — from 1909 named Fort Gomer Halt, to avoid confusion with the LSWR Meon Valley line station), Browndown Halt (1 mile 68 chains) and, from 1910, Elmore Halt (2 miles 43 chains), all of which had concrete platform faces. The platform for Lee-on-the-Solent at the junction station of Fort Brockhurst was adjacent to the LSWR station on the up side (but facing south). There was no direct connection to the branch except by means of a double shunt via a siding used for goods wagons. There were never any through services to Lee-on-the-Solent from the Gosport line. On leaving Fort Brockhurst the line curved westward and ran parallel to Military Road. There were level crossings at the first two halts, then some heathland was crossed before a 10-chain-radius curve took the line to the shoreline. The line then ran along the coast beside the original grassy strip of land referred to earlier, to the terminus, located just short of the pier, 3 miles and 3 chains from Fort Brockhurst. The terminus had a concrete-faced platform, waiting shelter and, in an adjoining brick building, a booking office, waiting rooms and conveniences.

There was a 25mph speed limit over the line and weight restrictions applied. There were no signals and the operation was conducted under the 'one engine in steam' principle. The line was single, but optimism was such that sufficient land for double-track conversion was purchased but never used. Operations commenced using the contractor's locomotive and some early tramcar-style coaches. These were followed by some very elderly LSWR four-wheelers that were sometimes coupled to the original coaches. By the early days of the Edwardian era two ancient locomotives were on loan from the LSWR. The first was a George

192

Above:
After 1953 the freight-only line to Gosport was popular with the organisers of enthusiasts' railtours. In this view a Southern Counties Touring Society special, the 'Southdown Venturer Rail Tour', is near Fort Brockhurst on the Gosport to Fareham run with 'N' class No 31411 seemingly making an effort with its modest 250-ton load. Originally the line was double track throughout. *John H. Bird*

Upper right:
The only intermediate station between Fareham and Gosport (as distinct from Stokes Bay) was Fort Brockhurst. The station was originally known as Brockhurst, but in 1893 it was renamed to avoid confusion with Brockenhurst on the Southampton to Bournemouth main line. Fort Brockhurst had the distinction of being adjacent to major Government sidings and from 1894 it was the junction for Lee-on-the-Solent. Here a 'Q1' heads a long freight down to Gosport.
Lens of Sutton

Lower right:
In 1933/34 the entire branch was singled, except for a passing loop at Fort Brockhurst. Once passenger services were withdrawn, the passing loop and associated signalling were removed, a single line being adequate for the daily goods that worked down to Gosport until January 1969. In this 2003 scene the old station and the platforms are still extant, but all other traces of the railway have disappeared. *JV*

Top right:
Other early
Lee-on-the-Solent motive
power included a George
England 1862-built 2-4-0T
purchased from the
Somerset & Dorset Railway
in 1871. Bearing the number
21, it was named *Scott* after
the General Manager of the
LSWR. The LSWR took
over the running of the line
(but not the ownership) in
1909, from which time the
company used its own small
locomotives and steam
railmotors. This view shows
No 21 at Fort Brockhurst
in about 1905.
LGRP/Bucknall Collection

Centre right:
By 1909 there were eight
trains per day on the line
and three on Sundays.
From 1923, after the
Grouping, the Southern
Railway often employed
ex-LBSCR motive power on
the 3-mile branch, including
the little 28-ton 'A1X' class
'Terriers', already featured
in this book on many other
lines. In this amateur but
nevertheless rare and
appealing photograph, a
'Terrier' and three ancient
compartment coaches are
seen at the Lee-on-the-Solent
terminus platform in the
1920s, the locomotive
already having run round
its train. *Lens of Sutton*

Lower right:
There were three small halts
between Fort Brockhurst
and Lee-on-the-Solent —
Fort Gomer Halt,
Browndown Halt and
Elmore Halt — but these
did not save the line from
omnibus competition.
The line lost money and
by 1923 debts of £14,000
had accumulated, a fortune
in those days. The line
inevitably succumbed and
was closed to passengers
from 1 January 1933 and to
freight on 2 October 1935.
Featured here is
Browndown Halt in August
1938, nearly three years
after final closure.
SLS/R. F. Roberts

England-built 17-ton ex-Somerset & Dorset Railway 2-4-0 tank engine, which was sold to the LSWR in 1871 and named *Scott* (after the LSWR General Manager). Built in 1862, it was rebuilt in 1887 and later renumbered No 21. The other locomotive was an ancient Manning Wardle 0-6-0ST of 1862 vintage. Originally named *Lady Portsmouth*, it was purchased by the LSWR from an Okehampton contractor in 1879 and numbered No 392; the name was removed in November 1889. These ancient machines, which would have been worthy of any Colonel Stephens line, are illustrated within. Although there was plenty of summer traffic, the railway struggled to pay its debts. Overtures to the LSWR to operate the line went unheard until 1909 when the company agreed to operate the line, but not to buy it! Debts of some £14,000 accumulated before the whole show was absorbed into the Southern Railway at the 1923 Grouping.

Once the LSWR took over it used its small and economical steam railmotors, and in 1910 it was running a total of nine round trips over the line, with the first train of the day leaving Lee-on-the-Solent at a leisurely 9.23am. Both First and Third Class accommodation was available! After World War 1 omnibuses started to make a serious impact on transportation in the area and the railway came under increasing pressure. The LSWR abandoned its railmotors for a more conventional engine and coaches (or quite often coach!), and after the 1923 Grouping often one of the

188 1st JUNE to 30th SEPTEMBER, 1909, or until further notice.

STOKES BAY, GOSPORT AND PORTSMOUTH TO SOUTHAMPTON.

FOR SPEED RESTRICTIONS SEE PAGES A, B, C, D, E, F & G.

Distance from Portsmouth Harbour (M. C.)	Distance from Stokes Bay (M. C.)	Nos.	1		2		3		4		5		6		7		8		9		10		11		12		13	
		UP TRAINS. WEEK DAYS.	Pass.		Goods. via Netley.		*Goods. Not Mons.*		*Engine. Not Mons.*		Pass.		Engine.		Engine.		Pass. Alton.		Pass. via Netley.		Horse Box Train.		Engine.		Pass Sarum.		Pass. Cardiff via Netley & Sarum.	
					A																							
M C	M C		a.m.	a.m.	a.m.	a.m.	am	am	a.m.	a.m.	a.m.	a.m.	a.m.	a.m.	a.m.	a.m.	a.m.	a.m.	a.m.	a.m.	a.m.	a.m.	am	am	am	am	a.m.	a.m.
— —	— —	**Stokes Bay**	...	...	...	...	...	...	...	...	...	...	...	...	...	...	...	...	...	...	...	...	...	...	...	...	...	...
— —	1 14	Gosport Road	...	...	...	...	...	...	...	...	...	...	...	...	...	...	...	...	...	...	...	...	...	...	...	...	...	...
— —	1 75	Gosport	...	...	...	...	...	...	...	*6 0*	...	6 15	...	...	...	...	...	7 25	...	...	...	...	...	...	...	8 0	...	...
— —	2 51	Fort Brockhurst	...	...	...	...	...	...	*6*	*3*	6 18	6 19	...	...	...	...	7 28	7 29	...	...	...	...	...	...	8 3	8 4	...	...
— —	6 14	**Fareham**	...	...	...	...	...	...	*6 11*	...	6 25	...	...	...	...	...	7 35	...	...	...	...	...	...	...	810	...	...	...
— —	— —	**Portsmouth H.**	...	...	...	...	...	...	...	...	...	...	...	...	...	...	...	...	...	...	...	...	...	...	...	745	...	...
— 67	— —	**Portsmouth T.**	...	1220	...	...	...	*5 0*	...	...	...	6 5	...	6 20	...	...	...	...	...	7 8	...	7 30	...	...	748	754	...	8 5
1 51	— —	Fratton	1222	1223	...	5A0	*5 5*	*520*	...	...	6 7	6 8	6	22	...	6 50	...	...	7 11	7 12	7	32	...	7 48	756	759	8 8	8 10
5 29	— —	Cosham	1230	1231	5	7	*530*	*540*	...	...	6 15	6 16	6	30	6 58	...	...	...	7 20	7 21	7 39	7 49	756	...	8 6	8 8	8 18	8 19
8 1	— —	Portchester	...	...	...	...	...	...	...	...	6 21	6 22	...	...	...	...	...	...	7 26	7 27	...	...	...	...	814	815	...	...
11 17	— —	**Fareham**	1240	1241	5A17	6 25	*555*	*6 0*	...	...	6 28	6 31	6	41	...	...	...	7 40	7 33	7 42	7 59	8 9	...	...	821	826	8 29	8 31
14 —	— —	Knowle Box	...	...	...	...	...	...	...	...	...	...	...	...	...	...	...	...	...	...	...	...	...	...	...	...	...	...
16 78	— —	Botley	...	1253	...	...	*615*	*520*	...	...	6 40	6 41	6	50	...	...	...	...	...	...	8 19	8 24	...	...	836	839	...	...
22 27	— —	Eastleigh S. Jun.	1	3	...	...	*6*	*33*	...	...	6	49	6	59	...	...	...	...	...	...	8	33	...	...	8	48	...	...
22 37	— —	**Eastleigh**	1 4	...	...	...	*635*	...	...	...	6 50	...	7 0	...	...	...	...	...	...	...	8 34	...	...	...	849	859	...	...
24 59	— —	Swaythling	...	...	...	...	...	...	...	...	...	...	...	...	...	...	...	...	...	...	...	...	...	...	...	...	...	...
26 13	— —	St. Denys	...	...	8 26	8 28	...	...	...	...	...	...	...	...	...	...	...	...	8 16	8 17	...	...	...	...	...	...	9 3	9 5
27 14	— —	Northam	...	...	8	32	...	...	...	...	...	...	...	...	...	...	...	...	8 20	8 22	...	...	...	...	...	...	...	...
27 75	— —	**Southampton**	..	...	8 36	...	...	...	...	...	...	...	...	...	...	...	...	...	8 25	...	...	...	...	...	...	...	...	...

Nos.	14		15		16		17		18		20		21		22		23		24		25		26		2[illegible]	
UP TRAINS. WEEK DAYS.	Pass. via Netley		2.55 a.m. Goods. Nine Elm- via Direct Line.		Pass. via Netley.		Pass. Yeovil via Sarum.		Pass. Sarum via Netley		Pass.		Pass.		Pass. via Netley.		*Special with Discharged Soldiers when required.*		*Engine Com'cing July.*		Pass.		Pass. Bristol via Netley & Sarum.		*Pass. Sarum June only.*	
							F				B		C				D									
	a.m	a.m	a.m	a.m	a.m.	a.m.	a.m.	a.m.	a.m	a.m.	a.m.	a.m.	a.m.	a.m.	a.m.	a.m.	a.m.	a.m.	a.m.	a.m.	a.m.	a.m.	p.m.	p.m.	p.m.	p.m.
Stokes Bay	...	...	...	...	...	...	.	9 35	..	...	...	1045	...	...	...	...	...	...	...	...	..	1153	...	...	...	...
Gosport Road	...	...	...	...	...	..	9 38	9 39	...	...	1048	1049	...	...	...	...	...	...	...	...	1156	1157	...	...	...	...
Gosport	...	...	...	...	...	...	...	...	...	10 5	...	...	...	...	...	...	...	...	...	...	12 2	12 7	...	...	...	...
Fort Brockhurst	...	...	...	...	...	...	9 44	9 45	...	10 9	1053	1054	...	...	...	...	...	*11 38*	...	...	1210	1211	...	...	...	...
Fareham	...	...	...	...	.	...	9 51		1015	...	11 0	...	...	...	...	...	*11*	*45*	...	...	1217	...	...	...	...	...
Portsmouth H.	...	...	...	...	...	...		...	...	...	...	...	..	1050	...	...	...	...	...	...	...	...	...	...	...	...
Portsmouth T.	...	8 37	...	...	...	9 4	...	9 25	...	9 50	...	...	1053	1055	...	...	...	...	...	*1155*	...	...	...	1220	...	*1230*
Fratton	8 39	8 41	...	...	9 6	9 7	9 28	9 30	9 53	9 55	...	...	1057	11 0	...	...	...	...	*11*	*57*	...	...	1223	1225	*1233*	*1235*
Hilsea Sidings	...	...	...	...	...	...	...	...	...	...	...	...	...	...	...	...	...	...	...	...	...	...	...	...	...	...
Cosham	8	48	8 53	8 59	9 15	9 16	9 38	9 40	10 3	10 4	...	...	11 7	1111	...	...	...	...	*12 5*	...	...	...	1233	1236	*1243*	*1247*
Portchester	...	...	...	9 9	9 22	9 23	9 45	9 46	...	...	...	...	1117	1118	...	...	...	...	...	...	...	...	1242	1243	...	...
Fareham	8 57	8 58	9 17	9 27	9 29	9 31	9 53	10 0	1014	1018	...	11 2	1124	1126	...	1136	*11*	*45*	...	...	...	1220	1249	1252	*12*	*57*
Knowle Box	...	...	...	...	...	...	...	...	...	...	...	...	...	...	...	...	...	...	...	...	...	...	...	...	...	...
Botley	...	...	9 45	1023	...	...	10 10	10 12	...	...	1113	1114	1135	1136	...	...	...	...	...	...	1231	1233	...	...	...	...
Eastleigh Sth. J.	...	...	10	36	...	...	10	23	...	...	B 11	23	...	...	...	...	...	...	...	...	12	42	...	...	...	...
Eastleigh	...	...	1038	...	...	...	10 24	10F35	..	...	1124	...	1146	...	...	...	...	...	...	...	1243	...	...	...	*1 17*	*1 22*
Swaythling	...	...	...	...	...	...		...	...	...	...	...	...	...	...	...	...	...	...	...	...	...	...	...	...	...
St. Denys	9	26	...	...	10 6	10 8	...	...	1055	1058	...	...	...	...	1214	1215	...	...	...	...	...	...	1 28	1 30	...	...
Bevois Park	...	...	...	...	...	...	...	...	...	...	...	...	...	...	...	...	...	...	...	...	...	...	...	...	...	...
Northam	9 28	9 30	...	...	1011	1013	...	...	...	...	...	...	..	...	1218	1220	...	...	...	...	...	...	...	...	...	...
Southampton	9 33	...	...	...	1016	...	...	...	...	...	...	...	...	...	1223	...	...	...	...	...	...	...	...	...	...	..

Nos.	29		30		31		32		33		34		35		36		37		38		39		41		42		43	
UP TRAINS. WEEK DAYS.	*Pass Brighton Sarum. Com'cing July.*		12.36 p.m. Engine Fareham via Stokes Bay Jct.		Pass. Sarum.		*Engine. Not Mons.*		Empty Wagons Sarum.		Pass via Netley.		Pass.		Pass. Bristol via Netley & Sarum.		Pass.		Pass.		Empty.		Pass. Sarum via Netley.		Pass.		Pass. via Netley.	
													E															
	p.m	p.m.	p.m.	p.m.	p.m.	p.m.	p.m.	p.m.	p.m.	p.m.	p.m.	p.m.	p.m.	p.m.	p.m.	p.m.	p.m.	p.m.	p.m.	p.m.	p.m.	p.m.	p.m.	p.m.	pm	pm	pm	pm
Stokes Bay	...	...	...	...	...	...	...	...	...	...	...	...	...	...	...	...	...	2 30	...	...	...	2 45	...	...	...	...	...	...
Gosport Road	...	...	...	...	...	...	...		...	...	...	...	...	...	...	...	2 33	2 34	...	...	2	48	...	...	...	...	...	...
Gosport	...	...	...	...	...	...	...		...	...	...	1 58	...	...	...	...	...	...	...	...	2 53	...	...	...	...	325	...	...
Fort Brockhurst	...	...	12	51	...	...	...	...	...	...	2 1	2 2	...	...	...	...	2 38	2 39	...	...			...	...	328	329	...	...
Fareham	...	..	1257	...	...	...	...	...	...	...	2 8	...	...	...	...	...	2 45	...	...	...	...	...	...	...	335	...	...	...
Portsmouth H.	...	...	...	...	...	...	...	...	...	...	...	...	...	...	...	...	...	...	...	...	40		...	...	...	...	...	...
Portsmouth T.	...	...	...	...	...	1245	...	...	...	...	...	...	...	...	...	2 5	...	...	...	2 15	Engine to Bishops Waltham		...	3 15	...	...	...	335
Fratton	...	..	...	...	1247	1249	...	...	...	1 33	...	...	...	...	2 8	2 10	...	...	2 17	2 19			3 17	3 20	...	...	338	340
Hilsea Sidings	...	...	...	...	...	...	...	...	1 37	1 45	...	...	...	...	...	...	...	...	...	...			...	...	...	...	...	...
Cosham	*1242*	*1247*	...	...	1256	1257	..	...	1	53	...	...	...	...	2 18	2 20	...	...	2 26	2 29			3	27½	..	...	348	349
Portchester	...	...	...	...	1 3	1 4	...	...	...	...	...	...	...	...	2 25	2 26	...	...	2 34	2 35			...	...	...	...	355	356
Fareham	*12*	*57*	...	...	1 10	1 12	...	*1 20*	2 8	2 20	...	2 12	2 34	2 42	2 32	2 34	...	...	2 41	2 49	...	3 45	3 36	3 38	...	...	4 3	4 5
Knowle Box	...	...	...	...	...	...	...	...	...	...	...	...	...	...	...	...	...	...	...	...	...	...	...	...	...	...	...	...
Botley	...	...	...	...	1 22	1 23	*1*	*32*	...	...	...	...	2 52	2 53	...	...	...	...	3 1	3 4	3 55	...	...	...	...	...	...	...
Eastleigh S. Jct.	...	..	...	...	...	...	...	...	2	43	...	...	3	3	...	...	...	...	3	13	...	...	...	...	...	...	...	...
Eastleigh	*1 17*	*1 22*	...	...	1 33	1 35	*1 42*	...	2 45	3 55	...	...	3 4	...	...	...	...	...	3 14	...	...	...	...	...	...	...	...	...
Swaythling	...	...	...	...	...	...	...	...	...	...	...	...	...	...	...	...	...	...	...	...	...	...	...	...	...	...	...	...
St. Denys	...	...	...	...	...	...	...	...	...	...	2 50	2 51	...	...	3 3	3 5	...	...	...	...	...	...	4	8	...	...	444	445
Bevois Park	...	...	...	...	...	...	...	...	...	...	...	...	...	...	...	...	...	...	...	...	...	...	...	...	...	...	...	...
Northam	...	...	...	...	...	...	...	...	...	...	2 54	2 56	...	...	...	...	...	...	...	...	...	...	...	...	...	...	448	450
Southampton	...	...	...	...	...	...	...	...	...	...	2 59	...	...	...	...	...	...	...	..	...	...	...	...	...	...	...	453	...

A Light Engine Fratton to Fareham. Goods thence to Southampton. The maximum load of this Train is 30 loaded Wagons. **B** When 10.0 a.m. Boat Train from Waterloo runs this Train must be held at Eastleigh South Box until the Boat Train has passed Eastleigh. **C** Horse Box and Carriage Truck Traffic, except that transferred from the L. B. & S. C. Railway at Havant, must not be conveyed by this Train. **D** When this Train runs a special Tail Board must be put on preceding Train. **E** This Train runs on the last Wednesday only in each month. **F** From 1st June to 10th July leaves Eastleigh 10.38 a.m.

Above:
For most enthusiasts the only memory of Gosport will be its use as a goods depot during the 1960s, when normally a daily train travelled the branch. After the end of steam it was Class 33 diesels that normally provided the motive power, and on 9 September 1968 it was No D6515 (later No 33012) that ran along the weed-covered track into Gosport, with four wagons and a brake-van. The direct spur from Gosport to the Stokes Bay line was on the left.
John H. Bird

Upper right:
Gosport station had a splendid overall roof and a centre road between the up and down platforms, but suffered bomb damage during World War 2. Just after the war a long rake of goods vehicles occupies the centre road while an old SR utility van stands at the up platform. The roof was later demolished, but the up-side buildings and colonnade are listed and survive to this day. *IAL*

Lower right:
Just before its closure to passengers in June 1953 the Stephenson Locomotive Society organised a special train over the Gosport branch. On 3 May 1953, and looking exactly like a typical branch working of its day, 'M7' class No 30110 shunts the compartment coaches of the special just outside the Gosport terminus. Note the signalbox on the right and the lower-quadrant starting signal. *S. C. Nash*

Left:
Part of the 1909 LSWR working timetable featuring the line from Stokes Bay and Gosport to Fareham. Destinations of passenger trains from the branch include Fareham, Alton, Salisbury, Yeovil, Eastleigh and Southampton.

diminutive LBSCR 'Terriers' normally provided the motive power. Freight facilities were available at Lee-on-the-Solent, and the wagons were normally conveyed in mixed trains. After passenger services ceased, an LBSCR Class D1 worked the goods trains. There was a goods siding at the terminus and goods traffic outlived passenger services by nearly five years.

By the late 1920s 'the writing was on the wall' for the Lee-on-the-Solent branch and arrangements were made for closure to passengers, services being withdrawn from 1 January 1931. Dwindling freight traffic soldiered on, but on 2 October 1935 the last goods train left the terminus behind ex-LBSCR 'D1' class No 2239. The weeds gradually took over and even by the advent of war the line had become nothing more than a weed-covered memory — see the 1938 photograph reproduced herein. Remains of the halts survived until the early 1960s, but everything has now been swept away except for the terminus platform and building and the crumbling remains of the platform at Fort Brockhurst.

Returning to the Gosport branch, the line continued to function, very much on branch-line principles, with local trains normally comprising two or three coaches. In 1933/34 the entire line was singled, but a passing loop at Fort Brockhurst was retained. There were about 18 round trips between Fareham and Gosport in September 1938, but with the advent of war there were travel restrictions in a sensitive military area and traffic diminished. Buses continued to make inroads into rail travel in terms of purely local journeys, and a shortage of coal in 1950 caused all branch-line services to be temporarily suspended. Some Gosport services were continuations of Meon Valley trains that had run down from Alton. By 1953 just two trains per day traversed the branch, nothing more than a token service, and unsurprisingly the line closed to passengers from 8 June that year. From that date Gosport had the doubtful distinction of being the largest town in the country without a train service. The normal motive power on the local trains in its last years had typically been LSWR 'M7s', although in earlier days other 0-4-4Ts, such as the 'O2' class, appeared. In terms of freight traffic in later years, members of the 'Q', 'Q1', '700', 'U', 'N' classes and Standard 2-6-4Ts were commonly seen. Once steam finished in 1967, Class 33 and 47 diesels were the normal motive power on the branch. The MOD shunters at Bedenham were latterly from the Hunslet stable. From time to time railway enthusiasts' specials visited the line.

There had been a reasonable amount of freight traffic to Gosport as well as Admiralty stores, but in common with the rest of BR this dwindled. In 1957 the down loop at Fort Brockhurst was removed, the siding layout simplified and signals removed. In January 1969 the entire line beyond the depot at Bedenham was closed to all traffic, and thus 16 years after the end of passenger services Gosport station was abandoned. From this date an as-required but often daily freight traversed the remaining 2¾ miles of track to Bedenham where freight was interchanged with the MOD, which had its own extensive railway network at the depot worked by domestic shunters. The truncated line continued to receive the MOD traffic as required plus an annual visit by the weedkilling train until 1995, when all traffic ceased. The track was kept *in situ* because there was a suggestion that a sophisticated new tramway system serving the greater Portsmouth area, including a tunnel beneath the water connecting Portsmouth with Gosport, would be built. The tracks are still there, but, as illustrated, the weeds are now taking over. In the latter part of 2003 the Government declined to back the tramway system because escalating costs had reached £250 million.

Until the last year or so the alignment was still clearly visible from Fareham station and the track can easily be traced down to Fort Brockhurst. In 2003 the exchange sidings at Bedenham were still in place but weed-covered. At Fort Brockhurst the old platforms and the station house survive, and hidden in the bushes is the old Lee-on-the-Solent platform (see photograph). Other parts of the trackbed to the south have been built on and Gosport station now faces a housing estate. The remains of the station, mostly the old up-side buildings, are listed and have been saved from demolition, and railings now protect them from local vandals. Across the road the line from Gosport down to Clarence Yard is covered by foliage and tarmac, but a few hundred yards of Queen Victoria's line can still be traced (see photograph). Unfortunately her personal station was demolished in the late 1950s. South of the triangle there are some allotments before the route down to Stokes Bay takes the form of a footpath/cycleway. The bridges across the inlets in the area of Little Anglesey are clearly discernible. Alas, the Gosport area is now completely devoid of railways. The area has had an interesting history, but in some ways it always seemed to suffer from being in the shadow of Portsmouth.

Adding to the long list of special trains on the Gosport branch was this LCGB example on Saturday 19 March 1966. The end of steam was rapidly approaching and the organisers were fortunate to secure the services of Bulleid 'Q1' class No 33006 of Nine Elms shed. This angle shows the goods yard on the left, or down, side, and the loading gauge above the brake-van. At this time some freight still worked beyond the station building, across the road and down a siding to Clarence Yard. *Gavin Morrison*

Above:
Goods traffic had almost petered out when the Locomotive Club of Great Britain 'Hampshireman' tour visited an increasingly empty Gosport on 3 November 1968. The signals and signalbox had long gone and the track was gradually being rationalised. Within a few years housing would cover this spot and a railway site that dated back to 1841 would be history. With more than 70,000 inhabitants, Gosport is now claimed to be the largest provincial town not to be served by a railway station. *John H. Bird*

Upper right:
In April 1863 a line was built from the Gosport branch, just outside Gosport station, down to Stokes Bay on the shores of the Solent. This was to have been the leading route to the Isle of Wight; however, once the railway extension to Portsmouth Harbour was opened in 1876 the commercial success of the Portsmouth to Isle of Wight route virtually destroyed the competition. The disruption of World War 1 finished the Stokes Bay line for ever, and it closed completely in 1915.

There was one intermediate station between Gosport and Stokes Bay: opened in 1865, it was originally known as Stokes Road, then Gosport Road and finally Gosport Road & Alverstoke. This is a view of the station, looking towards Gosport. *IAL*

Lower right:
Although the Stokes Bay line closed in 1915, the triangle of lines just outside Gosport remained open until 1965 and was used primarily for turning locomotives. South of Gosport on the alignment of the Stokes Bay line there are a couple of inlets, one of them at what is locally known as Little Anglesey. This 2003 scene shows the old railway bridge, which now carries a footpath/cyclepath through a highly populated area. *JV*

Right:
The wonderful preserved exterior of Gosport station is seen some 34 years after the last train departed. Sir William Tite designed the building and this shot shows the impressive south or departure side. There is a popular myth that this was Queen Victoria's station, which she used on her way to the Isle of Wight, but except possibly for the years 1841 to 1845 she always used her own Royal Victoria Station in Clarence Yard, across the road from Gosport terminus. *JV*

Below:
Beyond Gosport a track crossed the road in front of the station and made its way down to Clarence Yard. The line opened in 1845 to serve a Royal Navy establishment and, as already mentioned, Queen Victoria's station was located near the waterfront, where she would board the Royal Yacht *Alberta* for the journey to Osborne House on the Isle of Wight. Long after Royalty ceased using the line, it survived for freight-only use to supply the RN sidings in Clarence Yard. By 1969 the siding had closed, but after some detective work in October 2003, on land that was once Government property but which has now been sold off for barrack conversion and housing, these remains were located. Note the mature trees beyond the bridge. *JV*

21. Bishops Waltham Branch

THE Hampshire market town of Bishops Waltham is located approximately 9 miles from Southampton and is almost midway between Winchester and Fareham. The population in the mid-19th century was just over 2,000. Railways arrived in the area as early as November 1841 when the line from Bishopstoke (Eastleigh) to Gosport opened. The nearest station to the town was Botley, some 3¾ miles distant. At Bishops Waltham it was the same story as occurred so often during the heyday of railways when, deprived of a railway service by a major railway company, prominent members of the local community became proactive by establishing a local railway company for the purpose of seeking approval for construction and for subsequently raising the necessary finance to acquire land to build the proposed line. Accordingly the Bishops Waltham Railway Company was formed in 1861, and the proposed standard gauge branch line to Botley was authorised in 1862. The line was to run along the valley of the Hamble River, and although the line meandered like the river, construction was straightforward. Swift progress resulted in the line opening for passenger traffic on 1 June 1863. As was the case with so many other branch lines, the local company was taken over by the operating company, in this case the LSWR, which absorbed the Bishops Waltham Company during the year of opening.

There was a grand proposal to link Bishops Waltham with Petersfield on the 'Portsmouth Direct' line, and another plan for a route down from Ropley on the Mid-Hants line, but neither came to fruition, and throughout its life Bishops Waltham was to remain a terminus. In addition to general goods facilities, lengthy sidings were provided to serve both the local gasworks and the local brick and tile works. In fact, the brickworks owner, one Mr Blanchard, was one of the original proposers of the railway and his works

made a significant contribution to freight traffic on the branch. For the first couple of years of service a temporary station at Bishops Waltham was used, located south of the level crossing over the main Winchester to Portsmouth road; however, the permanent building, opened in 1865, was on the north side of the road. This resulted in the crossing gates being opened for every train movement, but fortunately the service was never frequent, so inconvenience to road traffic was not acute, especially as the line closed to passengers before the golden age of the motor car. The station had a single platform on the up side, and a fine decorative brick building was provided, noted for its striking use of both red and yellow bricks. Beyond the station there was a large goods shed and a small engine shed, also on the up side of the line. Although Bishops Waltham was a terminus, a single line continued for several hundred yards to serve the local gasworks, which was built by an old chalk pit and consumed large quantities of coal. Opposite the station on the down side another long siding served the aforementioned brickworks. The goods yard had a 5-ton-capacity crane, and a signalbox controlled movements from its position south of the road crossing on the up side.

In the early years there were about half a dozen round-trip workings between the junction station at Botley and Bishops Waltham, but no Sunday service. In Edwardian times the LSWR looked for operating economies and, in common with other lightly used lines, steam railmotors were tried; the first to arrive had been displaced from the steeply graded Basingstoke & Alton Light Railway. These small vehicles operated the branch from 1905 to the start of World War 1, and an intermediate halt at Durley Mill was opened on Thursday 23 December 1909 in an attempt to boost traffic. The halt was located 1 mile and 30 chains from Botley

Left:
The railway line through Botley opened in 1841, but it was 1863 before the established town of Bishops Waltham was connected to the outside world by rail. With a population of more than 2,000, the town was deserving of a railway, and although it was never anything but a single-track branch line, there were once plans to link it with the Portsmouth Direct and the Mid-Hants lines. On 7 November 1928 'O2' class No 236 (BR No 30236) pauses in the branch bay platform enticing passengers to change at Botley for Bishops Waltham. Within four years there would be no train to catch! *H. C. Casserley*

201

BISHOP'S WALTHAM BRANCH.

FOR SPEED RESTRICTIONS SEE PAGES A, B, C, D, E, F & G.

This is a Single Line, and is worked under the Regulations for working Single Lines by the Electric Train Tablet Block System.

Passenger Trains worked by Steam Motor Car, 1st and 3rd Classes only.   Goods Trains worked by Engine.

DOWN TRAINS.

Distance from Botley. M. C.	DOWN TRAINS.		WEEK DAYS.																SUNDAYS.						
—	Waterloo ... dep.	Gds. a.m. ...	5 35	6 10	...	7 40	9 20	1140	...	1250 (Eng or Goods p.m.) ...	2 20	3 0	...	5 0	6 55			...	...	10 0	...	...	...	6 40
—	Botley ... dep.	7 50	8 42	9 25	10 15	1116	12 0	1 45	3 6	3 55	4 10	5 12	5 55	6 40	7 47	8 55	9 36	1035	1 5	5 35	6 25	8 0	8 45
3 62	Bishop's Waltham ... arr.	8 5	8 52	9 35	10 25	1126	1210	1 55	3 16	4 5	4 20	5 22	6 5	6 50	7 57	9 5	9 46	1045	1 15	5 45	6 35	8 10	8 55

UP TRAINS.

Dist. fr'm Bishop's Waltham. M. C.	UP TRAINS.		WEEK DAYS.																SUNDAYS.						
—	Bishop's Waltham ... dep.	a.m. 8 20	9 5	Lgt. Eng. a.m. 9 16	9 55	10 40	11 40	1 5	2 48	3 38	4 45	4 56	5 37	6 20	7 20	8 35	9 15	1010	1220	5 15	6 5	7 30	8 25
3 62	Botley ... ... arr.	8 30	9 15	9 24	10 5	10 50	11 50	1 15	2 58	3 48	4 55	5 11	5 47	6 30	7 30	8 45	9 25	1020	1230	5 25	6 15	7 40	8 35
...	Waterloo ... arr.	11 4	...	...	12A28	1 31	2 45	4 45	5 39	...	7 31	...	...	...	10 5	12 2	1248	...	...	8 10	...	1040	a.m. 3 35

A—After 10th July arrive Waterloo 12.26 p.m.

Above:

This LSWR 1909 working timetable shows 13 passenger trains per weekday together with a daily goods train. At this time all passenger trains were worked by steam 'motor cars'. There were seven round trip workings on Sundays.

and 2 miles and 30 chains from Bishops Waltham, but, more importantly, 1 mile from the village of Durley! At opening, instructions to operating staff stated that 'the Guard, accompanying the Motor Car, will issue Tickets, which must be punched by the Bell-punch'. The instructions continued, 'When an ordinary coach is attached to the Motor Car as a trailer, the Passengers joining at the Halt must, if there be room, ride in the Motor Car', which suggests that the line did have strengthened peak-period workings. By 1910 the service had risen to 13 trains each way on weekdays and seven on Sundays. At this time the first train out of Bishops Waltham was not until 8.20am, while the last train from Botley was due to arrive at 9.5pm, hardly a 'workman's' service. After the end of the rail-motors LSWR 'O2' and 'M7' classes worked the line. Omnibuses soon arrived on the scene and by 1927 the train service had been trimmed by the Southern Railway to nine weekday workings and four on Sundays, with an extra lunchtime train on Saturdays.

One of the problems for rail passengers from Bishops Waltham wanting to travel to the major population centres of either Southampton or Winchester was the need to change trains at both Botley and Eastleigh. In this respect the buses had an enormous advantage; the train simply could not compete with the convenience of road transport, and closure of the little branch loomed. Notices were posted and all passenger services were withdrawn on 30 December 1932. The 16-lever signalbox at the terminus was closed in December 1935 and all signals were removed. The small engine shed was closed and demolished a year prior to the withdrawal of passenger services. However, despite the absence of passenger trains, goods traffic, somewhat surprisingly, continued to use the branch for a further 30 years! The traffic from the brick and tile company premises continued until just after World War 2, and a siding opposite the station was used by a brewery until 1949. Coal was a major incoming commodity and miscellaneous wagon loads were also handled. Bishops Waltham was also a distribution centre for light general goods and parcels.

The freight-only Bishops Waltham branch became a focal point for railway enthusiasts' special trains. The first special, in 1952, was a Railway Correspondence & Travel Society two-coach working from Eastleigh hauled by one of the curious LSWR short-wheelbase 'C14' class 0-4-0T locomotives, and a year later it was the turn of the Stephenson Locomotive Society, which ran a special

with two pairs of push-pull non-corridor coaches divided by an LSWR 'M7', a class associated with the line for many years. A final special, organised by the Branch Line Society, ran in 1959 and comprised an 'M7' and two SECR compartment coaches. Freight traffic continued and loadings were erratic, with sometimes a dozen or more wagons in tow, while at other times a single wagon made the only financial contribution to the line. In the early 1960s the service sometimes ran only two or three times a week, and freight was by then in the hands of the small but purposeful Ivatt 2-6-2T locomotives. The 'writing was on the wall', and sure enough the last goods train ran on 27 April 1962. A few days later a locomotive collected all remaining wagons. The line was lifted in 1965, and the attractive 1865 station was demolished. A roundabout and a relief road now occupy the site.

Branch trains always used a bay platform at Botley, a station that once had extensive goods facilities. After the opening of the Bishops Waltham branch in 1863 further sidings were added in 1885, 1907 and 1911. However, all goods traffic ceased at Botley in October 1967, and all staff were withdrawn from July 1968. The signalbox closed, except for local use, in June 1982. The line from Eastleigh to Fareham was later electrified, and although Botley station remains open, it is, in effect, little more than a halt with an approximately hourly service. A development worth mentioning, and one that has resulted in a short part of the Bishops Waltham branch surviving, occurred in 1972. A new stone terminal and distribution point was built at Botley by the Foster Yeoman company, and huge volumes of roadstone were transported from its quarries at Merehead in Somerset. About half a mile of the old branch trackbed was relaid so that loaded trains could be propelled along the branch and pulled forward through the unloading mechanism. The stone was then conveyed across the Eastleigh line to a Tarmac depot. The old branch bay platform was used as a headshunt/locomotive release some 40 years after the closure of the branch to passengers.

Other than for the occasional stone traffic at Botley, there is nothing left to see of the Bishops Waltham branch, discounting a grass-covered earth mound that once comprised Durley Halt. Of all the branches featured in this book, that to Bishops Waltham was one of the least known, and has now been closed for over 40 years, but it is nevertheless deserving of its own small chapter in this book.

Above:

From 1933 until 1962 the Bishops Waltham branch was freight only. Initially one train per day traversed the line, but in its final years the service was reduced to thrice weekly, as required. The old branch was eventually lifted, but in 1972 a new stone terminal was opened at Botley and part of the trackwork included the first few hundred yards of the Bishops Waltham branch.
In this view, looking west on 5 March 1983, the 08.00 Westbury to Botley, Yeoman stone train hauled by a brace of Class 37s, Nos 37272 and 37271, has just arrived and is positioned beneath the unloader. *JV/TTT*

Below:

In this summer 1968 scene the demolition of Botley station had yet to commence. It would appear that the line is closed and under the occupation of the engineers. There is a Class 33 with empty ballast wagons in the foreground and another on the line from Eastleigh. A Class 73 with loaded ballast wagons gives the erroneous impression that it is coming off the Bishops Waltham branch. All goods traffic and all station staff had just been withdrawn. The signalbox did not close until 1982, and the line has since been electrified. *John H. Bird*

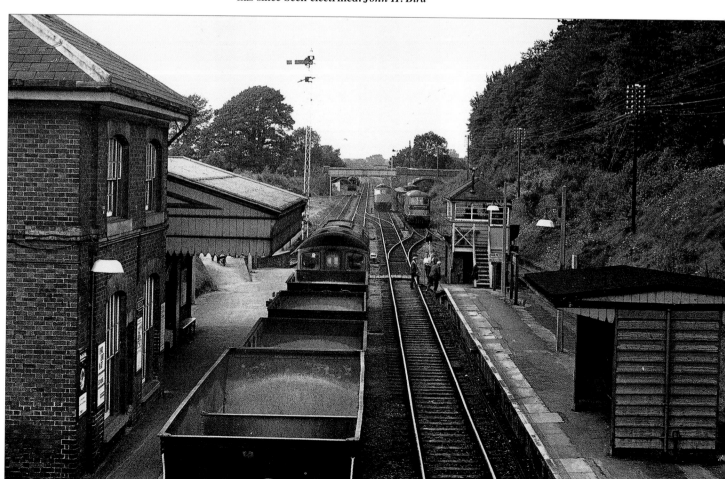

Above:
This fine study of the ornate terminus at Bishops Waltham dates back to 7 March 1959. Emulating scenes from the past, 'M7' No 30111 pauses at the platform with a Branch Line Society special train that was visiting freight-only lines in the area. There was one intermediate station on the line from 1909, when, in the age of the railmotor, Durley Halt was opened. *C. P. Boocock*

Upper right:
There was a large goods shed at Bishops Waltham, a goods yard, engine shed and long sidings serving the local gasworks and brickworks respectively, but the 16-lever signalbox was closed in 1935 and all signals removed. By 1962 many of the old LSWR and LBSCR classes had been withdrawn, and often the Bishops Waltham goods was in the hands of LMS Ivatt-designed 2MT 2-6-2Ts, such as No 41214.
The locomotive is about to travel to Botley with a single wagon and the brake-van, and complete closure is not far away. *David Fereday Glenn*

Lower right:
The single-platform terminus of Bishops Waltham was on the up side of the line, and the building was distinctive for the architect's attractive use of timber framing and yellow and red bricks. Compared with 1959, the station canopy has been demolished, a fate that the station would soon share to make way for a roundabout and a relief road. The line failed to reach its centenary by just over 12 months.
Maurice Dart collection

22. Andover Junction to Romsey and Eastleigh

AS long ago as March 1847 a railway line had been opened to passengers from Salisbury (Milford station) via Romsey to Eastleigh (then known as Bishopstoke), where it joined the London to Southampton main line. In June of the same year a line from Southampton (Blechynden) to Dorchester opened and slowly a network was established. The opening of Southampton Tunnel in July 1847 further facilitated the network. The LSWR had reached Andover from the Basingstoke direction in July 1854 (extended to Salisbury in May 1857) and it was just a matter of time before Southampton, Romsey and Andover were linked by rail.

In the latter part of the 18th century a canal had been built, broadly between Redbridge and Andover, which ran parallel to the picturesque Rivers Test and Anton, but which was nearly derelict by the mid-1840s. In 1847 the LSWR obtained powers to build the railway link, but the timing was poor because at that time there was what was called a 'post-railway mania' recession and no construction work was undertaken. In 1858 an independent Andover & Redbridge Company proposed a line along the route selected by the LSWR, and the rival Great Western Railway showed great interest, so much so that the line was to be built to broad gauge dimensions and link with an envisaged GWR 14-mile branch line from Pewsey to Andover. The GWR was anxious to gain access to the port of Southampton to tap some of the potentially lucrative passenger and freight traffic. The LSWR protested in vain with a submission that the line should at least be built with a mixed-gauge capability. A prospectus was issued under the grand name of the 'Andover Canal Railway' in an attempt to raise £130,000. In typical prose of the era, the prospectus stated that

'the Canal [route] is singularly adapted for the construction of a cheap line of Railway. There will be no Tunnel or Viaduct and the works will be of the most inexpensive character. The Landowners are most favourable to the undertaking, being very desirous of a Railway substituted for the Canal . . .'

Royal Assent was received in 1858 and Lord Palmerston cut the first sod near Ashfield Bridge on 28 September 1859. Although construction commenced, progress was slow, and a lack of capital resulted in the cessation of all activities by 1861. In 1862 there was a proposal for a railway between Newbury and Andover, but this also came to nothing. Subsequently in 1863 all parties agreed that the LSWR should take over and finance the project under the ARR/LSWR Amalgamation Act of June 1863. The initially single-track line opened on 6 March 1865, with four round-trip workings on weekdays and a single train on Sundays. The line closely followed the route of the old Andover Canal and there were several severe curves, so much so that in 1885 the line was partly realigned and doubled, but not before it had become known as the 'Sprat & Winkle' line. These changes were made at the same time as the opening of the Longparish branch (see next chapter). Northwards from Romsey the new line left the established Salisbury road at Kimbridge Junction. There were intermediate stations at Mottisfont, Horsebridge, Stockbridge, Fullerton, Clatford and Andover Town before Andover Junction was reached. The area was not heavily populated; in the 1901 census, Andover, with a population of 6,500, and Romsey, with 5,600, headed the list, but otherwise Stockbridge with 860 and Mottisfont with 504 were the only intermediate stations with a population worth mentioning.

Left:
During the heyday of the Ian Allan Locospotters Club, special trains were regularly organised for youngsters. Having subscribed to *Trains Illustrated* from January 1954, your author succumbed to advertising when an announcement appeared early in 1955 for an IA special to both Eastleigh and Swindon Works on a weekday during the Easter school holidays. Unaccompanied juveniles were permitted to travel and the fare was 12s 6d, an irresistible package for a 12-year-old! Who would have thought that half a century later I would have found a legitimate reason to include a photograph of that very train in a book? On Wednesday 20 April 1955 'T9' class No 30719, having travelled from Eastleigh via Romsey, leaves Andover Junction for a journey along the now-closed MSWJR to Swindon (see Miscellany section).
Bob Barnard

Before detailing the Romsey to Andover route, it is worth mentioning at this juncture the history of the line being used as a through route between the North, the Midlands and Cheltenham, via Swindon and Marlborough. In 1873 the Swindon, Marlborough & Andover Railway had been incorporated to link the towns mentioned in its title. A line from Red Post Junction, on the outskirts of Andover, to Grafton opened in May 1882 and throughout to Swindon in February 1883. The company was amalgamated with the Swindon & Cheltenham Extension Railway in 1884, and a single company, with the new collective name of the Midland & South Western Junction Railway (MSWJR), then controlled the Cheltenham to Andover route. The line was in financial difficulties at an early date, and in 1892 Sam Fay, one of the rising managers in the ranks of the LSWR hierarchy, took control of the line. As a result of his connections with the LSWR, he facilitated the MSWJR's running powers into Southampton, and from November 1892 through goods traffic used the Andover Junction to Romsey route as part of the journey from the Midlands and the North to the South Coast port. Through passenger trains between Cheltenham and the North and Southampton commenced in June 1894. Later services included a named train, the 'South Express', from Liverpool to Southampton. Fay was later knighted; he became the Superintendent of the LSWR and eventually the General Manager of the Great Central Railway.

The MSWJR ran through sparsely populated country and, based on only local services, it would never have become financially viable, but with through trains and freight traffic, especially military traffic during the two World Wars, it served a useful purpose for many years. Although primarily a link between the LMS and the SR, the line was taken over by the GWR at the 1923 Grouping, which gave that company running powers into Southampton. However, the GWR had operated the Didcot, Newbury & Southampton Railway for many years prior to 1923 so, effectively, it already had access to the southern port. Through workings from Cheltenham to Southampton did not finally cease until 1961, although by that time only one train per day was timetabled. From September 1961 the MSWJR closed, leaving only a freight branch from Andover Junction to Ludgershall, mainly serving military establishments. A branch from Ludgershall to Tidworth closed to passengers in 1955.

At Kimbridge Junction the original signalbox was on the south-west side of the line, but a wartime replacement box, opened in 1943 to cater for additional goods loops to accommodate wartime traffic, was built on the opposite side of the line; it closed on 14 June 1967. The first station on the dedicated Andover line was Mottisfont, just over 4 miles from Romsey. A signalbox was located on the west side of the line beside a gated road crossing just south of the station. There was a substantial station building and a single siding on the east side of the line, which comprised the goods yard; this closed on 3 October 1960. Some 2½ miles north of Mottisfont was Horsebridge station. Situated in a sparsely populated location, the local hamlet was just to the east of the station, but the much larger village of King's Somborne was about a mile to the east. The signalbox and quite a large goods yard were all on the eastern side of the line. Just beyond the station the line made one of its several crossings over the River Test. The yard handled agricultural traffic for surrounding farms and villages, such as Houghton and Broughton.

A further 3¼ miles to the north was Stockbridge. This ancient village of some 800 souls is located on the A30, the old London to Exeter turnpike, which the railway crossed just south of the station. On an east/west axis, the village lies about half way between the cities of Salisbury and Winchester. There were sidings on both the up and down sides of the line, and loading docks and cattle pens were provided. Goods facilities were withdrawn in January 1963. The slate-hung station building was on the west, or village, side of

the line, as was the signalbox. North of Stockbridge the line hugged the alignment of the River Test, passing near to the village of Leckford before reaching Fullerton Junction, 3 miles north of Stockbridge, where the river was again crossed.

Although the author passed through Fullerton Junction on an Ian Allan Locospotters special hauled from Eastleigh to Swindon by a 'T9' class on Wednesday 20 April 1955, it was not until 1970, and again in 1971, that the site was visited, some six and seven years after closure. The next visit was in the spring of 2003 in preparation for this book, and as can be seen from the photographs the contrast was startling. Fullerton was a magnificent site in the middle of a totally rural Hampshire setting. The site of the original Fullerton (Bridge) station was moved a couple of hundred yards to the south in 1871, and was known as Fullerton Junction from May 1889 until July 1929, although it was a true junction from 1885 until 1931 for passengers and 1956 for freight. From 1885 the station had four platforms, two for the Andover route and two for the Longparish branch (see the next chapter); each had a protective awning for passengers. After the singling of the line to Longparish and Hurstbourne in 1913, the down 'branch' platform was closed. There was no footbridge or subway at Fullerton and passengers had to cross the line(s) via track level board crossings. The signalbox was south of the station on the down side. There were sidings on both sides of the Andover line north of the station and another siding off the Longparish line.

Some 2¾ miles north of Fullerton was the little station of Clatford, which, unlike other stations on the line, would appear from photographs not to have had platform awnings. At the south end of the station was a gated road crossing with a small signalbox on the up side. At the north end of the station on the down side there was a siding used by goods trains until October 1960. By this time the line was following the course of the River Anton, and just beyond the station the road went through a deep ford. Some distance beyond the station was Upper Clatford Siding, but this was an early casualty. Two miles beyond Clatford was Andover Town station; with its two curved platforms, it was in a significantly better position to serve the town of Andover compared with the 'main' station at Andover Junction. The site had a significant goods yard on the up side with several sidings and a sizeable goods shed containing a lifting crane. Around the goods yard were several industrial installations including a gasworks, electricity works, an oil depot, several agricultural stores and a railway coal yard. The old canal basin was on the site of the goods yard, and was filled in at the time of the railway's construction. A wooden passenger footbridge was later replaced by an SR concrete example. The signalbox was at the north end of the station beside a main road crossing, and passing trains caused considerable traffic queues. The line between Andover Town and Junction was doubled in 1882, three years before the rest of the line. The distance from Town to Junction was just ¾ mile. After the closure of the line to Romsey in 1964, 'Junction' was dropped from the name, which became just plain 'Andover'. It should be noted that freight traffic between Junction and Town continued until September 1967, more than three years after the withdrawal of passenger services.

Andover Junction, 14¾ miles from Kimbridge Junction, was a major railway centre that had become established in July 1854 when the line from Basingstoke opened. The 'junction' status was established in 1865 when the line to Romsey opened, followed by the MSWJR in 1882. There was an MSWJR locomotive depot to the north of the station and an LSWR example to the south-east of the complex. The LSWR built a new depot on the site of the MSWJR original in 1904. The line from Romsey joined the main line on a sharp curve at the east end of the station. There was a branch bay platform, up and down main-line platforms and an island platform that was used primarily by MSWJR trains, which had their own dedicated single track to Red Post Junction. There

Left:
The cross-country MSWJR line to the north of Andover has now been truncated to the Army depot at Ludgershall (where another branch ran to Tidworth — see Miscellany). Those branches would be included in any Wiltshire branch project. On 14 February 1981 Class 47 No 47069 faces in the down direction at Andover Junction's up island platform with a Hertfordshire Railtours special for Ludgershall, while Class 33 No 33033 accelerates away with a down Waterloo to Exeter St David's train. Until 1964 this station was also a junction for the line down to Romsey, Eastleigh and Southampton, the junction being at the east end of the station. All the sidings on the right have now been removed.
JV/TTT

Right:
The line from Romsey, Kimbridge Junction, to Andover Junction opened on 6 March 1865, and the initially single line followed the routes of two river valleys, the Test and Anton. The route was doubled in 1882 and certain realignments were made. The first stop south of Andover Junction was the conveniently located Andover Town station, where there was a large goods yard, a goods shed and a number of sidings serving particular local industries. Heading south in SR days is Class C8 4-4-0 No 293; built in July 1898, it had 6ft 7in driving wheels and a boiler that was similar to the 'M7' and '700' classes. It was withdrawn in 1935.
R. K. Blencowe collection

Left:
Andover Town station is seen here in early BR days. The main station building was clad in corrugated iron. The signalbox in the distance controlled the crossing of the main road through the town, and especially when the line was dieselised in 1957 and a new 16-train timetable was introduced, delays were frequent. The SR influence is apparent with a replacement concrete overbridge and lamp standards. Note the unusual position for a crossover, on a curve between the platforms.
Lens of Sutton

Top right:
After passing Upper Clatford Siding, the next station on the line was Clatford, some 2 miles from Andover Town. The typical LSWR signalbox closed on 25 February 1962. In order for southbound passengers to cross the tracks safely to reach the nearby Upper Clatford and Goodworth Clatford villages, they had to 'STOP LOOK & LISTEN' in accordance with the warning signs. This photograph, looking south, is pre-1956, when the lower-quadrant starting signal was replaced by an upper-quadrant example. Note the delightful oil lamps. *Lens of Sutton Collection*

Centre right:
Fullerton Bridge station was opened with the line in 1865, but in 1871 the site of the original station was moved a little further to the south. Fullerton became a junction station when the line from Hurstbourne, on the Basingstoke to Salisbury main line, via Longparish was opened in 1885, and between May 1889 and July 1929 it was known as Fullerton Junction. The Romsey to Andover Junction line closed in September 1964 and this view, looking through the dereliction towards Romsey, dates back to June 1971. Half of the awning here was lost in 1956 and the white bands around the supports date back to World War 2, when they helped visibility during periods of blackout. *JV*

Lower right:
Fullerton Junction was sited at a remote location, but for a few decades it retained some importance as a country junction. In this post-closure scene we see the shell of the 28-lever signalbox and the junction station beyond. The line to Andover ran just to the right of the box, while on the right the up Longparish branch platform can just be detected. Passenger trains on the Longparish branch were withdrawn in July 1931, but goods soldiered on over part of the line until 1956. *JV/TTT*

Above:
On 2 November 1957, during the last days before dieselisation, a typical three-coach passenger train hauled by one of the graceful 'T9' class 'Greyhounds', No 30287, with the aesthetically pleasing eight-wheeled tender, crosses the River Test and arrives at Fullerton Junction. The train is the 12.53pm Portsmouth & Southsea to Andover Junction service. *S. C. Nash*

Below:
The entire Fullerton Junction area has now become heavily overgrown and the old platforms are buried in undergrowth. In 'before and after' terms this spring 2003 photograph is the best comparison now possible with the above photograph, before the surrounding trees come into full leaf. The railings over the river bridge should be compared with those seen just behind the last coach of the train above. *JV*

Right:
Stockbridge, with a population of about 1,000, is a pleasant small town located on the A30 highway, for years the main road from London to Salisbury, and the station was conveniently placed at the east end of the wide main street. It had a substantial station building, goods sidings on both sides of the line, goods shed, loading dock and signalbox. Goods traffic was withdrawn in January 1963 and the line closed completely in September 1964. This view, looking south, shows the scene in the late 1960s after closure when the track was being recovered. *R. K. Blencowe*

were two through roads between the main-line platforms, and 'A' and 'B' signalboxes were located at the east and west ends of the station complex; opened in 1882, both closed in 1973. There were goods sidings on both the up and down sides of the station, and while these were busy for many decades, in recent times only fertiliser and military traffic has survived. The site is now heavily rationalised with the through roads and most sidings removed, locomotive depot abandoned and signalboxes closed, and even the fertiliser traffic has been lost to road.

Initially the Romsey to Andover line had four round-trip workings per day over the single track, including one mixed train, and there was a single train each way on the Sabbath; it is now hard to imagine why the railway would bring in even a single shift of station staff, signalmen and crossing-keepers for the sake of a single return working. By 1888, after the doubling of the track, there were six round-trip workings, mostly through from South-ampton to Andover Junction via Redbridge and vice versa, and two trains on Sundays. By 1906 no fewer than 11 trains worked the line, three of which originated in the North of England and the Midlands and travelled via the MSWJR. On Saturdays there was even an 'Ocean Boat Express' as well as a southbound 'South Express' and a northbound 'North Express', which worked to and from Manchester (London Road). Some of the through trains did not stop at local stations. Although there were slight variations between the World Wars, there were normally about nine trains in each direction, two being long-distance through workings. At one stage after World War 2 the timetables showed only seven trains, but there was a radical change in September 1957 when the local services were dieselised and there were no fewer than 16 round-trip workings per day, with five on Sundays, a level of service that surprisingly lasted until the line's closure in September 1964. The majority of 'local' services ran to Southampton Terminus station via Redbridge, with a few running to Eastleigh and a handful to Romsey only. However, in later years, especially after the diesel units arrived, trains worked to and from Portsmouth & Southsea via Eastleigh. There was normally a daily pick-up goods along the line in addition to freight traffic that ran through to Southampton using the MSWJR.

In view of the fact that during the life of the Andover Junction to Romsey line some services worked to Portsmouth, Southampton and Eastleigh via the Chandlers Ford line, which in later years was to become something of a byway, it has been included in this chapter. As already mentioned, it opened in 1847, but its importance

was diluted once the Romsey to Southampton via Redbridge route opened in 1865. Chandlers Ford had a population of 1,085 in 1901 and was the only intermediate station on the double-track line. There was a signalbox at the up end of the down platform and goods sidings on both the up and down sides. Behind the box there was once a half-mile siding down to the Chandlers Ford Brick-works, which was horse-worked. This section of line closed to passenger trains on 5 May 1969, nearly five years after the Andover Junction to Romsey route. The signalbox closed on 22 May 1969 and the line was singled in 1972, except for double-track 'leads' at each end of the line. Chandlers Ford station was demolished and the entire site razed. The line remained open for freight trains, mainly stone traffic, and for diverted passenger trains. However, in 2003 the line was incorporated in a new Totton to Romsey via Eastleigh service, and a new station with a single platform face was built. The line had not been electrified in the 1990 Eastleigh to Portsmouth scheme and, accordingly, Class 170 diesel 'Turbostar' units work the new passenger service. It is refreshing to write about a railway branch and byway that has been reopened!

In the early days some 1859-built cabless Beattie-designed 2-4-0 tender locomotives worked the line, and towards the end of the century Classes A12, 415 4-4-2T and C8 were observed on the Andover line. However, for decades it was synonymous with the graceful Drummond 'T9' class. These remarkable engines, built between 1899 and 1901, performed tirelessly and were very much at home on the 47-mile journey from Andover Junction to Portsmouth & Southsea. The class was finally withdrawn in 1961, but they were replaced on the 'Sprat & Winkle' during 1957 by DEMUs. Drummond Class M7s also worked the line, sometimes operating in push-pull mode, and other vintage 4-4-0s, such as the 'L1' class, put in appearances from time to time. BR Standard and Fairburn tank engines worked the line in later years, while 'U' class Moguls also performed regularly, and shared freight duties with 'T9s' and '700s'. The through trains to and from Cheltenham via the MSWJR sometimes produced GWR motive power, with the Churchward '43xx' class and 'Manors' being the most frequent visitors. SR Moguls also worked these trains. Trains during the war years and various enthusiasts' specials brought more exotic motive power to the line, including the famous GWR 4-4-0 *City of Truro*. The English Electric 'Hampshire' diesel-electric multiple-units in both two- and three-car guise worked the line from the end of 1957 until September 1964. Class 33 diesel locomotives were sometimes seen in the final years, and the class hauled the

Top right:
Horsebridge station was located about 3½ miles south of Stockbridge. There was a small hamlet near the station, but the nearest village was King's Somborne, about a mile to the east. There was a signalbox at the Romsey end of the station, a three-road goods yard and a loading dock. Unlike so many sites, the station has been beautifully restored and is now not only a private residence but a site where various functions and wedding receptions are catered for. Note the old lamp room on the left, the awning and the former SR coach standing at the north end of the station. The original signalbox was demolished but a replacement was acquired from a station in Kent. *JV*

Centre right:
This charming view, looking south, finds the daily goods doing business, with a Standard 4-6-0 indulging in a little shunting. Goods facilities were withdrawn on 31 December 1962. The crossover is at the Romsey end of the platform, and a splendid lower-quadrant signal remains 'on' while the goods train is in the section. The yard handled mainly agricultural traffic for a large rural catchment area.
Lens of Sutton

Lower right:
Some 2½ miles south of Horsebridge station was Mottisfont. The goods yard here closed earlier than others on the line, on 3 October 1960. At this point the old Andover Canal alignment that the railway broadly followed was most obvious. The signalbox seen here also controlled a road crossing just south of the station. On 19 May 1957 'T9' No 30284 heads south with the 1.42pm Andover Junction to Portsmouth & Southsea train. There is one wagon in the goods sidings in the background. *C. Saunders/ R. K. Blencowe collection*

demolition trains in the late 1960s. 'Hampshire' units also worked the Chandlers Ford line until closure, and now Class 170 'Turbostars' provide the local service.

It seems ironic that in total closure terms so many cross-country routes and links in Dorset and Hampshire suffered so badly: the Somerset & Dorset, the Didcot, Newbury & Southampton and the Midland & South Western Junction all succumbed during the 1960s, and all ran through rural areas with only relatively low volumes of local traffic. The 'Sprat & Winkle' served a local community for more than a century, but despite modernisation in terms of motive power, if not infrastructure, it was a loss-maker under the criteria used in the 'Beeching' era and consequently its closure was inevitable. The last rites were executed on 7 September 1964, when the line closed completely save for the short stub from Andover Junction to Town, which, as already mentioned, lasted for a further three years for goods traffic.

There are plenty of remains along the old permanent way,

although in some locations all trace of the railway has been obliterated, either by building, ploughing in or simply disappearing into rapidly growing undergrowth — what is generally referred to as 'returning to nature'. In no particular order, perhaps Horsebridge is the most interesting survivor. The station is a private residence and has been beautifully restored, with platforms and awnings intact. The original signalbox was demolished but a redundant example has been acquired from a station in Kent. An old Southern Railway coach graces the up platform and the owners run a business catering for wedding receptions and other gatherings (see photograph). Mottisfont is another station preserved in private hands, but Stockbridge, Clatford and Andover Town have been razed. Several bridges have survived, the best example being south of Fullerton. This is a fascinating place to visit and every year the old platforms become more overgrown, to a point where they can only just be identified. When peering into the undergrowth it is hard to imagine that trains ever passed the place.

Right:
Mottisfont is another station on the line that has survived, and a fine home it has turned out to be. Now know as 'The Old Station', it is 40 years since a would-be passenger was able to buy a ticket. The only obvious relic south of here is one of the gateposts by the road crossing. *JV*

Upper left:
The 1865 line to Andover joined the 1847 Eastleigh to Salisbury route at Kimbridge Junction, to the north-west of Romsey. During World War 2 additional sidings were located on the Romsey side of the junction and a new signalbox opened in 1943. It was abolished in June 1967, three years after the Andover line closed, and a ground frame then controlled demolition train movements. The savings associated with diesel traction did not save the line. Here a 3H or 'Thumper' unit crosses the junction and makes for Romsey and Eastleigh. ***R. K. Blencowe***

ANDOVER, ROMSEY, and SOUTHAMPTON.—London and South Western.

Miles.		Week Days.																	Sundays.			
	Waterloo Station,	mrn	mrn	mrn	mrn	mrn	mrn	mrn	aft	aft	aft	aft	m	aft	aft				mrn	mrn		
	120London ....dep.	....	....	6 10	6 35	8 50	9 20	1115	m	2 10	....	3 50	5 50	....	m	....	....	....	....	1115	....	....
—	**Andover** Junction ....dep.	6 45	7 30	8 25	9 13	1118	1250	1 3	....	4 7	5 35	6 33	7 32	8 12	8 50	....	....	....	9 50	6 32	....	....
¾	" Town	6 49	Saturdays only.	Except Saturdays.	9 17	1123	....	1 8	2 10	4 11	....	6 37	7 35	Sats. only.	8 54	....	....	....	9 54	6 36	....	....
2¾	Clatford	6 54			9 22	1128	....	1 13	2 15	4 16	....	6 42	7 40		8 59	....	....	....	9 59	6 41	....	....
5¼	Fullerton Junction **149**	7 1			9 29	1136	....	1 21	2 22	4 23	....	6 50	7 48		9 6	....	....	....	10 6	6 49	....	....
8½	Stockbridge	7 8			9 37	1144	....	1 29	....	4 30	....	6 58	7 55		Saturdays only.	....	....	....	1014	6 57	....	....
11¾	Horsebridge	7 16			9 44	1151	....	1 36	....	4 37	....	7 5	8 2			....	....	....	1022	7 4	....	....
14¼	Mottisfont	7 23			9 50	1157	....	1 42	....	4 43	....	7 12	....			....	....	....	1029	7 11	....	....
18	Romsey **140, 142**	7 32		8 53	9 59	12 8	1 19	1 51	....	4 52	6 4	7 22	....	8 41		....	....	....	1038	7 21	....	....
21¾	Nursling	7 40		....	Via Eastleigh	1216	....	1 59	....	4 59	....	7 29	....	....		....	....	....	1045	7 28	....	....
23½	Redbridge **126**	7 45	8 6	....		1221	....	2 6	....	5 4	....	7 35	....	....		....	....	....	1050	7 33	....	....
25¼	Millbrook	7 50	....	....		1226	....	2 11	....	5 9	....	7 40	....	....		....	....	....	1055	7 38	....	....
26	**Southampton West**	7 53	8 12	9 8		1229	1 34	2 14	....	5 12	6 20	7 43	....	8 56		....	....	....	1058	7 41	....	....
27¾	" (Town and Dock)...arr.	8 2	8 21	9 16	1038	1237	1 42	2 22	....	5 22	6 30	7 53	....	9 4		....	....	....	11 6	7 51	....	....

SOUTHAMPTON, ROMSEY, and ANDOVER.—London and South Western.

Miles.		Week Days.																	Sundays.			
	Town and Dock Station,	mrn	mrn	mrn	mrn	aft	aft	aft	aft	aft	aft	aft	aft	aft	aft				mrn	mrn	aft	
—	**Southampton** ....dep.	....	7 25	9 *a*8	1042	1248	1 45	....	3 *a*0	4 14	....	6 7	....	Saturdays only.	8 22	....	....	....	7 58	8 53	4 51	....
1¾	" **West**	....	7 32	9 15	1050	1255	1 52	....	3 15	4 21	....	6 14	....		8 31	....	....	....	8 5	9 0	4 59	....
2¾	Millbrook	....	7 36	9 19	....	1259	....	....	....	....	....	6 18	....		8 35	....	....	....	8 9	....	5 3	....
4¼	Redbridge	....	7 41	9 24	....	1 4	1 58	....	3 22	4 28	....	6 23	....		8 41	....	....	....	8 14	9 7	5 9	....
6	Nursling	....	7 46	9 29	....	1 9	North Express.	....	3 27	....	....	6 29	....		8 46	....	....	....	8 20	....	5 14	....
9¾	Romsey **140, 142**	....	7 54	9 43	1110	1 17		....	3 47	4 40	....	6 38	....		8 56	....	....	....	8 28	9 17	5 23	....
13¼	Mottisfont	....	8 2	9 51	North Express.	1 25		....	3 55	....	....	6 46	m		9 4	....	....	....	8 36		5 31	....
16	Horsebridge	m	8 8	9 57		1 31		....	4 1	....	....	6 52	8 7		9 10	....	....	....	8 43	North Express.	5 38	....
19¼	Stockbridge	7 36	8 15	10 5		1 38		m	4 8	....	m	6 59	8 14	m	9 17	....	....	....	8 51		5 46	....
22¼	Fullerton Junction **149**	7 49	8 22	1012		1 45		1 53	4 15	....	6 52	7 6	8 22	9 15	9 24	....	....	....	8 59		5 54	....
25	Clatford	....	8 28	1018		1 51		1 59	4 21	....	6 58	7 12	8 28	9 21	9 30	....	....	....	9 5		6 0	....
27	**Andover** Town ..{**123, 147**	....	8 33	1023		1 56		2 4	4 26	....	7 4	7 17	8 34	9 27	9 35	....	....	....	9 10		6 5	....
27¾	" Junc. **117, 120,** arr.	....	8 37	1027	1136	2 0	2 32	....	4 30	5 6	7 7	7 21	8 37	9 30	9 39	....	....	....	9 14	9 44	6 9	....
94¼	**123London** (Waterloo).arr.	1011	....	12 8	2 30	....	4 40	....	6 1	8 10	....	1034	1034	....	1159	....	....	....	12 9	....	8 6	....

a Via Eastleigh. **m** Motor Car, 1st and 3rd class.

☞ For **OTHER TRAINS** between Southampton and Romsey, see pages 140 to 143; between Southampton and Redbridge, see pages 126 to 135.

Lower left:
In 1910 some Andover to Southampton trains ran via Redbridge while others ran via Eastleigh. The few fast trains were those working over the MSWJR on an inter-regional basis. In the final years most trains ran from Andover through to Eastleigh and Portsmouth.

Below:
Quite possibly the oldest photograph in this volume is this study of a down train at Romsey, featuring a 2-2-2 locomotive and four four-wheelers. Although speculative comment, it could have been the first ever train to work to Andover in 1865. The scene undoubtedly illustrates a special occasion and there is no doubt that photography then existed, even though in its infancy. Certainly the picture is pre-1884, because the station canopy has not yet been extended.
J. Hicks collection

Above:
On 3 December 1977 the author, in his capacity as MD of Railway Pictorial Publications Railtours, ran the 'Class 74 Farewell Tour' in conjunction with the Diesel and Electric Group. To add spice to the tour it was important that the 'Big Edward' electro-diesel completed some mileage using its auxiliary 600hp diesel engine. The ideal candidate was the non-electrified freight line from Eastleigh to Romsey via Chandlers Ford. Here No 74003 prepares to leave Romsey for Eastleigh shortly before its withdrawal.
JV/TTT

Below:
From 1865 Romsey effectively became a four-way junction, with lines to Eastleigh, Southampton (via Redbridge), Salisbury and Andover. Trains from Southampton must negotiate a tight curve before they reach Romsey station and they are restricted to a line speed of 20mph. Suitably accentuated by a 300mm Nikkor lens, a Class 47/7 working a down Exeter train joins the Eastleigh line at Romsey in September 1990. Most of the old signalbox at the junction (now controlled by Eastleigh panel) was moved into the grounds of a local school after it closed in 1982. *JV/TTT*

Top right:
The line from Romsey to Eastleigh was not part of the branch from Andover, but a glimpse has been included here because for many years it was a byway (and in some ways still is) and it was part of the route for many trains travelling to and from Andover Junction. These three photographs show three stages in the life of Chandlers Ford station, which opened in 1847 and was the only intermediate station. After a life of 122 years it closed on 5 May 1969. The first view is looking towards Eastleigh on 20 March 1968. Originally there were sidings on both the up and down sides of the line, but the goods yard closed on 4 May 1964. The signalbox closed on 22 May 1969, just after passenger services ceased. *J. Scrace*

Centre right:
After the passenger service ceased, the line was used for freight (mainly stone trains), diversions and empty stock movements. Track rationalisation started in 1971 and by 1972 the line from Eastleigh to Romsey had been singled, except for double-track feeds at either end. Eventually the Chandlers Ford site was levelled, with only a trace of the down platform remaining. Making for the terminal at Fareham in September 1991 is one of the impressive General Motors Class 59s, No 59102 *Village of Chantry*, with a heavy stone train that has travelled from Whatley Quarry via Westbury. The old platform can just be seen beside the sixth wagon. *JV/TTT*

Lower right:
The avenue of trees disappearing into the distance towards Romsey can still be identified in this October 2003 view, but there has been a further transformation and another episode in the railway history of Chandlers Ford. In 2002 it was announced that a new Totton to Romsey via Eastleigh service was being introduced, and included in the specification was the reopening of Chandlers Ford station. A modern functional station was built with a single platform face, booking office, waiting area and pedestrian overbridge. Class 170 two-car 'Turbostar' units are employed because the Chandlers Ford section is not electrified. No 170307 pauses on the single line in the late autumn of 2003. *JV*

23. Longparish Branch

ANOTHER significant development along the Andover to Romsey line took place on 1 June 1885 when a line to Fullerton opened from Hurstbourne on the LSWR London to Salisbury main line (to the east of Andover), from which date Fullerton became a junction. This double-track line had an interesting history, and yet again its construction was essentially strategic to keep other railway companies at bay. Although there had been an element of co-operation between the LSWR and GWR over the Romsey to Andover line, the GWR was still anxious to gain access to Southampton, and its golden opportunity came with the advent of the cross-country Didcot, Newbury & Southampton Railway, which had been authorised in 1873 and would enable through traffic from the Midlands and the North to reach the Channel port. The DNSR would pass under the LSWR Salisbury main line at Whitchurch, and was originally intended to join the LSWR Southampton line north of Micheldever; this would of course mean a high degree of dependence on the LSWR between Micheldever and Southampton. A spur between the DNSR and the LSWR Salisbury line at Whitchurch was included in the plans.

Although the DNSR opened between Didcot and Newbury in 1882, there were delays to the south of Newbury while various discussions were held with organisations in the Southampton area, including the Harbour Board, Chamber of Commerce and Corporation. As a consequence of these discussions the viability of the DNSR was endorsed, but a revised routeing for a direct line to Winchester and thence to Southampton was recommended. In the meantime, alarmed by the DNSR proposals, the LSWR proposed that a new route for north/south traffic, deviating from its Salisbury route at Hurstbourne, should be built, and that this 7½-mile line would travel in a south-westerly direction to meet the Romsey to Redbridge line at Fullerton, with trains continuing onwards to Southampton via the established LSWR route. At the northern end of the route trains would travel over the DNSR via a junction at Whitchurch, just east of Hurstbourne.

After the two railway companies objected to each other's plans, a Parliamentary Committee adjudicated over the situation and, after considering at length submissions from the two sides, it found in favour of the DNSR proposals. The LSWR appealed against the decision and the House of Lords allowed the LSWR to proceed with its proposed line, both railways being authorised on 10 August 1882. The LSWR plan had the grand name of the Northern & Southern Junction Railway. Although construction started right away, major earthworks were required over difficult terrain and the line, together with the aforementioned improvements to the Romsey to Redbridge section, was not completed until May 1885. The line opened on 1 June of that year, and intermediate stations were located at Longparish and Wherwell, villages of little significance in terms of population.

The link with the DNSR at Whitchurch was never built, and it quickly became apparent that the LSWR line was a 'white elephant'. Just after the turn of the century a spur was planned so that trains travelling south from Fullerton and Romsey could head west at Redbridge, with a through train potential to the Bournemouth and Weymouth line. However, the spur was never built and planning permission lapsed. This inaction really committed the Longparish branch to nothing more than a rural branch line. There was little diversionary value to the line, and although it was heavily used in both World Wars, it served little purpose and was uneconomic to operate.

Left:
Although the Longparish branch from Fullerton Junction joined the Basingstoke to Salisbury main line at Hurstbourne, train services mostly worked to and from Whitchurch. Whitchurch station survives to this day, although the outer face of the old island platform, seen here on the right and once used by Longparish branch trains, has been abandoned. Pounding up to Waterloo is the 06.26 service from Exeter St David's on 2 May 1981, headed by Class 50 No 50011 *Centurion.* **Goods facilities were located in the right background of this view, and there was once a siding on the left.**
JV/TTT

Right:
Prior to the opening of the Longparish branch there had been a private siding near the proposed junction with the main line, and it was decided to locate Hurstbourne station at the same site. This view shows the wooden station soon after opening, looking in the up direction towards Whitchurch. The branch opened in 1885 and passenger services ceased in 1931. The line from Longparish to Hurstbourne was lifted by May 1934, and the junction signalbox was closed in the following October. Perhaps surprisingly, Hurstbourne station remained open until April 1964.
JV collection

From Whitchurch, trains for Fullerton travelled down the main line for about 2 miles until Hurstbourne station was reached. At the location of an existing 1871-built siding, a station with both up and down wooden platforms, together with wooden shelters and awnings on both platforms, was constructed in conjunction with the opening of the line to Fullerton. Just west of Hurstbourne Viaduct there was a double-track junction with the main line and all movements were controlled by a junction signalbox on the up side of the main line. The branch veered off to the south-west and passed through several cuttings and over a number of bridges on undulating gradients until the station of Longparish was reached, some 4¼ miles from Hurstbourne. In the 1888 Bradshaw the station appears as 'Long-Parish', but from 1890 the name became one word. As was so common on rural lines, the actual village of Longparish, which was spread out along the River Test, was 1½ miles from the station. The station buildings here and at Wherwell were very substantial structures. Again, up and down platforms were provided and each had awnings with curved roofs. There was a large goods yard on the up side and a loading dock. A 15-lever signalbox was located at the up end of the down platform.

A little over 2 miles from Longparish was the second of the two intermediate stations, at Wherwell. Generally the line descended to Wherwell, and the station was approached in a deep cutting that can still be located today, albeit heavily overgrown. Two road bridges crossed the line at Wherwell. Again, two curved roof awnings were provided and the station building and 15-lever signalbox were both on the down side. There was a goods yard at the down end of the up platform. The picturesque village is located in the immediate vicinity of the station and is noted for a profusion of thatched cottages. The double track then continued to Fullerton Junction, originally Fullerton Bridge, to join the Andover to Romsey line. Both lines had up and down platforms, all four having awnings for passengers as protection from the elements. A signalbox was located on the down side of the Andover line south of the station.

At the opening of the line there were four trains in each direction on weekdays, with no Sunday service. It is amusing to relate that at the time of the opening the local paper said that the line was 'intended to expedite the journey between London and Bournemouth'! By 1888 there were five trains in each direction, with three down and four up trains working between Basingstoke and Fullerton. Of the two down trains, where a change at Whitchurch was required, there was a 40-minute wait for the Fullerton connection. The service gradually declined, with four trains in 1914 and only three in 1920. There was a reasonable amount of local freight traffic, but passenger loadings were so light that a single coach normally sufficed, and the LSWR used a steam railmotor, working out of Andover depot, in the

Edwardian era, and a Drewry petrol railcar was tried during the late 1920s. With a meagre timetable, few passengers and no through train prospects, the entire line was singled in 1913 and the signalboxes at both Longparish and Wherwell became redundant and were replaced by ground frames.

In 1914 a sawmill was established near Longparish station, and in 1916 this was followed by a wood distillation factory in the same area. For a time a special train ran from Whitchurch to Longparish for the factory's employees, and its large output, estimated at 1,000 tons per week, was mostly conveyed by rail. Traffic from the sawmills required up to 30 wagons per day. During World War 1 the Longparish branch was extensively used for troop movements. Longparish continued to be used, primarily for coal traffic and wood products, and Wherwell was still a centre for agricultural traffic, but generally there were no encouraging signs regarding overall viability. In 1927 the movie-makers moved in when, during April, scenes from the silent film version of *The Ghost Train* by Arnold Ridley (of *Dad's Army* fame) were filmed on the line. The end of passenger services became inevitable, and in July 1931 the service was withdrawn. Goods services continued, but by then Wherwell could boast only a single siding. To make matters worse, the section of line from Hurstbourne Junction to Longparish was closed and lifted in May 1934, from which time all goods traffic ran from the Fullerton direction, reducing the branch to little more than a siding.

There was a significant increase in freight traffic during World War 2 when, in 1942, an RAF military depot in Harewood Forest, near Longparish, was used as an ammunition storage depot. This resulted in a large number of trains working over the line, and military personnel also used the line until the end of the war. The highlight was when 14 troop trains were handled in a single day. Activity was so great that 15 mobile cranes and one heavy over-head crane were used to move bombs weighing up to 4,000lbs each. By April 1944 four ammunition trains a day were using the line, and during a single month no fewer than 1,200 wagons were dealt with. This era was undoubtedly the busiest in the line's history. After the war the depot had to be cleared of all ammunition, and this took many years to complete. The RAF continued to use the railway until January 1955, by which time the line was served by a daily train, only coal and other fuel comprised the diminishing traffic, and a single freight clerk was sufficient to handle the paperwork. By 1956 there was but a single wagon handled on some days and the service was reduced to Mondays, Wednesdays and Fridays only. On 28 May 1956 the goods service finally succumbed and the last freight left Longparish behind 'T9' class No 30288.

After formal closure the line was used for testing the then brand new diesel-electric multiple-units, and on 30 October 1957 an inspection special traversed the line. After this date, part of the line

Upper right:
The Longparish branch was built as a main-line double track, but once the prospect of through trains from Waterloo to Bournemouth evaporated, it became a lightly used rural branch line. It was singled throughout in 1913, and after passenger services finished in 1931, it was severed just beyond Longparish station, 4¼ miles from the junction. From that time the line from Fullerton Junction to Longparish was merely a freight siding. At Longparish there was a sawmill, a wood distillation plant, two coal yards and a military depot. The steel gantry seen here was erected by the RAF to lift heavy bombs. Some time in the 1950s 'T9' class No 30730 shunts the yard, with the old station on the right. *R. K. Blencowe collection*

Lower right:
During World War 2 there was an enormous amount of activity at Longparish, almost certainly (and somewhat ironically) the traffic zenith during the life of the line. An RAF Maintenance Unit was set up as an ammunition storage depot in October 1942, and during 1944 there were no fewer than four trains traversing the remaining line every day. There were plenty of troop train movements, which served a transit camp at Longparish, and almost unbelievably there were once 14 troop trains on the line in a single day! The RAF stopped using the line in January 1955, and although it soldiered on for coal traffic, it closed on 28 May 1956.
By the end the service was thrice weekly. On 30 October 1957 the grasses are growing long at the disused and forlorn station. *S. C. Nash*

Below:
Happily, the 1884-built Longparish station was eventually saved and converted to a private residence.
Many thousands of servicemen will have used this approach road, but when photographed in April 2003 it was very tranquil indeed. The station was 1½ miles from the village — a familiar branch-line situation. After closure the line was used for testing the then new 3H 'Hampshire' diesel-electric units and also for withdrawn wagon storage. Later, at Fullerton, condemned pre-war electric stock was stored on the remaining stub. *JV*

Upper left:
Wherwell station was 2 miles beyond Longparish, and the village, adjacent to the station, was and still is noted for its delightful thatched cottages. It must have been fascinating to have been on board this inspection saloon that traversed the line 17 months after closure — perhaps back in 1957 there was far less chance of local youngsters putting obstacles on the line. 'T9' class No 30707 arrives at Wherwell on the return trip from Longparish with officials peering from the windows.
S. C. Nash

Lower left:
When the author first visited the line in November 1969 the track had been lifted but the trackbed could be clearly identified, and this view should be compared to the previous plate. There was a busy goods yard at Wherwell in its heyday, whereas on this day a couple of beehives just off the end of the old up platform was the only sign of life.
JV/TTT

Below:
It is doubtful whether the occupants of the foreground bungalows ever think of the branch goods passing their washing lines on Mondays, Wednesdays and Fridays. This view, looking towards Fullerton from the main road into the village from the north, taken in April 2003, should be compared with the next photograph, especially the chimneystack at the top of the photograph, which locates the original station building. *JV*

Upper right:
A staff of only three could be mustered for this Edwardian view of Wherwell, looking south-west. The stationmaster is almost certainly the one with the beard in the centre. Passenger traffic was so light that the line was singled in 1913, and the 15-lever signalbox in the distance was closed on 13 July of that year. A single goods siding survived until the line closed. *JV collection*

Lower right:
Photographs of the daily, and later thrice-weekly, goods in action between the stations on the Longparish branch are not common, but in this composition, taken on 12 July 1954, 'T9' No 30289 heads a typical branch goods of six wagons and a brake-van back to Fullerton Junction. The train is a modeller's delight, but not one to swell the coffers of British Railways, when compared to running costs. *E. W. Fry/R. K. Blencowe collection*

Left:
In the days of passenger trains they usually comprised an elderly locomotive, such as an LSWR 'A12' class 'Jubilee' 0-4-2 or an '0460' class 4-4-0, hauling a single coach. In later years a small steam railmotor was used, and a petrol railcar was tried in the late 1920s. Emulating a branch local, this inspection special, with saloon at the rear, passes beneath the Wherwell road bound for Longparish on 30 October 1957. Note the fancy headcode configuration. *S. C. Nash*

Left:
This good view of Fullerton
Junction station is looking
eastward towards the
Longparish branch platforms.
'T9' No 30730 is waiting for
the road on to the Andover
Junction to Romsey line with
a diminutive goods train.
Either a '700' or a 'T9'
normally worked the
Longparish goods train,
although Bulleid 'Q1s'
occasionally appeared.
Note that the old down branch
platform on the far side
is without track.
R. K. Blencowe collection

was used for the storage of withdrawn wagons and rolling stock until it was finally taken out of use in April 1960. A short stub at Fullerton survived until June 1964, which, curiously, was used to store some withdrawn 4SUB EMUs in the early 1960s. As mentioned in the previous chapter, even the Andover to Romsey line closed from 7 September 1964, and although the track remained *in situ* long after closure, the history of the Longparish branch had already come to a rather sad end.

Of all the branches featured in this volume the motive power used on everyday trains on the Longparish branch is perhaps the simplest to describe. In the early days small LSWR Adams and Drummond tank locomotives such as the 'O2' class and the diminutive 2-2-0T 'C12' class worked the line with either one or two compartment coaches. As already mentioned, services were in the hands of Class H13 steam railmotors between 1906 and about 1910, and a Drewry petrol railcar was used in 1928. Otherwise it was the elderly Adams 'A12' 'Jubilee' class that plied to and fro between Whitchurch and Fullerton. For most of the line's life goods trains were either in the hands of Classes T9 or 700, but during World War 2 the motive power would have been considerably more varied.

The primary remains of the line comprise cuttings, embankments and the two original station buildings (see accompanying photograph). South-west of the junction at Hurstbourne the earthworks are truly impressive, and the brickwork of surviving overbridges has survived the passage of time. Most of the cuttings were through chalk, and although now heavily wooded many can still be identified. The alignment is most visible at Wherwell, although bungalows have been built on part of the former trackbed. The Fullerton site is now heavily overgrown, although with some 'bramble-bashing' the branch platform edging can still be found. On reflection the line served little purpose, except for the war years. It closed to passengers so long ago that few living people would have travelled over the line as fare-paying passengers. It has now peacefully returned to nature.

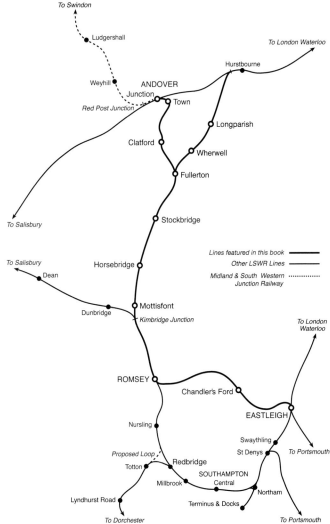

Above:
Map of the Longparish branch
and Andover to Eastleigh lines.

Left:
The 1927 public timetable
provided by Bradshaw.

Mls	WHITCHURCH, FULLERTON JUNCTION, and HORSEBRIDGE. Week Days				Mls	Week Days			
		mrn	aft	aft			mrn	mrn	aft
—	Whitchurch ....dep.	9 5	5 13	6 56	—	Horsebridge ....dep.	7 3	10 1	5 54
1¼	Hurstbourne	9 9	5 17	6 54	3½	Stockbridge	7 13	10 9	6 2
6	Longparish.............	9 20	5 26	7 3	8½	Fullerton Junction........	7 21	10 10	6 15
8	Wherwell................	9 26	5 34	7 9	7½	Wherwell................	7 27	10 23	6 18
9¼	Fullerton Junction 187 ...	9 30	5 40	7 13	9½	Longparish..............	7 34	10 29	6 24
12½	Stockbridge	9 42	...	7 20	14½	Hurstbourne 179.........	7 46	10 42	6 35
15½	Horsebridge 184 .....arr.	9 49	...	...	15½	Whitchurch H 49, 179 arr.	7 52	10 49	6 41

H About 1¼ miles to G.W. (late D.N. & S.) Station.
☞ For LOCAL TRAINS between Fullerton and Horsebridge, see page 184.

※ ※ For other
Trains
BETWEEN PAGE
Whitchurch and
Hurstbourne 179

24. Fawley Branch

OIL and oil-based products are the mainstay of traffic on the Fawley branch. The vast Esso plant on the western side of Southampton Water is an establishment for refining oil into other products such as petroleum and aviation fuel. In the late 1950s and the 1960s rail traffic to and from Fawley was truly impressive. For example, in 1957 some 13 trains per day traversed the branch, and by 1961 this had risen to 25. Some of these oil trains turned the scales at a gross weight of 2,000 tons, especially the workings to Bromford Bridge, near Birmingham. However, in recent years improvements in pipeline technology and distribution systems, combined with lower costs, have been to the detriment of the railway. For example, Fawley once supplied Gatwick Airport by rail via a terminal at Salfords, but it is now supplied by pipeline from another source. By contrast, there are now merely a couple of trains per day to and from Fawley, comprising tanker wagons destined for a multiplicity of locations, together with one military train working (as required) to MOD Marchwood and back.

Military traffic over part of the branch has also performed a strategically important role as stores, munitions and Army vehicles are transported to the establishment at Marchwood, where a military railway runs down to the wharves on Southampton Water. Passenger trains no longer serve Marchwood, Hythe or Fawley, but the future potential for the branch, should the proposed Dibden

Bay container port ever come to fruition, would be enormous; frequent Freightliner trains would branch off from the Southampton to Bournemouth main line at Totton to reach their destination south of Marchwood.

Although plans for a branch line to Fawley go back into the 19th century, the branch was a latecomer, not opening until 1925. It is located just a few miles west of historic Southampton, with its great maritime traditions; in fact, access to the open sea was one of the reasons for the development of small towns along the western side of the estuary of the River Test, where it meets Southampton Water and the Solent. Other than by the circuitous journey by road (and previously rail), the area is still linked to the city of Southampton by the Hythe Ferry, a journey that either starts or ends by a narrow gauge pier railway at Hythe.

The railway had come to Southampton in 1839 when Southampton and Winchester were linked by rail, and by May 1840 Southampton was connected to the capital. Construction of a line from Southampton to Dorchester commenced in July 1845, and it was opened on 1 June 1847. The line, known as 'the Water Snake' or 'Castleman's Corkscrew' (Castleman being a proactive solicitor from Wimborne who promoted the $60\frac{1}{2}$-mile line), connected the two towns in its title by running via Brockenhurst, Ringwood and Wimborne. However, it was to be 1860 before any proposals for a

Below:
The Fawley branch will always be primarily associated with oil and the military. Although plans for a railway down the western side of Southampton Water go back to the 19th century, and Light Railway Orders were approved in 1903 and 1921, the branch was, surprisingly, not opened until 1925. In 1920 650 acres of land at Fawley were acquired for the purpose of building a large oil refinery. The plans were agreed and the refinery built, but within a short time the Anglo-American Oil Company (later Esso) took over the site and started distributing oil and petrol products in some volume. In the 1950s and 1960s four-wheeled tankers with the prominent 'Esso' logo on the side were commonplace. Crossing the River Test between Redbridge and Totton with empties for Fawley on 24 August 1962 is powerful 'W' class tank No 31911. *Michael J. Fox*

The frequency of passenger trains between Totton and Fawley was never high. In 1927 there were five round-trip passenger journeys over the line, but by 1938 this had shrunk to three workings. In August 1937 Adams 'A12' class No 611 approaches the junction station of Totton with the 11.55am train from Fawley, comprising four old ex-LSWR coaches. The main Southampton to Bournemouth line is on the right. *SLS/R. F. Roberts*

The January 1927 Bradshaw shows five trains to Fawley on weekdays only, either beginning or ending their journeys at Redbridge, Southampton Terminus or Eastleigh.

A number of powerful tank locomotives were tried on the Fawley branch. Due to the many road and path crossings, including 10 public crossing, 32 private crossings and a footpath, tank locomotives were preferred to tender engines for reasons of visibility and safety. On 18 September 1960 the first of Urie's five 'H16' class locomotives, No 30516, was used on the LCGB 'The South Western Limited' railtour. The train has just joined the branch at what was originally Eling Junction, but which became Totton Junction from 5 February 1950. *J. C. Beckett*

EASTLEIGH, SOUTHAMPTON, TOTTON, and FAWLEY.

Week Days only.

Miles		mrn		mrn		mrn		aft		aft	
	Eastleigh ....dep.	6 40		..		..		..		..	
2½	Swaythling...............	6 45		..		..		..		..	
3½	St. Denys................	6 50		..		..		..		..	
5½	Southampton Terminus			9 25		..		3 35		5 33	
7½	Southampton West ..... arr.	6 57		9 31		..		3 41		5 39	
	{dep.	7 3		9 32		..		3 42		5 41	
8	Millbrook...............	7 8		9 36		..		3 46		..	
9½	Redbridge...............	7 13		..		11 5		..		..	
10½	Totton B................	7 18		9 43		11 8		3 54		5 51	
14	Marchwood	7 29		9 54		1130		4 5		6 0	
17	Hythe (Hants.)...........	7 39		10 4		1151		4 15		6 10	
20	Fawley (Hants.).......arr.	7 50		1015		1211		4 26		6 21	

Week Days only.

Miles		mrn		mrn		aft		aft		aft	
	Fawley (Hants.).......dep.	8 10		1023		1220		4 45		6 30	
3	Hythe (Hants.)..........	8 18		1031		1228		4 53		6 39	
6	Marchwood	8 30		1042		1239		5 4		7 1	
9½	Totton B 154............	8 43		1055		1252		5 18		7 30	
10½	Redbridge 187...........			1038		1255		5 20		..	
12	Millbrook...............	8 48		..		1 0		5 25		..	
12½	Southampton West 159,.. arr.	8 52		..		1 4		5 29		7 37	
	1132 {dep.	8 53		..		1 6		5 30		7 38	
14	Southampton J 1132......	9 0		..		..		5 37		7 45	
16½	St. Denys...............			..		1 13		..		..	
17½	Swaythling..............			..		1 17		..		..	
20	Eastleigh..........arr.			..		1 23		..		..	

B Station for Eling.

J Southampton Terminus (for Docks).

☞ **For Local Trains and intermediate Stations**
BETWEEN   PAGE
Eastleigh and Southampton 208

*** For other Trains
BETWEEN   PAGE
Southampton and Redbridge... 187
Southampton and Totton....... 154

railway line to Fawley were tabled. The Southampton & Isle of Wight Railway proposed to build a line from the Southampton & Dorchester via Marchwood and Fawley to the tiny coastal fishing village of Lepe. Nothing came of this proposal, but in 1872 the Swindon, Southampton & New Forest Railway (later the Swindon, Marlborough & Andover Railway) planned to build a line that would terminate at Stone Point, near Lepe. However, the Bill that emerged failed to include the southern portion.

A plan to build a railway tunnel under the Solent lapsed, but in 1881 the SM&AR, which became the Midland & South Western Junction Railway in 1884 and was intent on invading the Southampton area from the north, was again active. Its Bill was for a line from Cheltenham, Swindon and Andover via Romsey and Redbridge, where a west-facing spur connecting its proposed line to the, by then, LSWR line would give access to Lepe. At Lepe a short route to the Isle of Wight would be available (the distance from Stone Point, near Lepe, to Cowes is only 2½ miles, whereas it was 11 miles from Cowes to Southampton). The Act received Royal Assent on 10 August 1882. However, at about the time all of this was happening, access to the Isle of Wight via Portsmouth and Southampton was improving and the LSWR was broadly content with its own arrangements. When the SM&AR approached the LSWR in 1883 in an effort to progress its route, the larger company became obstructive by imposing a string of conditions and stipulations before it was prepared to enter into any arrangement. The terms offered by the LSWR were so demanding as to make the (by then) MSWJR's plans financially non-viable.

In 1885 another scheme to link Cowes and Southampton via Stone Point was proposed by venture capitalists, and in June 1886 the resulting South Hampshire Railway & Pier Act was given Royal Assent. The MSWJR, which was still broadly linked with the proposed route, had been put into receivership in 1884 and its financial position was parlous. Unfortunately the South Hampshire venture failed, and these proposals were also abandoned. In 1902 the LSWR took advantage of recent legislation permitting 'light railways' to be built, with certain cost-cutting economies allowed compared to normal railway standards, subject to line speed limits and other operational limitations. The railway company submitted a case to the Light Railway Commission for a line from a point on its main line between Totton and Lyndhurst to Hythe and Fawley. There was a slight departure from normal light railway practice in that it was intended to provide a number of overbridges. Also, as it transpired, the railway would terminate at Stone Point, and not Fawley. The area was at that time sparsely populated, with Fawley showing about 1,900 residents in the 1901 census. The overall journey time from Southampton was estimated at 35 minutes, and the fare would be about a shilling. Following discussions it was later agreed to terminate the line at a point some 2½ miles short of the original plan, and accordingly a formal application was made in February 1903 for a Light Railway Order for a branch from Totton to Fawley.

At about this time in the Edwardian era motor buses started to appear, although by today's standards the vehicles were cumbersome, unreliable, uncomfortable, and ran on solid rubber tyres. The Great Western Railway had been conducting some experiments in Devon and, not to be outdone, the LSWR thought it timely to conduct trials by buying two second-hand buses and putting them to work between Lyndhurst Road station and Lyndhurst village. The experiment was a failure. However, before giving up the ghost the General Manager of the LSWR said buses would be tried between Hythe and Fawley to see whether passenger traffic developed. On 13 August 1906 a bus service run by the LSWR was inaugurated between Totton and Fawley. The bus could seat 16 passengers and two round trips per day were scheduled. A second bus joined the 'fleet' of one and the timetable was doubled in frequency from June 1908. In the meantime, the five-year time

limit in which to build the light railway was rapidly approaching, yet there was no sign of railway construction. After a row with local authorities regarding the buses cutting up the primitive local roads, the service was discontinued in November 1908. The time limit duly lapsed and still the west side of Southampton Water had no railway.

Various developments were starting to take shape in the area. Although basically a farming and fishing stronghold, a Naval seaplane base had been constructed at Calshot, just beyond Fawley, between 1913 and 1916, and a 1¾-mile narrow gauge railway from there to the Spit had been commissioned. Also, with the advent of World War 1 activity had increased at Marchwood Magazine. In previous years the Anglo-American Oil Company (later Esso) had been distributing oil and petrol products all over the country, due to the increasing use of these fuels for the propulsion of road transport and shipping, and its name was eventually to become synonymous with Fawley. In 1920 the Anglo Gulf West Indies Petroleum Corporation Limited was registered, and selected some 650 acres in the environs of Fawley on which to build its refinery. In addition to the refinery, deep-water berths and storage tanks, and all the necessary infrastructure, would be required, including pipework. Building progressed rapidly and a point at Ashlett Creek, about ½ mile south of the refinery, was chosen as the location for the wharves. A 2ft-gauge railway was also built to convey materials to the construction site, and great use was made of Eling Wharf near Totton because the roads down to Fawley were in such poor condition. In 1921 the Totton, Hythe & Fawley Light Railway was formed with the objective of building a railway line of 9 miles and 16 chains to link the towns incorporated in the name. The line would terminate about ¼ mile north of the ancient Fawley Church, some distance from the town centre. The estimated cost was just over £250,000, with a forecast annual income of £30,000. The plans were lodged with the Light Railway Commissioners, and following a full public inquiry in May 1921, when a wide range of issues were raised, discussed and largely resolved, the Order was approved by the Ministry later in that year.

The LSWR was a supporter of the scheme and agreed to work, maintain and administer the line; an Order allowing it to do so was made in January 1922. There followed some discussion about the precise alignment of the railway, and certain changes were made to the original proposal. The relevant land was purchased and the tendering process was won by Sir Robert McAlpine and Co Ltd. The contractor used a temporary narrow gauge railway along the trackbed to transport excavated materials from cuttings and, where necessary, to infill embankments. Totton yard became the depot for track-laying operations, including sleepers, ballast and track. For the purpose of track-laying and haulage, the contractors provided their own standard gauge locomotive. All of the station buildings at Marchwood, Hythe and Fawley were primarily block-built with rendering and pebbledash on the outside, and tiled roofs. By the date of construction the SR had absorbed the LSWR and much use was made of concrete produced at Exmouth Junction, for example in the form of lamp posts, fencing posts, coping stones and platform faces. In accordance with past traditions, many Irish navvies were used in the construction of the branch.

There was considerable public concern about the design of road crossings on the line, and the railway company assured critics that cattle grids would be provided at ungated crossings. Along the standard gauge single-track route there were no fewer than nine crossings either over or under the railway, 10 public road crossings, two of which had crossing gates, and the rest were cattle grids (which was more in keeping with light railway standards). There were also 32 private crossings and one footpath, in all more than enough for the footplate crews to be looking out for! The stations all had 350ft-long platforms, sufficient for a branch train comprising a locomotive and four or five coaches.

Above:
As with most freight-only lines, the Fawley branch has been a popular part of many railtour itineraries over the years. The Class 33s were much associated with Esso oil tanker trains in the mid-1960s, and on 5 November 1988 the 'Wessex Adventurer' tour brought Class 33/1s to the line in the shape of Nos 33102 and 33114. The duo are powering away from Marchwood on the return leg with Class 45/1 No 45106 at the tail end, thus avoiding the need to run round at Fawley. *JV/TTT*

Upper right:
This vintage view was taken at almost the same location back in the summer of 1937. One of the Adams 'Jubilee' 'A12' class, No 611, makes for Redbridge and Southampton with an afternoon train comprising four compartment coaches. The class were all built between 1887 and 1895, and later benefited from the fitting of Drummond boilers. They had all been withdrawn by 1948. *SLS/R. F. Roberts*

Lower right:
The dear old Class A12s were more likely to be found on freight workings than passenger trains, which were mostly handled by Classes O2, M7 and T1. When photographed in August 1938, No 628 was heading a Fawley to Eastleigh goods at Marchwood. Just south of Marchwood station is the junction for the Marchwood MOD complex, and in 1960/61, with increasing oil traffic, a passing loop was provided here to increase line capacity. *SLS/R. F. Roberts*

Above:
Another somewhat bizarre special to visit the Fawley branch in March 1983, at least in terms of motive power, was Hertfordshire Railtours' 'Thames Piddle Executive', referring to the rivers not to the end-of-day habits of the revellers! Passing through the down road, and the only platform line, at Marchwood are 'Hastings' units Nos 1032 and 1017. The signal is 'off' for the through line, the lower 'peg' being for the line to Marchwood sidings. *JV/TTT*

Upper left:
The MOD site at Marchwood has its own internal railway system, and at the far end of the complex the military has access to wharves on Southampton Water, where Army vehicles and supplies can be transferred from rail to ship for despatch to any trouble spot in the world. Arguably the sight of light tanks on low-loaders is the most forceful impression of such traffic. In preparation for operations in Iraq, special train 7X13, headed by Class 66 No 66075, passes Marchwood with a long line of armoured vehicles in desert livery on 25 February 2003. *Stephen Green*

Lower left:
The number of trains using the Fawley branch has hugely diminished in recent years. With most of the oil now travelling by pipeline, two Fawley oil trains and one MOD Marchwood train would be regarded as a good weekday tally. Marchwood is undoubtedly the best place on the line to view trains. There are semaphore signals and manually controlled crossing gates, and all trains must pass the old station.
In March 2003 signalman Stephen Green closes the gates behind Class 66 No 66238 and its load of tanker wagons at Marchwood, as the load disappears towards Totton. *JV*

Above:

The traffic to and from MOD Marchwood is erratic, similar to the old 'as required' principle adopted on freight-only branch lines. In the past small four-wheelers were used, including box vans loaded with ammunition, but now more modern rail wagons appear, including containers on Freightliner trains. Creeping around the corner and passing from military property to BR land in October 1989 is grubby Railfreight-liveried Class 47 No 47256. Note the old wooden protecting gate, so unlike the large metal security gates around the corner. In the foreground is the line to Fawley. *JV/TTT*

Below:

Once the Class 33 appearances on oil trains diminished, but before the latest generation of freight locomotives from North America arrived, the standard oil train on the branch usually comprised a Class 47 and either 50-, 80- or 100-ton tanker wagons. Class 37 and 58 locomotives were also regular performers. This powerful telephoto lens shot from July 1989 shows the 'kink' at the southern end of the Marchwood loop. The Class 47 and its up train from Fawley are obscuring the entrance to the Marchwood site as they run through the 'down' side of the loop. *JV/TTT*

The line finally opened on 20 July 1925. The local press commented unfavourably on the first train because it comprised three old SECR coaches that had 'a shabby appearance'. The criticism continued with a comment that the stations were lit by oil lamps and had 'not yet aspired to such modern methods of lighting as gas and electricity'! Initially the service was sparse and 1926 saw no improvement, but by January 1927 five trains in each direction, weekdays only, plied between Fawley and Totton. One train in each direction worked from and to Eastleigh, there was one short working in each direction to and from Redbridge, while the other three worked to and from Southampton Terminus. The first train arrived at Fawley at 7.50am, and the last left there at 6.30pm. Throughout its years the Fawley branch never generated large volumes of passenger traffic, and by 1938 the SR provided only three return workings on the branch with an extra one or two on Saturdays. By 1953 there was but a single down train from Southampton to Fawley, effectively a workmen's train, which arrived at 7.43am. On Saturdays there were two down trains, a later one catering for returning shoppers. There were, however, three up trains but just two down on Saturdays. Throughout its passenger-carrying life journey times never changed, and at least half an hour was deemed necessary to cover the 9½ miles (from Totton), an average speed of less than 20mph! However, there were so many crossings with a 10mph speed limit that there was little opportunity of journey time improvements. By the 1960s, and against the 'Beeching' background, with only an up and down train per day and minimal loadings, the line had to be a candidate for closure, and predictably, on 11 February 1966, the last passenger train left Fawley. The line had survived as a passenger route for a mere 40 years.

While there were thus few significant developments in terms of the basic passenger traffic, the growth story was based on military and oil traffic. The branch layout of a single track with a run-round loop at Fawley changed shortly after opening when the loop was extended, followed shortly by the first dedicated sidings running to the refinery. Oil, petrol, bitumen and asphalt were all transported by rail; in 1927 the amount of crude oil refined at Fawley was 350 tons. In the same year a goods shed, which once resided at Tisted on the Meon Valley line, was transported to Fawley. By 1934 the Esso brand-name was being promoted by the Anglo-American Oil Company, which was by then affiliated to the Standard Oil Company ('SO') of the USA. The refinery was extensively enlarged and modernised at the end of the 1920s, and by the start of World War 2 Fawley refinery was processing no less than 700,000 tons of crude oil per annum. It should be added that the freight facilities at the intermediate stations also made a useful, if small, contribution to the railway's coffers. However, with Fawley producing 92% of the freight tonnage, Hythe 6.5% and Marchwood 1.5%, the focus was clearly on the southern end of the branch.

Marchwood became an increasingly important military establishment over the years. As already mentioned, a magazine, which stored large amounts of ammunition and explosives, was established at Marchwood, and in 1939 a long 1½-mile siding was built from Marchwood Junction on the Fawley branch down to Cracknore Hard on Southampton Water. The site was hugely enlarged and later dealt with all manner of military stores as well as providing a useful connection between railhead and shipping wharf for a variety of traffic. This included, by way of example, a loading point for shipping military vehicles to trouble spots throughout the world. The complex became so large that, including all sidings, there were some 30 miles of track controlled by the military. There were reception sidings, sorting sidings and a multiplicity of other sidings, including some served by a traverser. The site was large enough to have its own passenger train service and there were three stations at Mulberry Platform, Park Gate and Model Room.

The military used its own locomotives, originally steam engines and more recently diesel power, and former main-line stock was employed on passenger services. Although a secure MOD site, from time to time railway enthusiasts' specials have been allowed on to the premises. Open days have also been held, providing general public access.

From the Fawley branch, the single-line connection to MOD Marchwood passes through some now unused wooden protective gates and through some much larger modern security gates before entering military property (see photograph). There is a path in the working timetable for a daily train to and from Marchwood, and the train normally runs. Often it was comprised of small four-wheel box vans used for the transportation of munitions, but on occasions wagons of the VDA type are used for stores and general equipment, while arguably the most exciting trains are those conveying tanks and other military vehicles. In recent times much MOD traffic has been loaded into containers, and from 2001 this has resulted in Freightliner trains hauled by new green-and-yellow-liveried Class 66 locomotives entering the site. Whether it was the conflict in Bosnia, the Gulf War or, more recently, the war with Iraq, the Marchwood branch has served an important strategic role in overall operations.

Returning to the oil scene, the entire refinery was shut down during the war because of its vulnerable geographical location, but by 1946, following a post-shutdown maintenance and refurbishment programme, the installation was again processing some 600,000 tons of crude oil. By 1949 grand plans for a large new oil refinery were implemented and the scale of operations was to become truly impressive. Some 3,000 additional acres of land were acquired from the Cadland Estate and the refinery itself occupied 1,000 acres. New buildings and large storage areas were constructed and there was an extensive internal pipeline system, adding to the operational flexibility of the site. Most important was the new 3,200ft-long deep-water jetty, completed in 1951, enabling four of the largest ocean-going tankers to use the Fawley complex at one time. The Fawley branch contributed to the new-build operations by conveying men and materials in some volume. In 1949 the early down workmen's train regularly comprised 10 coaches! In 1950 a second, relief, workmen's train was provided for a short period. The Prime Minister formally opened the new refinery; such was its commercial importance to the area and much of the UK.

The main site was on two levels and a large number of new sidings appeared on both levels, including some that contained loading racks for the speedy loading of tanker wagons. The refinery and storage tanks were above the shore level (where Fawley station was located) and a single-line railway connection was built between the sections. At the station level the multiplicity of sidings on the western side of the site became known as Cadland Yard. There were also a few sidings on the eastern side of the line, including track serving a liquid petroleum gas (LPG) depot. In fact, from 1973 LPG was to become the source of considerable rail traffic, but unfortunately for Fawley and the railway, natural North Sea gas ended the LPG era. The area was riddled with points and ground frames, and the private refinery sidings were served by the refinery's own motive power. As already mentioned, in the late 1950s and 1960s oil traffic boomed. However, all of this extra activity disguised the fact that as modifications were being made, technology was changing rapidly, and this included the wider use of pipelines, sometimes over long distances. This would result in a downturn in oil by rail traffic. On 3 March 1958 Hardley Halt, about 1 mile north of Fawley, was opened for the benefit of refinery workers but it never appeared in public timetables.

The development of North Sea oilfields caused Esso to review the future role of Fawley, even though by the mid-1970s production had escalated to 19½ million tons of crude oil. However, only 8%

Right:

A misty March morning in 2003 provides plenty of atmosphere as the headlights of Class 66 No 66238 serve their purpose on the approach to Marchwood. The up oil train, 6V34 ThO 10.56 Fawley to Margam, is using the up loop, whereas on the left is the down loop and the feed to the Marchwood line, controlled by the two semaphores (Marchwood signals 4 and 5) on the old lattice gantry. *JV*

Below:

It is so refreshing to think that this sort of branch-line picture can still be captured in 2003. Immaculate Class 66 No 66049 has just three empty four-wheeled tankers in tow as it leaves the south end of the Marchwood passing loop with an Eastleigh to Fawley 'short' working. The Marchwood signalman has pulled off the signal for the run down to the refinery. The station and crossing gates can just be glimpsed in the background. There will be significantly more traffic on the line if the Dibden Bay Container Terminal on the west side of Southampton Water ever comes to fruition, but with planning permission declined in May 2004 such a prospect is unlikely to occur. *JV*

Left:
The Marchwood Military Railway was established in 1939 when a 1½-mile siding from the Fawley branch down to Cracknore Hard on the waterside was opened. Over the years the establishment has been hugely enlarged, and at its peak the installation contained 30 miles of track. There were scores of sidings, wharves, a traverser and even a passenger service, with three stations on site, viz Mulberry Platform, Park Gate and Model Room. Over the years steam traction has given way to diesel, but in the late 1970s 0-6-0ST *Waggoner* was photographed leaving Mulberry Halt for the Jetty with two ex-BR Mark 1 coaches.
Harry Tabeart

of production was transported by rail, as against 50% by coastal tanker and 40% by pipeline. Other bad news included the end of Gatwick traffic, delivered to Salfords, as a new pipeline from Alton opened. In the early 1980s Tiverton Junction and Northampton oil traffic ended, and, as if that was not bad enough, oil delivered to Langley was transferred to a refinery on Humberside. In an ever-changing industry, following the opening of various on-shore oilfield sites, there was a time in 1986 when there was more oil arriving at Fawley by rail for refining than outgoing tonnages in oil-based products. Again, a pipeline reduced rail traffic potential as Fawley was connected to British Petroleum's Wytch Farm site on the old Swanage branch in Dorset. By the end of the 20th century traffic on the branch had dwindled to a daily train to and from Marchwood (as required) and either one or two oil trains to and from Fawley.

As regards future traffic, there have been rumours for more than a decade that a new power station and jetty might be built beside the existing Fawley 'A' power plant and that this would result in increased rail traffic by the importation of coal. But by far and away the most promising development is the plan for a massive new container depot at Dibden Bay on the western edge of Southampton Water. The site would have its own siding from the Fawley branch just to the south of Marchwood, and there is no doubt that considerable traffic would be generated. It is almost certain that double track would be necessary, at least as far as Marchwood. However, the project has been opposed on environmental grounds, with no doubt a large amount of 'nimby-ism'.

The junction for the Fawley branch is just west (34 chains to be precise) of Totton station, where the closed line to Eling Wharf, often referred to as the Eling Tramway, also branched off. The last of Totton's signalboxes closed in 1987 when Eastleigh panel was activated, whereupon Eastleigh controlled all train movements on to the branch. The single-line branch runs parallel with the main line for some yards west of Totton and a branch loop is provided. On leaving the main line the line curves towards the south and heads on a relatively straight and fairly level alignment, across numerous crossings, in a south-easterly direction to Marchwood, 3½ miles from Totton. Marchwood is a location that retains manually-operated road crossing gates. These were initially controlled by a small gate box and, from 1943, by a signalbox, which was built as an extension to the station but appeared, at a glance, to be an integral part of the original station building. This was the

same year that the Marchwood Military Railway was connected to the main branch. The line, which runs from the Fawley branch down to Southampton Water over MOD property, curves to the east just south of the station and was opened on 23 November 1943. As already mentioned, this became a huge complex with over 30 miles of track available for use. At this time Marchwood became a signalling block post. Originally there was a single line through the station with the platform on the down side. There was also a small siding at the down end of the down platform, which was disused after 1962 and taken out of use in 1971. To increase operating flexibility a passing loop was constructed at Marchwood, which was ready for service in July 1960. The signalbox remains extant and enjoys interface with Eastleigh signalling panel. Even in 2004 the area is still controlled by upper-quadrant semaphore signals and the crossing gates are still opened manually by the signalman.

The branch gently meanders to the south-east and, after passing yet more crossings, the closed station of Hythe is reached, approximately 3 miles from Marchwood. The station is in the same style as Marchwood, with the single-face platform on the down side of the single line. At the end of the platform was a small loading bay that had a single siding controlled by Hythe East ground frame. More than 30 chains beyond the station was Hythe West ground frame on the down side, which controlled a reverse siding that ran down to a much lower level and divided into two roads, comprising Hythe goods yard. This yard closed in January 1967 and the tracks were finally taken out of use in December 1970. Some 47 chains beyond Hythe station is Frost Lane Crossing. A modern signalbox using an old ex-Meon Valley Railway frame was opened here in October 1960, when various modifications were made to the branch, and just beyond that point a new crossing loop was opened at the same time. The crossing loop lasted just 20 years and, in the following year, 1981, the signalbox was reduced in status to a crossing ground frame until automatic half barriers were installed. Next in line was Hardley Halt, already referred to, which opened for Fawley workers in March 1958 and closed in April 1965, less than 12 months before the entire line closed to passengers. Before reaching the Fawley complex Union Carbide siding is passed. Fawley is 3 miles from Hythe and 9½ miles from Totton.

In 1925 the Fawley track layout comprised a single line that opened into a couple of oil sidings on the up side, followed by sidings to a goods shed, then the signalbox, station building and platform, all on the up side. A conventional run-round loop completed the fairly simple track configuration. Just after the start of World War 2 an Air Ministry fuel reserve depot opened, but it was as a result of the colossal developments of the 1949/51 period, already described, that the track layout became really complex. There were arrival roads, departure roads, sidings with loading racks, sidings to various depots, and even wagon repair sidings adjacent to the station. There was additional trackwork in abundance at the refinery top site, together with the LPG sidings on the east side of the station, already mentioned. From 1957 there was a siding between Hardley Halt and Fawley for the International Synthetic Rubber Company. During the period of decline Fawley signalbox was closed on 9 July 1978. It all seems rather sad that this huge complex is now little used compared with the halcyon days of the 1951 to 1971 period.

The locomotives using the line on passenger and freight trains during the past 79 years have been hugely varied. In the early days of the SR many minor ex-LSWR branch lines were the favourite haunts of 0-4-4T classes such as the 'O2', 'M7' and 'T1', and these all saw service on the Fawley branch. Generally tender locomotives were used less often because when running tender-first the train crews had problems with visibility at the large number of road crossings. However, the old 'Jubilee' 'A12' class locomotives had low tenders and they regularly found work on both passenger and freight trains. As regards freight locomotives, a variety of 0-6-0s were diagrammed to work the branch, including 'Qs', 'Q1s' and occasionally '700s'. LSWR 'L11' and 'K10' classes appeared, and shortly after nationalisation in 1948 ex-LBSCR 'E4', 'E5' and 'E6' classes all appeared, the latter only on freight duties. In the 1950s a number of large and powerful tank locomotives were used, including 'H16', 'W' and 'Z' classes. Over the years other regular performers included Ivatt 2MTs and BR Standards, and from 1960 some of the first '9F' class. Less common types included, by way of example, ex-LMS, WD and ex-GWR 2-8-0s. Most visits by other classes could be called rarities. Diesel-electric two- and three-car multiple-units commenced working the branch from 1958, and operated the majority of services until closure to passengers in 1966. Class 33 diesel-electrics started working oil trains in the early 1960s, and since then Classes 37, 47, 56, 57, 58, 60 and 66 have, in turn, provided the staple motive power on the branch. Again, railway enthusiast specials have from time to time brought unusual classes to the line, the farewell-to-steam specials in 1966 finding pairs of 'USA' class tanks appearing in bunker-to-bunker formation, and in 1988 a 'Peak' Class 45 diesel appeared on a Chartex special. Most unusually, in 1983 a pair of 'Hastings' six-car diesel-electric units appeared.

The Fawley branch is an interesting Hampshire branch line survivor. It seems strange to relate that following all the promise of the early 1960s there has been such a rapid decline in freight traffic and the complete withdrawal of passenger trains. The terminus at Fawley was never in a good position for travellers, being some way to the north of the town, but when one views the truly massive refinery complex it is hard to believe, even in the face of pipeline technology, that the output can justify merely a train or two per day. The military presence at Marchwood is a useful source of traffic, but many military lines, such as the relatively nearby Bedenham, were not saved from closure just because the MOD was involved. Unless the Dibden Bay project really takes off, or the Council Tax-payers of the greater Southampton area want to contribute to what is likely to be, in pure profit and loss terms, an unremunerative branch line, there is a very real risk that closure may not be too far away. Undoubtedly the place for viewing trains is Marchwood, where all traffic on the branch can be seen, where semaphore signals survive as something of an anachronism in the area, and crossing gates are manually opened and closed. However interesting this may be, patience in waiting for a train is the only down side for the casual observer.

Below:
Except when the refinery was being enlarged, passenger loadings on the Fawley branch were never large, and consequently the service was always infrequent. By the mid-1960s there was just one down and one up train per day (mainly for Fawley workers), and on 11 February 1966 the service was, predictably, withdrawn. Although final services were in the hands of DEMUs, closure broadly coincided with the end of steam traction on BR. This resulted in a number of special trains such as the LCGB's 'The Hampshire Branch Lines Rail Tour', which ran on 9 April 1967 and was double-headed by 'USA' class Nos 30069 and 30064. The train is passing Frost Lane Crossing south of Hythe station. The loop here was opened in 1960 and closed in 1980.
Brian Stephenson

Hythe's small station was 3 miles south of Marchwood, and had a goods yard on the down side at a lower level than the main branch line. In transport terms, Hythe is still important in that a ferry service continues to operate from the town's pier to Southampton. On the journey along the pier it is still possible to travel on a vintage narrow gauge electric railway (see the Miscellany section). The station has survived and at the time of writing is used by the Waterside Heritage Centre and incorporates their museum, seen here in March 2003. *JV*

Lower right:

On 3 March 1958 the small concrete single-platform Hardley Halt was opened for the benefit of refinery workers who worked towards the north end of the huge Fawley site. The platform was about a mile north of Fawley, but curiously it never appeared in public timetables. The halt was near the Union Carbide sidings and was rarely photographed. However, Hugh Davies captured this Class M7-hauled train pausing at the halt on 17 May 1958, hauling set No 812. The halt closed in April 1965. *Hugh Davies*

Below:

Fawley station was some distance north of the town, and although the multi-level track complex was enormous (see text), the passenger platform was a modest single-faced affair, which was extended in 1951. General goods were catered for in the early years, but the signalbox closed in 1978, 13 years after it was regularly used for passenger workings. This charming scene at the Fawley terminus is unusual in that it was taken on 13 April 1940, during World War 2. Standing beside 'M7' No 357 (later No 30357), from left to right by grade, are the Shunter, Porter, Guard, Station Master, Engine Driver and Fireman. *SLS/R. F. Roberts*

25. Lymington Branch

THE town of Lymington lies at the mouth of the river of the same name and on the shores of the Solent, and has a maritime history and association with shipbuilding that goes back to the 14th century. In naval terms Lymington was once more important than Portsmouth, and became a significant port for international freight shipments in the days when commercial vessels weighed but a few hundred tons. In the mid to late 19th century the population was a little over 4,000 but by then both Portsmouth and Southampton had become the leading ports along the central South Coast. As the port became less important some silting up of the creek reduced the scope for shipping, and by the early 19th century it had become a secondary destination for commercial vessels, especially after the abovementioned larger ports had become rail-connected in the 1830s and 1840s. However, from 1830 there had been a ferry link from Lymington to the Isle of Wight, and to exploit this and to boost local business it was 'on the cards' that the feasibility of a railway line would be contemplated. This duly occurred in 1844 when the Town Council approached the Southampton & Dorchester Railway Company, which was building a line through Brockenhurst, just 4 miles to the north of Lymington. This became more of a reality when one year later the SDR (not the Somerset & Dorset!) agreed that a branch line should be built from its proposed Southampton to Dorchester main line down to Lymington. The proposed route of the branch was sur-

veyed in 1846, and on 1 June 1847 the new line from Southampton reached the New Forest town of Brockenhurst (and beyond).

There then followed a most unfortunate delay as a result of conflict between the Town Council and the railway company as to the location of the junction station, with the railway company preferring a station near the site of the present junction, while the local authority was adamant that Brockenhurst, a town with a population of 1,500, was the only practical location if maximum potential of the branch line was to be exploited. These delays took some six years to resolve, and by then the LSWR had taken over the Southampton & Dorchester. A move to progress the railway in 1854 was thwarted by the LSWR shareholders, and consequently Lymington businessmen established the Lymington Railway Company, with a Bill for the construction of a branch being passed by Parliament in an Act dated 7 July 1856. Total funding would be in the order of £27,000 with a further £5,000 for the purchase of the toll bridge over the Lymington River, the town quay and ferry.

The first sod was cut in January 1857, and a time limit of four years was stipulated for the construction of the 4-mile branch line. Progress was steady and one year later the line had been laid from just outside Lymington to the junction, approximately 1 mile to the west of Brockenhurst. However, landfill for the purposes of building Lymington (Town) station took several months, and the first trains ran in May 1858 to a temporary wooden station building

Left:
As was common on many branches, one of the scheduled afternoon services was effectively a school train. On 25 October 1966 the author noted that this train at Brockenhurst was one such working! Basking in the afternoon sunshine, but so filthy as to not produce a glint from the backlighting, is Standard tank No 80016. Note the 'yesteryear' infrastructure, with old wooden goods trucks, early generation container, water crane, two types of luggage trolley and SR lamp standard. The children would soon arrive in Lymington. *JV/TTT*

Left:
During the last weeks of steam haulage there was great debate as to whether the Lymington branch was, as the headboard proclaimed, 'The Last Steam Branch'. Some cited the 'Kenny Belle' from Clapham Junction to Kensington Olympia as deserving of that label, but in reality the latter was far removed from most definitions of a branch line. The very last steam-hauled branch train, the 9.40pm from Lymington Town on 2 April 1967, hauled by Ivatt No 41312, arrives at Brockenhurst to be greeted by adoring crowds.
E. J. S. Gadsden

by the toll bridge road, short of the new substantial station. Although the line passed the Board of Trade inspection on 11 May, the LSWR insisted that additional sleepers be placed beneath the track at a number of locations, and as a consequence the branch did not formally open until 12 July 1858. The LSWR was holding all the aces because it had earlier agreed to work the line for 50% of receipts. On the formal opening day the local band played and the church bells rang to celebrate the event. Just 11 days later Lymington was provided with a goods service, despite the absence of the brick-built goods shed that was not ready for use until November of that year, and the new permanent station building was not completed until 1860. It is amusing to relate that the station boasted First, Second and Third Class waiting rooms!

In the meantime, and under new ownership, work was progressing on building a new jetty near the Town station for use by ferries. Although this was completed in 1861, the ferries to Cowes and Yarmouth on the Isle of Wight could not tie up at low tide, which caused some inconvenience to passengers. The LSWR main line in the Brockenhurst area was doubled in 1857/58, and in 1860 a small intermediate halt with a single wooden platform at Shirley Holmes, some 1½ miles from Lymington, was opened. The hope was that traffic might be generated from the villages of Sway to the west and Boldre to the east. It should be remembered that the main line at this time ran from Brockenhurst to Dorchester via Ringwood (known as 'Castleman's Corkscrew'), as the town of Bournemouth was in its infancy and barely deserving of a train service. From March 1888 a direct line from Lymington Junction to Bournemouth was built, and the village of Sway was then served by its own local station. Shirley Holmes Halt was used only in daylight hours and trains stopped only by request; rarely used, it closed a few years after the new main line opened. Curiously, it never appeared in public timetables and no tickets were issued bearing the name Shirley Holmes!

On more than one occasion plans were prepared to bore a railway tunnel beneath the Solent to link up with the railways of the Isle of Wight, but after several attempts the scheme in all of its guises was abandoned.

Notwithstanding the through trains to and from London in later years, branch trains normally started their journey at Brockenhurst. The station has for decades comprised two island platforms, and in years gone by the up branch train would use the outer face of the up island platform, affording up passengers cross-platform interchange with main-line services. Branch trains departed from the outer face of the down island platform, greatly assisting holidaymakers arriving with mountains of luggage on down main-line trains. Nowadays the branch EMU shuttles backwards and forwards from the down island platform. Until a single dedicated line was provided for the branch in 1979, branch trains would join the down main line for the journey to Lymington Junction, a mile west of the station. As mentioned earlier, a station was never provided at the junction. The signalbox was located on the down side of the line and the signalman would exchange the single-line token with the branch train driver.

After crossing under and over a couple of bridges, the line continues across some gorse-covered heathland, affording passengers views of some typical New Forest scenery. After passing through a cutting and some woodland the line passes the site of Shirley Holmes Halt at a falling gradient of about 1 in 70. It then gently curves its way in a south/south-westerly direction running under and over bridges and past the now closed Ampress Works Halt, generally on a falling gradient, to the outskirts of Lymington and Town station, 4 miles and 70 chains from Brockenhurst and 97 miles and 56 chains from Waterloo. The signalbox, single-road engine shed and coaling stage were on the down side, while the three roads that led to the goods shed and coal yard were on the up side, together with cattle pens and a wagon turntable. The commodious station building, with its decorative brickwork, is also on the up side. Until 1884 the site was the terminus of the branch, but today the line curves sharply left, or east, beyond the station on an 11-chain-radius curve and crosses the river on a 10-span viaduct. Crossing the mud flats on an embankment, the line finally curves sharply right past the now abandoned 1956 signalbox into the single platform that comprises Pier station, 5 miles and 31 chains from Brockenhurst. Four miles beyond is the Isle of Wight.

The initial service of seven trains on weekdays with three on Sundays was later cut back to four down and five up per day with no Sunday service. The line settled down, providing a useful local service but one that was only just profitable in the early years, providing the shareholders with a modest but regular dividend payment. In 1879 the LSWR exercised its option by purchasing the Lymington company outright, with the shareholders receiving a like value of their holdings in LSWR stock. The new owners

Above:

On 16 March 1967 No 80146 passes Lymington Junction signalbox and joins the main Southampton to Bournemouth line with two Bulleid coaches. Note how soon the double-track junction became single track. What is surprising is that a main-line Bournemouth to Waterloo express, headed by 'Merchant Navy' class No 35028 *Clan Line*, has been held at the home signal. Only electric trains would soon pass this spot. The signalbox closed in October 1978. *JV/TTT*

Below:

During 1979 a third track was provided from Brockenhurst to Lymington Junction for the exclusive use of Lymington branch trains, preventing the situation featured in the above plate from occurring. Assuming that the milepost has not been moved very far, the new track alignment would seem to be across the base of the demolished signalbox. Leaving the branch in April 2003 with a Lymington Pier to Brockenhurst train is the newly formed 3-CEP unit, No 1199, which shuttles backwards and forwards to provide Lymington with an excellent half-hourly service. *JV*

Upper right:
One of the highlights on the Lymington branch, especially in the days of steam, was the full-length through trains from Waterloo to Lymington Pier and vice versa. These trains gave holidaymakers the opportunity of travelling to Lymington Pier, for Yarmouth on the Isle of Wight, without having to change trains. Due to weight restrictions on the branch a 'Q' class was often diagrammed for these trains, but only to and from Brockenhurst. Emerging from the woods north of Ampress Works Halt is No 30541 with the 1.28pm Lymington Pier to Waterloo train on 5 September 1959. *S. C. Nash*

Lower right:
In October 1956 a new halt was opened to the north of Lymington to serve a new industrial complex.
The running-in board on the new SR-style concrete halt proclaimed '[Wellworthy] Ampress Works Halt'.
The halt never appeared in public timetables because it was mainly the workers at this and other nearby establishments that used the train service. The main works closed in the late 1980s and the halt then also closed. In April 2003 the halt was still *in situ*, and a down branch train is seen speeding past the crumbling concrete. *JV*

Top right:
This photograph depicts a typical branch train of the era, comprising an 'M7' and two coaches, leaving Lymington Town station in April 1964. The following month the 'M7s' were withdrawn (including No 30480 seen here), and Ivatt 2-6-2Ts took over operations. Although there are a sprinkling of goods wagons in the sidings, freight facilities were withdrawn from Lymington Town on 9 August 1965. *J. D. Mills*

Centre right:
Lymington Town station was graced with this delightful overall roof until the demolition men moved in and dismantled the 80ft-long structure. Since the days of steam the semaphore signals at the end of the down platform have gone, the small engine shed (right background) and the goods shed have been demolished, the foreground track has been removed and, with just a single-line branch, the point rodding has long gone. *IAL*

Lower right:
Although the main Lymington Town station, with its Gothic styling and multi-coloured bricks, is, thankfully, still standing, it is difficult to find anything at all that is aesthetically pleasing in this 2003 scene when compared with the previous view. Far removed from its Kent Coast origins, an EMU of the CEP family leaves for Lymington Pier. *JV*

wasted little time in securing the necessary powers to extend the Lymington branch line beyond Town station by just under ½ mile, across the river estuary on the abovementioned 10-span, 70yd viaduct, then along an embankment to the new Lymington Pier station. Here ferries could berth at both high and low tide, with rapid rail/ship interchange arrangements for passengers (and in later years motor cars). The first train ran in April 1884 and just three months later the railway company took over the Solent Steam Packet Company that ran the Isle of Wight ferry service. In 1889 there were some alterations to the track layout at both Lymington stations and two new signalboxes were provided.

The railway had an impact on the population of Lymington and there were growing residential areas to the west at Milford-on-Sea and New Milton. From 1905 the LSWR introduced a bus service connecting Lymington to these growing towns. The single-line branch saw an upsurge of strategic traffic during World War 1, and by the time the war had finished the LSWR had introduced push-pull passenger train workings. In the early 1920s there were further changes to the track layout at Town station, and the signalbox was moved to improve visibility and to save crossing-keeper wages. Between the World Wars traffic boomed as the middle classes were able to afford seaside holidays in southern Hampshire, but more particularly on the Isle of Wight. During the 1920s and 1930s, by which time the SR was in control, services peaked at around 16 trains per day in each direction. Also, Lymington had become a centre for the yachting fraternity, and from the end of the 1930s the motorist was targeted when the first double-ended 'Ro-Ro'-type ferry arrived. This utilised a new wide loading/unloading ramp that had been built into the river at the landward end of the platforms, and which was accessed via a level crossing over the railway. Access to the Lymington area was limited during World War 2 and passenger services were much reduced. There was also a large amount of military activity due to Lymington's strategic position.

After the war and the creation of BR the old *status quo* only gradually returned, but by the 1950s traffic was sufficiently buoyant for the push-pull local services to be supplemented by Lymington Pier to Waterloo (and return) through trains. From 13 local trains each way in 1948, the frequency increased so that in 1979, by which time electric trains had been operating the line for 12 years, no fewer than 19 trains traversed the branch in each direction on weekdays. In 2003 a staggering 30 round trips per day worked over the branch, providing a half-hourly service. From the 1858 timing of 13 minutes for the journey from Brockenhurst to Lymington Town, the 2003 journey time from Brockenhurst to Lymington Pier is just 9 minutes. There is no scope for improvement, with a 45mph limit from Lymington Junction to Lymington Town and 20mph beyond Town station. In addition to passenger services there was also a daily freight train that was normally worked by a tender locomotive. Trains were limited to 22 wagons, but with light traffic comprising mainly incoming loads of timber, coal, fertilisers, livestock and other sundry wagonloads, that restriction was unlikely to be tested. Nevertheless, freight was conveyed by rail over the branch for 107 years until all goods traffic was withdrawn on 9 August 1965.

Other changes on the branch included the opening of Ampress Works Halt in October 1956. The single concrete platform built in traditional 'Southern Railway' style was provided to serve the adjacent Wellworthy factory and, although well used by factory workers for many years, it was an unadvertised station. A new signalbox was built at Pier station in 1956. As an aside, the old main line from Brockenhurst to Ringwood and Wimborne closed in 1964, although freight continued to visit Ringwood until 1967, when the old 'corkscrew' line was abandoned. In conjunction with the electrification of the main line to Bournemouth in 1967 it was decided also to electrify the Lymington branch, a move that augured well for the survival of the line. There was a two-month gap between

the end of steam traction on the branch and the commencement of electric services, and this was filled by one of the ubiquitous 'Hampshire' diesel-electric multiple-units. Changes came thick and fast in the following years, nearly all of which rationalised the infrastructure and led to the demolition of many buildings, eventually reducing the branch to a single-line stub from Brockenhurst.

The signalbox at Lymington Junction was closed in October 1978 when the Lymington branch was provided with its own single bi-directional line from Brockenhurst station, effectively giving the impression of a three-track main line east of the junction. All sidings were removed, as were the engine shed and watering facilities at Town station. Ampress Works Halt was closed in the late 1980s along with the works it served. The Town signalbox was demolished and the Pier box decommissioned. The crossing gates at Pier were removed when alternative car-loading arrangements were built in 1976, the run-round loop already having been abandoned after the end of steam. Perhaps the saddest act in all of this destruction was the pulling down of the original 80ft-long all-over roof at Town station, leaving a very desolate platform scene. Needless to say, with the changes in signalling came the removal of all semaphore signals and the installation of colour lights.

Over the years a variety of motive power has worked the Lymington branch with, not surprisingly, a heavy LSWR bias. In the earliest days a small 2-4-0T named *Nelson* was a regular performer, and a truly ancient machine, a 2-2-2 rebuild of a locomotive originally constructed by Summers Groves & Day, way back in 1839, later provided support! It was given the name *Southampton*. Two Sharp 2-2-2WT locomotives of 1852 vintage joined the ranks in 1864. Beattie well tanks followed, but the intervening years saw a variety of motive power, all of which is now far beyond living memory. Occasionally tender locomotives such as the 0-6-0 'Ilfracombe' goods type worked the branch. Once push-pull workings commenced, classes of the 'T1', 'O2' and 'M7' variety provided the motive power. However, above all else it was the Drummond 'M7s' that will be for ever associated with the branch, lasting until May 1964. After that date only Ivatt 2-6-2Ts and Standard 2-6-4Ts worked the line, before steam finally ended in April 1967. During the last weeks of steam traction trains carried a headboard proclaiming that the Lymington line was the last steam-hauled branch line in the UK. Other than for narrow gauge and preserved lines, together with the suburban Clapham Junction to Kensington Olympia services, this claim was accurate; the end of an era had truly arrived. Special mention must be made of the through trains from Lymington Pier to Waterloo and vice versa, which over the years numbered between one and five through trains on Summer Saturdays. This brought Classes D15, T9, Q and Q1 to the line, and SR Moguls and Standard 2-6-0s and 4-6-0s were not unknown. On occasions in the mid-1960s Class 33 diesels also worked the line. After a short two-month spell operating with a 'Hampshire' DEMU unit, 2-HAP/2-SAP two-car EMUs worked the line, and later 4-VEPs were in charge. Other EMU types appeared, but during 2003 a specially constituted three-car unit of 4-CEP origin took over all branch shuttle services.

The significance of the Lymington branch is simply that, compared with most branches and byways featured in this book, it has survived the passage of time. The journey along the single-track railway is quite scenic with, arguably, the view of the town of Lymington across the water from the pier extension and the run across the heathland being the most attractive. For visitors hoping to see other railway artefacts there will be disappointment, with the exception of the magnificent Lymington station building, which still impresses, and the Ampress remains. At Lymington Town most of the railway land, such as the area once occupied by the old engine shed, has been built upon, and now modern factories, with no architectural merit, crowd the railway. The short 9-minute journey is, nevertheless, well worth the effort.

Above:
At the height of the 1959 season there were five up and three down through services between Lymington Pier and Waterloo. At other times there were just two through trains each way, a short period when such trains ran on a summer Saturdays-only basis, and several seasons when they were withdrawn altogether. Adding to the motive power variety on 1 September 1962 is Standard 2-6-0 No 76027 crossing the Lymington River with the 1.28pm Lymington Pier to Waterloo train. *Michael J. Fox*

Below:
The town of Lymington has recently spent time and money 'sprucing up' the waterfront, and a huge new marina has brought an ever-increasing number of visitors to the town. Although the branch has changed significantly over the years, the trains still rumble across the river and the frequency of service is better than it has ever been. In early South West Trains (Stagecoach) livery, 3-CEP No 1199 shuttles north past the pseudo gas lamp on 20 March 2003 with the 15.45 service from the Pier. *JV*

Above:
Bustling the 10.34am Lymington Pier departure towards Town station on 24 February 1966 is grimy 2-6-4T No 80138,
with one BR and one Bulleid coach. The train crew seem to be taking in the view across the river towards the town of Lymington.
It seems hard to believe that the author pressed the shutter nearly 40 years ago. Note the trio of home signals, although only
the centre 'peg' relates to a platform road. *JV/TTT*

Left:
From an early date Lymington Pier and the route to Yarmouth catered for motor vehicles, and pre-World War 1 advertisements advocated the 'shortest and most sheltered' route to the lovely 'Garden Isle'. The vessels used were effectively 'Ro-Ros', where cars travelled down a slipway under their own power and on to specially constructed boats. The main slipway was located just to the right of this picture. One track feeds a short bay platform, while the other tracks are the platform road and run-round loop. No 80016 simmers as the crew have a chat under the running-in board on 25 October 1966. Note the unusual lower-quadrant semaphore signals. *JV/TTT*

BROCKENHURST, LYMINGTON, YARMOUTH, TOTLAND BAY, and FRESHWATER.

Miles	Down.	Week Days.														Sundays.	
		mrn	mrn	mrn	mrn	arn	mrn	aft	aft F	aft V	aft	aft	aft	aft	aft		
					R	R		R	R	R	R	R	R	R	D		
—	London (W.) 154..dep.	..	5 40	..	8 30	9 30	1130	..	1 30	1 30	2 30	3 30	4 30	5 30	6 30	8 10	
93	Brockenhurst 154 arr.	..	8 19	..	1056	1158	1 50	..	3 50	3 50	4F41	5 50	6F41	7 52	9F48	11J39	
—	Brockenhurst.....dep.	7 25	8 29	9 44	11 6	1210	2 7	..	4 8	4 8	5 6	5 6	6 43	7 57	9 2	11 40	
97¾	Lymington Town B arr	7 37	8 41	9 56	1118	1222	2 19	..	4 20	4 20	5 17	6 17	6 56	8 7	9 14	11 52	
98¾	" Pier ... "	7 42	8 47	..	..	1225	2 22	..	..	5 20	5 20	..	6 59	..	..	..	
—	Lymington Pier ...dep.	7 50	9 8	..	..	1230	2 28	..	..	5 35	5 35	..	7 5	..	..	..	
102¾	Yarmouth Pier.... arr.	8 20	9 38	..	..	1 0	2 58	..	..	6 5	6 5	..	7 35	..	..	..	
—	Totland Bay Pier.. "	..	..	..	..	..	..	..	..	..	..	..	..	..	..	..	
104	Totland Bay } C.. arr.	9 0	1020	..	1 40	3 40	..	..	6 45	6 45	..	8 15	..	..	..	..	
104	Freshwater }	9 0	1020	..	1 40	3 40	..	..	6 45	6 45	..	8 15	..	..	..	..	

Miles	Up.	Week Days.												Sundays.	
		mrn	mrn	mrn	mrn	mrn	aft	aft	aft	aft	aft	aft	aft		
		R	R	R	R	R				R					
—	Freshwater } C.. dep.	..	..	7 45	..	1025	..	1225	..	4 10	..	5 35	7 0	..	
—	Totland Bay }	..	..	7 45	..	1025	..	1225	..	4 10	..	5 35	7 0	..	
—	Totland Bay Pier..dep.	..	..	..	..	..	..	..	..	..	..	..	..	..	
—	Yarmouth Pier.... "	..	..	8 25	..	11 5	..	1 5	..	4 52	..	6 15	7 40	..	
—	Lymington Pier.... arr.	..	..	8 55	..	1135	..	1 35	..	5 22	..	6 45	8 10	..	
—	Lymington Pier...dep.	..	..	9 5	..	1143	..	1 40	..	5 32	..	7 10	8 18	..	
—	" Town B arr.	7 45	8 15	9 10	1145	..	1 42	4 30	..	5 34	6 24	7 12	8 20	..	
—	Brockenhurst 154 arr.	7 55	8 25	9 19	10 11	1156	..	1 53	3 15	4 40	5 46	6 34	7 25	8 32	
—	Brockenhurst 159 dep.	8 1	8F35	9 35	10F23	12 4	..	2 3	4 7	..	5 54	..	8 28	..	
—	London (W.) 159.. arr.	10 7	1059	1144	12 49	2 20	..	4 24	6 36	..	8 24	..	1132	..	

B Station for Milford-on-Sea (3¾ miles). Connection by Motor Bus.
C By Coach from and to Yarmouth.
D Wednesdays and Saturdays.
F Tuesdays, Wednesdays, and Thursdays.
F Change at Southampton West.
J Change at Eastleigh.
R Restaurant Car between London (Waterloo) and Brockenhurst.
R Restaurant Car between London (Waterloo) and Southampton West.
V Mondays, Fridays, and Saturdays.

MOTOR CARS FOR THE ISLE OF WIGHT.—Special arrangements are made at Lymington Station for this traffic, including slipways and tugboats which obviate lifting. Enquiries from Station Master, Lymington. Tel.: No. 7.

Above:
This January 1927 timetable shows only the Waterloo and Brockenhurst train connections
with sailings on the Lymington to Yarmouth route.

Upper right:
This wonderful scene shows the rail/ship interchange at Lymington Pier in June 1956, with the good ship *Freshwater*, a paddle-steamer built in 1927, tying up at the pier having just arrived from Yarmouth. Behind is one of the small car ferries, being loaded via the slipway.
On the right the branch train waits at the platform for passengers to transfer. A new car ferry terminal has now been built to the right of this picture. *A. Wilson*

Lower right:
This view of the end of the line shows just how close Lymington is to the Isle of Wight. With the island clearly visible across the Solent in the background, No 80146 runs round its train in March 1967. There is little margin for error! As mentioned in the text, other than for Chandlers Ford, the line to Lymington is the only one of 13 Hampshire branches, comprehensively dealt with in this book, to remain open to passengers. *JV/TTT*

26. Sussex and Hampshire Miscellany

THE following pages show a miscellany of other lines in the counties of Sussex and Hampshire for the sake of virtual completeness. It has not been possible to include every line, especially freight sidings, large industrial installations, narrow gauge and pleasure park lines, ancient quarry plateways (such as the first Sussex railway at Offham), brickworks lines, airport 'people-movers', certain military railways (such as the Bramley complex), docks sidings, the Isle of Wight network (except for a mention), street tramways (for example, the Portsdown & Horndean Light Railway or the Crumbles line at Eastbourne) or small preserved sites (for example Amberley Chalk Pits), etc.

Below:
The route from Ashford in Kent to Hastings in Sussex via Rye is an old line dating back to 1851. Although a glimpse at the railway map would indicate otherwise, the line has never been developed as part of a through route, and even today the 26¼-mile line has not, unlike connecting tracks, been electrified. Parts of the route were singled in the late 1970s, and at one time it was scheduled for closure. Featuring this delightful old windmill at Rye, a six-car formation headed by 'Oxted' DEMU No 1303 arrives from Hastings, on the singled track on 24 April 1981. *JV/TTT*

Top right:
On the Hastings Direct line between Etchingham and Robertsbridge, near the site of the closed Mountfield Halt, is a long siding and small works network belonging to British Gypsum. For many years the traffic flow has been from Mountfield to Northfleet in North Kent. Seen in the 1970s, British Gypsum shunters Nos 1 and 2 shunt wagons at the works before proceeding to the interchange sidings. *JV/TTT*

Centre right:
The famous Kent & East Sussex Railway will be included in any volume on the Branches and Byways of Kent, but nevertheless the old Colonel Stephens line is worthy of at least a mention because a significant part of the route is in Sussex. Propelling its single coach back into the bay platform at Robertsbridge in 1953 is 'A1X' class No 32678. The main Hastings route is on the right and there is evidence of a little coal traffic in the goods yard. *JV collection*

Lower right:
Another branch line that straddles county boundaries is the Horsham to Guildford line, which will be included in any volume on the Branches and Byways of Surrey. Opened in October 1865, the line lasted until June 1965, just short of its centenary. Beyond Christ's Hospital (see Chapter 10) there were two stations in Sussex, Slinfold and Rudgwick, and three in Surrey. A Guildford train arrives at Slinfold in about 1908. *IAL*

Top left:
The Volk's Electric Railway along the seafront at Brighton is said to be the world's first passenger-carrying electric railway. Opened in August 1883, the line was extended over the years to run 1½ miles from the Aquarium, near Palace Pier, to Black Rock — just short of the modern marina. The line is of 2ft 8½in gauge and services now operate only in the summer months. Cars once ran singly as seen in this *circa* 1906 view, but the vintage cars now run in pairs. The line carried over ¾ million passengers in 1952 and it has just celebrated its 120th anniversary. *IAL*

Centre left:
In 1899 the incredible 'Daddy Long Legs', alias *Pioneer*, the only car on the 2¾-mile Brighton & Rottingdean Seashore Electric Railway (which was another innovation by the redoubtable Magnus Volk), approaches Brighton. It has been said that the elevated car, which ran 15ft above the water line at high tide, was a cross between a tramcar, a yacht and pier! The car stood on four braced legs that were 23ft high, and ran on two 2ft 8½in gauge tracks set 18ft apart. Electric current was supplied via a trolley pole, and the overhead wires are visible in this shot. The line opened in 1896, but following severe storms in December 1896, when a pier was demolished, and with the line repeatedly being covered by sand and shingle, it closed in 1901. *IAL*

Lower left:
Although many towns along the South Coast had sidings to adjacent docks, this Victorian scene at Kingston Wharf, at Shoreham by Sea in (West) Sussex, was a major source of income for the railways for many years. The line from Brighton to Shoreham opened in 1840, over a year before the London to Brighton line, because Kingston was going to be used to land construction materials. Also, by way of example, as early as 1848 no fewer than 21,000 tons of coal were landed at Kingston Wharf for onward transportation by rail to Brighton. In the later years a small 'P' class 0-6-0T worked the wharf and took wagons up to the exchange sidings, before being replaced by a Class 03 diesel shunter. *IAL*

Upper right:
When the line from Brighton was extended westward from Worthing to Chichester in 1846, Littlehampton station was a couple of miles to the north of the town in the village of Lyminster. However, in 1863 a line 2 miles 14 chains long from Ford (originally Arundel, and for some time 'Ford for Littlehampton') into the centre of the town was opened, and the station at Lyminster was closed on 1 September of that year. This line thus effectively became the Littlehampton branch, but direct access from the Brighton and Horsham directions was established in 1887 (creating a triangular junction), and in a way Littlehampton ceased to be a conventional branch and became part of a main-line network. There was a locomotive shed, goods yard and shed, dock sidings and signalbox at the new terminus. On 4 August 1920 there was an accident at Littlehampton when the brakes failed on 'D1' class No 360, which ran through a wall and into a street. *JV collection*

Lower right:
Littlehampton grew as a town and the terminus was tantamount to a main-line station, with through trains to London. There is still a comprehensive service to London, Brighton, Bognor and Portsmouth, although direct trains to Arundel and Horsham have dwindled over the years. Upon electrification in 1938 a carriage shed capable of holding three 12-coach trains was built. The engine shed and docks sidings went years ago, but semaphore signalling survives at this busy location, something of an anachronism today. In this 6 November 1988 photograph, 4-BIG Class 422 No 2205 has been comprehensively derailed on some points. The terminus and signalbox can be seen in the far distance. *JV/TTT*

Above:
Bognor Regis was just plain Bognor until 1929, when a seaside convalescence visit by King George V entitled the town to use the suffix. The (initially) single-track Bognor branch opened on 1 June 1864 from a new station called Barnham Junction. In common with Littlehampton, before the branch was built passengers were encouraged to alight at another station, in this case Woodgate for Bognor, and as with Lyminster, Woodgate closed upon the opening of the Bognor branch. With a rich choice of slam-door electric stock at the platforms, in the centre road and the carriage sidings, 4-VEP Class 423 No 7870 departs for Barnham. *JV/TTT*

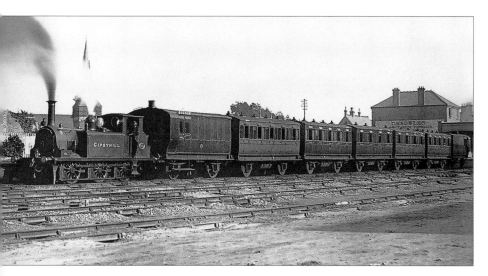

Upper left:
This photograph shows a truly delightful train of four-wheelers at Bognor, waiting to depart for Barnham in 1899. There is a 'Bognor' carriage board on the guard's vehicle because until 1903 there was no through road from main line to branch and the train was therefore a shuttle working. The train engine is 1877-built Class A1 No 43 *Gypsy Hill*, which was later sold to the Weston, Clevedon & Portishead Railway. The Bognor line was eventually doubled and became part of the main-line network rather than a conventional branch, although even today many passengers still 'change at Barnham for Bognor'.
O. J. Morris/Bucknall Collection

Lower left:
Early Bognor stations were either destroyed by storms or burnt down, and the splendid current terminus dates back to 1902. Bognor had many sidings and a goods yard, signalbox, engine shed, turntable and all the usual facilities. The line was electrified in 1938 when a brand new, and surviving, 66-lever signalbox opened. Today Bognor Regis still retains its semaphore signals and the 100-year-old station has recently been refurbished. Here a pair of the venerable pre-war 2-HALs, with No 2686 leading, wait for the off at Platform 1 in 1969.
JV/TTT

Right:
The Longmoor Military Railway, located between Liss and Bordon, was a major undertaking and the vital statistics of the total complex were mind-boggling. For example, from 1939 to 1945, during the World War 2 years, track mileage increased from 17 to 71 miles, and locomotives allocated to the railway increased from five in 1939 to 27 in 1944, plus hired locomotives. The population of the garrison was 7,000, and there was a wartime throughput of 80,000 trainees in the transportation arm of the Royal Engineers. From 1949 until 1969 the LMR became well known for its public open days, and on the last to be held, on 5 July 1969, 0-6-0ST No WD 196 nears Hogmoor with a Longmoor Downs to Oakhanger train composed of the railway's 'Blue Saloon' stock.
JV/TTT

Left:
The LMR ran internal passenger services and there were two railway links with the outside world. The southern section was covered by a Longmoor Downs to Liss service, which connected with Liss station on the Portsmouth Direct route. The northern section ran from Longmoor Downs to Bordon LMR station, which was adjacent to the terminus of the Bentley to Bordon branch (see Chapter 16). In the early 1940s passenger numbers amounted to more than 3,000 per day. Freight movement was very high and in one day in 1944 no fewer than 497 goods wagons were transferred. More than 150 different locomotives worked on the LMR in its lifetime, and one of the most impressive was WD 2-10-0 No 600 *Gordon*, seen here at Liss Junction with the 12.14pm Liss to Oakhanger train on 28 September 1968.
S. C. Nash

Right:
The LMR comprised one major through route but also scores of sidings and mini-branches to obscure depots. There was also a long training loop, known as the Hollywater Loop. Although the LMR passenger service was for military and civilian personnel, it was possible on some days to simply turn up at Liss LMR station and cadge a ride. In the final decade, especially at off-peak times, there were usually only one or two other passengers travelling, and the general attitude was pleasantly casual. Motive power could be a steam tank locomotive or diesel shunter and an old compartment coach, while at other times it was a small petrol-driven Wickham trolley.

The final closing ceremony was held on 31 October 1969, and although an abortive attempt was made at preservation, all the tracks of a great institution were finally removed. In 1968 a train from Longmoor has just arrived at Liss and the only passengers, a couple of civilians (and the author!), alight. *JV/TTT*

Top left:
The Southsea branch should never have been built. The line ran for 1¼ miles from Fratton Junction to a terminus at Southsea, later called Southsea East. There was never a direct/through connection to the branch and passengers had to change trains at Fratton. The line opened in July 1885 and it was extravagantly built with double track, a substantial three-platform terminus and 15 trains per day (some with through London coaches!). Despite the additions of single-platform halts at Albert Road Bridge and Jessie Road Bridge, the introduction of railmotors and a 20-minute service, the singling of the track and the removal of all staff, the line closed in 1914, and formally in 1923. The first railmotor to arrive, on 31 May 1903, was No 1, seen here as rebuilt, at Fratton in 1904. *IAL*

Centre left:
As an important South Coast port with a great naval tradition, Portsmouth had a number of dock lines and sidings. Opened in the 1840s but realigned in 1876, the Portsmouth Dockyard branch ran from Portsmouth & Southsea (High Level), past Victoria Park and Unicorn Road to Unicorn Gate. There were regular freight hauls along the line for over a century, with a peak of activity during the war years. The line closed in 1977. Photographs of the line are few and far between, but in this early 1960s view the crew of a Class 08 diesel shunter with some early container wagons and box vans give up the token to the Portsmouth High Level signalman on leaving the branch. *Roger Holmes*

Lower left:
The main line to Portsmouth was extended to Portsmouth Harbour in 1876. A branch was built to South Railway Jetty and Watering Island, with a junction just short of the Harbour terminus. The line was known as the South Dockyard branch and was much used by troop trains and special passenger traffic, including the Royal Train. This 1906 view shows the Royal Train about to leave for London (Victoria) via Chichester, Arundel and Sutton, hauled by immaculate 'B4' class No 42 *His Majesty*. There were weight restrictions on the line that resulted in only 4-4-0s appearing, for example 'T9', 'L12' and 'B4' classes. No doubt the sailors would soon be offering 'three cheers'. Portsmouth Harbour station is in the right background. *IAL*

Above:
The 1½-mile line from Hamble Halt on the Fareham to Southampton line down to an oil depot at Hamble, on Southampton Water, was one of the more significant sidings. The siding ran across an aerodrome and down to a pier and storage depot owned by Shell-Mex and BP, which operated its own diesel shunters. The siding is now closed. On 22 March 1975 branch-line fans travelled down the siding on board a BLS special comprising 'Hampshire' DEMU No 1124. The gates across Hamble Lane are being closed on the return trip. *John H. Bird*

Upper left:
The substantial Royal Victoria Hospital at Netley was constructed to care for the casualties of the Crimean War. Situated on Southampton Water, it had its own pier where the sick and the wounded could be landed from troop-ships. In 1866 a line from Southampton to Netley was opened, but it was 1900, during the Boer War, before a ½-mile siding from Netley goods yard to the hospital opened. The line was not only used for the casualties of war but also for goods and supplies. There was much activity during the two World Wars, but the line closed in the 1950s and the hospital was subsequently also closed and demolished. Here LSWR 'M7' class No 106 is seen at the hospital — note the red cross on the leading coach. *Maurice Dart collection*

Lower left:
Much has been written about the Didcot, Newbury & Southampton Railway, which ran through both Berkshire and Hampshire. This cross-country line was established to create a north-to-south link that would exploit the port of Southampton and, after takeover, give the GWR the access it so desired (see Chapter 23). South of Newbury, stations within Hampshire included Woodhay, Highclere, Burghclere, Litchfield, Whitchurch, Sutton Scotney, Worthy Down, Kings Worthy and Winchester Cheesehill. The DNSR joined the LSWR main line at Shawford Junction, south of Winchester. The line opened throughout in May 1885 and closed to passengers (through trains) in 1960, with freight following in 1964. BR Standard Mogul No 76019 leaves Winchester Chesil (as it became known) with a train for Southampton terminus. *David Lawrence*

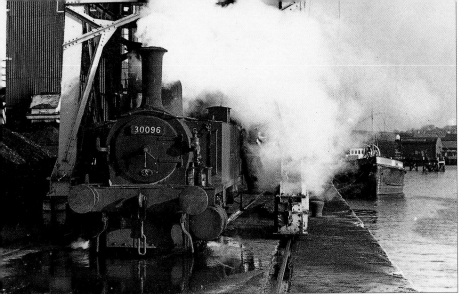

Top left:
Corrall's (and later Powell Duffryn), a coal distribution company, operated an interesting little siding that ran from Northam near Southampton to Dibbles Wharf on Southampton Water. The siding attained fame for being steam-worked after steam had been withdrawn on BR (SR), and adding interest was the fact that 'B4' class No 30096, later named *Corrall Queen*, worked the line, which is seen here under a dockside crane on 31 January 1967.
The locomotive, formerly (and subsequently) named *Normandy*, is now preserved on the Bluebell Railway. *Alistair McIntyre*

Centre left:
The Hythe Pier Tramway is a wonderful anachronism. To be able to travel down a 700yd pier to catch a ferry to Southampton on an 85-year-old, 2ft-gauge, 110V third-rail locomotive-hauled train is an unforgettable experience. Trains meet every ferry, although operations were interrupted in 2003 when a dredger sliced through the pier. Nearly ¾ million passengers use the service every year.
This 1950 shot shows the tramway, which, except for livery, looks just the same today.
JV collection

Left:
The Eling Tramway was a very old line that dated back to 1851. The line gave a connection to Eling Wharf, which in turn had access to the River Test and hence Southampton Water. For many years the line was used to transport a wide variety of commodities, and was used during the construction of the Fawley branch. In later years ARC used the line for stone, and Redland for tiles. On 30 July 1979 Class 47 No 47106 leaves Eling for Totton with empty stone wagons for Westbury. The line has now closed. *R. E. Ruffell*

Right:
The line from Brockenhurst to Dorchester via Ringwood was once the LSWR main line, and dated back to 1847. In 1862 a branch line from Ringwood to Christchurch (for Bournemouth) was opened, but it was not until 1870 that the line was extended to the growing town of Bournemouth. When the direct and shorter line through Sway to Bournemouth opened in 1888 the Ringwood line decreased in importance, as purely local traffic was modest indeed. The route was used for diversions, but was closed to passengers on 4 May 1964. On 13 July 1963 'West Country' No 34107 *Blandford Forum* is seen at Ringwood with the 11am SO Weymouth to Waterloo, avoiding Bournemouth. *Michael J. Fox*

Lower left:
It would be impossible to find the space to deal with the very comprehensive subject of Southampton Docks. The LSWR took over the Southampton Dock Company in 1892, and in the age of the great steamers and with the increasing size of commercial vessels and international trade, the area expanded hugely. There were extensive lines in the Eastern and Western Docks, and at the eastern end there was access to the docks via the crossing over Canute Road adjacent to Southampton Terminus. In the docks such locations as Empress Dock, Ocean Dock, Ocean Terminal and Town Quay were all rail-served. In freight terms containers now rule the roost and two large terminals at Millbrook and Maritime serve the docks. Boat trains are catered for at both Eastern and Western Docks, but the two areas are no longer joined by rail. In September 1991 a P&O boat train leaves the Western Docks behind Class 33/1 No 33101. *JV/TTT*

Upper right:
A line that ran mainly through
Wiltshire and Dorset was the
Salisbury & Dorset Junction Railway,
from Salisbury to Bournemouth West
via Wimborne. The line opened on
20 December 1866 and the 'heart'
of the route, between Alderbury
Junction and West Moors on
'Castleman's Corkscrew', was
19 miles of single line, which included
two Hampshire stations at Breamore
and Fordingbridge. The line served
a purpose for some years, including
local goods traffic, but in profit and
loss terms, under the scrutiny of the
Beeching criteria, it failed the test
and was closed at the same time as
the Ringwood line, on 4 May 1964.
In this now historic view, '700' class
No 30317, heading a classic pick-up
goods, leaves Fordingbridge with
a Salisbury to Wimborne working
on 18 July 1953. *S. C. Nash*

Lower right:
Two Hampshire branch-line stations
not included in this volume, because
they are more relevant to Wiltshire,
are Tidworth, which was located at
the end of a branch from Ludgershall,
and Weyhill, just north of Andover
Junction on the old MSWJR.
However, this study of No 6395,
one of the beautifully proportioned
Churchward '4300' class, entering
Weyhill with the 9.35am Swindon
Junction to Andover Junction on
10 September 1961 was impossible
to resist! Although the station closed
on 11 September 1961, the line is still
open for freight and special traffic
between Andover Junction and
Ludgershall. *S. C. Nash*

Right:
Although there are close historical links between the county of Hampshire and the Isle of Wight, from 1971, before the reorganisation of county boundaries, the two became quite separate and several entities in local government and 'county' terms. Therefore, strictly speaking, the Isle of Wight is beyond the scope of this book. Nevertheless, for the sake of historical completeness at least, mention should be made of the extensive IOW network. The first line opened was from Newport to Cowes in 1862, followed by Ryde to Shanklin and Ventnor in 1864/66. A Ryde (Smallbrook) to Newport line opened in 1875, another from Sandown to Newport via Merstone in 1879, Bembridge to Brading in 1882, Newport to Freshwater in 1889, and finally Merstone to Ventnor Town in 1897. When the SR took over the 55-mile complex of IOW lines in 1923, it set about replacing ancient motive power. Class O2s were drafted in for passenger trains (and, until just after World War 2, some 'A1Xs') and four Class E1s for goods traffic. Taken by the then 13-year-old author on a 620 box camera in the summer of 1956, No 4 *Wroxall* simmers outside Newport shed. The 1874-built 44-ton locomotives were withdrawn between 1957 and 1960. *JV/TTT*

Left:
Between 1952 and 1966 all the Isle of Wight lines closed except for the section from Ryde Pier to Shanklin, which was retained and electrified. Fortunately, the 5-mile line from Smallbrook Junction, on the outskirts of Ryde, to Wootton via Havenstreet was also saved by the Isle of Wight Steam Railway.

The old IOW atmosphere has been re-created and some truly magnificent sights can still be experienced. In this wonderful period scene (from 2002!) 'A1X' class No 8 *Freshwater* poses at Smallbrook Junction with two vintage compartment bogie coaches and three four-wheelers, before leaving for Wootton. *JV*

Right:
From 1967 the line from Ryde Pier to Shanklin was electrified, and because of tunnel and bridge clearances some redundant 1920–30-built ex-London Transport underground (or 'tube') stock was refurbished and modified for island use. Designated 4-VEC and 3-TIS (later Classes 485 and 486), a total of six four-car and six three-car units were formed. Brading station, seen here, was once the junction station for Bembridge, but the branch closed in 1953. After electrification the track was singled, leaving only the old up line. Four-car No 485041, showing the 'RydeRail' marketing logo and in Network South East livery, is seen at Brading in May 1985. Passengers no longer have to 'mind the gap'! *JV/TTT*

Bibliography

Bancroft, P. *Railways Around Alton* (Nebulous Books, 1995)

Bird, J. H. *Southern Steam Sunset* (Runpast Publications, 1997)

Bradley, D. L. *The Locomotives of the LBSCR* (RCTS, 1972/74)

Casserley, H. C. *London & South Western Railway Locomotives* (Ian Allan, 1971)

Clark, P. *The Railways of Devils Dyke* (Turntable Publications, 1976)

The Chichester & Midhurst Railway (Turntable Publications, 1979)

Course, E. *The Railways of Southern England: Secondary and Branch Lines* and *Independent and Light Railways* (Batsford, 1974 and 1976 respectively)

Dean, M., Robertson, K. and Simmonds, R. *The Basingstoke & Alton Light Railway* (Crusader Press, 1998)

Elliott, A. C. *The Cuckoo Line* (Wild Swan Publications, c1989)

Fairman, J. R. *The Fawley Branch* (Oakwood Press, 2002)

Fereday-Glenn, D. *Rail Routes in Hampshire and East Dorset* (Ian Allan, 1983)

One Hundred Years of Roads and Rails Around the Solent (Ensign Publications, 1991)

Gray, A. *The Railways of Mid Sussex* (Oxford Press, 1975)

Grayer, J. *The Lymington Branch* (*Steam Days*, January 2003)

Griffiths, E. C. *The Hundred of Manhood and Selsey Tramways* and *The Basingstoke & Alton Light Railway* (Edward Griffiths, 1968 and 1970 respectively)

Harding, P. A. *The Rye & Camber Tramway*, *The Bordon Light Railway*, *The Hellingly Hospital Railway*, *The Longparish Branch Line*, *The Kemp Town Branch Line*, *The Dyke Branch*, *The Bexhill West Branch* (Peter A. H. Harding, 1985 to 2002)

Jordon, S. *The Bognor Branch Line* (Oakwood Press, 1989)

Kidner, R. W. *The Newhaven and Seaford Branch* (Oakwood Press, 1979)

Mitchell, V. and Smith, K. *Andover to Southampton* (Middleton Press, 1990)

Branch Lines to East Grinstead (Middleton Press, 1984)

Morris, O. J. *LB&SCR* (Ian Allan, *circa* 1950)

Morrison, Brian *British Rail DMUs and Diesel Railcars* (Ian Allan, 1998)

Nash, S. C. *Southern Region Steam Album* (Ian Allan, 1974)

Newell, L. *Catching the Train to Hayling Island* (Havant Borough Council, 2002)

Pallant, N. *The Brighton to Portsmouth Line* (Oakwood Press, 1980)

Paye, P. *The Lymington Branch* (Oakwood Press, 1979)

Reade, L. *Branch Line Memories: Southern* (Atlantic, 1984)

Riley, R. C. *Brighton Line Album* (Ian Allan, 1967/1972)

Robertson, K. *Hampshire Railways in Old Photographs* (Alan Sutton, 1989)

Ronald, D. W. and Carter, R. J. *The Longmoor Military Railway* (David & Charles, 1974)

Stone, R. A. *The Meon Valley Railway* (Kingfisher Railway Publications, 1983)

Vaughan, J. A. M. *Modern Branch Line Album* (Ian Allan, 1980)

Diesels on the Southern (Ian Allan, 1980)

Branch Lines Round Britain in the Diesel Era (Bradford Barton, 1975)

Welbourn, N. *Lost Lines: Southern* (Ian Allan, 1996)

Welch, M. S. *Branch Lines to Horsted Keynes Then and Now* (Author and Runpast Publications, 1995)

White, H. P. *A Regional History of Railways of Great Britain: Southern England* (David & Charles, 1961)

Various issues of *Trains Illustrated*, *Railway Magazine*, Bradshaw, LBSCR/LSWR/BR timetables, Ian Allan ABCs, W. G. Tilling's *SR Locomotives 1935*, etc

Left:
The sun has now set on so many Sussex and Hampshire branches and byways. Most were born at an exciting time in the Victorian era, before the age of the motor car and the omnibus. For some years the railway dominated the transportation scene, but these mainly rural lines serving scattered communities were doomed because in the long run, and without public subsidy, they could not survive financially. More than 80% of the lines featured in this volume have now closed completely, and as a result a way of life has gone for ever. Just days before withdrawal in 1966, an Adams 'O2' class locomotive climbs away from Ryde towards Smallbrook with three ancient coaches. The end was nigh and we would never see such sights again outside the preservation movement. *JV/TTT*

Acknowledgements

IN ADDITION to lengthy personal research at a number of learned institutions, it has been necessary to rely on the authors of a number of specialised railway publications for some of the detailed information contained within. The author knows only too well from previous activities that many hundreds of hours are required to wade through old documents and reports in order to produce a definitive history of a particular line or area. I have mentioned all books and magazines of reference in the Bibliography and I take this opportunity to thank all of the authors and their publishers mentioned therein for their hard work.

A number of individuals have been particularly helpful in making valuable photographic material available. This has involved many of them in long searches through personal collections to find required illustrations. My thanks go to all the photographers acknowledged in the caption credits. In addition, a number of friends and acquaintances have helped in a variety of ways, and in no particular order I acknowledge their invaluable assistance and express my sincere gratitude: Sid Nash of Eastbourne, Phil Barnes of Roffey, Maurice Dart of St Austell, Hugh Davies of Godalming, Rod Blencowe of Romsey, Brian Morrison of Sidcup, Gavin Morrison of Mirfield, Dick Riley of Beckenham, John Hicks of Highams Park, John Bloom of Horsham, and Steve Chandler of Sheffield. The British Library provided valuable assistance, as did the East and West Sussex and Hampshire Library Services. I also acknowledge the help afforded by the Stephenson Locomotive Society and my publisher, Ian Allan Publishing, particularly Peter Waller, for the availability of material but also for the freedom and latitude afforded regarding content and layout. I would also like to publicly recognise the understanding shown by my long-suffering wife, Maureen, who had to watch all of the TV 'soaps' on her own for over a year!

Worthy of special mention is my old friend John Frith of Guildford, who travelled with me over many of the old branch lines featured in this book. Indeed, we travelled in the brake-vans on many branch freights and mutually revelled in the delights that the fascinating hobby produced. We had great times and now have great memories. John volunteered for the onerous task of proof-reading the sizeable manuscript and made a number of helpful suggestions at business meetings held in various public houses! However, any inaccuracies that have survived the vetting process are the sole responsibility of the author. The author has great pleasure in dedicating *Branches & Byways: Sussex and Hampshire* to John Frith, in recognition of a lifelong friendship.

Picture Credits

Photographic credits identifying the photographer, source or supplier are shown at the end of every caption:

JV: The photograph was taken by the author and the copyright rests with the author.

JV/TTT: The photograph was taken by the author but the copyright rests with 'The Transport Treasury', Gate House, North Road, Insch, Aberdeenshire, AB52 6XP.

Abbreviations and Wheel Notations

LBSCR	London, Brighton & South Coast Railway
LSWR	London & South Western Railway
SECR	South Eastern & Chatham Railway
SR	Southern Railway
BR	British Railways
BR (SR)	British Railways Southern Region

To avoid repetition, the following are the wheel arrangements of the various classes of locomotive frequently mentioned:

'A12'	0-4-2
'B4'	0-4-0T
'A1', 'A1X'*, 'E1', 'USA' (*unless otherwise stated)	0-6-0T
'B4', 'C8', 'D', 'E', 'L', 'L12', 'T9', 'Schools'	4-4-0
'I1X', 'I2', 'I3', 'I4'	4-4-2T
'D1'	0-4-2T
'D3', 'M7', 'O2', 'T1'	0-4-4T
'E4', 'E4X', 'E5', 'E5X', 'E6'	0-6-2T
'C', 'C2X', '700', 'Q', 'Q1'	0-6-0
'K', 'N', 'N1', 'U', 'U1', '4300', Standard 4MT	2-6-0
Ivatt 2MT	2-6-2T
LMS Fairburn, Standard 4MT, 'W'	2-6-4T
'H2'	4-4-2
Standard 4MT, 'Black Five', 'Manor'	4-6-0
'BB', 'WC'	4-6-2
'H16', 'J'	4-6-2T
'Z'	0-8-0T

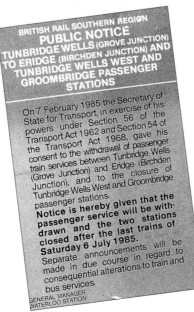

BRITISH RAIL SOUTHERN REGION
PUBLIC NOTICE
TUNBRIDGE WELLS (GROVE JUNCTION) TO ERIDGE (BIRCHDEN JUNCTION) AND TUNBRIDGE WELLS WEST AND GROOMBRIDGE PASSENGER STATIONS

On 7 February 1985 the Secretary of State for Transport, in exercise of his powers under Section 56 of the Transport Act 1962 and Section 54 of the Transport Act 1968, gave his consent to the withdrawal of passenger train services between Tunbridge Wells (Grove Junction) and Eridge (Birchden Junction), and to the closure of Tunbridge Wells West and Groombridge passenger stations.

Notice is hereby given that the passenger service will be withdrawn and the two stations closed after the last trains of Saturday 6 July 1985. Separate announcements will be made in due course in regard to consequential alterations to train and bus services.

GENERAL MANAGER
WATERLOO STATION

Marchwood

255

Geographical Index by Chapter